The Boys of
Adams' Battery G

The Boys of Adams' Battery G

*The Civil War Through the Eyes
of a Union Light Artillery Unit*

Robert Grandchamp

Foreword by Glenn Laxton

McFarland & Company, Inc., Publishers
Jefferson, North Carolina, and London

Illustrations are from the author's collection
unless otherwise noted.

LIBRARY OF CONGRESS CATALOGUING-IN-PUBLICATION DATA

Grandchamp, Robert.
The boys of Adams' Battery G : the Civil War through the eyes of a
Union light artillery unit / Robert Grandchamp ; foreword by Glenn Laxton.
p.   cm.
Includes bibliographical references and index.

ISBN 978-0-7864-4473-1
softcover : 50# alkaline paper ∞

1. United States. Army. Rhode Island Light Artillery Regiment, 1st (1861–1865).
Battery G.   2. Rhode Island—History—Civil War, 1861–1865—Regimental histories.
3. United States—History—Civil War, 1861–1865—Regimental histories.
4. Rhode Island—History—Civil War, 1861–1865—Artillery operations.
5. United States—History—Civil War, 1861–1865—Artillery operations.   I. Title.
E528.81st .G73   2009   973.7'445—dc22   2009022286

British Library cataloguing data are available

Cover image: *Battle of Cold Harbor*, 1890, courtesy of Richmond National
Battlefield (National Park Service); background ©2009 Shutterstock

Manufactured in the United States of America

McFarland & Company, Inc., Publishers
Box 611, Jefferson, North Carolina 28640
www.mcfarlandpub.com

For Shirley Arnold,
a historian's best friend,
and
Dr. J. Stanley Lemons
for proving that Rhode Island
history could be done.

Just before daylight we formed with our detachment in the front line and, at the booming of the signal gun, started. We were successful, and on reaching the line of works our little squad took charge of the guns. We brought with us lanyards, sponge-staffs, and other tools as we thought necessary. It was a grand undertaking, well executed, and many of the enemy bit the dust from their own guns.

—Private George W. Potter
Battery G, First Rhode Island Light Artillery,
April 2, 1865

Contents

List of Maps

Acknowledgments

The entire process of writing history is a collaborative effort, and this book was no different. Over the course of my nearly decade of research, I have traveled the path of Battery G from Providence to Appomattox, and have met scores of individuals and organizations who graciously opened up their vaults and museums to allow me to conduct research. From these vast collections came the records of the past, which made this project possible.

I owe my deepest regards to Glenn Laxton. Through his early research, he laid the foundation for this book to be written. He truly assisted in getting this project downrange through freely sharing his research and knowledge of "The Seven." In addition, Glenn kindly agreed to read a draft of the book and write a heartfelt foreword. To him I will always be grateful.

During my research, I met several remarkable individuals who are directly connected to Battery G's story and contributed greatly to this work. Midge Frazel, a descendent of James Barber, provided superb material on her distinguished forebear, she freely gave of her insight and help into uncovering some of the mysteries relating to Battery G and provided a welcome relief during the weary months of researching. Furthermore, Bill and Jean Barber provided some interesting anecdotes on Barber's service. James' descendents carefully preserved his wartime diaries before they became part of the collections at the Hay and Providence Public libraries. Together these three volumes represent the most detailed representation of Battery G's service available; without them, this project would not have been possible. It was an honor to work with the Barber family on this project.

General Richard Valente and Sergeant Major Tom Caruolo, veterans of the Rhode Island National Guard's 103rd Field Artillery and members of the Providence Marine Corps of Artillery, provided important insight into the history of Rhode Island's distinguished artillerists and kindly opened those massive doors of the Benefit Street Arsenal so I could see firsthand where Battery G was recruited and where the veterans met after the war. Although the Civil War did not take place in North Dakota, Connie Cordner Anderson kept the past alive by preserving Albert Cordner's wartime diary and other papers; I am grateful to her for allowing their use. Colonel Bill Havron, United States Air Force, gave important clues on his ancestor, Sergeant John H. Havron.

Kris VanDenBossche is again to be commended for his kind replies to my many questions pertaining to the military history of southwestern Rhode Island and for the use of several images from his collection. Again Kris' *Pleas Excuse All Bad Writing* saved the day on more than one occasion. Phil DiMaria and the cannoneers of the reactivated Battery B, First Rhode Island Light Artillery showed me how the men of the Rhode Island Artillery lived and drilled. I owe Phil a great deal; he first introduced me to the role the Rhode Island Artillery played in the Civil War, and showed me how to load and fire a Civil War–era artillery piece, in addition to providing much information.

Rangers John King, Dennis Frye, Melinda Day, and Jeff Bowers at Harpers Ferry

National Historic Park freely gave of their time to answer my many questions relating to Harpers Ferry in the Civil War and the 1864 campaigns in the Shenandoah Valley. In addition the following National Park Service rangers all contributed in various ways: Steward Hendersen, Greg Metz, and Eric Mink at Fredericksburg and Spotsylvania National Military Park; Ted Alexander and Mannie Gentile at Antietam National Battlefield; Robert E.L. Krick of Richmond National Battlefield; Eric Campbell and John Heiser at Gettysburg National Military Park; Barbara Justice at Monocacy National Battlefield; and Jim Burgess at Manassas National Battlefield. They all gave vital access and guidance into the National Park Service's vast library system and the battlefields Battery G fought on.

I owe much to the professors and librarians at Rhode Island College, which I proudly call my alma mater. They taught me how to write history and are responsible for insuring that this project was accomplished. Dr. J. Stanley Lemons first introduced me to the vast history of the smallest state on the academic level; to him I will always be grateful. Drs. Ron Dufour, Robert Cvornyek, and Gary Donato taught me much and guided me on the path to becoming a historian. At the James P. Adams Library Dr. Marlene Lopes allowed me free access to the special collections. To Corrine Kilpeck and Moira Blanc of the circulation and interlibrary loan departments I owe special thanks for checking out and ordering scores of books that allowed me to complete this project.

The overwhelming majority of this book was researched at the United States Army Military History Institute, the Library of Congress, and the National Archives. I was fortunate to meet many talented librarians and archivists at these institutions who kindly answered my questions and gave me all the material I needed to piece together Battery G's complicated history. I am especially grateful to Jill Abraham for helping me wade through thousands of "finding" aids and guiding me to exactly what I needed in the Military Records at the National Archives. At the Adams County Historic Society in Gettysburg, Pennsylvania, Lisa Malandra and Al Ferrenato kindly opened the collections and showed me around. To Tim Smith of the Society, the "world's leading expert on the Granite Hill fight," a huge thank you is extended for sharing all of his knowledge of this important engagement. Dean Thomas kindly took the time to direct me to the site of the fighting at Granite Hill and shared his findings from surveying the battlefield.

I am again indebted to Ken Carlson of the Rhode Island State Archives for helping me sift through the mountains of material held within the Rhode Island Adjutant Generals' Office Records. His patience and mentoring over the years has definitely been rewarding. Rick Ring and Phil Weimerskirch of the Special Collections Department at the Providence Public Library are truly a researcher's best friends. They allowed me free access to the vital C. Fiske/Harris Collection, where many of the printed primary source books were found. In addition, Rick kindly gave permission to copy James Barber's 1862 field diary and the use of an image of this noble man.

Elizabeth Demars at the Rhode Island Historical Society and the staffs at the Hay Library and the University of Rhode Island were all of superb service in guiding me through their collections. Nina Wright of the Westerly Memorial Library was invaluable in her expertise of southern Rhode Island history; I owe her and the library a deep debt for allowing me to use their material to study the "Westerly Boys" and their community. Patricia Millar and the Richmond Historical Society kindly provided a listing of men from their town who served in the battery, and an image of the veterans from Shannock.

I am very fortunate to have connections within the Civil War community. During the course of my research, many of my fellow students of the conflict came forward to lend their support and comments to my writing. J.D. Petruzzi and Eric Wittenberg helped to uncover some of the mysteries involving the skirmish at Granite Hill, which proved to be vital in understanding the battery's sojourn in Pennsylvania. Scott Patchan, the undisputed master of the 1864 Valley Campaign, carefully reviewed my thesis, offered insightful critiques, and provided important material to understand this vital campaign. The incredible Ed Bearss kindly answered an important question on the performance of the Rhode Island Light Artillery in the Civil War. Kudos to John Hoptak who kindly reviewed my work on the Maryland Campaign and offered important comments. Furthermore, fellow artillery historian Bob Trout offered his views towards this overlooked and very important branch of the service.

Pete George kindly offered guidance into light artillery tactics and carefully tutored me in the difference between Dyer and Hotchkiss ammunition. Furthermore, Mike Stewart and the men of the re-created Battery C provided valuable information on the soldiers who suddenly found themselves in Battery G.

Don Troiani and Jeannie Sherman proved that the historian should never give up. William H. Lewis' letters were finally located after six months of searching, and added greatly to this work. Thanks are also to be extended to the Connecticut State Library for allowing me to quote from these letters and use several images of Battery G veterans. Philip Laino contributed to this work immensely through his superb maps. Brent Nosworthy kindly listened to my theories on the advancement of rifled artillery and pointed out several overlooked sources that proved to be very useful. At the Sterling Town Hall, town clerk Catherine S. Nurmi assisted in locating George W. Potter's probated will, which gave an understanding of his latter years.

Mike Lannigan and Jennifer Snoots were of great assistance in relaying information and photographs of many of the Battery G veterans' final resting places. Just as the Rhode Islanders turned to the Green Mountain Boys on more than one occasion, I found myself drawn to Vermont in the later stages of my research and wish to thank Paul Zeller, Howard Coffin, Tom Ledoux, Bill Smythe, and Tom O'Connor, who provided important documents and information on Battery G and its relationship to the Green Mountain Boys. Linda M. Welch and Margo Caulfield provided some welcome information on Major William Sperry and how his actions led to Battery G's feat at Petersburg. Reinhard Battcher of the Bristol Historical Society kindly allowed me to examine several important artifacts in the collection and helped to fill in the picture of Captain Adams' last years in Bristol, including locating his final resting place at Juniper Hill Cemetery.

At Cedar Creek, Daniel Ambrose, Jenny Powell, and Jerry Sands identified the locations of Battery G and its actions in the battle, in addition to providing some welcome Confederate accounts of the "rough and tumble fight." A. Wilson Greene and Randy Quinn of Pamplin Historical Park in Petersburg, Virginia, helped to solve the mystery of the actions of April 2, 1865, and permitted the examination of several items in the collections, in addition to carefully reviewing my chapter on the Forlorn Hope. Thomas White of Shepherd University kindly acquainted this Rhode Island Yankee with the correct pronunciation of the word "Opequon." Cherry Bamberg and the Rhode Island Genealogical Society permitted me access to their fine collection of early Rhode Island books, in addition to assisting in finding the descendents and burial sites of Battery G veterans. Kevin O'Beirne and Chris Piering both gave superb material on Sixth Corps operations, particularly on the Forty-Ninth and Seventy-Seventh New York regiments, respectively. Brian Downey assisted in understanding the Maryland Campaign through his excellent "Antietam on the Web" Website.

I had the honor of working two incredible years at Harpers Ferry, and my fellow NPS rangers assisted greatly in this project by helping find sources and accompanying me to battlefields, but most important they put up with the rants of "the Rhody." They are John Rudy, JEB S. Inge, Polly Root, Christy Tew, Anna Goodwin, and Skye Montgomery. Patricia Grandchamp and Joyce Knight Townsend, my mother and grandmother, cajoled me constantly to close it up, to be steady, and to keep going forward no matter what obstacle was in my path.

Foreword by Glenn Laxton

Late on the night of April 1, 1865, Captain George W. Adams of Battery G, First Rhode Island Light Artillery, selected volunteers to accompany the Sixth Army Corps in an assault on Confederate works at Petersburg, Virginia. It had been four years since the deadliest war in American history had begun, and the smallest state in the young Union had been heroically represented in its defense. On every battlefield, from Pennsylvania to Texas, the Rhode Islanders had more than proved their worth, sacrificing much along the way. Although they did not know it, hostilities would be over in a week. The men from Battery G would play a large role in ending the Civil War.

Sixth Corps commander General Horatio Wright had tasked these men with capturing enemy guns at Petersburg to open a path directly to Confederate general Robert E. Lee, who had been holding Richmond. Seventeen men from Battery G were finally chosen among those who had volunteered. They were armed with only gun spikes, lanyards, and sponge-rammers. At first light, the soldiers of Battery G charged the enemy positions. In the bloody battle that followed, they assisted some Vermonters in taking possession of the cannon, which were turned around on the startled and fleeing troops. In the midst of the battle, the Rhode Islanders stood by two captured howitzers. As resistance grew, the men began blasting away at the enemy, forcing them to retreat for good while the rest of the Sixth Corps charged in; in total, 100 rounds were fired in the deadly fight. A day later Lee withdrew from Richmond and on April 9 he signed the papers of surrender at the Appomattox Court House. For their efforts, seven cannoneers were awarded the Medal of Honor.

When I was commander of the 110th Public Affairs Detachment of the Rhode Island National Guard some twenty years ago, I happened to notice that books had been written about most of the batteries of the First Rhode Island Light Artillery Regiment that served in the Civil War. There were detailed histories of Batteries A, B, C, D, and so on but when I got to Battery G, there was none. No one seemed to know why so I did some research about Battery G; all I found were details on the April 2, 1865, Battle of Petersburg. During that fight, which ended a week before the entire war did, an incident stood out that made me become an instant fan of Battery G. Seven men in the same unit had been awarded the Medal of Honor for only one incident, an unbelievable feat. I dubbed these soldiers "The Seven." A further check into the historical record struck me dumb that nothing had been written about Battery G except the citation on the Medal of Honor. Unlike every other Rhode Island battery, no veteran ever wrote about the deeds "Adams' Battery" performed in the Great Rebellion. I eventually accumulated more than 100 pages of notes but never went any further with my work until a National Guard friend introduced me to Robert Grandchamp. The rest, as the saying goes, is history.

The exciting story of Battery G has never been told in book form until now. Robert Grandchamp has brought to life in gripping detail each of the seven brave soldiers as well as their comrades and commanders who fought, and in many cases died, defending their country. Two sergeants, two corporals and three privates were among those lured from their farms and factories by a sense of patriotism and the promise of a quick war and quicker money for just a few months' service. They ended up spending four years of life-altering horror on Southern battlefields with names such as Antietam, Gettysburg, and Cedar Creek. The soldiers would continue to deal with the war after it was over, as they tried to readjust to civilian life, coping with the injuries they received in the service. Even the most decorated would have problems. Most of the seven did not receive their medals for years and in some cases decades after the war. One of them, Charles Ennis, had to wait until 1892, when he was fifty-eight years old. He would live longer than any of his other comrades. The story of these seven men is just part of the overall history of a gallant Rhode Island unit. With the death of Private Ennis in 1930 went the story of Battery G until Robert came along.

The Boys of Adams' Battery G represents a first rate job of reporting. The digging, the research to come up with details of each member of the battery and their service makes for a crackin' good story that is all true.

Glenn Laxton, a former major in the Rhode Island National Guard, is a retired television reporter and an Emmy Award recipient. He has had a deep interest in Adams' Battery for years and is the author of Rhode Island: A Genial History.

Introduction

History is defined as the study of the past. Historians study all aspects of what occurred before in order to gain a better understanding of those events. This can be any aspect of the documented record. In my pursuit of what happened, I have decided to study the most written about and studied part of American history: the Civil War. Countless books have been written and will be written about this most volatile period that destroyed the old and gave rise to the new. Although many aspects of Civil War history have been uncovered, many more remain to be discovered.

Among these is the role of the smallest state in the Union: Rhode Island. During the four years of war, the smallest state with the longest name sent 24,000 men into the field; over 2,000 of these soldiers paid with their lives for the Union to be restored. The Civil War touched each Rhode Island community, and every family was forever affected by the conflict. This is a topic that has engrossed me for many years, and will for many more to come.

The subject of this study first piqued my interest in high school. One day while sitting in the library, I noticed small book titled *The High Road to Zion*. This volume chronicled the early history of the Pawtuxet Valley, the home of my family since the early 1700s. In one small paragraph was a story about three men from Coventry who earned the Medal of Honor for one of the most daring acts of valor in the Civil War. They ran forward in the midst of an infantry charge, helped to capture a Confederate cannon, and turned it upon its former owners. Through research, I later learned that seven Rhode Islanders earned the Medal of Honor for this action. Ten more were nominated and received the award, but the War Department failed to mail it to the veterans and no record of it was ever filed. This was the most earned by a single unit for one battle in the Civil War and the most awarded to one battery in the history of the United States Army. These men were from Battery G, First Rhode Island Light Artillery.[1]

Every historian has their own distinct style of writing. It is in their work that the past comes alive and those who are long gone return to life through the simple words they left behind, now residing in musty archives and libraries. Some Civil War historians study strictly the military campaign, trying to grasp how one side maneuvered to victory in a particular engagement. Still others study the social side of history and how the lives of ordinary people affected the larger war efforts. For others, such as this author, there is a gray area in the middle, in which both the social and military blend together to form a distinct version of history, and where those powerful human stories are told against the backdrop of a terrible conflict.

I can easily remember my first family trips. While other people went to Florida or visited relatives in distant states, we spent each summer in Pennsylvania, where the United

3

States was founded and saved. These vacations to the fields of Gettysburg first gave me a deep respect and understanding of the soldiers, North and South, who fought for four years over a series of ideals that resulted in a reunited country and freedom for so many. Upon learning of a family member who had fought and died in the conflict, I became engrossed in its study. This work has taken me across the country to most of the nation's battlefields and libraries as I have tried to understand and research the men from my state who went South between 1861 and 1865.

Much of my research is performed in cemeteries. In small, abandoned graveyards throughout Rhode Island, I find peace among those who came before us and am able to conduct vital research among old, barely legible gravestones of people who lived in days gone by. The inscriptions on the stones present important information about the individual, because it was placed there by the family, who knew them better than what might be revealed in a piece of paper, which is often the only thing that survives. Since my teens I have been an active participant in the process of placing flags upon the graves of Civil War veterans each May to commemorate their final resting spot as a Rhode Island hero. Much of this work has been conducted in southern Rhode Island, large portions of which remain untouched and preserve a distinct antebellum look.

One cold January day in 2004, while traveling through the old mill village of Carolina, I decided to visit White Brook Cemetery, a rather large, by Rhode Island standards, rural cemetery. Entering the cemetery I parked the vehicle and began to walk among the old stones and to read the names upon them, all the while bundled up against a frigid New England winter's day. Traversing the neat rows of graves, I saw several names and units that were familiar; but remembering that Battery G had been recruited in part from Washington County, I looked for a faint glimpse of stones from men of this battery. I was not disappointed. There was Corporal Daniel Hoxsie, thrice wounded severely in action, who would later live a life of poverty. A little way up the row were Artificers Peleg and Welcome Tucker, brothers who went to war together. As I walked around a sharp bend at the rear of the cemetery, I saw something that did not seem right. There was a standard government issue grave marker, but it had gold paint on it, rather than the standard black. Kneeling down I knew why. This small block of granite marked the grave of Private Charles D. Ennis of Charlestown, Rhode Island. He served in Battery G and was one of those seven men who were awarded the Medal of Honor. This field encounter convinced me I had to learn more about this unit; unfortunately, I soon found myself at a dead end.[2]

When the Civil War was over, the veterans of Rhode Island were proud to retell their stories. Indeed, the first published regimental history of the war was written by a Rhode Islander in 1862. During the war, Rhode Island sent ten batteries of light artillery into the field; all but one published a history. Each one of these books, richly illustrated and quite compelling, tells the story of the war as the artillerists saw it. As I glanced through the holdings of regimental histories at Rhode Island College one day, I again found myself disappointed. Somewhere between Appomattox and the death of the last survivor in 1930, Battery G had fallen by the wayside. Except for a small sketch in a state sponsored publication, no written history of Battery G was ever recorded.[3]

Nearly a decade after reading *The High Road to Zion*, and several years into my quest to find more information on the seven medal recipients, I decided to reread General Harold Barker's *History of Rhode Island Combat Units in the Civil War*. Barker was the first writer since the Civil War to chronicle Rhode Island's role in the conflict. The general presented a small history of each Rhode Island unit and their contribution to every battle of the war. Except for the campaigns in central Tennessee and the Atlanta Campaign, at least one

Rhode Island unit was represented in each major engagement of the war. This was an unbelievable occurrence for such a small state. Unfortunately, Barker's sections on Battery G were somewhat disappointing. With only a small sketch, he could not properly give the unit's actions in the battles. Indeed the general was forced to write, "Because no history of Battery G has been published, specific details of its operations are regrettably lacking." Further research indicated that Barker attempted to write a history of the battery, but his premature death prevented it. Two others, including an officer in the command, attempted to do the same thing, but never could finish the story. With General Barker's comments in mind and the unfinished work others had begun, I decided to undertake this: a history of Battery G, First Rhode Island Light Artillery.[4]

A chance encounter in the winter of 2007 led to a remarkable meeting with Glenn Laxton, a distinguished reporter, historian, and veteran. A former member of the Rhode Island National Guard, he had always had an interest in the Rhode Island batteries, and Battery G in particular. The story of "The Seven," as Glenn called them, had to be told. He conducted research, traveled to the graves of the men, and uncovered much. In the end, though, this was one story that could not be reported on. On a cold January day, I met Glenn near the grave of Corporal Samuel E. Lewis, one of the Medal of Honor recipients, and Glenn quite literally gave the fruits of his labor to me. It was a passing of the torch from one generation to another. I was being entrusted to tell the story of this distinguished unit. I fully accepted the burden. I was going to "Play the Game," as the motto of a local Guard battery, descended from the Civil War unit, goes. It was going to be a tough game, but the results would be more than worth the effort. With Glenn's material at hand, I knew I had my bedrock.

Because no history of the unit exists, I was forced to begin my research from the ground up. Without printed materials, the individual letters and diaries of the soldiers of Battery G became very important. Even though written long ago and today barely legible, these pieces of paper told me the story as the cannoneers experienced it. Combined with valuable unpublished federal and state government resources I knew I had hit the mother lode. Historians call the history behind the history historiography. The historiography of Battery G is simple. The soldiers' written material, government records, and the comments of fellow Union soldiers were combined to write this narrative. With only the guide of the six-page narrative, others writings proved valuable to fill in the missing gaps caused by the lack of printed material on Battery G. Still, the unpublished records provide the reader and scholar with the best view into the history of this unit.

The actions relating to the assault on Petersburg have been widely circulated in the resurgence of interest in military history and the Medal of Honor. Unfortunately, all of the volumes simply give the names of the cannoneers and the same brief government citation issued by the United States War Department that accompanied the medal. One account from 1958 simply read, "Trained artillerymen were to accompany the infantry so they could man any guns that were seized and turn them against their former owners." Nearly all accounts fail to mention that the artillery men were the Rhode Islanders of Battery G. Here, for the first time, is the gripping account of what actually transpired in the Petersburg trenches on April 2, 1865. This small action is the sole reason Battery G is remembered today; it was, however, only a small half hour in the larger image of a very distinguished history of a group of brave soldiers.[5]

The history of Battery G goes beyond that morning in April of 1865. Initially assigned to duty on the Potomac River, Battery G went on to fight through the grueling Peninsula Campaign and fought well at Antietam. They were heavily engaged during the Battle of

Marye's Heights, were present at Gettysburg, fighting in a rearguard action, and served throughout the Overland Campaign during the spring of 1864, including the brutal contests at Spotsylvania Court House and Cold Harbor. During the summer of 1864, they were transferred to the Shenandoah Valley and played a prominent and memorable role in four major engagements that decided the course of the war; the guns were one of the main reasons for these victories. At Cedar Creek, they held on against desperate odds—buying critical time for the Union forces to regroup—while losing a third of their command. Eventually transferred back to Petersburg in 1865, Battery G made history during the final assault on Petersburg. Between all of these engagements was a group of men who depended upon each other for survival. They would stay together through all the disease, incompetence, and mud the battery had to march through. On the opposite side was a group of officers, mostly culled from the elite of Providence, sometimes more concerned with their own well-being than they were with that of the men under their command. They trained their soldiers to become experts in the deadly duties before them.[6]

The men who comprised the unit were the last of the volunteers who left Rhode Island in 1861 to fight for the preservation of the Union. They were different though; a large proportion were of foreign birth and they were generally older than the earlier Rhode Island volunteers. Many skilled workers were in the ranks. Furthermore, each would leave his mark in the history of the battery. Some would be heroes; others would be constantly intoxicated while on duty; one would be sentenced to death.

Throughout the war, Battery G would be commanded by three men who held the exalted rank of captain. Of these, only one would be remembered for his mark on the command. George William Adams was born into a prominent Rhode Island family, was Brown educated, trained by the Providence Marine Corps of Artillery, and worked as a merchant before the war. Rising through the ranks, he quite literally turned Battery G around overnight into one of the finest combat batteries in the Union Army. To this day, his command is remembered as Adams' Battery.

The Rhode Islanders who served in this command were unique because they were artillerists. Comprising less than 10 percent of the army during the Civil War, the Federal artillery became the elite of the United States Army. Highly drilled, disciplined, and readied for action, the batteries proved their worth in every battle of the war. This was seen especially at Malvern Hill and Gettysburg, where they stopped attacking Confederate columns in their tracks. The Union artillery was even held in a high degree of respect by their adversaries. Confederate general D.H. Hill once said, "Confederate infantry and Yankee artillery, side by side on the same field, need fear no foe on earth." Unlike an infantry soldier, who simply had to stand, load, and fire his musket, the artillery had to work as one body, each man "on time and in time." If they did not, the entire gun crew were at risk of suffering violent deaths. A great deal of responsibility was thus leveled on each man, even the privates. There were hundreds of batteries that served during the war, but none contributed more than those from Rhode Island.[7]

Much has been written about the supposed fact that Civil War field artillery, especially rifled guns, were largely ineffective on the battlefield. The long accepted theory has been that field artillery was only used effectively in the defensive role, against attacking infantry or as a morale booster. With the advent of the minié ball and the rifle-musket in 1855, the perceived notion was that cannoneers were relegated to the status of noisemakers; they could no longer bring their guns effectively to bear against an attacking column armed with the most advanced killing weapon of the time. Indeed, in his groundbreaking 1960 study on the Army of the Potomac's field artillery, VanLoan Naisawald recorded this statement: "No offensive operation on either side was decisively effected by the offensive use of artillery; it was beyond the capabilities and fire-control systems of the era." As Naisawald goes on to state, he did not have access to much of the rich and vast primary source material available today. These sources, primarily from Federal infantrymen who felt the benefit of the supporting artillery fire, combined with the written accounts of the cannoneers and in some cases the archaeological record, have proved that the old theories of Civil War era light artillery were indeed wrong. In his book, *Battle Tactics of the Civil War,* Paddy Griffith wrote, "A major function of artillery was not so much to win the battle at close quarters, although it could also do that very well, but rather to keep the enemy at bay so he would not come to close quarters at all." Although it would take two years to develop, by 1863 the Army of the Potomac's field artillery was the most potent combat force on the continent.[8]

Throughout the war, the Federal artillery evolved into an offensive force, able to take the war to the enemy at ranges and with accuracy never before seen on the battlefield. This was due in large part to three main factors: excellent combat leaders, rigorous training of both officers and men, and a strong tradition of excellence in the artillery arm. Furthermore, new rifled cannon and better ammunition played an important yet rarely studied role on the field. While casualties inflicted, or destruction on the receiving end of the fire, were not always great, the artillery played a crucial role in supporting the efforts of the Federal infantry. On more than one occasion, it was the sheer firepower of the guns that won the day for the Union. One author wrote, "The effect of artillery in these battles should not, in any case, be measured in terms of casualties inflicted, but in terms of tactical advantages gained. Artillery had a shock power and a deterrent effect that is beyond statistical reckoning. It could break enemy units, and disperse attacks even when it did not hit enemy soldiers." During the conflict, the cannoneers of Battery G were able to overcome the limitations of their cannon and ammunition to become one of the premier batteries in the Union army.[9]

This volume is essentially a history of the Army of the Potomac as seen by one small group of men, but it is a human story as well—of normal men placed in abnormal circumstances who tried everything possible to survive the hell they were forced into. The men formed a unique culture, based on brotherhood, to safely operate their cannon in combat. In this manner, this study is akin to a regimental history; but at the same time it is not. Battery G was a company of the First Rhode Island Light Artillery Regiment, one of eight that comprised the command. While a regimental structure was in place to handle the daily operations of the individual batteries, the regiment never served together as a whole. At various times in July of 1863, the units were stationed in Pennsylvania, North Carolina, Virginia, and Kentucky. Without a regiment, the individual battery took on more significance as men from the same state and community shared in the "perils and glories" of the war. The battery was the building block of the artillery in the army; to study it is to better understand the Civil War as a whole. Indeed, Napoleon himself said, "No history of an army can be written without the history of each company and regiment is written first."[10]

While studying the background of the men who composed Battery G, I noticed an interesting trend. They came from nearly every town in Rhode Island, while nearly a third were of foreign birth. Forty percent came from the city of Providence. During the research of my book *The Seventh Rhode Island Infantry in the Civil War*, I took a special interest in the small town of Hopkinton. Not only were its soldiers extremely literate, leaving behind a vast record, but the town suffered much during the Civil War. Throughout the research phase for this project, I was constantly drawn to Hopkinton's neighbor, Westerly. This community of seamen, mill workers, and farmers contributed the most men to Battery G outside of the capital. They would form a unique portion of the battery and would suffer more than others, on the battlefield and off. While they were fighting to preserve the Union on the battlefields of the South, life continued very much unabated in Westerly.

Today, behind a thick pane of glass at the Rhode Island State House, is the small tattered and faded American flag of this battery. Emblazoned upon it are the battles these Rhode Islanders fought in. From Yorktown to Appomattox, they were at the front with one of the greatest armies ever to march into battle. Although these artillerists are long gone, they live on in the pieces of paper left behind through the generations. This is the story of Battery G, First Rhode Island Light Artillery, the Civil War's most gallant artillerists.

Over the last few years, this study had been a sort of modern day case of "consumption," once one of the deadliest killers in rural Rhode Island. Battery G truly has consumed a large amount of my time, energy, and skill as a historian. Now the writing is over and I firmly hope this tome serves its purpose: to tell the full story of this battery. I am often reminded of the epitaph on the headstone of Private William O. Tabor of Richmond, Rhode Island, who gave his life in the brutal struggle. Part of it reads, "His toils are passed, his work is done. He fought the fight, the victory won & entered into rest." 'Tis sweet to finally hear the haunting sound of taps.

1

Traditions

Rhode Island furnishes the best light artillerymen.
—*New York Commercial,* September 19, 1862

These words were recorded by a New York newspaper correspondent two days after the bloodiest day in American history: the Battle of Antietam. Flashed throughout the United States, they served as a testament to the officers and men of the First Rhode Island Light Artillery Regiment. Raised from the cities, towns, and villages of the smallest state, these units became the elite of the Union field artillery in the Civil War; ranking on par with the professional Regular Army batteries they served with. The Rhode Islanders who composed the batteries were soldiers who joined a hazardous brotherhood in working the cannons. These men fought in every engagement with the Army of the Potomac from Bull Run to Appomattox, including small skirmishes in between that would never make the history books. After the war, the veterans would be proud to quip that the generals would not begin an engagement until a Rhode Island battery was on the field. The Rhode Island artillerists of 1861–1865 were carrying on a tradition that began a century before and continues to this day in the deserts of Iraq.

The tradition of artillery in Rhode Island began in 1741 with the founding of the Artillery Company of Newport. First engaged in the French and Indian War, the unit remains the oldest continuously chartered militia unit in the United States. This company was joined in 1774 by the United Train of Artillery. Headquartered in Providence, the unit was chartered by the Rhode Island general assembly to provide supporting fire for the militia companies then in the state. Activated to service in May of 1775, the Rhode Islanders joined the Grand American Army besieging the British in Boston. Even from a distance, there was no mistaking these men were Rhode Islanders. They wore a distinct wave-shaped helmet, with the motto of their state upon it: *In Te Domine Speramus* (In Thee, Lord, We Hope). Moving to New York in 1776, the battery was one of only eight in the Continental Army. The legendary status of the Rhode Island artilleryman began in the summer of 1776, during the Battle of Long Island. The Rhode Islanders became part of the rearguard as the Americans retreated off the island. They lost half of their strength, while significantly contributing to the successful American withdrawal. By war's end, the United Train of Artillery remained in service, fighting in every major engagement with Washington's Main Army. It served as a learning platform for the senior officers of the Continental Artillery; two of its officers rose to senior positions of leadership in the artillery ranks.[1]

The tradition was revived in earnest in 1801 with the founding of the Providence Marine Corps of Artillery. Formed as a response to feared French and British encroachments on shipping during the Quasi-War, the corps was chartered by the Providence Marine Society. This elite group was composed of wealthy merchants and sea captains from Providence. The organization was created "for the purpose of improving themselves in the art of military discipline." The corps became a repository of the well-to-do and influential of Providence to learn the military drill of the time; muskets were used and no artillery pieces were present. Meeting weekly, the men who comprised the command became very proficient in the use of their weapons. During the War of 1812, the unit erected a fort near Providence to defend the capital in the event the British returned to Narragansett Bay.

In the late spring of 1842, Rhode Island erupted in armed rebellion as two governors were elected using two different systems. Samuel W. King was elected under the original charter of 1663, which allowed only landowners to vote. His challenger, Thomas W. Dorr, ran on a platform of a new constitution that allowed all Rhode Island males that privilege. Dorr tried to seize weapons stored in Providence, but he failed. His followers erected an armed camp in the western reaches of the state in Glocester. The Rhode Island Militia was called out to put down the rebellion. Among the units that responded was the Providence Marine Corps of Artillery as they marched to Chepachet as part of the Law and Order Army to suppress the rebellion. They brought two old coastal artillery pieces with them, which were not utilized because Dorr retired into Connecticut.[2]

During the Mexican War, the American artillery dominated the field. Called "flying artillery," the pieces were of small caliber and drawn by horses. Using a series of complicated drill maneuvers, the batteries could instantly change positions in the heat of combat. Throughout the conflict the Americans were able to overwhelm the Mexicans with their firepower, resulting in victory every time. In light of these actions and to emulate the glory of the Regulars on the fields of Mexico, the Rhode Islanders procured funds and in 1847 purchased a complete six-gun battery for the use of the marines. Their first parade was held on October 17, 1847, in Providence. The Providence Marine Corps of Artillery became the first battery of light artillery outside of the United States Army. They came to national attention in 1852 when the unit traveled to Boston and performed the light artillery drill on Boston Common, moving constantly and firing rapidly. Upon seeing the exhibition, the Bostonians promptly organized their own battery, which was instructed by the Rhode Islanders.[3]

In the mid 1850s a young millionaire named William Sprague took command of the unit. A son of the murdered textile giant, Sprague expended a large amount of time and money in continuously upgrading the battery. When Sprague's tenure as commander ended, the Providence Marine Corps of Artillery was a thoroughly uniformed, drilled, and equipped organization. The unit had already built a large medieval style arsenal on Benefit Street to store the cannon and other equipment. By 1860, the battery was commanded by Charles H. Tompkins, a twenty-seven-year-old merchant with flaming blue eyes; he had a long beard to cover his young age. In February 1861, the men received an ominous warning from Thomas Clark, the Episcopal bishop of Rhode Island: "Days of terrible contests and nights of weary watching may await you. The turf may be your dying bed and the roll of the drum your requiem." The drills became more frequent as the war clouds loomed. From this series of complicated and often hectic maneuvering, a cadre of leaders soon appeared whose names would become legendary in the coming storm: Adams, Hazard, Monroe, Weeden, Brown, Randolph, Tompkins.[4]

With the Providence Marine Corps of Artillery refitted and readied, the unit became the crack instrument of the Rhode Island Militia. With the election of Abraham Lincoln to the presidency of the United States in 1860, there was little doubt that a war would be coming soon. In late 1860, Governor Sprague sent Major Joseph Balch of the corps to visit General Winfield Scott to offer the Rhode Island Militia for service. Scott rebuffed Balch, knowing that a war was not yet occurring; so as to not strain tensions between North and

South, the offer was not accepted. Remembering his War of 1812 service, Scott told Balch, "I know the stuff they are made of. The Rhode Island men were the best troops I commanded." Scott's compliment would soon be put to the ultimate test. In February, Balch was again dispatched south to visit Lincoln's private secretary and to ask if the guns would be of any service during the inaugural in March. There was a perceived fear that Lincoln would be assassinated as he entered the city. The president elect did not accept the offer of the escort. Eager for his state to show their ardor, Sprague wrote another letter to Lincoln on April 11. In it, the boy governor promised the president that Rhode Islanders "would do their utmost to maintain the Union." Sprague then reported on the military conditions in the state, "We have a Battery of Light Artillery, 6 pdrs, horses + men complete—Unsurpelled or at any rate not surpassed by a similar number in any country—who would respond at short notice to the call of the government for the defence of the capital. The artillery especially, I imagine would be very serviceable." The time had come for the Rhode Island artillerists to show their mettle.[5]

With the firing on Fort Sumter on April 12, 1861, the Civil War began in earnest. On the fifteenth, President Lincoln issued a proclamation calling for 75,000 men to suppress the rebellion in the south; within three days, Rhode Island raised one infantry regiment and a battery of light artillery to serve for three months. Captain Charles Tompkins' Providence Marine Corps of Artillery would provide the artillerymen for the command. They were called the First Rhode Island Battery. Composed of 146 men, the unit spent the sixteenth and seventeenth of April loading their guns and horses at the Fox Point docks. Finally, on the morning of April 18 among thousands of well-wishers, they left Rhode Island. They were the first unit of Northern militia to answer Lincoln's call. Stopping at Jersey City, New Jersey, the battery then went to Easton, Pennsylvania. They had left Rhode Island still using their six cannon. These were six-

This 1850s broadside shows a member of the Providence Marine Corps of Artillery and their arsenal on Benefit Street.

The Providence Marine Corps of Artillery often performed their drill to the delight of crowds around New England. Here they muster on Boston Common in 1852.

pound smoothbores, capable only of short-range fire. They were returned to the Benefit Street Arsenal to be used in the training of the future artillerists to pass through the building.[6]

At Easton, the Rhode Islanders reequipped with a revolutionary piece of equipment: the James Rifle. Charles T. James of East Greenwich, Rhode Island, had developed an ingenious solution to converting old Mexican War era cannon into modern pieces, by drilling rifling into the barrel. James was able to rebore the cannon into a powerful long-range weapon. The First Rhode Island Battery became the first unit in the United States equipped with rifled artillery pieces and they were not even in the Regular Army. After remaining in Easton for a week, the battery proceeded to Washington where they joined the First Rhode Island Detached Militia at Camp Sprague, located north of the city. On May 2, Tompkins' Battery marched in review before President Lincoln. The new commander in chief could see for the first time the artillerymen promised by Governor Sprague. A Washington correspondent recorded the moment: "The magnificent Providence Marine Corps Artillery passed in review before President Lincoln, who expressed himself as much pleased with the completeness of the battery, and with the patriotism of the noble little State which has come out so nobly in defence of the Union."[7]

There remained behind at the Benefit Street Arsenal a small cadre of men. Now, in May, Lincoln issued another call for men to serve for three years. Rhode Island was again tasked with raising an infantry regiment and a battery. Within two weeks the Second Battery was full and on its way to Washington to join the First. With artillery sorely needed in the Shenandoah Valley, Tompkins' Battery was dispatched to that area. With the three months' enlistments set to expire in early August, Lincoln knew that action needed to be taken. Thus, he ordered the Federal forces to engage the Confederate.[8]

The Rhode Islanders set forth on the afternoon of July 16 to Manassas, Virginia. Because they had been the first to respond in April, they were allowed to be placed first in the line of march. The Second Rhode Island Battery was the second unit in line. At 9:00 on the morning of July 21, 1861, the Rhode Islanders opened the Battle of Bull Run. They held on for nearly an hour, alone and unsupported, before other Federal forces entered the field. The Second Battery was in the heat of the early morning fight, losing three killed and a dozen wounded, while expending hundreds of rounds of ammunition. Although the battle had gone against the Union forces, the Rhode Islanders performed exceptionally well, opening the battle and covering the retreat. As the Second Battery fled towards Washington with the panic-stricken Federal forces, they discovered the main route over the Cub Run Bridge blocked by a throng of carriages and disorganized soldiers. Faced with the blocked road and fearing a Confederate counterattack, the Second Battery was forced to abandon its guns: only one piece was saved. After the battle, the rallying cry of the Providence Marine of Artillery became "Don't Give Up the Guns." George W. Field of the Second Battery wrote, "If ten regms. of our troops had fought as well as the R.I. boys did we would have gained the day."[9]

Following the Battle of Bull Run, Lincoln issued a call for 500,000 men to serve for three years to put down the insurrection. The state again responded with ardor, this time with another battery and infantry unit. Because they comprised only 150 men, Rhode Island, with her small size, could quickly raise and equip the batteries rather than the 1,000-strong infantry regiments. The state was given permission to raise two more batteries. With their three-month service over, the men in the First Battery returned to Providence. Although engaged in only one skirmish, they had been the first to answer Lincoln's call, and, even more important, comprised a trained and disciplined cadre from which to draw experienced officers. Upon returning home, the veterans reenlisted in the batteries then forming, providing them with solid leadership to be found nowhere else. Others remained behind on Benefit Street to train the new men traveling to the armory to enlist. In effect, the Providence Marine Corps of Artillery became the "Mother of the Rhode Island Batteries."

Colonel Charles Tompkins of Providence made the Rhode Island Light Artillery into one of the best combat forces in the Union army (USAMHI).

Captain Tompkins was promoted to major of the new unit, which was called the First Rhode Island Light Artillery Battalion. The batteries were designated as individual companies of the battalion; the Second Battery became Battery A and so on. By the time

Top: The mythical status of the Rhode Island cannoneers was born on the Plains of Manassas (Library of Congress). *Bottom:* Part of a light artillery battery on the drill field. The cannoneers stand by their ten-pounder Parrotts, while the drivers and limbers are directly to their rear. Standing by each detachment in the distance is a caisson (Library of Congress).

Battery D left Rhode Island in September, even more men were there to enlist in the Rhode Island batteries. The War Department now gave Governor Sprague permission to equip a full regiment of eight batteries of artillery. Major Tompkins became a colonel and set his command at Camp Sprague to drill the units; his second in command remained in Providence, forwarding the batteries to the front. From August until the end of the war, the Benefit Street Arsenal was a hub of activity for men wanting to enlist in the artillery.[10]

On October 21, at the Battle of Ball's Bluff, Battery B was among the first Federal units to cross the river and was heavily engaged. It lost a cannon and several men to the enemy. By this time, the batteries had fought in only three battles, but the enigma of the artillerists from the smallest state was already in place. This was seen in the fact that men came to the Benefit Street Arsenal from Connecticut, New York, and Massachusetts for the chance to join the First Rhode Island Light Artillery. By the end of October, two more batteries had left for the front. The new Federal commander, General George B. McClellan, was taking his time to organize the forces properly before embarking upon another campaign. McClellan's plan was to acquire hundreds of field pieces to overwhelm the enemy. John Rhodes of Battery B wrote, "In this mass of power Rhode Island was fairly represented."[11]

It was in these traditions that Governor William Sprague issued orders on October 26, 1861, for 150 more Rhode Islanders. These men would form the eighth battery of artillery to answer their country's call within six months. This unit became Battery G, First Rhode Island Light Artillery.

2

Organization and Equipment

No arm of the service calls for greater intelligence,
capacity, and judgment than the light artillery.
—Lieutenant Colonel J. Albert Monroe, 1886.

During the Civil War, field artillery was unique among the three main branches of both the Federal and the Confederate armies: infantry, cavalry, and artillery. The officers who commanded and the men who carried out their orders each had a specific function as they performed their deadly duties. At their hands were the most modern killing machines of the time, capable of dealing out death and mayhem at ranges never before seen on the battlefield. They were also equipped and organized along different lines than their counterparts in the infantry and cavalry. The tactics, weapons, and drill of the mid nineteenth century deserve to be told in full in order to better understand their function on the battlefield.[1]

The basic building block of the artillery was the battery. A battery was the equivalent of a company in the infantry or cavalry. It was composed of either four or six artillery pieces, referred to as guns. The unit contained 150 men at full strength and was commanded by a captain. During the Civil War, Rhode Island raised ten batteries, eight of which served as part of the First Rhode Island Light Artillery Regiment. Although a regimental structure was in place, the units served independently of their regiment, reporting directly to the adjutant general's office in Providence. In the Union Army, the batteries were formed into commands of four to eight units called artillery brigades; they were then attached to the much larger corps, which formed the Union army in the field.

An individual battery rarely mustered its full strength, often only numbering one hundred men when in combat. As casualties mounted, they were allowed to draft men from the infantry regiments who would serve a given period as an attached man, working for and assigned to the battery. Once the command left the state, recruits were sometimes hard to obtain, even though they wanted to join the light artillery. Politicians sent them to the infantry regiments where more commissioned officers would bring more political favor. A soldier was normally always at home acting as a recruiter, trying to draw additional men to the battery, which sometimes worked and oftentimes failed. The Rhode Island batteries would always be short of men in the field. The field artillery was considered the safest branch of the service to join, but it would often see the most hazardous service on the battlefield. Although relatively small, a battery provided as much firepower as an infantry regiment and at a greater distance.[2]

A battery organization was broken down into two to three smaller commands called sections, each containing two guns. They were designated as the right, center, and left sections. The sections were commanded by a lieutenant. The next level of organization was called a detachment, under a sergeant, and contained not only the actual artillery piece, but a caisson as well. The cannon and caisson had a corporal in command of each piece of equipment.[3]

A captain commanded the battery. His was a position of great responsibility, honor, and scrutiny. A guidebook for officers said, "A battery commander should possess not only executive ability, but he should be mentally qualified, as well as naturally inclined, to acquire a familiarity with every detail of the material under his charge." The captain was positioned in the middle of the battery so he could keep an eye on the action around him. Always near him was a musician and the guidon bearer, a soldier who carried a small American flag and served as the captain's orderly. In the initial assignment to the Rhode Island batteries, all of the first captains were members of the Providence Marine Corps of Artillery. At the end of the war, with one exception, all of the battery commanders had begun the conflict as enlisted men and were promoted through the ranks to receive the double bars of a captain, the insignia of his rank. This position required the officer to perform many minuscule duties such as maintaining order and inspecting the men daily. The captaincy brought with it a certain sense of pride because a battery was a reflection of its commander; it was

A brilliant and gifted artillerist, General Henry Hunt commanded the Army of the Potomac's field artillery and was fond of his Rhode Island batteries (Library of Congress).

only as good as he was. When assigned to the larger artillery brigades, field officers were often in short supply. At such times, the senior captain would command the brigade. The Regulars were often hampered by the fact that the artillery captains left their batteries to become generals in the infantry. During the Civil War, a captaincy was often the highest an artillery officer could aspire to. Most states did not have a full regiment of artillery as Rhode Island did; few of the artillerists made it to these higher ranks.[4]

In a six-gun battery, two first and two second lieutenants were assigned to the unit. The two first lieutenants commanded the right and left sections, while the junior officer commanded the center section so the senior officers could watch him and cover his flanks. The lieutenants identified the target, called out the range, and ordered what type of ammunition was to be used upon it. An artillery lieutenant had a far greater responsibility than an infantry platoon commander. He not only had this duty but also had to act as an ordnance officer, engineer, topographer, and adjutant, all during a battle. The senior second lieutenant commanded the caissons, baggage train, artificers, and other spare men. In addition, the senior first lieutenant served as the second in command, and took care of the long trails of paperwork the battery produced. When the captain was absent, he commanded the unit. Because the larger artillery brigades often did not contain the requisite staff necessary to properly operate them, one subaltern was normally always permanently detached on staff duties ranging from being a judge advocate to an aide de camp. When this occurred, the first sergeant or a duty sergeant commanded his section. If too few officers were present with the battery, the officer in command would divide it in half and give each lieutenant three guns to command.[5]

One of the most crucial positions in the battery was that of the first, or orderly, sergeant. Designated by three stripes surmounted by a diamond, this man insured that the day to day operations of the battery as ordered by the captain were carried out. Wherever the captain went, the first sergeant was close by and answered only to him. He also maintained the books and accounts of the battery. This sergeant could hold the noncommissioned officers and privates to discipline on his own accord and report it to the captain only after the fact. In addition, he always knew where the privates were; those failing to report were bound to be assigned to extra fatigue duty. The first sergeantcy, as with all noncommissioned positions, was directly appointed by the captain and this honor was given to only the most qualified, sober, and respected of the sergeants.[6]

Unique to the light artillery was a quartermaster sergeant. Because the units were separated from their parent regiments, this noncommissioned officer collected and distributed food for the men and forage for the horses. In addition, he maintained a supply of clothing, which he was responsible for. The position was often filled by a clerk or merchant from civilian life, for they had the experience necessary to maintain the many required accounts for each army department. A recruiting poster for a Rhode Island battery announced, "Every company is allowed a Quarter Master Sergeant, thereby dispensing with red tape circumlocution in this department." The quartermaster sergeant did not

Artificers were skilled mechanics who repaired the battery's broken equipment.

The Providence Marine Corps of Artillery pioneered the use of horse-drawn field artillery which was passed down to the members of the Rhode Island batteries.

have to go into combat and remained in the rear watching the baggage wagon and other equipment left behind.[7]

Every battery had six duty sergeants called Chief of the Piece. These men were the true leaders in any battery, commanding a detachment of sixteen men. "He should have all the dash and impetuosity of a cavalry and, all the coolness of an infantry commander, for at times he must throw his piece forward like a whirlwind to the very front line and fling his iron hail into the very ranks of the enemy," wrote one Rhode Island battery commander. Under the command of the Chief of the Piece were the artillery piece and the men who performed the work. The Chief of the Piece required a cool head and calm demeanor, but had to be stern and insure all was moving smoothly on his gun. The position also required the sergeant to have the same knowledge as a lieutenant; oftentimes the officers would allow the sergeant to work his own gun in combat, as they knew the pieces best. When not engaged in battle, the sergeant lived with and supervised the daily fatigue details of his men. An artillery sergeant had the same responsibility as an infantry first sergeant. He called the roll of his men and issued them their rations.[8]

The corporal was the living embodiment of the soldier, clean, disciplined, and well drilled. In a battery there were twelve corporals, two assigned to each detachment. The first corporal was called the Gunner and supervised the cannon. After the sergeant identified the target, the gunner sighted the piece using a pendulum sight and an elevation screw near the breech of the gun. Since there was no indirect fire capability, as such, the corporal had to see the target and have a clear line of sight for the round to find its mark. When the gun was loaded and ready, he gave the order and the cannon were fired. The second corporal was referred to as the Chief of the Caisson. He was positioned near the second vehicle in the detachment. This corporal supervised the ammunition being supplied and maintained a listing of what type of rounds were being fired. When the ammunition was gone in a limber chest, the Chief of the Caisson supervised the changing of the chests containing the rounds to insure the Gunner always had a constant supply. When a sergeant was disabled, a corporal would move up to command the detachment; likewise, when there was no corporal present, a private became a lance, or acting, corporal. In camp, the corporal directly supervised the men and led fatigue duties, guard mount, and other mundane camp tasks. Because of the small size of a battery, and a larger number of noncommissioned officers, privates in the artillery had a far better chance of sewing on the coveted two stripes of a corporal than in an infantry company.[9]

Each battery was assigned two musicians who played the bugle. In order to insure they were proficient with the task, professional musicians were ideal for the position. In the smoke of the battlefield, oftentimes the sounds of the bugle were all that could be heard to command the men. The bugler had to memorize thirty calls. So vital was this task that musicians were paid an additional dollar per month. In order that he would be seen on the battlefield, the bugler was mounted on a white horse and wore a distinct red herring-bone trimmed jacket.[10]

Due to the mobile nature of the battery, equipment was bound to wear out and break down. Consequently each battery was assigned two blacksmiths who operated a small forge from which they could make and shod the over 100 horses assigned to a battery, in addition to fixing the metal on the vehicles. Two harness makers maintained the yards of leather harnesses needed to hook the horses to the carriages, and the other leather implements in use. Furthermore, two wheelwrights did as their name implies; they replaced the broken wood on the carriages and performed other duties given to them. Furthermore, several wagoners drove the necessary wagons containing the vital supplies. These soldiers remained in the rear during battle, often completing repairs while the carnage raged around them so the guns could quickly return to the front. All of these men were referred to as artificers.[11]

The most important men in the battery and the ones that it could not function without were the 122 privates who composed the bulk of the unit. In the light artillery, privates were divided into two categories: cannoneers and drivers. During the forming of the command, the privates had a choice as to what position they wanted to take. Many considered the drivers to have a safer position in combat, but serving on the gun was seen to be a higher honor.

The drivers were responsible for the horses that pulled the guns and caissons. Each vehicle was assigned six horses, which were harnessed together in three sets of two. The drivers rode on the left side, and had to control both horses; their equipment was carried on the right horse so that if they had to switch them, the other horse was used to the weight of the driver. From the front, the pairs were named the lead, swing, and wheel horses. The driver had to be watchful for the horses colliding together while the battery galloped into action and wore a metal brace on their right leg to protect it. During combat, the drivers remained mounted on their horses in the event the battery had to quickly limber up and change position. The horses assigned to the command were often sick and unused to the rigorous service of the artillery. They were often leftovers, after the cavalry and medical corps had received the best mounts. However, the drivers were proud of their horses, spending many idle hours grooming and tending to the animals. Veterinarian care was unknown and many horses died along the road during the long marches. One of the few ways to stop a battery in combat was to shoot at the horses. In their after action reports, battery commanders always gave two counts of their losses: men and horses.[12]

The cannoneers were part of a brotherhood and depended upon each other for their very survival. Each man was assigned a position, which in turn had a specific task. The men had to work as one on the battlefield; if they did not, chaos would occur. Not every man was suited for the light artillery. Sergeant John H. Rhodes of Providence wrote of the ideal qualities of an artilleryman:

> A first class cannoneer had to be cool, intelligent, keen, and quick to understand, also being able to perform the duties of two or more posts at the gun, as was often necessary when in action. A slow, awkward person should hold no place in a gun detachment. A detachment

of artillery was like a machine, no one worked individually but all in unison and with the precision of clock-work, every man on time and in time; one mistake or awkward movement would cause confusion and tend to dire results. If one or two men were suddenly disabled it would cause confusion and retard its working; but such was not the case, provision was made for casualties but none for mistakes or blunders.

Each soldier learned the details of the job above him, and indeed those below him. As a result the field artillery became the crack branch of the Union army.[13]

Every member of the gun crew was assigned a number and was known by that number in action. The Number One Man stood to the right muzzle of the cannon. He was equipped with a large staff called a sponge rammer. On one end was a wool swab that was dipped in a bucket of water attached to the front of the gun and then inserted into the cannon to extinguish any embers remaining from the last shot. This was one of the most significant actions in the battery. If there were any sparks remaining in the barrel, the next round inserted would explode. In the heat of combat, to ensure a faster firing of the gun, Number One would sometimes forego sponging, which often resulted in an explosion. On the opposite end of the piece was a flat rammer used to push the round down the muzzle and seat it at the breech of the gun. Across from Number One was Number Two. His task was simple; he inserted the round into the piece.[14]

Of all the men in the detachment, Number Three held the lives of the others by his thumb, and was the most important man on the entire team. He stood near the breach of the cannon, in back of Number One. On his left thumb was a small glove called a thumbstall that was placed over the vent at the rear of the piece as the tube was sponged. The

Once the cannon has been loaded, the Number Four man prepares to pull the lanyard, as the other cannoneers prepare to instantly reload.

Change in front to fire to the right, left wing to the rear.

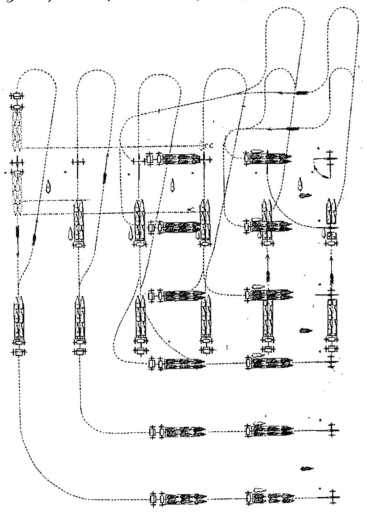

Civil War light artillery tactics were demanding on men, horses, and guns.

vent was the small opening into the powder chamber that permitted the fire from a primer to ignite the powder charge, which fired the gun. If Number Three did not properly seal the vent, air would enter the hole and fuel the glowing embers in the tube. When the round was inserted the entire gun crew was at risk. Even in combat and fast firing, the vent was covered. The devotion of Number Three to his comrades was so much that if his thumbstall was burned away, he would stick his bare thumb over the vent, allowing it to burn down to the bone rather than give up the vital task. He also carried a small brass pick. This implement was inserted into the vent to open the powder bag below so it would ignite. Standing across from Number Three was the Number Four man, who actually fired the gun. He was equipped with a small box called a fuze pouch, which held friction primers, a copper tube containing fulminate of mercury and gunpowder. Four also carried a yard long lanyard, which was hooked to the primer. When the gun was sighted,

Number Four stepped to position and inserted a primer into the vent. With a steady pull, the fulminate of mercury exploded, sending a flame into the powder bag and the round out the cannon.[15]

The remaining cannoneers were stationed at the limber, which was the key to the American light artillery system. A two wheeled vehicle, the limber was used to pull the cannon and caisson. Upon it was an ammunition chest. Each cannon was assigned a caisson. This vehicle carried two additional chests of ammunition, a shovel and ax, spare limber pole and wheel; in addition, it served as a place for the cannoneers to place their personal equipment. In the light artillery, the cannoneers walked; only the officers, sergeants, and staff rode. If the battery needed to get into action quickly, there was room for the men to ride three abreast on the limber chests. As there were no shocks, they were in for the army version of a "Nantucket sleigh ride." The caisson was required to always follow the cannon it was attached to, as a Gunner could go through a large amount of ammunition in a short time. The drivers were told they should follow the piece, "even if it went to hell." The caissons were often bristling with the enlisted men's personal gear so that orders had to be given to reduce the equipment so the vehicle would not resemble a baggage wagon.[16]

Number Five stood to the left of the limber and moved the ammunition up to Number Two in a large leather bag. Instead of the standard black leather worn by the infantry and cavalry, all of the artillery equipment was made of russet colored leather. Number Six retrieved the ammunition from the chest and had a vast array of tools to cut fuzes for the explosive types of ammunition. Number Seven handed the ammunition to Five and also alternated in running rounds forward. Number Eight was also the Chief of the Caisson and tended to that vehicle.[17]

Upon arrival into position during battle, the cannon would instantly be detached from the limber and swung into action. The lieutenant or sergeant would identify the range to the target as they relayed the information to the gun crews. Number Three stepped forward and stopped the vent as One sponged the tube. Number Six selected the round, inserted the fuze if called for and passed the round to Seven, who gave it to Five to run forward and hand to Number Two. He took the round and inserted it into the gun, as One quickly rammed it home. The Gunner sighted the piece, Three pricked the cartridge, and Four inserted the primer as he attached the lanyard. Once all was clear, the piece was ready to fire. When the command was given, Number Four pulled his hand to the left and the cannon was fired. A battery could unlimber and begin firing in under a minute, while a good crew could fire two aimed shots in a minute.[18]

An artillery battery in combat was no place for those without a stout heart or an iron will. As soon as the gun was fired, mountains of smoke bellowed out of the muzzle, obscuring the battlefield. The recoil and noise was immense; after each shot the piece had to be rolled back into position. The first few rounds were critical for a commander to see where the shells were landing. Through the smoke, the musicians would be heard echoing their shrill bugle calls as the officers and sergeants screamed commands to the men as they loaded and fired as fast as they could. As they were exchanging fire, enemy shells screamed into the position. It was here that both officers and men showed their mettle: "Amid the noise of the guns, the tearing and bursting of the enemy's shot, the blinding smoke and general uproar, he can preserve all his facilities unimpaired." Men and horses would be shot down, and the privates instantly stepped into position to relieve their dead or wounded comrades. All of this chaos led to its being called an "artillery hell."[19]

The tactics used by the artillerists in the Civil War were updates of those used by the

American artillery in Mexico. The standard manual was titled *Instructions for Field Artillery*. It was 404 pages long and was written by three experienced Regular Army artillery officers, all of whom rose to the highest ranks during the war. One of the authors was Henry Jackson Hunt, who would go on to command the artillery in the Army of the Potomac. The manual combined tactical thoughts, with the duties of each man, including how to maneuver by section and battery. In addition, it contained information on ordnance, vehicles, and other pertinent information of the battery's operations. Handsomely wrapped in red Moroccan leather, the tome was commonly referred to as "the red book" by the officers. A battery officer would not be found without a copy; it was sold at several locations in Providence for three dollars.[20]

Due to the three-section complement, the battery could engage separate targets at the same time. Principal dictated two main types of firing practices; counter–battery fire was used to suppress enemy artillery and antipersonnel fire to stop advancing infantry or cavalry. A commander's goal was to place his battery in a position to enfilade an enemy's flank with fire, thus causing it to collapse. Standard principle in the early stages of the war directed that guns be used mainly on the defensive, while remaining stationary; it seemed as though what had brought success on the fields of Mexico had been forgotten. Beginning at Chancellorsville, some brash young commanders would revive the old system by using the guns as an offensive weapon. This included moving while under fire, shooting over the heads of friendly troops at extreme long range, and using the right type of ammunition on targets. The artillery remained vulnerable to an assault, so an infantry regiment was usually stationed near it to protect the guns. Frequently the rigorous gun drill was laid aside so the men could get the pieces into action and firing in the shortest amount of time, but also assuring that every round hit its target.[21]

The field artillery was divided into two main types; rifled and smoothbore pieces. In the Union army, a battery contained the same caliber guns; this was so that the same ammunition was present, making it easier to supply from the quartermaster. Furthermore the pieces were named after the size of the ammunition they fired. A twelve pounder Napoleon shot a twelve pound iron ball and had a 4.62 inch bore. An artillery brigade would have pieces of different types and calibers to insure a corps could provide its own firepower at different ranges. Confederate artillery was hampered by having several different caliber pieces in one battery, often placing one section out of combat when the guns could not hit at that range.[22]

The rifles, as their name implies, had a series of lands and grooves giving a spin to the round, which allowed it to hit targets at a maximum distance of up to two miles away. Some gunners could accurately place a round through a window at one mile. Two types of rifles were the mainstay of the Federal light artillery; both fired a three inch diameter round, which weighed ten pounds. The three-inch ordnance rifle was the preferred rifle of the Union field artillery. It was also the lightest of the field guns, weighing slightly over 800 pounds. The ordnance rifle was made out of welded iron bands, which strengthened the piece so it would not burst. The gun never failed in combat and was favored by all who used it—Federals who were issued the cannon and Confederates who could capture it. On the opposite side, cannoneers hated to be on the receiving end of its fire, as the rounds were bound to hit their target at long range.

The counterpart of the ordnance rifle was the ten pounder Parrott, identifiable by a large metal jacket welded around the breach to strengthen the weapon. Two types were issued, one with a 2.9 inch diameter barrel, the other three inches, creating logistical nightmares for the overworked ordnance officers. These cannon were made of cast iron, which

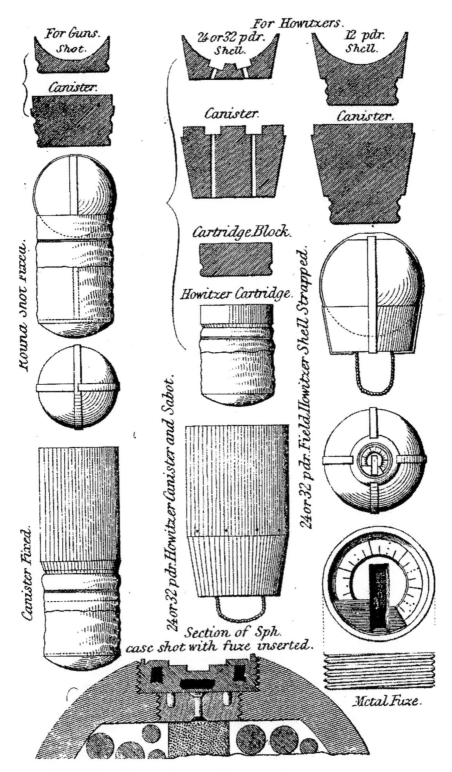

Civil War field artillery used a variety of ammunition, depending on the target.

often resulted in air bubbles forming in the metal. The poor construction often resulted in the gun exploding on the battlefield. The Parrott earned the sobering title of "the cannoneer killer." A larger version of the Parrott firing twenty pound projectiles was sometimes utilized by both sides.[23]

The first Rhode Island units were armed with the James rifle, the first piece of rifled artillery used by the United States Army. They were designed by Charles Tillinghast James, of East Greenwich, who developed a unique way to transform old, worn-out smoothbores into new, highly effective rifled pieces. Because they were bronze tubes firing an iron projectile, the rifling in the barrels quickly wore down. In addition, the shells did not always explode properly upon impact. Furthermore, in their three engagements—Bull Run, Bolivar Heights, and Ball's Bluff—the weapons had proven to be very inaccurate, so much so that at Bull Run the rounds were later found three miles from their intended targets. As a result, the Rhode Islanders turned the guns into the Ordnance Department and were reequipped with standard field pieces. James would be killed by his own invention in 1862.[24]

This soldier wears the typical uniform and combat load of a soldier from the First Rhode Island Light Artillery (courtesy Phil DiMaria, Battery B 1st Rhode Island Light Artillery Inc.).

In the Mexican War, all American artillery pieces were brass smoothbores, most of which fired a six pound projectile. As the Civil War began, the six pounders were relegated to training duty and in its place came the twelve pounder Napoleon. Based on a French design, the smoothbore Napoleon could fire a projectile up to 1,300 yards. This gun was made of bronze instead of iron; like the ordnance rifle, it never failed in combat. This cannon was also the heaviest in the Federal field arsenal, weighing over 1,200 pounds. The Napoleon was referred to as a gun-howitzer in that it replaced the older howitzers—guns that fired explosive shells at a high degree of elevation. This cannon was the preferred smoothbore weapon of the Civil War.[25]

A battery or section commander had four different types of ammunition to fulfill his mission, each designed for a specific purpose. Solid shot was a ball of iron used to punch a hole in the target or engage in counter–battery fire. The old Regular Army officers put much faith into this round, and often scolded their young subordinates for relying upon explosive rounds. Shell was similar to solid shot, but it was hollowed in the center. The cavity was packed with gunpowder. Shell was used to engage enemy troop formations and could go into a target before exploding. Corp. George W. Field related his experiences firing solid shot and shell at Bull Run: "My shot dropped into their Battery & rank. I sent a heap of them to their reckoning & hope to help along ten time as many next time."[26]

Case shot and canister were the two most lethal types of ammunition. Case consisted of a hollow cavity, which was packed with lead balls and powder. It could be used in any capacity and wreaked havoc on enemy infantry columns or disabled artillerymen in counter–battery fire. It required the Number Six man to cut a fuze for it to work properly. Canister turned the cannon into a giant shotgun; it was a tin can containing large iron balls. Canister was an antipersonal weapon, used at distances of under 400 yards. It left the container and scattered upon being fired. This round was most effective fired from a smoothbore, as it had a greater scattering effect. Canister was particularly harsh on a rifled gun as it damaged the rifling; in addition, it was not as effective because of the smaller bore of the barrel, which negated the scatter effect. If a battery was facing the enemy at extremely close range, double and even triple rounds could be fired to keep the foe at bay. If a commander ran out of canister, he could switch to shell or case shot without a fuze, as it would explode upon leaving the muzzle.[27]

Smoothbores used the same type of ammunition, manufactured in government arsenals. It was made into a single round with the powder bag attached; the whole projectile was inserted into the cannon. The United States government issued many contracts to private contractors for the rifle ammunition, named after the company it was made by. This ammunition had to be the caliber of the cannon, but it varied in quality; rifle ammunition would pose a problem throughout the entire war, as rounds blew up in the gun or did not take to the rifling. In addition, the rifle required two actions to be loaded; Number Five first had to bring a linen powder bag to Two, which had to be rammed home before Seven brought the round up.[28]

Each branch of the army had a designating color; for the artillery it was red. The enlisted man was allotted forty-two dollars per year in order to purchase clothing from the quartermaster; any excess funds were returned. A forage cap or black hat was worn with a vividly piped mounted serv-

A member of the Providence Marine Corps of Artillery, Governor William Sprague activated Battery G.

The Benefit Street Arsenal was the birthplace of the Rhode Island Light Artillery.

ices jacket. The waist length jacket contained twelve buttons and a chin length collar, which caused much aggravation among the men, who cut it down. The jacket was accented by four yards of scarlet piping, which let all know that these soldiers were artillerists.

The men were also issued a four-button fatigue blouse to be worn during stable duty or when the jacket was not worn. Many favored the jacket, as it was more practical to wear. The trousers issued to the men were the same sky blue as the infantry, but were reinforced in the seat to prevent them wearing faster from riding. Battery G was only the second Rhode Island battery to receive this uniform in 1861. The jackets were issued with Rhode Island buttons featuring an anchor and the word "Hope." After the initial issue had been worn out, the soldiers were supplied by the United States government. In addition, ankle high shoes called bootees were also given to the men. A sky-blue winter overcoat shielded them from the winter cold, while government issued underwear left many chafed from the sandpaper-like texture.[29]

The men of Battery G were issued red wool blankets, manufactured at Governor Sprague's mills in Cranston. When the Confederates saw the color, they knew they were facing a Rhode Island unit. The blanket was either rolled over the shoulder or carried in a knapsack with other personal equipment, often thrown onto the caisson. In addition, a rubber blanket was issued to be used as a ground cloth or raincoat. A canteen held water, while a haversack contained rations and other personal equipment. Each man also was issued a sword belt and saber. This weapon was useless in combat and was carried in the wagons during the campaigns. Each noncommissioned officer and some of the privates if they purchased them carried a small caliber revolver. This was less likely to be used in combat than to put down wounded horses or as a sidearm during picket or fatigue duties. The burden of the light artillerymen was far less than the infantry or cavalry, and the men were much simpler to outfit.[30]

The officers were dressed and accoutered in uniforms of much better quality than their men; this was because they were privately purchased. In addition, they had a far better selection. This ranged from an elegant tailored frock coat to a waist length jacket, or a baggy sack coat; an officer could wear about anything as long as it looked like a uniform. The officers in a battery even had their own wagon to carry their belongings, while a servant, usually a freed slave, cooked and maintained their equipment. In this way, they could have large tents and more personal equipage then the officers in the other branches of the service. The officers also had to purchase their own food, oftentimes of much better quality than the private's fare. A pair of shoulder straps with a red background, cynically referred to as "sardine cans" by the men, signified his rank, while an "A" on his buttons gave his branch of service. While the enlisted men carried their sabers in the wagons, the officer always had his on; it was his badge of honor and rank. One piece of equipment any battery officer never went without was a good pair of field glasses to identify targets and report the damage inflicted.[31]

Thus armed, equipped, and organized, the artillerymen of Battery G prepared for battle on the fields of the South.

Recruiting

*We will endeavor to make this Battery equal to any in the Service and
that we will use all of our exertion to uphold and sustain the honor of the cause,
the dignity of the flag, and the ancient fame of the Rhode Island Line.*
—Muster Roll of Battery G, October 30, 1861

Captain James Cutts of the Eleventh United States Infantry stood before 129 anxious and proud men on December 2, 1861. Among the names recorded upon the books were Barber, Chace, McDonald, and Young. While the men were formed into seven detachments, the captain told each man to raise his right hand and repeat the words as he began: "I do solemnly swear." The captain had already administered the oath of allegiance to hundreds of other Rhode Islanders. With the formality of being mustered into the service complete, the men before Captain Cutts were now the soldiers of Battery G, First Rhode Island Light Artillery.[1]

The story of Battery G began on October 26, 1861, when Governor Sprague issued orders calling for yet another battery of light artillery; already two were considered veteran units, and a further three were training at Camp Sprague. Battery F was preparing to leave in late October for Washington and had a half dozen men left over who could not go because the battery was already complete. As the First Rhode Island Light Artillery Regiment needed two more batteries for its authorized strength, Sprague directed that an eighth battery be raised immediately. With the return of cold weather as November began, the recruits were moved from the Mashapaug training camp to the Benefit Street Arsenal to further their training. Slowly they came, like the first few drops of rain, residents of Providence hiked up the steep streets of College Hill to the arsenal. Entering the massive doors of the structure, they approached the clerk of the corps and signed their names to a small green book. The roll was headed by these words[2]:

> We, the undersigned hereby agree to accompany the 8 Battery of Marine Artillery as members thereof to any place or places that may be designated by the military authorities of the United States of America hereby agreeing to serve for the war unless sooner discharged under such officers the Commander in Chief may be fit to appoint. And it is hereby understood that all orders from our officers will be most implicitly obeyed and that we will endeavor to make this Battery equal to any in the Service, and that we will use all of our exertion to uphold and sustain the honor of the cause, the dignity of the flag, and the ancient fame of the Rhode Island Line.[3]

In one week, one detachment was full; now only five more were needed to make yet another Rhode Island Battery.

On the morning of November 6, the initial detachment of men who formed the command and some marines harnessed twelve horses to one of the Providence Marine Corps of Artillery's old six pounders and a caisson as they began a march to the west down the Plainfield Pike. They were going to recruit fellow Rhode Islanders for Battery G. The force was commanded by Lieutenant William H. Dyer of the corps, who would receive one hundred dollars for his efforts. The first three Rhode Island batteries had drawn almost entirely from Providence and the neighboring areas. Batteries D and E both recruited out of Kent County, in the central part of Rhode Island. When Battery F was being raised in September and October 1861, the officers decided on a new tactic to encourage men to join. A detachment of the battery each took a gun and caisson to Newport and Bristol counties, while another went to northern Rhode Island to show local inhabitants the light artillery service. The tactic worked; by the time, the men returned to Providence in mid October, Battery F was full and ready for war.[4]

As the detachment marched down the Plainfield Pike, they did so in the footsteps of history. It was on this very road that the Count de Rochambeau had marched his 4,000 Frenchmen in 1781 to victory at Yorktown and in 1842 the Rhode Island Militia to fight

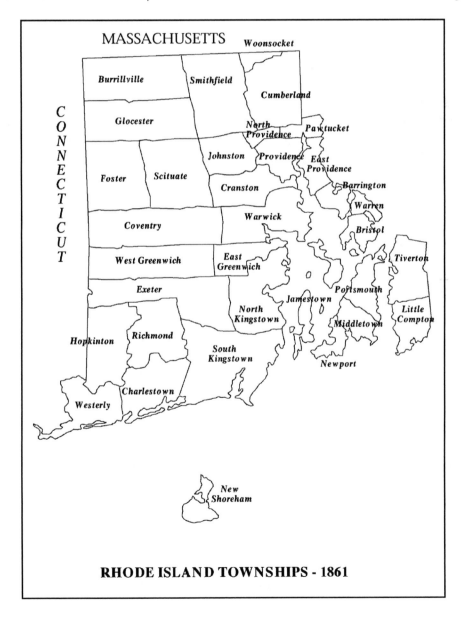

RHODE ISLAND TOWNSHIPS - 1861

against the Dorrite insurrection. The first night was spent at Hope in the large farming and manufacturing community of Scituate. The men fired a salute and waited for recruits.

Due to the cold weather, and contrary to the Third Amendment, the soldiers were quartered in the houses. This first night was dismal; only five men signed the rolls. Scituate was picked clean, as were the local apple trees. The town had already sent nearly 200 men into the Second and Third Rhode Island regiments, in addition to forming a detachment for both Battery D and Battery E. The next night was spent in Foster, where the results were the same; only two men joined from that town, while others

Recruiting posters such as this encouraged soldiers to join the Rhode Island Light Artillery.

came from neighboring Coventry to constitute a full detachment. Rather than follow the gun on its mission, the recruits were immediately forwarded to the Benefit Street Arsenal, where they began learning the principals of artillery tactics. From these early simple maneuvers, leaders among the men arose as the officers could identify those capable of holding rank. On November 8, the cannon and its crew turned south onto the Ten Rod Road, followed by the New London Turnpike, which brought them to an untapped source of manpower.[5]

Located in southern Rhode Island was Washington County; it remained the frontier of the state. This was the ancestral home of the Narragansett people. In the seventeenth and eighteenth centuries, agriculture had been the primary form of subsistence. Since the 1820s, however, the inhabitants had been erecting cotton and wool mills on every small stream; soon manufacturing overtook farming in the area. The funds created in these mills were larger than farming wages, which allowed the citizens to live comfortably. Still something remained in the villages, many young men unable to enlist in the service of their country. Washington County had sent only four companies to the front, while few of the men had yet to enlist in the batteries. Indeed so many attempted to enlist in these four companies that many were turned away; one farmer even offered his gold watch and a large sum of cash for the privilege of fighting for his country. Unable to join the Rhode Island regiments, many simply crossed the line and enlisted in Stonington, Connecticut. The men from Providence believed that they could recruit a significant portion of their battery from this area.[6]

The first stop in Washington County was Richmond, a rural community of 2,000 citizens sandwiched between five neighboring towns. Incorporated in 1747, Richmond contained fourteen villages with names like Brand's Iron Works, Wood River, Usquepaugh, and Kenyon. One of its small claims to fame was as a large producer of the white flint corn needed to produce johnnycake, a dish many native Rhode Islanders enjoyed. Like much of Washington County, Richmond also had many mills running on its small streams. Five men joined from Richmond, while others came from bordering Charlestown and Hopkinton.[7]

After remaining in Richmond for a time, the column turned west to Westerly, a large commerce center and seaport of 3,800 on the Pawcatuck River and Block Island Sound. Although a rural community, the town had a railroad, telegraph office, and several highways passing through it. Furthermore, there was a weekly newspaper and a small free black population. This community had a rich military history and had sent soldiers to fight in King

Adjutant General Edward C. Mauran ran the Rhode Island war effort from a small office in Providence and was the only official connection between Battery G and their regiment (USAMHI).

Phillips' War, the Franco-Colonial conflicts, American Revolution, War of 1812, and the Mexican War. In addition, the town had always kept an active militia; during the War of 1812, the British had struck the neighboring town of Stonington, sending fear throughout Westerly. It was here that the detachment met with its greatest success. Except for sending a company to the First Rhode Island Detached Militia, only a few men had gone into the Fourth Rhode Island. Now the men of Westerly saw the battery as a way to serve their country. Each week those who attended the local Freewill Baptist Church had heard their fiery minister, Frederic Denison, give impassioned patriotic speeches. He told the young men that "a great wrong" had been done to their country. Denison also reminded them that "In every hour of our country's trials the inhabitants of Westerly have been prompt to pledge their honor and their blood."[8]

The citizens welcomed the artillerists, furnishing them with food and shelter. However, the vital task at hand was to find men willing to travel north to Providence. Indeed, some of the boys from the outlying villages, such as Potter Hill and Watch Hill, where most of the recruits came from, had never ventured to the capital city. The highlight of their otherwise dull existence was winters spent at the local schools gaining a basic education. The one-day stop at Westerly was successful; nineteen men were recruited in the twenty-four hour span. Among them were four sets of brothers, including identical twins Alexander and Charles Sisson. Another recruit was Nathaniel Champlin. He was one of the few veterans in the battery, having fought at Bull Run with the Westerly Rifles. The Westerly recruits would soon be designated as the First Detachment. The local *Narragansett Weekly* would give the volunteers the title of "the Westerly Boys." Those men left over from the First Detachment were placed in the other detachments with men from Charlestown, Richmond and Hopkinton. They would be retransferred as casualties mounted or promoted if a vacancy occurred in another detachment.[9]

Upon enlistment, the Westerly men were each given two dollars by Lieutenant Dyer to pay for their train fare to Providence; the officer trusted the men he had just enlisted with state money. All of the recruits used it in the appropriate ways. Over the next five days, the new men returned home to Watch Hill, Potter Hill, and Westerly itself to collect some personal items that many thought would be needed on the campaign. Then in detachments of three to five, they left their homes and boarded the daily Stonington Railroad cars to Providence amid a throng of tears and cheers. In Westerly, they had been sailors, mill workers, and farmers. Now they were going to the capital of Providence to learn how to become soldiers. As their family members bade them farewell, little could they have imagined the suffering these men would go through.[10]

The men who were going north to comprise the First Detachment had known each other their entire lives. They included John Babcock, a descendent of Westerly's founder (in 1669), who would have many eventful wartime experiences. John Hallam would stoically do his full duty and would come through without a scratch, while Private John Smith would be the first to fall. These men would serve together, all knowing that each man in the detachment was from the same town; they could be depended on in times of crisis. Whatever lay ahead of them was only a distant thought as the Westerly Boys left their homes for long days and short nights in a distant land.

Following the success at Westerly, the detachment marched east down the Kingston Road and encamped at the village of Wakefield in South Kingstown. They then followed the Post Road to East Greenwich, where another stop was made, gathering men from neighboring Warwick and North Kingstown. Following this, they proceeded back to Providence. Although only gone a week, this vital mission was a smashing success; nearly half of the battery was recruited in this one week. Only fifty more men were needed to complete the battery. The gun detachments were filling out, but spare men were always needed. While this was occurring, the officers at the Benefit Street Arsenal again turned their attention to the citizenry of Providence. In even the most ethnic unit from the smallest village or town, Providence men were always present.

Unlike the previous Rhode Island units, the officers only needed to take out one advertisement—for trained artificers and buglers to join the command. Without circulars, the arsenal on Benefit Street and the drills provided the best recruiting tool. The few recruiting posters sent out were targeted at those men of foreign birth or those unsure if the light artillery was for them. Among the statements were "In marches, the private soldier may usually ride or walk according to his choice and is not cumbered with heavy muskets and accoutrements. Far less drilling is required to secure efficiency in action, than in some other branches of service." Unless taken by an infantry assault, the artillery was generally a safe place to be in combat; the batteries mostly stayed in the rear, shelling the lines. The statement in the recruiting poster was true in all but one regard; the Rhode Island batteries would be drilled constantly to yield a high degree of professionalism that all would see on the battlefield.[11]

The Third Rhode Island was the first unit to contain a large amount of soldiers of Irish birth, while French Canadians were represented in the Fourth Regiment. The foreign soldiers represented a significant change. Battery G would be the first battery to have a large amount of nonnative Rhode Islanders in its ranks. For these men the most important article listed on the broadsides was the $115 bounty. This was paid as fifteen dollars cash upon enlistment and one hundred dollars as a bounty after the three years were over. Only nine months later, the state would be forced to pay up to $400 to send men into the Seventh Rhode Island and Battery H. For now, though, these large bounties were deemed sufficient to stir patriotism and those wanting to prove themselves as Americans.[12]

As with the other light batteries, the recruits again flocked to Battery G; it would be the last unit to leave Rhode Island in 1861. However, something was different. The many young soldiers who had left in the summer and fall of 1861 were gone. Many older men enlisted; the average age of the soldier in Battery G was twenty-six. The ages were very varied, however. The youngest three were sixteen; the oldest was in his sixties. The officers ignored those with boyish looks or gray hair so the unit could quickly be filled up. Rhode Island had already sent nearly 6,000 of her sons into the service in four infantry

Chaplain Thomas Quinn fought hard for the rights of the many Irishmen in Battery G but was eventually overruled by the Protestant state hierarchy (USAMHI).

and one heavy artillery regiments, two battalions of cavalry, and seven batteries of artillery. In addition, hundreds of men joined the United States Navy and the Regular Army.[13]

The men who joined Battery G represented all occupations and all parts of Rhode Island. Despite being heavily drawn from Providence and Washington County, the soldiers came from nearly every town in the state. Among the ranks were eight sets of brothers. The oldest soldier was Private George R. Norton, a sixty-one-year-old laborer from Providence. The maximum enlistment age was supposed to be forty-five, which Norton attested he was. There were two sixteen-year-olds. One of them was William Henry Lewis, a musician and student who enlisted as a bugler, but was appointed as a corporal. He was to leave behind a mother and three brothers; his father was a notorious liar and had recently abandoned the family. Lewis enlisted with his best friend and neighbor, Henry Seamans, who was a cigar maker.[14]

With the crops harvested, and nothing to do in the winter, the men could leave their farms to join their brothers at the front. Many of the men in the battery were skilled workers, not just farmers, as was common in the earlier regiments. They included clerks, mill workers, sailors, students, and teachers. All would find the army equivalent of their civilian occupation and put it to good use in the service. In addition, these men represented an interesting cross section of the United States population. All but eight of the men (all from Ireland), could sign their names to the enlistment papers. This represented a huge step in Rhode Island's public education system. Now, for the first time in history, the majority of the participants of a conflict could write home with the news of what was occurring around them; most important they could read and understand the government documents they were signing. In addition, the math skills that they learned would be of immense use in the artillery as they calculated ranges and set fuzes.[15]

As the men were being gathered for Battery G, Governor Sprague and Adjutant General Edward Mauran selected the officers for Battery G. Three of them came from the elite of Providence, having had a Brown University education. Another came from Warwick, while yet another came from Sweden. There could not have been a more marked contrast between the latter two; it was not only a difference in cultures, but in soldiering as well. For the captaincy Sprague promoted First Lieutenant Charles D. Owen of Battery A. Only nineteen years old, Owen had been a member of the Providence Marine Corps of Artillery and dropped out of Brown in his second year to join the army. He hid his boyish looks with a pair of sideburns and the massive sword he wore at his side. Owen was already a veteran of Bull Run and Bolivar Heights. In early November, he returned home to Providence suffering from "abscesses upon the legs." Owen not only spent a month at home, but he also won a new commission. Sprague's second in command was First Lieutenant Edward H. Sears, the son of Brown's president. Like Owen, he had left school to join the army as a first lieutenant in the Second Rhode Island Infantry. Fighting at Bull Run, Sears earned a captaincy. Now in the fall of 1861 he resigned that rank and took a demotion to join Battery G. A fellow officer in the Second Rhode Island wrote of Sears: "He is now a Capt and will make a very poor one ... a man who I do not respect."[16]

First Lieutenant William B. Rhodes commanded the left section. A jeweler from Warwick, Rhodes was a veteran of the Rhode Island Militia and an expert on rifled cannon, having participated in the testing of the James artillery system. He provided invaluable knowledge into the inner workings of an artillery battery, having served in a Warwick militia company since 1850. Second Lieutenant Crawford Allen was a Brown graduate who had toured Europe and China extensively. In April of 1861, he was in San Francisco and hurried home to the offer of a commission in a light battery. Although ambitious for further promotion, Allen was popular with the men under his command and would become the most respected of the early officers.[17]

The oddest officer in Battery G was Second Lieutenant Otto L. Torslow. He was a Swede by birth and was a veteran of service in the Swedish army. Moving to Providence in the 1850s Torslow had some political connections, which allowed him to gain a commission while also being a veteran officer. While the other officers wore plain jackets with simple rank insignia, Torslow purchased an expensive jacket and cap based on a Russian design, heavily piped in gold and scarlet. Although he could not win a commission, First Sergeant Benjamin E. Kelley was among the officer elite. He was twenty years old and still a student at Providence High School. Kelley was the only son of his widowed mother, who let him go to war. Prior to the war, he had served in the Providence Marine Corps of Artillery where he had learned the art of soldiering. He was a veteran of Bull Run, having fought with the First Rhode Island. Kelley did not return to school in the fall, preferring to rejoin the army.[18]

James Barber was a sailor who joined from Westerly with his half-brother Ellery. James was twenty-two and was employed as a fisherman, in addition to taking part in the local intercoastal trade. He was different in this, as the majority of the men from southern Rhode Island were farmers, or like his brother, employed in the mills. From Warwick came another set of brothers, William and Gilbert Westcott. William became a sergeant, while his older brother served in that capacity and as an artificer. Among the first men to join Battery G was German immigrant Kirby Steinhaur, a thirty-five-year-old farmer from Providence. Steinhaur had originally enlisted in Battery F, but was one of those who remained behind to form Battery G's original detachment. His good friend Lieutenant George W. Field of Battery F wrote to his father, who had some clout with Governor Sprague, asking for Steinhaur to be transferred back to Battery F: "I should like very much to have him with me. For we cannot have too many good men & I know his pluck to be good." Much to his friend's chagrin, Steinhaur remained and was one of the first to become a sergeant.[19]

Men of foreign birth were well represented in Battery G. Of the 273 men who served, thirty-four listed a foreign land as their place of birth, while others from New York, Boston, and New Jersey were recent immigrants who had become Americanized. Many of those giving their residence as Providence were Irish. For the Irish, the service represented a way to pay America back for the provisions sent over during the famine, and to prove that they wanted to be Amer-

Only nineteen years old, Captain Charles D. Owen led Battery G throughout the 1862 campaigns.

icans by fighting for the United States. Promotion for these men was difficult; only four became noncommissioned officers. A third of the membership of Battery G had a direct connection to a foreign land.[20]

Many of these immigrant-soldiers were Catholics, which stood in sharp contrast to the many Protestant faiths represented in the battery. Governor Sprague settled the problem of Catholics and Protestants in the First Rhode Island Regiment by appointing two chaplains, one for each faith. He had also decided to adopt this system for the light artillery, but it represented a unique problem. Because the companies of an infantry regiment served together, the men could attend Sunday worship as a body. The batteries were different; they were sent to different departments. The regimental chaplain could often not reach a battery to perform his duties. This upset Chaplain Thomas Quinn, a priest from Providence appointed as the Catholic chaplain of the First Rhode Island Light Artillery Regiment. Quinn felt that the beliefs of his constituents were being crushed by the elite Protestant officer class who commanded the batteries. He wrote, "The feelings of all should be equally represented." The officers in the other batteries went so far as to arrest men for leaving camp to attend to their Catholic duties, overstepping their roles as commanders. The matter was never fully settled; Chaplain Quinn resigned in January of 1862 and returned to his pulpit in Providence.[21]

As November closed and December began, the battery came together as an organization. In the three-story Benefit Street Arsenal, the men bunked together on the top floor and messed together in the basement. As the new soldiers of Battery G spilled into the building, one of the clerks assisting in recruiting noted that they were "tough and muscular, most excellent material to make a serviceable and efficient corps." The most important floor of the armory was the central drill floor, where the men from all corners of the smallest state and beyond prepared to learn from the veterans of earlier engagements the art and mystery of the light artillery tactics.

The men drilled twelve hours a day at the arsenal, preparing for their duty at the front. The new soldiers rotated clockwise around the pieces, each one learning the duty of each position and how they all fit together. In time the well-oiled precision machine that Sergeant Rhodes had described was made; the men were not just farmers or mill workers learning how to operate a cannon, but thoroughly trained soldiers. The drill hall was filled with many different accents, representing the nationalities of the men in Battery G. The Canadians, English, and Irish all spoke uniquely, while the most distinct speech came from the nasal-sounding native Rhode Islanders who replaced "er" in every word with "ah." Their voices resounded throughout the entire army, as all knew where they hailed from. In the tight confines of the arsenal, the veterans of Providence Marine Corps of Artillery and other members of the militia were adamant that every minor detail, each step, be perfect; if not, the entire detachment was at risk. These soldiers were discharged veterans. They had seen what had occurred at Bull Run when an untrained mob was thrown into combat. Furthermore, they also knew that this war was real; the chances of not returning home were very real indeed.[22]

Prior to leaving for Washington in April of 1861, Lieutenant Governor Samuel Arnold, himself a member of the Corps had given an impassioned speech to the men at the armory. Even eight months later, the message still spoke true for the recruits of Battery G:

> It is no holiday sport for which you have volunteered. A firm resolve on your part to submit cheerfully to the most rigid discipline without regard to personal comfort, can alone bring to that state of efficiency, which the crisis commands. Anyone who hesitates to endure every hardship, to obey without question every order, to think of himself merely as part of the corps, or to merge his individuality in the organization should leave at once. A glorious

cause demands that life itself should be given up if need be, a willing sacrifice upon the altar of our country.

Little did the newly enlisted Rhode Islanders know, that many would be called upon to give the supreme sacrifice in the long years ahead.[23]

Uniforms were issued, and the men learned that the recruiting posters had indeed lied as to the amount of drill in a light battery. Many of the clothes did not fit, so the soldiers simply exchanged with each other until they did. Because they were leaving in the winter months, each soldier was allowed two of the red wool Rhode Island blankets, made in the Sprague Mills in Cranston. Combined with an overcoat, the blankets would shield the men from the harsh Virginia winter that lay ahead. Governor Sprague had already issued the officers' commissions, while the enlisted men eagerly waited to see if they were among the fortunate eighteen who would become a sergeant or a corporal. The artificers looked over their new equipment, including a new traveling forge for the two blacksmiths. After countless hours of drill, the men kept waiting for the orders to be received to send them to the front.[24]

Quartermaster Sergeant J. Russell Field tried to keep the men well supplied but was court marshaled for cowardice on the Peninsula (courtesy Kris VanDenBossche).

On November 30, 1861, the Rhode Island Militia held its first large review in several years. The entire division of six regiments marched in the formation. Each company was attired in a different distinct uniform, ranging from scarlet red for the First Light Infantry to green for the Scituate companies. For the first time many were outfitted in Federal blue. Most of the companies traced direct lineage to the same famed units in the Revolution. The lead unit in the parade was Battery G. This would be their first opportunity to display themselves before the people of Rhode Island and to know if the weeks of hard training had paid off. Captain Owen ordered the six guns hooked up and had Battery G in position at eight o'clock in the morning. The men waiting in the ranks could already see the difference between militia and properly trained soldiers.

Because the majority of the militia had to travel into Providence by train, the line was not formed until high noon. Some came from as far away as Westerly, or by steamer from Newport. At that hour, the battery fired a signal of a cannon salute as 1,850 Rhode Islanders formed up and were inspected by Governor Sprague and Adjutant General Mauran. Following this, the companies began a three-hour parade through downtown extending into the east side of the city. Everywhere the companies went, American flags hung from each house and business. At four in the afternoon, the division returned to Exchange Place, the hub of downtown Providence and where all the regiments mustered before leaving for the war. Battery G unlimbered and fired another salute as the Stars and Stripes was run up a large flagpole. In addition, a Confederate flag captured by the Third Rhode Island Heavy Artillery in South Carolina was displayed. The soldiers stacked their arms and were treated to a fine meal while listening to several patriotic orations. Governor Sprague addressed the artillerists, claiming, "They are a noble example of patriotism, and give renewed assurance that the cause of the country will never want for defenders." Following the supper, the units were dismissed and Battery G returned to the arsenal, satisfied with their first public display. That night Captain Owen addressed the men; he had the piece of paper they had been waiting for.[25]

Because Battery G was nearly fully outfitted and ready for the front, Adjutant General Edward Mauran issued Special Orders 136 on November 30. Captain Owen, and Lieutenants Sears, Allen, and Torslow were to proceed immediately to Washington with the majority of the battery. Lieutenant William Rhodes was ordered to remain behind with his section for a very important task. The First Rhode Island Cavalry was also being raised at the same time, and any day the regiment was expecting a shipment of 1,500 Morgan horses from Vermont, considered the best for cavalry and artillery duties. Battery G would draw its first mounts from this shipment. In addition, Rhodes could recruit any additional men that might go to the arsenal. The next two days were full as the men said farewell to their loved ones, packed their knapsacks, and readied themselves for the journey south. Some traveled to Westminster Street to purchase items advertised in the Providence papers that might add to their comfort in the field; others went to have their pictures taken for family members in the event they did not return. In total, the state had spent $8,835 recruiting, uniforming, and equipping the battery, including the bounties to be paid upon muster out. This was the most spent on a single battery to that time. On December 2, Captain James Cutts swore the men into the service. Although still Rhode Islanders, they were now United States soldiers, subject to the laws and orders of the officers above them. With this act complete, each man received the fifteen dollar advanced bounty as advertised, in addition to a belt and saber.[26]

Captain Owen commanded three officers and eighty-seven enlisted men in the first detachment. Lieutenant Rhodes and his section would follow two weeks later. Owen's two sections would leave Providence on the evening of the second of December. Every other Rhode Island command that had left the state had received rousing speeches from the state officials and a farewell parade through the streets of Providence. Unfortunately, Battery G was left out of this important ceremony; no one saw them off to war. Instead, Captain Owen and his ninety men marched silently the half mile to the Stonington Railroad depot, where they boarded a train for the South. As the men marched, perhaps they thought of an old man with a white beard and a fire burning in his eyes. It was two years to the day since John Brown had been hung for trying to end slavery at Harpers Ferry. Now the Rhode Islanders were going south to join their brothers gone before in an attempt to carry on Brown's fight. Waiting at the railroad station was Carrie Smith, a seven-year-old girl from Providence; her father was a member of the Providence Marine Corps of Artillery. As each soldier prepared to enter the cars, she gave them a gift. Wanting to do something patriotic for her country, the young girl had personally sewn over one hundred needle cases and pincushions. Without their wives and sweethearts present, the men would need to learn how to repair their own clothing. The artillerists accepted the small tokens and placed them in their already burgeoning knapsacks. Finally, Captain Owen and the officers boarded the train and ensured all was in order. The engine was fired up and Battery G was off to war.[27]

4

Duty on the Potomac

A soldiers life is a hard one but I can endure and am ready to do whatever is needed.
—Private George L. Gaskell, December 27, 1861

They had volunteered for a hazardous duty and now the State of Rhode Island was sending ninety more of her sons off to the front of war. Leaving Providence on the night of December 2, Battery G began its journey to the South. The train carrying Captain Owen and his men passed through southern Rhode Island, Connecticut, New York and New Jersey before arriving in Philadelphia. Here the men spent the night of December 4 at the Soldier's Rest, a civilian hostel that offered quarters and meals to Union troops going to and from the war zone. Finally, on December 5, the battery arrived in Washington and was promptly sent to Camp Sprague, the rendezvous for all Rhode Island units. Here a formidable sight awaited them: Colonel Charles Tompkins. Under his guidance, the men would become soldiers.

Almost as soon as the command arrived in the South, the first major incident occurred in the battery. Privates Henry Camsteen, John Higgins, and August Hidelbrand, all from South Kingstown, deserted. The men had been among the first to join, having been left over from Battery F. This was the beginning of a serious problem that would plague Battery G for years. On December 8, Major Alex Webb conducted the first inspection of the command, taking note of the new battery to his battalion. The First Rhode Island Light Artillery Regiment had two battalions, each commanded by a major. The following day Captain Owen appointed eight privates as corporals "to be obeyed and respected as such." Four more would be appointed when the third section arrived in camp.[1]

With the first two sections already at Camp Sprague, the enlisted men were assigned to their barracks. The change from the Benefit Street Arsenal to the new camp in Washington had both a positive and a negative benefit. "Discipline here is more strict. We are encamped in a pleasant place on a hill overlooking Washington and the Potomac having in sight several federal camps," wrote one private. The officers gathered the over thirty forms they would need to complete their duties. They had to report to the adjutant general, as well as the ordnance, quartermaster, and commissary departments. One good article of equipment did arrive when Quartermaster Sergeant J. Russell Field issued the artillerists boots, which extended halfway up the calf and were much more practical for mounted service than shoes. However, they were charged to the men in the regimental books; the boots were optional, but many took the opportunity to wear them. Furthermore, the officers went to the Ordnance Department and put in their request for a battery of guns; without them, the men would be useless. Lieutenant Rhodes remained in Providence awaiting the arrival of the horses from Vermont.[2]

Finally, the guns arrived—four of the massive twenty-pounder Parrotts and two twelve-pound field howitzers. This interesting combination was conceived of as a way to engage targets at both long and short range. The Parrotts fired a large twenty-pound pro-

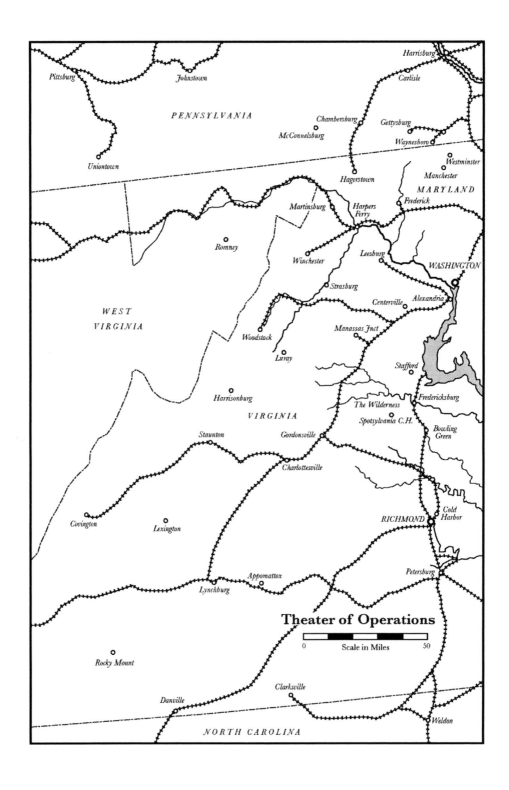

Theater of Operations

jectile over two miles. The gun was disliked by Union artillerists because of its massive weight and the fact that the limber chests carried far less ammunition than the other guns. Furthermore, the howitzers were of Mexican War vintage and fired a twelve-pound shell; they were outdated as field pieces.[3]

Although this armament was placed on the battery, Captain Owen continued to drill the men daily in their use, resuming what had begun at the Benefit Street Arsenal. The complicated light artillery drill was stressful to both mind and body, but it became vital that the men learn it thoroughly so they would not make a critical error when enemy shells started to hit their position. The noncommissioned officers also had much to learn, studying the tactics and getting to know the capabilities of their individual pieces, in addition to supervising their men to insure that they were well behaved. The last became a difficult process for many of the recruits. Neighbors and friends that had grown up together and known each other all their lives now had two or three red stripes on their arms, which put them in a different class than those with none.

Camped alongside Battery G were several other Rhode Island units. Elisha Hunt Rhodes of the Second Regiment was pleased to visit his neighbors, Gilbert and William Westcott from the Warwick side of Pawtuxet. Because of the state's small size, many of the men in Battery G were related or had grown up in the same small villages as their comrades. Among the other regiments present was the Fourth Rhode Island, which had left the state in October and had recently completed a grueling 150-mile forced march into Maryland to protect the fall elections against Confederate infiltration. "Cananicus," a member of this regiment, was a correspondent to the *Providence Journal.* One day he observed Battery G at drill: "Lieut Owen is zealously engaged in the office of instructor. For the time to arrive is soon when it too shall 'take the route.'" In addition, he reported that the unit had been "culled from the very flower of Rhode Island." The drills were made difficult by the fact that there were no horses present. This was about to change.[4]

After waiting in Providence for two and a half weeks for the mounts to arrive, Lieutenant Rhodes finally received 116 of the Morgan horses. Chaplain Frederic Denison of the First Rhode Island Cavalry described the animals assigned to Battery G: "They were of the small Morgan and Canadian breeds, yet not of very light weight. These beasts found in the north of New England and parts of Canada proved to be of superior constitution and metal." Rhodes' detachment was ordered to leave on December 16, the same day his men were sworn in. In only two weeks, the lieutenant had recruited forty-four additional men for the command.[5]

Among them was Private George L. Gaskell, who would quickly be appointed the guidon bearer. He came from Tiverton and represented a unique position in the battery. Only twenty-one years old, he had sailed around the globe as a merchant sailor before the war. He was fluent in French and Latin in addition to several native languages, and was fond of visits to Madagascar and the east coast of Africa. Gaskell was also devoted to his married sister, Mary Call, who lived in Central Village, just over the border in Connecticut.[6]

Finally, on the night of December 16, all was in order as Lieutenant Rhodes and his men prepared to depart. The men signed the muster roll and received their premium. As a Regular, Captain Cutts, the mustering officer recorded the incredible amount of baggage Rhodes' detachment was taking with them: "Eight ambulances, ten thousand pounds baggage stores, one hundred+ ten horses belonging to the United States, which had been previously inspected, branded, and accepted on the part of the Quartermaster General, + six officers horses." As Captain Cutts and Lieutenant Rhodes went through their muster rolls, the enlisted men took the time to bring the horses and stores to the Stonington Railroad Depot. An anxious Private Gaskell took the time to scribble a short note to his sister: "We leave the State for the South tonight. I am in fine health and spirits. So don't worry on my acct. We have a fine company of young men and I think I shall like. I shall write to you again soon."[7]

The horses proved far more difficult to transport then the men and their baggage. The section took a train to Groton, Connecticut, followed by a steamer to New York, then another train to Washington. Because of the horses, the men did not sleep for three days. All of the beasts arrived safely in camp, where the horses were assigned to the detachments and Battery G was now officially a complete light artillery battery prepared for service at the front.[8]

After the men remained at Camp Sprague for several weeks, the time had again come for Battery G. After a brief respite on New Year's Day, when the men were granted passes to tour Washington, Captain Owen prepared the command for the great task before them. The battery had solidified its organization; all of the soldiers knew how to work the guns and the officers had learned their duties. All of the harnesses were hooked up to the mounts as they began to feel, just like the men, the grueling duties of the artillery service. Finally, on January 3, 1862, Owen received his marching orders; he would join a division of Union troops northwest of Washington performing guard duty along the Potomac River. Many of these regiments were badly demoralized and broken after their defeat at Ball's Bluff the previous October. Marching in a column, the battery took two days to reach Poolesville, Maryland. For some the abrupt change from the barracks at Camp Sprague to the life in camp was drastic; many came down with colds as the sleeping conditions changed overnight. The roads were muddy due to recent snowstorms, thus impeding the march.

In addition to the change in weather, the men also had a drastic change in their diet. In Providence and at Camp Sprague the men ate cooked and prepared meals issued to them daily. Now on the march, they lived on hardtack, salted meat, and coffee. The meat was often rotted, while the hardtack was as hard as a brick and could barely be eaten. This did not deter the soldiers, who came up with creative ways to eat the cracker, ranging from frying it in lard to toasting it and even drinking pieces down with coffee. The Civil War soldier lived on a diet of flour, caffeine, and liquid grease. The food provided no nutrients and quickly wore down the men's immune systems to the point they would develop chronic dysentery. Although they did not know it, the food provided by the United States Army would kill more Battery G soldiers than the Confederates ever did. Private Gaskell confessed, "A soldiers life is a hard one but I can endure and am ready to do whatever is needed."[9]

Battery G arrived at Poolesville on January 5 and made their camp in a pine grove, using the trees to string ropes on for the horses. The camp was set in the standard fashion as found in the officer's red book. Much to their surprise, Colonel Tompkins was relieved of duty at Camp Sprague and was placed in command of all of the artillery on the upper Potomac. Battery G was assigned to a good station; located in camp nearby were Batteries A and B of their regiment. Many of the men in these commands instantly recognized their comrades and were allowed to visit them. As the column first came into camp and passed Battery B, the men in G scorned B for having smaller ten pounder Parrotts, which were not capable of the range of the twenty pounders. The men in Battery B took it in jest, as they were fellow Rhode Islanders. The adjustment to camp life was difficult and interesting to the men; it was a trying time, but they felt it was their duty to go through it. This experience also brought together men who prior to enlisting had never even talked to each other. A Battery G soldier reported, "The rich man's son can now experience a little of the hardships and trials which meet the poor laborer from day to day; now all share alike." Through this common bond of living in the same conditions and working together on the guns, the men became comrades in arms.[10]

One tent was issued to each detachment. Called a Sibley tent, it looked like a teepee and could sleep a full detachment of eighteen men lying around a small stove like the spokes of a wheel. When one man wanted to turn over, all had to. There was hardly any space for personal items, as the men had to deal with the cramped tents, which were often filled with casks of gunpowder, large chests, and other superfluous items, all of which would disappear once the battery went on campaign. The small stoves often gave out in the middle of the night, making all cold and miserable. The thick overcoats and two red Rhode Island blankets worked somewhat, but did not fully protect the men of Battery G. After waking up one morning, George Gaskell described his misery of sleeping in a Sibley tent: "I lay shivering in the *infernal* cold listening to the snow pattering on the canvas." Although the men lived in tents, they built a small hut of timber to cook their rations; rather than issuing hardtack, the officers allowed the men to build a small oven to bake bread in.[11]

On January 8, Captain Owen issued three sets of orders to guide his men in their duties as they adapted to field service. The first directed the care and grooming of the battery horses. This task had to be done daily, as the horses made it possible for the unit to move and were hard to replace. The drivers were responsible for their care, while the sergeants were to watch their men perform the duty; an unfortunate private was detailed daily to groom the sergeant's horse. While the sergeants monitored the daily care of the horses, a lieutenant was detailed each day to oversee the general operations in the camp. In the other

Sergeant Jacob F. Kent of Warwick died of tuberculosis at home, shortly after receiving his discharge (USAMHI).

branches of the service, the task of officer of the day was rotated among the ten captains. In the artillery, the lieutenants each performed the duty every four days, more if an officer was on detached duty. The most important order was General Orders Number 4: "The ammunition chests must at all times be properly packed and the cartridges secure from rolling." This had been a directive to all Rhode Island batteries since the previous year. On July 9, 1861, a caisson belonging to Battery A had exploded in Washington after the men simply threw the rounds into the chests, killing two and severely injuring three. The corporals were responsible for seeing the orders were carried out. These principles would carry the men through the war.[12]

The typical day in camp for a light battery began at 5:00 A.M. with the sounding of reveille by the musicians; the men would throw out expletives such as "throw the bugler in the guard house" as they awoke and were given fifteen minutes to get dressed and packed up. After reveille, the sergeants would call their detachment to make sure all of the men were present for duty. The first sergeant would report the findings to the captain, while the clerk prepared the morning report. Following the roll call, the drivers would repair to the stable area to groom and clean the horses, which were fed and watered as well. At the same time, the cannoneers would check over the guns, insuring the chests were in order. Only after these tasks were complete were the men allowed to eat breakfast. After this, those reporting an illness could see the doctor if one was available.

The light artillery did not have a large amount of fatigue duty to perform and only had to police the camp. Drill was held in the morning and the afternoon for two hours at a time. The morning drill consisted of individual detachments and sections training together. In the afternoon, the entire battery put on a drill, often to the delight of throngs of infantrymen. Sometimes they would end it by firing blank cartridges. The horses were again fed and watered in the evening as the men ate their supper; there followed two roll calls, with dress parade in between. Here orders and other battery transactions were relayed. Finally, at 9:00, after a grueling day the men retired to their tents, ready to begin it again.[13]

The light artillery did not have to perform picket duty frequently, which consisted of monotonously waiting at night for the Confederates to attack; they were the outer line of defense for the camp. The artillerists did, however, have to defend the canal boats on the Chesapeake and Ohio Canal, one of the major east-west supply routes. In the line of this duty, the men broke camp on January 10 and went the short distance to "Muddy Camp" near Edward's Ferry. Here they saw interesting sights as the pickets from both sides ice-skated across the frozen Potomac River. One day a private from the Fifteenth Massachusetts ran across the river and yelled "Three cheers for the Union;" he was almost captured by the Confederate pickets.

The guns were arranged along the riverbank as the cannoneers worked tirelessly to perfect their drill. At the new camp, Private George Gaskell was pleased to receive a promotion to company clerk. In this position, he was relieved of all duties and reported directly to the captain in order to assist him in the company paperwork. In addition, Gaskell served as the captain's orderly and carried the battery guidon. This position allowed the private to gain a view into the inner-workings of the battery. Furthermore, he messed with the officers and shared a tent with the first and quartermaster sergeants. Gaskell continued to complain about the cold, asking his sister to make him a quilt to supplement the clothing issued in Providence.[14]

Only four miles from the position was Leesburg, Virginia, which remained heavily fortified by a large Confederate force. It was the duty of the soldiers on the Maryland side of the Potomac to insure that the enemy did not go anywhere unnoticed. The seventeenth of January was an interesting day for the battery. Captain Owen's tent caught fire after his stovepipe erupted; it spread to two other tents before being extinguished. By January 19, the boots Private Henry Farnsworth drew from the quartermaster became uncomfortable. He had to seek Owen's permission to exchange them for a pair of shoes from Esek Bowen, who had decided not to use his clothing allowance to purchase the item. The captain consented and the two wore each other's footwear.[15]

Battery G finally had its full complement of officers and men by this time, with an aggregate enrollment of 153. On January 21, the men received a welcome surprise in the form of Governor Sprague; but even more welcome was the paymaster, who arrived to pay the men for the one-month service, which was a rare occurrence. Later in the war, they would sometimes go without seeing the paymaster for six months. A private received thirteen dollars per month, while corporals, buglers, and artificers got fourteen. A sergeant saw seventeen and the first sergeant twenty-one dollars per month. The officers were paid at $117 for a lieutenant and $150 for the captain. Although these wages were much higher, the officers had to pay for their own uniforms, food, horses, forage, and servants; in addition, any government property unaccounted for was taken out of their pay. The payday brought joy to the camp, but sadness rained in on January 24. Private John Taft, a weaver from Ireland, died in Washington of disease; his was the first death the battery suffered. In it, they could see that soldiering was no gentlemen's sport; it was real, as were the consequences.[16]

Enlisting as a private, Lieutenant Benjamin E. Freeborn was wounded at Gettysburg and brought Battery G home as its last commander (USAMHI).

The first day of February brought the first court martial in Battery G. Corporals William W. Potter and Charles Jennings had been caught drinking whiskey in their tent against orders. Captain Owen, Lieutenant Allen, and Private James Barber found them while conducting an inspection. The threesome kicked down the door of the tent, dragged the two men out and clapped them in irons. Potter and Jennings were charged with being intoxicated on duty and "gross misconduct." Both men were found guilty. They lost their rank, but were further sentenced to a week in solitary confinement and to wearing a ball and chain for an additional week. Captain Owen meant the punishment to be a deterrent to others. The sentence was imposed "for the deep disgrace they have brought upon themselves, to the company, and to the positions they occupy." The two men would prove to be good soldiers. Within months, they would have the two stripes of a corporal again and would end the war as sergeants.[17]

The duty remained monotonous at Muddy Camp; all the men did was wait for the Confederates to appear. In the off time, Owen and the officers drilled the men constantly. Their comrades in Batteries A and B nearby brought a welcome relief. On February 17, it was announced that General Ulysses S. Grant had scored a brilliant victory against the Confederates at Fort Henry in Tennessee. To commemorate the event, Lieutenant Edward Sears fired a salute of thirty-four shells into Virginia, one for every state in the Union. On February 27, Colonel Tompkins ordered Lieutenant Rhodes to take his section to Ball's Bluff, opposite Leesburg, Virginia. A strong force was stationed here, and the long range Parrotts could handle any threat from the opposite side. Any time the Confederates were observed Rhodes ordered the men to fire the guns. Private Barber recalled, "We fired at the rebel pickets posted in Virginia." One day the fire was accurate enough to score a direct hit on a caisson. The vehicle exploded, "which caused a general stampede." Captain Owen, watching, commented: "Good shooting."

This was the exception, not the rule. Private Gaskell wrote, "Every day or two we are out shelling the rebel batteries on the Virginia shore, but with only indifferent success." Furthermore, Gaskell believed General Charles Stone, in command of the troops on the upper Potomac, should be brought up on charges for allowing the Confederates to remain directly across the river instead of ordering the attack. Lieutenant Rhodes and his section were gone for a week before returning to Muddy Camp. His policy of firing at any living target across the river became doctrine, as the men fired the guns daily. Because target practice was frowned upon in the army as a waste of ammunition, this allowed the sergeants and corporals to accurately guess the ranges of their guns for certain types of rounds, in addition to providing for the most realistic training they could receive. Only the massive Parrotts of Lieutenants Sears' and Rhodes' sections were used, as the smaller howitzers would not have been as effective at long range; thus the men of Crawford Allen's center section missed out on this valuable exercise.[18]

While the battery remained at Muddy Camp, Captain Owen and the regimental surgeons were making preparations for the upcoming campaign. Because the battery had been recruited in such haste, there were men in the ranks who were not capable of service in the field, and they were ordered to be discharged from the service for medical disability. They were seven in number; the majority were over the age of forty, but one of them was only eighteen years old. Private Charles Webb, a spinner from Providence, was discharged "by reason of mental imbecility produced by the habit of masturbation." In September of 1862, Webb would reenlist into the Twelfth Rhode Island and would die of typhoid. In addition, Battery G suffered its first real deserter at the front. Four other men had already left while the unit was in Washington. Now Private James McCabe, an Irishman, took his leave on February 24. He was never heard from again. In addition, Captain Owen took stock of his horses. Due to the harsh weather at Muddy Camp three had died, reducing the number to 113. Now rather than receiving the best from Rhode Island, the left-over horses would be sent from Washington. Each month the captain had to file a monthly return to the Rhode Island adjutant general and the United States Army chronicling his losses and accounting for all men and government property.[19]

By the first week of March the Confederates at Leesburg had pulled back; indeed the main Confederate forces around Manassas had also left and had gone into the Shenandoah or towards Culpeper. This gave Union forces their first real opportunities to cross into Virginia since the previous summer. The Rhode Islanders were anxious to return to Bull Run in order to retrieve the bodies of those who died that morning on Matthews Hill. On March 9, Captain Owen and his orderly, Private Gaskell, crossed the Potomac into Leesburg to investigate where the Confederates forces had relocated: the town was abandoned. Gaskell called it "one of the greatest events of my life parading the streets of this beautiful Secesh town." While they were on the opposite bank of the river, a heavy rain fell, almost trapping the two men. Finally, they returned to camp in the afternoon. That night Captain Owen was summoned to Colonel Tompkins' tent; orders had again arrived.[20]

On March 11, the ominous sounding of "Boots and Saddles," the artillery call to arms, was called as the cannoneers limbered up the pieces and the drivers harnessed their horses. Battery G was going into enemy territory. All baggage that was unnecessary, including tents, was to be left behind. Under these circumstances, the men would place a heavy canvas tarp over the gun and limber at night and go to sleep. The battery crossed the Potomac at Harpers Ferry and was ordered to proceed to Winchester in a perceived move up the Shenandoah Valley. The expedition was nearly 200 miles in length and tested the men and their horses for the rigors of field service. Although it was strenuous, the Rhode Islanders were thrilled with the beautiful valleys and rugged mountains of the Shenandoah; it was vastly different than the geography of their native state. Private Gaskell called it "the finest country I ever saw."

A battle was thought imminent, but there were no Confederate forces in the area. This brief campaign was just what the commander in chief wanted so the men would not be worn out on the first actual march. Some parts of the expedition proved hazardous, as the Virginia spring yielded large amounts of mud, thus causing the guns to become stuck in the mud. On one occasion, sixteen horses were required to pull a piece out. After remaining at Berryville, near Winchester, for several days they returned to Harpers Ferry, where the orders were countermanded. The battery would rejoin Tompkins' command on the Potomac. Thus, Battery G missed an opportunity with destiny to fight Thomas "Stonewall" Jackson for possession of the Shenandoah. Little did the Rhode Islanders know that two and a half years later, they would fight their own bloodbath in the Shenandoah Valley.[21]

While the battery was on duty in the Valley, they received their first issuance of recruits. Unlike the bounty men and shirkers who would plague the army in 1864, these men had volunteered under the same principal as the men in Battery G, to preserve the Union. They were seventeen in number and were distributed among the different detachments; the majority came from Providence, while several came from Westerly and Charlestown. One of these men was Albert D. Cordner, a twenty-six-year-old mechanic from

Sergeant William W. Potter (right) and his brother George (left) both enlisted from rural Coventry. William was court-martialed for drunkenness and was wounded at Antietam. His brother George would survive the war almost unscathed only to lose an eye in the war's last grand charge; but he would be awarded with the nation's highest honor for his bravery.

the village of Shannock in Charlestown. Like some of the men, he was married with children. The men without a detachment were called "spare men" and were assigned general duties such as grooming the horses or fatigue duty until a berth opened in a gun detachment.[22]

Battery G remained at Harpers Ferry, waiting for orders. Located at the head of the Shenandoah Valley, the town was only a shell of its former glory as one of the largest manufacturing centers in the world, having been destroyed at the start of the Civil War to prevent the armory machinery from falling into enemy hands. On March 18, Lieutenant Otto Torslow went absent without leave and returned quite intoxicated. He stole a bugle from one of the musicians before finally passing out while playing the instrument. The men took the time to view the sights in the abandoned town (where only 100 people remained out of 4,000 before the war) while contending with muddy country roads yet again. After two weeks in the Shenandoah, Battery G received orders on the twentieth directing them to Washington itself; they completed the journey in thirty-six hours. The unit was now receiving orders from a new commanding general: George B. McClellan.[23]

Only thirty-eight years old, he was a West Point graduate and a Mexican War veteran. At the beginning of the war, McClellan organized the Ohio militia and led them to several important but small victories in the mountains of western Virginia. After the Federal forces were defeated at Bull Run he was placed in command of all the Union forces in the Washington area and spent the following nine months preparing the massive army for battle. Now in the spring of 1862 he and President Abraham Lincoln thought they were ready for the ultimate test of a soldier. McClellan was loved by his men, being affectionately referred to as "Little Mac" or the "Young Napoleon." He knew how to make an army; now the United States would see if he could use it.

As the thousands of men were gathering for the campaign, McClellan took the time to organize the army. The force would be called the Army of the Potomac. Prior to the Civil War the largest organization in the army was the division, created only during wartime. With so many troops at his disposal, McClellan created five corps. Each was to be commanded by a major general and was in effect its own army. These new units would allow the general to monitor a smaller number of commands. In each corps would be three divisions, each with three brigades, containing four infantry regiments apiece. The artillery would be divided at the rate of four batteries to a division. This was a slight improvement over the Revolutionary and Mexican War policy of assigning batteries piecemeal to individual infantry brigades. Here they were totally ineffective for massed firepower and were often controlled by infantry commanders who had no idea of artillery theory. The infantry organization would remain unchanged throughout much of the war. The artillery organization would change drastically, though. One thing that would remain was a vast logistical supply line that kept plenty of ammunition in the field to supply the batteries. Each gun carried 200 rounds in the limber chests and caissons for the detachments, fifty in each chest, while an additional two hundred followed in the army wagons assigned to each corps.[24]

The troops on the upper Potomac were designated as the Second Corps. This unit was to be commanded by Major General Edwin Vose Sumner, at sixty he was the oldest field commander in the Army of the Potomac but also one of the most qualified. His second division included all those troops involved in the Ball's Bluff fiasco. This division was commanded by John Sedgwick, another veteran officer who was called "Uncle John" by his men; the general did not mind the sobriquet. He was a Connecticut Yankee and had served for thirty years on the western frontier. Like the men under his command, Sedgwick had been a career artillerist prior to becoming a dragoon officer in 1855. His artillery brigade was commanded by Colonel Charles Tompkins. Tompkins was one of the few field grade artillery officers in the army at the time. Under his command were four batteries, one from New York and three from Rhode Island. Among them was Captain Charles Owen's Battery G.[25]

Arriving in the city, the men were met with interesting scenes that they had not experienced in several months during their tour of duty on the Potomac. "One soon gets weary of seeing long crowds of brainless dandies and half drunken soldiers on the side walks," wrote Private Gaskell. The Ordnance Department summoned Battery G to the Washington Arsenal to exchange their cannon. The odd combination of Parrotts and howitzers would be tried by the other two Rhode Island batteries. Now Battery G had six three inch ordnance rifles, one of the best guns in the light artillery. This gave the cannoneers a far safer instrument of war and one that would be used on many bloody fields to come. In addition, more horses were received from the government to replace those that had died or broken down. As the men were preparing to leave, death again struck the battery. Private Eliza H. Brown of Providence died of pneumonia on March 22. In addition, Michael Kingsley deserted the same day. Nevertheless, by March 25, Battery G was ready for the campaign.[26]

Using their *Artillery Tactics,* the officers directed the men to break down the batteries' guns and other vehicles and to place them in boxes to be reassembled later onshore. The horses were stabled aboard the *Ella,* while the *Delaware* and *Charles Gorge* transported the cannoneers and baggage. As the battery left, the men were forced to turn in their large tents as they took up too much room in the wagons; the officers were allowed to retain the larger tents. The men in Battery G became some of the first in the army to be equipped with the shelter tent. Each soldier carried a square of the canvas in his knapsack. At night, two soldiers would button their halves together, thus creating a small tent. The men pitched them only in poor weather, as they mostly slept under the stars or the guns. These tents provided a ready means of shelter that only took several minutes to erect. By the end of the campaign, the entire Army of the Potomac was outfitted with them.[27]

On March 29, all was ready as Battery G departed Alexan-

A native of Charlestown, Private Albert D. Cordner was active in the 1862 campaigns and acted as a forager on the Peninsula.

dria for Fortress Monroe. As they left the city, they passed Mount Vernon and the men gazed at the house where George Washington once lived. The only thing to eat that night was pork stew, which contributed to the already miserable conditions of men not used to being on the ocean; many became seasick. This was not the first time Private Gaskell had been to sea. He wrote, "I would like to be on the quarter deck of the Ariel again bounding over the blue waters of the Mozambique or still better to recline under the Mango trees. But that is past." In addition, Gaskell was also hoping for a commission, because a vacancy had opened on Colonel Tompkins' staff. The armada proceeded slowly down the Chesapeake. On the night of March 30, a severe storm hit the *Delaware,* which was carrying Battery G's wagons, artificer equipment, ammunition, and other vital instruments. The crashing of the waves ignited a fire, which quickly spread. With few options, Lieutenant William Rhodes, who was onboard with his section, ordered the men to abandon ship. The next morning the vessel was found as the fires were extinguished. The battery lost a wagon and two ammunition chests; but most important, many of the men's knapsacks were gone, leaving the men with only the clothes on their backs.[28]

Finally, on the morning of April 2, 1862, Battery G arrived at Fortress Monroe. First Sergeant Benjamin Kelley wrote, "great difficulty in disembarking." All of the equipment had to be remounted and the ammunition checked to insure that it was still usable. Among the first sights viewed was the USS *Monitor,* only a few weeks removed from her battle with the *Virginia.* Up a peninsula separated by the York and James rivers was Richmond. Standing in the path of the Union Army were thousands of entrenched Confederates waiting to give battle.[29]

5

The Peninsula

We came to the bridge that crosses a little stream before entering the first woods.
Here the road was very poor indeed. The remainder of the night was spent
in crossing the river with the other half of battery.
—Captain Charles D. Owen, June 1, 1862

Long lines of men wearing blue gathered on the eastern tip of the Virginia Peninsula in April of 1862. After a year of war, the Union had now produced a combat force in the East thought capable of ending the rebellion. Each week word of victory came in the West, including the recent Battle of Shiloh; both sides were horrified at the massive casualties, but the Confederates were stopped and repulsed. Now George B. McClellan stood poised to strike. He had spent the entire winter of 1862 preparing the massive army around Washington for battle. These men were no longer a mob; they were now soldiers. After much debate with President Lincoln, McClellan decided to take his army of 120,000 men and sail down the Chesapeake Bay to Fortress Monroe on the tip of the Peninsula. From here, he would march the seventy miles up the narrow strip of land to besiege and capture Richmond. With a trained army such as he had, the general was sure that the war would be over soon. The forces assembled south of Washington and from there steamed to the fortress. Once all of the troops were in order, McClellan would march.[1]

Battery G disembarked from their ships after the rough voyage; some of the men needed new uniforms and the entire battery had to be unpacked and reassembled. Most important, the horses needed to be exercised. The men also prepared both physically and mentally for what many thought would be a battle in the near future to decide the fate of the war; somewhere to the west lay the Confederate army. With no food at hand, one detachment built a raging bonfire to keep themselves occupied.

The first major objective for the Army of the Potomac was the Warwick Line. It stretched the length of the Peninsula, with a large base in the historic village of Yorktown. McClellan knew that he would have to lay siege to the town, in order to force the retreat of the Confederates. Here lay his one problem: he always hesitated. Throughout the campaign, he outnumbered the enemy but never used this to his advantage. The Confederate commander, John Magruder, staged elaborate displays in front of the Union troops, marching in circles to show that he had more troops. In reality it was all a show to make the Union think there were more Confederates present than there actually were.[2]

Sedgwick's Division began to move towards Yorktown as soon as they arrived on the Peninsula on the fifth. The path was somewhat difficult, as trees and other debris had to be cleared from the road before any progress could be made. The soldiers cheered wildly as General McClellan rode by them. The First Division of the Second Corps, commanded by Israel Richardson, had yet to arrive. The Confederate lines ran directly across the Peninsula: there was no way to flank it. Federal soldiers probed the front daily, trying to find a weakness. Meanwhile, in front of Yorktown, the main body of the Union army prepared for a siege. Trenches were dug, and all was placed in order for the siege to begin. Because of the relatively short space that the Army of the Potomac occupied, the batteries would each be rotated in the trenches daily, so each command could gain combat experience. Battery G was so close to the enemy that men were forbidden to talk after dark and buglers William H. Lewis and Thomas F. Mars were prohibited from calling on the bugle.[3]

McClellan planned to bring up siege artillery from Fortress Monroe, but he would depend upon the field guns for now. Battery B was given the honor of firing the first shot at Yorktown. An onlooker remembered that the "The lanyard jumped from the gun, there was a flash, a deafening roar, the gun recoiling backwards, and away flew the shell on its aerial flight, bursting over the enemy's fortifications." This was the beginning of a tradition that would be carried throughout the rest of the war: to always depend upon the Rhode Island batteries.[4]

The Federal artillery fired constantly, trying in vain to drive the enemy out of the works. They became so precise that the artillerists could put one round after another into the same position with pinpoint accuracy. Although the guns were having good effect on the enemy, sometimes the Confederates would reply. The men from Richmond in Battery G received news that one of their fellow townsmen was killed during the siege; he was a private in Battery C.

When the siege of Yorktown began, the men in Battery G began to adapt to the trials and trepidations of being soldiers on the front lines. They had to perform guard duty each night, while the poor roads caused by constant rain forced Quartermaster Sergeant Russell Field to cut the rations because no more could be forwarded to the battery, as

Edward H. Sears resigned his captaincy in the Second Rhode Island to become a lieutenant in Battery G. He later served in the United States Navy.

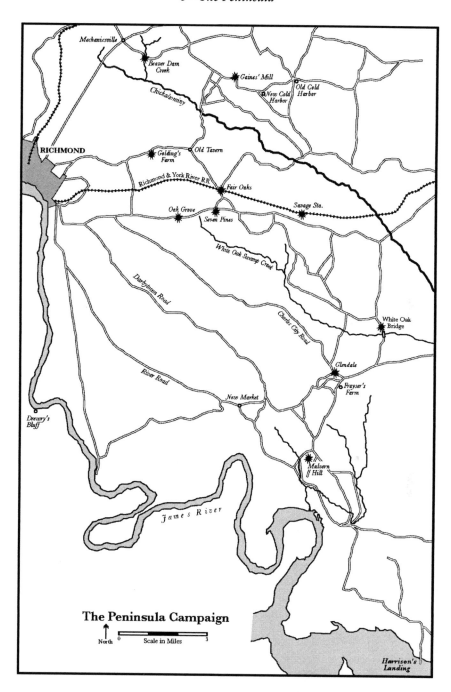

The Peninsula Campaign

North 0 Scale in Miles 3

the wagons could not move. Albert Cordner wrote, "The mud is so deep that the Army can't move. Some of the boys want to go home."

Grain for the horses was also in short supply, as many of the horses from units other than Battery G died along the road. On the ninth of April, Private Cordner was sent to fetch some grain from the transports at Fortress Monroe. He became lost and was almost captured by a Confederate patrol; eventually he was directed back to camp by McClellan himself. The soldier made a poor appearance after not bathing or washing his clothes in three days. Governor William Sprague appeared in camp to pay a visit to the soldiers from Rhode Island on the thirteenth of April; he was drunk in front of his fellow statesmen. The fifteenth was a busy day as the cannoneers limbered up their guns and began to move. Captain Owen and his Rhode Islanders were about to receive their baptism by fire.[5]

With the trenches in place, Battery G advanced to within 1,000 feet of the Confederate works when the rebels opened fire on April 17. This was the moment the battery had waited for. After months of countless hours of drill and occasionally firing across a river, now Battery G was finally going into combat. James Barber wrote, "Day comes in pleasant a sharp skirmish broke out between our men and the rebels." As Private Cordner's detachment deployed into action, the axle to their gun broke; this did not stop them, however. The six guns came abreast, unlimbered and began to fire shells into the enemy earthworks, some of them simply rebuilt from the British defenses in the Revolution.

Since Battery G was a state unit, Governor Sprague was often seen in the field exercising his role as captain-general of the state militia; he held no United States military rank. During the height of the bombardment, Sprague rode up to the battery. Dismounting, the governor promptly sighted two of the guns, smiling with delight as the rounds hit the Confederate fortifications. Satisfied he had made a good impression, the governor mumbled he had "wasted ammunition enough," and he rode off to the next Rhode Island unit. During the day rumors spread through the other batteries that three Battery G men had been severely wounded in the exchange. As with most army rumors it proved to be false.[6]

Built by soldiers of the Fifth New Hampshire, the Grapevine Bridge allowed the Second Corps to arrive at Fair Oaks on time, but it almost collapsed under the weight of Battery G (Library of Congress).

The unit was "engaged day and night" in the second siege of Yorktown, the first having occurred in 1781. Each gun fired up to 300 rounds per day. In Battery G, this caused some problems, as the cannons were fired constantly. On April 23, the axles, which held the gun carriage together, broke in two or three pieces as a result of poorly made government equipment. It was impossible to keep them at the front in this condition because the accuracy of the sights would be thrown off. The guns were pulled off the line, welded back together by the blacksmiths and were quickly back in action. The firing was having its effects on the men's nerves, not just on the Confederate works. "While I write the cannonading shakes the ground," remembered Private Gaskell as he wrote another letter home to his sister. McClellan's plan was to keep up a show of force in order to reduce the Confederate defenses before the infantry would carry them. A cold rain fell constantly as the soldiers kept up the duty. In Battery G, the men "slept as soundly as though we were on feather beds." This lying in the rain would begin to cause problems for the artillerists as they began to come down with diseases that they had never experienced or heard of before. The hospitals were soon filled with the sick and those malingering soldiers who did not want to complete their duty. Lying on the cold ground produced rheumatism, which left many with sore joints and bones.[7]

At least one section of the battery was engaged daily in the trenches. The Rebels did return fire occasionally, but their shells often failed to explode. Off duty, the men kept themselves occupied by ducking from the Confederate fire and digging trenches to move the siege lines forward. Because the supplies had to be brought up from Fortress Monroe, the drivers were constantly engaged in bringing up fresh supplies and ammunition, and in doing so they had to run a gamut of fire. On April 28, Lieutenant Allen was ordered to shell Redoubt Number Seven with his section. The men of the center section soon found the accurate range of the fort and were placing their shells within it. However, Allen was dissatisfied with the way his guns kept on recoiling to the point that the tired cannoneers could not place them back in the same position after each shot. The lieutenant decided to try something new. He ordered the trail of a three inch ordnance rifle placed against a large tree nearby; Allen thought the tree would absorb the recoil. The plan quickly turned into a bad idea when the gun did not recoil at all. The force was absorbed into the wooden carriage as the gun buckled under the immense force and was thrown off the carriage. This brought an end to Allen's new experiment; the piece was remounted and put back into action the traditional way.[8]

The day after the accident, a pleasant surprise came when the battery received two months' pay. McClellan finally prepared to assault the fortifications on the night of May 4, but Magruder withdrew. The Confederates fired their guns incisively as the rain fell and covered the movement. Battery G had attained its first battle honor, "Yorktown," to emblazon on its guidon.[9]

As the Confederates pulled out of Yorktown, they regrouped as the Federals pushed further west. Some of the men took the time to visit the abandoned earthworks and the location where Cornwallis surrendered; for some of the men from western Rhode Island their ancestors had been here nearly a century earlier fighting in the Revolution. On May 5, the Confederates counterattacked at the Battle of Williamsburg, the first land battle of the campaign. The engagement was in effect a draw, but was claimed as a victory by the Union as the enemy again retreated.[10]

The most important equipment in Battery G were also considered members of the unit: the battery horses. Ever since Lieutenant Rhodes had brought the horses south from Providence, they had been of concern, as the beasts often fell ill and the men tried every-

Battery G had a difficult experience passing through the Chickahominy Swamp on their way to the Battle of Fair Oaks.

thing they could do to help them without a veterinarian present. Once the battery retired for the evening, the horses were unharnessed and groomed by the drivers as the cannoneers greased the wheels on the limbers, guns, and caissons for another day. Private Barber complained, "They must be attended to at all times." At night, the infantry around them simply had to drop their knapsacks and muskets and go into bivouac. Sometimes the artillerists were up all night preparing for another day at the front. Despite this, some men developed a special attachment to their mounts. Private George Gaskell rode his gray Morgan daily and wrote, "I prize him most highly. He is kind, gentle, and faithful and stands first rate."[11]

Small skirmishes were fought up the Peninsula as the vast Army of the Potomac advanced closer to Richmond. The artillery and the infantry were loaded onboard steamers and taken to West Point, farther up the Peninsula. Here McClellan hoped to establish another base of supply. All baggage except for overcoats, canteens, and haversacks were left behind at Yorktown and would be brought up later. Battery G had only been on the Peninsula for a month and was already starting to show the effects of the campaign.[12]

All they had to eat daily was six hard crackers and dirty water to drink; it caused a severe amount of illness in the battery, but nothing could be done to help those in need. Private Gaskell described his condition:

> Exuberent spirits, and an appetite that would astonish a cannibal: black as a negro a nose that blushes at the sun continually a beard and a moustache are distinctly visible. Several dirty shirts and one ragged pair of pants. My face is black, fingers ditto. Crouched under a blanket spread under two crouched sticks and you have a total of G.L.G. I cannot but feel first rate as they say. I have seen enough (not of fighting) but of hard fare, sickness and vicious horses, to say nothing of no mail.[13]

As the men advanced closer to Richmond, they began counting down the miles. Some nights it was savagely cold as the rain came down; it also hailed stones "the size of peaches." The men eventually did not care, just trying to keep the horses moving and the ammunition dry.[14]

By the end of May, McClellan had dispatched two corps across the south bank of the Chickahominy River to Fair Oaks, a railroad stop on the Richmond and York River Railroad. In Battery G, despite their ragged condition, Lieutenant Torslow was excited that his battery would soon be engaged in a real, pitched battle; the lieutenant had not seen any combat since his service in the Swedish army. On May 24, the Westerly Boys suffered their first sense of dishonor when George Church, a twenty-seven-year-old farmer who had joined in March, deserted and was never heard from again. One of the vital cogs in the artillery machine was missing, but the weak link was replaced by another Westerly soldier

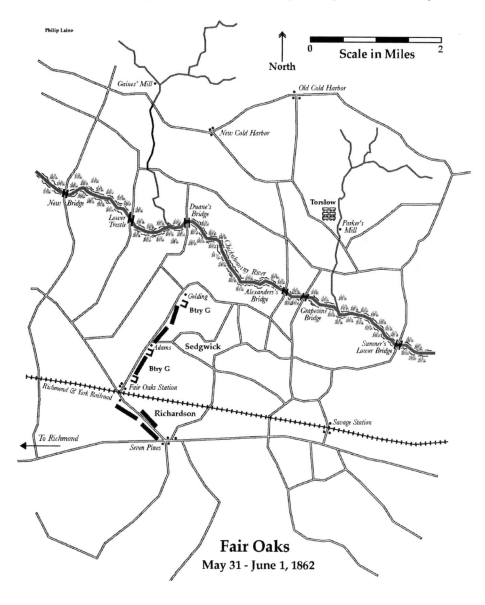

Fair Oaks
May 31 - June 1, 1862

who would stay by his comrades in the engagement sure to come. Only three days after Church left, yet another major incident occurred. Private Jesse Young deserted on the eve of battle and made his way back to Providence; his case would be dealt with severely.[15]

In order to support the Third and Fourth corps on the Confederate side of the Chickahominy, General Sumner ordered a bridge built across the span. The weeks of bad weather contributed to the flooding of the stream, making the project an almost impossible task. For three days straight it had rained, leading Private Cordner to write, "Thundered and rained the hardest. It was the worst I ever knew." The Fifth New Hampshire of the Second Corps built the bridge in two days, allowing the Union forces to reinforce their comrades at Fair Oaks.[16]

On May 31, Joseph Johnston, commanding a large Confederate force, attacked the Third and Fourth corps along the line. The sole feature on this battlefield was a grouping of seven pine trees. The Confederates fought hard and soon the Union troops were buckling and on the verge of running away. Confederate reinforcements got lost in the forests and could not exploit the breach. At 2:00, on his own initiative, Sumner sent Sedgwick's Division into the mass of confusion that was the Federal army. These Union reinforcements arrived just in time to prevent a total rout within the Army of the Potomac. With additional troops arriving on the field by the hour, both sides prepared for the second round of combat on June 1. This would be the first large action of the Peninsula Campaign. Battery G was only five miles from the battlefield, but would have a perilous journey getting there.[17]

It was 2:00 in the afternoon as the batteries of Colonel Tompkins' brigade left camp and proceeded to the front. In the woods to the front the heavy crashes of musketry could be heard, letting everyone know they were about to enter a desperate engagement. The artillery, as always, brought up the rear of the column as the rest of the Second Corps advanced into battle. Battery I, First United States, led the column, followed by Battery A, First Rhode Island, and then the Rhode Islanders of Battery B, with Captain Owen's G bringing up the rear. The wagons, forges, and other noncombat equipment were left behind on the north bank of the Chickahominy near Parker's Mill so the advance would not be slowed. Owen further ordered Lieutenant Torslow's caissons to remain behind. The lieutenant was going to miss the battle he wanted to be part of. In order to reach Fair Oaks, the artillery had to cross the swollen Chickahominy River over the rickety Grapevine Bridge. The river by this time was more of a swamp than an actual body of water. As described by Colonel Edward Cross of the Fifth New Hampshire, "The swamp itself was a mass of sorry vegetation, huge trees, bushes, grape vines, & creeping plants. Beneath the water lay a thick bed of rich, soft earth about the consistency of mortar."[18]

The raging river, combined with the Virginia mud in the roads, made it all but impossible to move the guns. Finally the small wooden structure that functioned as a bridge was reached and Battery A and Battery B went over it cautiously. The bridge groaned under the tons of weight put on it by the batteries and their heavily loaded limber chests. One Battery A soldier wrote, "It was a great miracle that the Grapevine Bridge held together as it did." Finally, it was Owen's turn to bring Battery G across; five guns were cautiously brought over, but then disaster almost struck the command. As the last gun of Battery G was being pulled over the Grapevine Bridge, the cannoneers had to jump into the swamp, which was up to their chests, and hold the bridge together so it would not be swept away by the current. With the bridge cleared, the battery continued onward. The infantry columns had destroyed the roads as they ran into the fight, so the drivers had to use spur and whip while the cannoneers frantically tried to push the guns along. In many places, the cannon were simply unlimbered and dragged by the weary artillerists. First Lieutenant Nelson Ames of Battery G, First New York Light Artillery recorded. "No one living who was engaged that night trying to get the battery through the swamp can forget the difficulties encountered, or fails to remember the struggle that was almost paralyzing."[19]

In the front, three miles away, the soldiers could continue to hear the fighting and wanted to join in the fray. Colonel Charles Tompkins galloped into the swamp to encourage his command forward. Another small stream was soon encountered; the men went into the creek as the horses were unharnessed and the guns dragged through it. Each battery took four and a half hours to make it that far. After the obstacle of the creek, yet another one was faced in the form of a small muddy road that led to the battlefield. By 7:00, Owen managed to bring three pieces through. He left orders for Lieutenant Edward Sears to carry on the mission as the half battery continued onward in hopes of joining in the fighting. After the New Yorkers had passed the narrow road, it became necessary for the two Rhode Island batteries to take the axes off of the caissons and corduroy the roads in order for them to pass. This consisted of laying logs over the roads to prevent the wheels from going into the mud: even this failed. In some places, a new road had to be cut. The men simply wanted to lie down to sleep, but knew they had to keep on moving. Finally, the Forty-Second New York was relieved from the battle line as they helped to drag the cannons through the quagmire. Captain Owen delivered his guns and instantly returned to the swamp to bring in the other three: it took all night.[20]

The rest of Battery G arrived by eight o'clock in the morning; it had taken eighteen hours for the entire battery to go five miles. General Sedgwick was pleased that Colonel Tompkins managed to get his brigade across the nearly impassible river; he knew the artillery would be needed in the counterattack to follow. The Confederates counted on the river being so swollen that no artillery would cross, but they misjudged the Rhode Island Light Artillery. Tompkins singled out Captain Owen and Major James Bowe of the Forty-Second New York, among others, for the task of getting the artillery over the stream. The colonel wrote, "The zeal and energy of these officers are worthy of the highest praise, it being a matter of difficulty to bring the artillery across the Chickahominy."[21]

With all of his guns on the field, Captain Owen reorganized his battery; if called to support the battle, the command would have only the fifty rounds in the limber chests. With the caissons on the other side of the river, there was no chance for resupply. Colo-

Battery G encamped at the Adams' House after the Battle of Fair Oaks.

nel Tompkins placed the three sections at different positions on the field. The cannoneers were exhausted after the ordeal and wanted to rest. A member of Battery G recorded, "We arrived at the scene of action, completely dragged out from the night's work, and felt more like sleeping than getting into position for action." Owen would not let his men rest and ordered them to be prepared to go into combat at any moment. As soon as the battery was positioned, the engagement began. During the bitter engagement, known as Fair Oaks, one section supported General Napoleon Dana's Brigade at Fair Oaks Station; the second was placed near the Golding Farm, while the third remained at the Adams House, covering a field hospital but in general reserve. In this manner, the battery covered the entire field. Throughout the day, Battery G waited in the woods to engage the Confederates but was never called upon to fight. One private in a letter to the *Providence Journal* recorded, "We had a fine view of the whole affair until our forces drove them through the thick woods. After which we listened to the incessant rattle of musketry, intermingled with the cheers of our boys as they tried the power of cold steel."

Richardson and Sedgwick fought hard to hold their position. The Fifteenth Massachusetts, comprised of men from neighboring Worcester supported the Rhode Island batteries. General Sedgwick wrote of the Union counterattack: "Without wavering, repeated and furious charges of the enemy finally charged him in turn with the bayonet with such impetuosity as to rout him from his position." Although they did not fight in the battle, several of the men in Battery G disgraced themselves by running away from the battery during the engagement, even though the command was not involved in direct combat. These men were not cowards, but simply could not stand the din of the battle. Because Battery G was a state unit, recruited in the same community, these men were considered to not dishonor only themselves, but their detachments as well. No news of the disgraceful affair was ever carried by the newspapers at home. Rather it would be handled within the unit.[22]

The artillery of the Second Corps contributed immensely to the battle. Lieutenant Edmund Kirby placed his guns some 100 yards from the Confederate line when he began to engage them. The South Carolinians "were mowed down where they stood." Owen's Battery remained in readiness all day, but the tight, compact area of the battlefield made the use of rifled guns all but useless. The Napoleons were used effectively to drive back the Confederates. Private Barber was amazed by the experience of being in combat for the first time; he had missed Yorktown, being detailed to remain in camp and care for horses. The young Westerly soldier wrote, "Our men poured a heavy volley of balls in the rebel ranks which caused a great panic." The drivers stayed in the saddle, but at dusk it was clear that the fighting was over; neither side had won any ground and the only result was thousands of casualties for both armies.[23]

With the battle over, the horses needed watering. Privates Henry Farnsworth and John L. Rathbun took their teams to a nearby stream for water, but both men got lost in the tangled forest and swamps of the area. They ran into a Confederate patrol and were taken prisoner. The Confederates stole the four horses and took the two Rhode Islanders to prison in Richmond. Private Rathbun was never seen alive again; these two drivers were Battery G's first combat casualties.

While the cannoneers were recovering from the sights, sounds, and smells of their first battle, another group of Battery G men arrived on the field. This was Second Lieutenant Otto Torslow and the six caissons that had remained behind at Parker's Mill. Now the heavily loaded vehicles carefully maneuvered over what remained of the muddy roads and the Grapevine Bridge, now all but submerged beneath the black Chickahominy. The lieutenant and his six corporals carefully managed the process, as they only had a few spare men to accomplish the same mission that had required 100 cannoneers and a battalion of the Forty-Second New York. It was a difficult process, but the Rhode Islanders met the challenge with their usual ardor. As had happened before, the mission was successful and the caissons were reunited with their detachments. Upon arriving on the battlefield, Torslow was disgusted: "Our battery would have been engaged if the roads had not prevented it."[24]

In the Battle of Fair Oaks, the Federals lost 5,000 men compared to 6,000 Confederates. The lines remained in place as the surgeons began to perform their gruesome work. The men in Battery G visited their friends in the neighboring infantry regiments to insure that all had survived. The other Rhode Island units were not heavily engaged as well. Private Gaskell learned something from the engagement: War truly was all hell. "There human life has its end, and glory enough to satisfy me, was his conclusion." Albert Cordner saw "dead lain on the field burning." Private Barber added, "[I]t was horrible." The worst Union casualty was Oliver Otis Howard, commanding a brigade in the Second Corps who lost his arm. The greatest outcome of the battle for the Confederates was a strange one. Joseph Johnston, the Confederate commander, was wounded on June 1. Jefferson Davis replaced him with his personal military advisor. In 1861, this replacement was among the highest ranking Union officers to go South; now he would lead one of the greatest armies in history to victory and defeat. His name was Robert E. Lee.[25]

After suffering his first real casualties of the campaign, McClellan paused for three weeks on the battlefield. It was a fatal delay. Lee returned to Richmond, where he gathered additional reinforcements and prepared to strike. Skirmishes continued to be fought each day as both sides probed each other's lines; the Second Corps was usually always engaged. The Union artillery and infantry threw up crude fortifications to protect the camp from enemy attack. Private Gaskell described the camp: "We are now in a wilderness of swamps and woods with scattered open patches." Even if the Confederates did not attack, stray shells would always land in camp, often unnerving the men, but sometimes inflicting horrendous wounds to soldiers in other regi-

Quartermaster Sergeant William B. Westcott served with his brother Gilbert and provided the men with food and clothing; he rose to the command of Battery B (courtesy Phil DiMaria, Battery B 1st Rhode Island Light Artillery Inc.).

ments. On the fourth of June, the battery fired three rounds at some Confederates they observed in the distance, the only shots they fired at Fair Oaks.

While the soldiers adapted themselves to camp life once again, they realized that this camp would be different from any other they had bivouacked on. The sights of the June 1 battlefield continued to have their effect on the men. Gaskell wrote, "I have seen men fall at Edwards Ferry and Yorktown but never before witnessed such wholesale slaughter as that on the field from which I write." The thoughts of Richmond, some ten miles away, were very provoking. "Next week: perhaps tomorrow, will decide the fate of Richmond and the War. Many a brave fellow will sleep in death before our flag waves above the city."[26]

Battery G remained encamped at Fair Oaks for three weeks after the battle, waiting for action. Private Barber wrote, "We are all hoping to meet the enemy before long." The battery pitched a semi-permanent camp several yards from General Sumner's headquarters at the Adams House, near where one of the sections had been posted during the battle. The house had undergone significant destruction during the battle as described by a member of the command in a letter to the *Providence Journal*. "If the owner of this plantation should conclude to visit his former abode again after the present struggles have been adjusted. I hardly think he will recognize it. All traces of the fence which once surrounded it have disappeared long ago, leaving the gate-posts as landmarks and even these bear the marks of canister and minie balls."

Instead of cutting wood, the artillerists took the nearby split rail fences as a convenient fuel supply. The house was a frightening location to live near. It was a hospital and all of the windows had been removed to provide circulation of air for the sick and wounded. Their moans could be heard constantly. Inside presented a grislier sight: "The floors are stained with blood, marking the spot where some poor soldier lost his arm or leg, and in some cases both. The whole house is almost ruined and it will be some time before it recovers its former condition and beauty." Fortunately none of the wounded in the house were members of Battery G. Unfortunately, however, the battery was about to be attacked in waves by an enemy even more deadly than the Confederates.[27]

The only water available to drink had to be recovered from hand-dug wells, and it was often tainted with the blood of their comrades who fell at Fair Oaks. Many in Battery G came down with dysentery, caused by the dirty water and poor food. "I have lain on the ground since March 10th and have been exposed to cold, heat, rain and hunger. My health is broken. Our situation before Richmond is a very unhealthy one, having located in a varied range of swampy fields and woods. If one could ensure a sufficient and nutritious diet there would not be so much sickness among our troops," recalled Private Gaskell. The horrid sanitation conditions at this camp, combined with the swamps, and malaria, caused many Rhode Islanders to become sick. The illness became known as Chickahominy Fever, named after the river, which contributed to many of the soldier's deaths nearby. The intense labor involved in erecting the fortifications, in addition to spending nearly every night on alert, left many severely fatigued. The swamps "were reeking with the poisoned air." In addition, few of the soldiers had a change of clothing and were forced to wear the same dirty, grimy garments daily. This included sleeping each night in soaking wet uniforms. The fevers infected those at the highest ranks as well.

The months of active campaigning had accustomed the men to the harsh realities of a soldier's life; the poorer men and immigrants in Battery G were long used to living under such conditions. The diseases came as a reality to some who still romanticized the glories of war. Surgeon George Stevens of New York recorded the horrifying conditions of his patients: "Burning with fever, tormented with insatiable thirst, racked with pains, or wild with delirium; their parched lips, and teeth blackened with soars, the hot breath and sunken eyes, the sallow skin and trembling pulse, all telling of the violent workings of these diseases." The army brought new illnesses that many were susceptible to receiving. A frightful outbreak of scurvy hit the Army of the Potomac at the same time as the fever. The only food to eat was rotted meat and moldy hardtack. There were tons of fresh potatoes and other supplies at White House Landing, but there was no way to ship them to the soldiers at the front.

This disease contributed to the vast misery of the army. "Men are rotting," recalled a Massachusetts surgeon. Daily, hundreds of men were shipped to hospitals in the North; some simply lay down and died. Even the officers suffered poorly from the conditions, Lieutenant Rhodes was one of them. Indeed, the lieutenant was on the verge of dying and desperately wanted a leave of absence to go home to Warwick; he was rebuffed by the bureaucrats, who felt the illness was not severe enough. Meanwhile, Captain John Tompkins, the brother of the regimental colonel, was only slightly ill and received a two week furlough. The only remedies for many were whiskey or quinine, which helped to break fevers but could not stop the dysentery ravaging Battery G.[28]

The "swamp fevers" from the Chickahominy infected the artillerists in many different ways. Among those to suffer was Private Henry Heap, a thirty-two-year-old German immigrant from Providence. Heap was a strong man, before enlisting he had been engaged every day in manual labor with a sledge hammer. A neighbor recorded, "Prior to the war he was a rugged, sound, able man; who frequently worked at stone cutting." After drinking "impure water" from the river, Heap fell ill and was sent to a hospital in Washington. He was discharged from the service in January of 1863 "a perfect wreck." Heap moved to Coventry and later to Connecticut trying to find steady employment. Seven months of service in Battery G destroyed Heap: "He was not able to do ½ days work." Many feared he would soon die of the illness he brought home from the Peninsula. Private Henry Heap surprised his friends and lived until 1900.[29]

The longer Battery G remained at Fair Oaks, the more the strict discipline for which the battery was known began to break down. Part of the problem was the four ounce whiskey rations being distributed to all of the men twice a day to combat fevers, not just to the ill. In addition, the general disillusion with camp life left many with menial tasks that they did not want to complete.

Captain Owen was still fuming over the men who deserted in the face of the enemy at Fair Oaks. On June 9, the captain lashed back with far-reaching consequences. Quartermaster Sergeant J. Russell Field was demoted to private, in addition to Sergeant Charles H. Bogman and Corporal William H. Lewis. "Men who are qualified for the positions of sergts and corpls are wanted and not those who when danger or a little hard work is ahead deliberately stop and refuse to try," wrote Owen. Sergeant Bogman had earned a stellar combat record. He fought at Bull Run with the First Rhode Island, where he was wounded before joining Battery G. Despite this, he still committed one of the worst crimes a soldier could engage in while on the battlefield.[30]

To replace these three men, the captain completely rearranged his noncommissioned officer corps. Men were promoted who had shown an interest in helping others or had stood by their posts in the midst of the danger. Those sergeants and corporals that remained were transferred to different detachments to insure they did not carry on with the old ways. Sergeant Kirby Steinhaur was among those who performed their soldierly duties. He was rewarded with a promotion to second lieutenant and a reassignment to Rhode Island. Here he would help to recruit for Battery H, the last remaining company necessary to complete

The July 1, 1862, Battle of Malvern Hill showed what massed artillery could do to an attacking force. Battery G was one of five Rhode Island batteries in the engagement.

the First Rhode Island Light Artillery Regiment. Even while Captain Owen dealt out discipline, the men were just as displeased with the captain himself. George Gaskell recorded, "Our Capt. has not done just for what he should in all respects, and many think that he shall retire in disgrace from the seat of war." Outside of his personal opinion of the captain, the private enjoyed serving as Captain Owen's orderly. He was excused from all other duties, but unlike on the Potomac, he received the same rations as the other enlisted men.[31]

The generals also became dissatisfied with the condition in the battery. The problems continued to stem from the lack of supplies and unsanitary conditions, in addition to the whiskey. Instead of drinking the alcohol, Private Cordner found some cider and after taking it, became violently ill. On June 13, Private James H. Horton somehow lost his trousers and sack coat: he was charged for their loss. The men became restless as McClellan failed to move; he believed he was vastly outnumbered by the Confederates and pleaded daily to President Lincoln for more troops.[32]

In Battery G, the artillerists simply sat and waited under their tents for the orders to move on to Richmond and win the war. Private William B. Thurber used the time to make small sketches "from nature." George Gaskell also took note of the beautiful flora in the area, including the Virginia creeper, a vine he found most peculiar. As with all of his observations it was a comparison to his trips to Africa; he wished he was there rather than at Fair Oaks. On the seventeenth, First Sergeant Kelley took the time to record the most exciting occurrence in the battery in two weeks: "had a drill this morning." Despite the waiting, some men still had faith in their commander, as recorded by Private Albert Cordner: "Gen. McClellan understands his business and we are willing to wait while he forms and carries out his plans."[33]

In one month Robert E. Lee took an army that was almost pushed into the Richmond defenses and reorganized and reequipped while the Federals waited. McClellan finally advanced some units but the progress was pitifully slow; some patrols made it to within six miles of Richmond itself before they were called back. Lee counterattacked on June 25, at a small battle named Oak Grove, near the Second Corps' camp at Fair Oaks. The Army of the Potomac was thrown off balance when Lee again attacked the next day at Beaver Dam Creek. Unable to withstand the constant blows of Lee's force and with timid Federal leadership, the Army of the Potomac retreated in haste.[34]

Over the next four days, engagements were fought at Gaines' Mill, Golding's Farm, Savage's Station, and White Oak Swamp. In each battle, the Union forces were hurled back. The Confederates suffered massive casualties, but won the day as McClellan ordered his army ever backwards, giving up all the ground they had captured in May and June of 1862. In this set of battles Confederate leaders began to emerge who would play an important role in events to come, namely Thomas J. Jackson and James Longstreet. On June 27, the Confederates struck the Second Corps near Fair Oaks. Sumner held his position "with great determination," but like all others was forced back. As Colonel Tompkins ordered his batteries to leave the camp which had been their home for three weeks he was struck by a sudden attack of an illness he had suffered from since arriving on the Peninsula. His surgeon advised him to yield the command of the brigade and go to the rear for treatment. If this happened, Captain Owen, as the senior captain, would take command. Ever stoic in his duties, Tompkins did not take the advice, and although deathly ill, remained in the saddle. His orders to the artillery were the same for the rest of the army: fall back. Battery G participated in the marches along with the Second Corps; but as the dense undergrowth prevented it, they could not engage the enemy. Private Gaskell described the fighting to his sister: "It was evident to us all that we could not longer hold our position before the city. Everyday saw an action of more or less event in all of which I can tell you Mary we were with one exception the losers."[35]

On June 28, Battery G was at Charles City Cross Roads as the situation turned desperate. Still believing he was facing a superior foe and being pressed on all sides, McClellan ordered the Army of the Potomac to retreat towards the James River and abandon the campaign. Theodore Reichardt of Battery A recorded the following: "Our situation is very critical, our right flank is being turned." The drivers in Battery G rode their horses, while the cannoneers rode on the limbers for sixteen hours straight, only stopping for one fifteen minute rest. The roads were backed up with a seventeen mile long caravan of Union supply wagons. With no use for artillery, the batteries continued to retreat while the infantry conducted most of the fighting in a desperate and continuous rearguard operation.[36]

On June 30, Captain Owen detached his orderly, George Gaskell, to General Sumner to convey orders. The roads were jammed with soldiers as the young Rhode Islander completed the hazardous task. Upon reaching General Sedgwick, he was told to return to his unit as the battery was not on the field and Gaskell was unneeded. Gaskell remained on the field for a half hour watching as the shells and minie balls flew around him, but he was not hurt. Lee was trying to prevent the Federals from crossing a small bridge through White Oak Swamp. Only a bayonet charge by Thomas F. Meagher's Irish Brigade saved the day for the Union forces. Private Gaskell had to travel through even more throngs of retreating soldiers to find Battery G when the battle was over. The battle this day was fought near Glendale. Battery G was three miles from the fighting and the men could hear the battle in all its horror. Albert Cordner wrote, "Heavy fighting with the rear guard, fight all day, whipped the Rebs, and drove them back in White Oak Swamp, we fell back."[37]

Finally, after seven days of nonstop combat, Lee had succeeded. McClellan inflicted heavier casualties on the Army of Northern Virginia, but they had pushed the Army of the

Potomac to the James River. By July 1, he stood by to deliver one final death blow to the Union Army. General McClellan prepared his men, massing the entire army on the slopes of Malvern Hill some twenty miles south of Richmond. The Second Corps was placed in the forefront of battle, on the right slope, while Battery G again positioned itself near Battery B. In total, some thirty Federal batteries lined the crest, five from Rhode Island, waiting for the Confederates to attack. The galloping of the artillery horses kicked up large amounts of dust that obscured the field. It was brutally hot as the two armies prepared for the deadly work before them. This day would be decisive to both armies.

Lee was a military genius who developed brilliant techniques to defeat the Army of the Potomac in the campaign. However, they went awry in the complex undergrowth and swamps of the Peninsula. Now he would send them up the bare hill in the open to attack the Federals. Lee had much faith that his forces could crest the hill and finally drive the Army of the Potomac from the Peninsula. The plan went haywire as the Union artillery opened fire upon the advancing Confederates, delaying them for two hours while they deployed and waited for additional reinforcements. Finally, the Confederate artillery responded and at 4:00 the Army of Northern Virginia began the assault up the long slopes towards the summit of the hill ringed with Federal troops.[38]

On the Peninsula, Federal artillery organization had been a problem from the start. Despite the reforms enacted by McClellan, batteries still were assigned to individual brigades or acted under the authority of infantry commanders, unused to the demanding tactics this special branch of the service used. The generals felt they were in control and often did not consult the chief of artillery assigned to each division to supervise the batteries. At Malvern Hill, McClellan finally let Colonel Henry Hunt, the chief of artillery for the Army of the Potomac, arrange his guns as he wanted them; the plan worked. The Union artillery tore into the advancing Confederate ranks as they charged up the hill. Private Barber was there, working a gun and remembered: "We got in a murderous fire of about 150 pieces of artillery which mowed them down like grass as they was thrown in such a panic they fled towards Richmond." The Federal gunboats anchored in the James supported the field guns with their long range fire; however sometimes it landed onto the Federal positions. Battery C lost four killed and a dozen wounded in this manner. Battery G soon found itself coming not only under Confederate fire, but friendly fire as well. For George Gaskell and Battery G the fire became too much: "The shell and shrapnel flew into our Battery like hail."[39]

A shell burst overhead as Private Gaskell was galloping along the line, acting as a courier for General Sumner. His horse bolted from the incident as the young Rhode Islander was thrown to the ground. This pitched him onto a cannon wheel, knocking him insensible. Despite suffering immensely, the stoic young man refused aid: "I had a dread of the hospital, so the boys carried me along on a caisson." Again, Battery G could only engage in the battle sporadically because of the other batteries and the infantry crowding the hill. After throwing a few shells towards the enemy, Captain Owen ordered the battery to a reserve position on the opposite crest of the hill. The battle was over by nightfall. Without the Union artillery, McClellan would have been driven into the James. The Union held the field, inflicting 5,000 casualties to 3,000 of their own. McClellan, however, decided once more to evacuate the field and retreat to the James. Lee had been successful. Taking command of the forces on the Peninsula, he managed, through heavy losses, to repel the Army of the Potomac.[40]

On July 2, Battery G left Malvern Hill. It was 110 degrees that day as the men struggled onward. The roads were completely filled with Union soldiers, large flies pestered the men constantly. The men inhaled the pests, which flew everywhere; there was no escaping them. As the Rhode Islanders continued the march, the soldiers became more concerned with defeating the flies than defeating the enemy. For the final time McClellan ordered the entire army to retreat, this time to Harrison's Landing, on the James River. From here, the Union navy could cover the battered army if Lee counterattacked. Instead, Lee retired to the Richmond defenses to nurse his battered army. It rained that night as the tired men in Battery G trudged to the coast. Private Gaskell remained on the caisson, covered by a blanket. Finally, they arrived at the vast Union supply depot at Harrison's Landing. Only four months earlier, the Army of the Potomac had been traveling in the opposite direction. Richmond was nearly taken; only indecision on the part of the Union high command, and a bril-

Lieutenant Crawford Allen was a young and ambitious officer who was wounded at Marye's Heights and rose to command his own battery.

liant Confederate leader, had prevented them from capturing the capital. Faced with the need for more troops, President Lincoln issued a proclamation on the first of July calling for 300,000 more men to serve for three years. The Union was on the verge of collapse unless something was done.[41]

The battery and indeed the entire Army of the Potomac remained at the landing while McClellan plotted his next move. Still unsure about Lee's strength he ordered General Ambrose Burnside, a Rhode Islander commanding troops in North Carolina, to advance his corps to Newport News to join in the next campaign. On the Fourth of July, the men of the Second Corps paid homage to the eighty-sixth birthday of the United States by firing long range artillery shots at some Confederate pickets and being reviewed by General McClellan. Four days later President Lincoln arrived as the cannoneers put on their best appearance for the commander in chief. Due to the tens of thousands of Federal soldiers clambering among Harrison's Landing, a dozen men had their knapsacks stolen containing everything they owned. Many freed slaves flocked to the Union army; they came seeking protection, freedom, and to sell their goods to the unpaid soldiers. George Gaskell compared it to trading with natives in Africa.[42]

The weather and illness again proved to be a problem for the army, Battery G in particular. Half of the men were ill with dysentery, yellow fever, and other swamp diseases. James Barber said it quite plainly when he wrote, "I have been sick with the diarrhea." The most severe cases were transferred to hospitals in Baltimore, Philadelphia, New York, or Portsmouth Grove, located in Rhode Island. The men were stable at first; the diseases took several weeks to kill. One of the main problems was the doctor at Artillery Brigade headquarters. This was the surgeon of the First Rhode Island Light Artillery Regiment, Major Caleb Thurston. Corporal David B. Patterson, who served in a Rhode Island battery complained, "There is quite a number of sick now. A man may be a very good doctor at home, but when he gets out here & gets his bars on, he is a different man altogether. His pay runs on wheter kill or cure."[43]

As the men waited longer at Harrison's Landing some became disgruntled at McClellan's leadership in the campaign. Private Gaskell wrote, "Our cause looks gloomy to us here, but we hope and pray for the best." The general was loved by his men; they knew he would not needlessly risk their lives. However, he had been pushed back into the James River by an overly aggressive and determined Confederate leadership, despite the fact that the Army of the Potomac had the advantage in numbers and materiel. McClellan had taken false intelligence that he was greatly outnumbered and used it to believe he would be defeated; the Union forces fought aggressively, but continued to retreat because of poor leadership. Constant camp rumors began to infiltrate into Battery G: one day the men were going home, the next they were being transferred to the west. This led to the already stressful conditions in camp. In the defeat, Gaskell took stock on why the Confederates were fighting: "I don't blame the Virginians for fighting—they have everything at stake, home, liberty, property, and all." Although some could appreciate this, they remained loyal to the flag. The desertion and intoxication had stopped for the moment, and the battery had gained back some of the reputation that had been lost at the Fair Oaks encampment.[44]

Battery G along with Battery B were detached from General Sedgwick's Second Division and assigned as a general reserve to the entire Second Corps, to be called upon to provide support wherever it was needed. As they remained at Harrison's Landing the men in defeated commands such as Battery G waited for another battle so they could prove that their cause was not lost. The food situation remained very poor. Albert Cordner recorded the situation in the battery: "most all sick." The soldiers in Battery G had not been paid since April, leaving many to rely upon the slim government rations of hardtack, salt pork, and coffee. For no apparent reason, Battery B was paid off during the campaign, while G missed the opportunity. Albert Cordner had lent money to men in Battery G and the Second Rhode Island during the campaign and now came to collect on those debts to send home to his family in Charlestown.

Copies of the *Providence Journal* circulated for ten cents a copy, instead of the two cents paid at home. Some of the artillerists used their prewar occupations to good use. A fisherman in civilian life, Private James A. Barber went out into the mud flats in the James River and collected a large amount of oysters for him and his brother Ellery. Borrowing a mess kettle, the private began to cook the tasty treats when the rest of the Westerly detachment appeared, hoping to enjoy part of the meal. As they gathered, Barber promptly spat in the kettle and the other soldiers departed. That night the two Barber brothers had a good meal.[45]

The Sanitary Commission was comprised of civilians devoted to the well-being of the army through donations of food, writing material, and kind aid. They made an appearance in the camp of the Artillery Brigade of the Second Corps on July 15 with a meal for the weary artillerists. The artillery officers, as usual, were only looking out for their own welfare. Instead of their men eating, they took the food and ate it that night. The enlisted men were aghast that the officers committed such an act. Furthermore, gambling and drinking among the officers became a constant problem. In an infantry regiment, with thirty company officers, the problem officers could be removed and men could be promoted to fill their ranks, but with only five officers to battery, those with the red shoulder straps became more difficult to replace. As sergeants proved themselves on the battlefield, they would replace the officers. For now, Battery G remained with the same five who had left Providence; several men had shown great promise during these first campaigns and would rise to great prominence in the years ahead.[46]

The water, as it would throughout the campaign, remained horrible at the landing.

The dysentery spread very rapidly, infecting all. Unable to be filled on the government rations, the Rhode Islanders lived on the oysters in the area. Some men were fortunate to steal some potatoes and cabbage. Private Gaskell continued to write about the dysentery, and vent his frustration that nothing was being done to help his fellow soldiers: "The Army sickness continues to increase and scores are buried daily from the hospital. Unless some new sanitary arrangements are speedily devised the command will soon be decimated one third." Even the private soldiers knew what needed to be done: "If one could ensure a sufficient and nuticius diet there would not be so much sickness among the troops." The latrines were placed next to the camp, which further led to the spread of dysentery, while the brackish water at Harrison's Landing was often tainted with sea water. Despite the many problems at the landing, many thought it was a better camp than Fair Oaks.

On July 28, Captain Owen received a shipment of pecans and cake from home; he did not share it with his men. Despite the poor food, many were surprised they gained weight; others simply wasted away. There was no in-between in the army; men either lived and thrived or wasted and died. Those not ill took the time to view the sights. The woods were full of many exotic plants and animals; for many of these Rhode Islanders the scenery would always be remembered. Rain fell daily; the soldiers pitched their small shelter tents, trying to keep dry, and more important, alive. With nearly 100,000 men, half of whom were ill, the Army of the Potomac consumed mountains of supplies, and the forest closest to the camps quickly disappeared.[47]

Two important events occurred in the history of Battery G on August 7. First on this day, a long forgotten sight arrived back in camp. This was Private Farnsworth, who had

Major General Edwin "Bull" Sumner commanded the Second Corps (Library of Congress).

been captured at Fair Oaks. He escaped his captors and made it back to Union lines, but was gravely ill. Farnsworth was sent to a hospital at Hampton, Virginia, where he died on September 20. Second, the orders finally came. Instead of containing instructions for a second campaign against Richmond, the orders were far different. The Army of the Potomac was going to abandon the Peninsula and retreat to Washington.[48]

The seventeenth brought a welcome relief to the sick and tired battery, when a dozen recruits came from Rhode Island. Most were from Washington County and joined their friends or, in two cases, brothers in the battery. Only one new recruit came from Westerly. Although the manpower supply in the town was hit hard by the raising of Company A of the Seventh Rhode Island Infantry, Westerly was playing a far more important role now in the formation of the regiment. Because of its location on the railroad to Providence, and its commercial district, the town served as the recruiting headquarters for southern Rhode Island. Now, instead of just forwarding men to Battery G, other recruits came from nearby Charlestown and Hopkinton, and from as far as Coventry and North Kingstown to join the light artillery. Unlike their previous comrades who had joined up for only $115, these men received $400. One of them was Charles W. Hudson, a twenty-four-year-old lawyer from Smithfield; it was quite odd for a man of his education to be a private. Only twenty days after enlisting, on August 24, Hudson died of typhoid at a hospital in Philadelphia.[49]

Another new recruit was Charles D. Ennis. Prior to Ennis enlisting, Albert Cordner had communicated with him weekly. Now he came to Battery G to join his friend in the struggle. Artificer Welcome Tucker and his brother Peleg, a private, came south with their brother-in-law, who happened to be Private Ennis; he had married their sister Mary against the conventions of the time. In 1845, Ennis' father had died and the young boy and his siblings were sent to live at the neighboring Tucker farm; the Tuckers were experienced blacksmiths and mechanics. Charles learned the trade and prospered. Welcome and Peleg were both welcome reinforcements, as they were combat veterans already. Peleg had seen service at Bull Run with the First Rhode Island, while Welcome had served in Battery B. Discharged in February of 1862 for illness, he recovered and had now gone to war again. By serving together, these three Charlestown men maintained a close family bond that transferred directly to their action on the guns—to never abandon each other and to perform their duty.[50]

On August 16, Captain Owen had received orders for Battery G to limber up and leave Harrison's Landing. Only five months earlier the battery had entered the Peninsula with full ranks, all of the men ready to begin the life of soldiers on campaign and end the war by capturing Richmond. Now most of the command was ill as they trudged the forty-seven miles back down the Peninsula to Fortress Monroe. After a five-day journey, the guns and horses were loaded onto the steamer *Star Island* to be sent ahead of the battery under the command of Lieutenant Allen; the men left two days later for Alexandria. The recruits had not even had time to be exercised in the manual of the piece as they helped load the guns and other equipments aboard the vessels; the most realistic training available would soon be before them. A fellow Rhode Islander who had observed Battery G in the campaign wrote, "The battery had maintained a good reputation."[51]

The Peninsula Campaign was over, but another would soon be occurring and Battery G would be in the thick of it. This time they were going north on a campaign that would decide the fate of the United States. Waiting for them along a quiet creek in western Maryland was Robert E. Lee and the Army of Northern Virginia.

6

"A Savage Continual Thunder"

Commence the fight at daylight. First we drove them and then they drove us.
Then we drove them back again. The fight lasted all day.
—Private Albert D. Cordner, September 17, 1862

A demoralized Union army stumbled into Washington in late August 1862, as the Army of the Potomac had been driven from the Peninsula by determined Confederate assaults and timid leadership. Throughout August, a second thrust to capture Richmond had been attempted under John Pope in central Virginia. He was repulsed at Cedar Mountain and Groveton, culminating at the Second Battle of Manassas in the last three days of August. Reinforced by units from the Army of the Potomac, Pope's Army of Virginia fought on the exact same ground as First Bull Run some thirteen months earlier. After leaving McClellan on the Peninsula, Lee and Jackson had maneuvered to perfection, sending Pope reeling in retreat, while threatening Washington D.C. Now they stood poised on the banks of the Potomac.

To complicate matters for the Army of the Potomac, President Lincoln had removed McClellan from his command for failing to defeat Lee on the Peninsula. This further demoralized the men as they stumbled to defend the capital; some even threw away their muskets, not wanting to carry on the fight. Battery G was part of this ragged band of veterans. Having fought in three battles on the Peninsula, the Rhode Islanders were now veteran troops, well trained and disciplined in their deadly duties. Owen's Battery arrived in Alexandria on August 29. After retrieving additional ammunition and unloading the equipment, they moved to Arlington Heights on September 3, waiting for events to transpire.[1]

With the victories in the summer of 1862, Lee, in three months, had transformed the Army of Northern Virginia into one of the finest combat forces in all of American military history. After clearing all Union forces out of Virginia, Lee turned his eyes to another target: the North itself. His army was already in a position to attack Washington, but his men were tired, ragged, and on the verge of starving. With no move on the part of the Federal forces for several days, Lee had to take the initiative. In tandem with a Confederate invasion into Kentucky, Jefferson Davis hoped that this invasion would end the war once and for all. As such, Lee pushed the lead elements to the fords of the Potomac River on September 5. In front of these soldiers was an enemy land, the United States of America. For the first time since the War of 1812, a foreign army was about to invade the United States. However this army was not composed of soldiers from another country. It was made of people who, until eighteen months earlier, had been fellow citizens. The rest of the Army of Northern Virginia crossed over the next three days and began pushing north.[2]

The Confederates had much to gain by invading the United States in the late summer of 1862. The objective was Harrisburg, Pennsylvania. Here the Rebel army could capture a large amount of supplies, destroy a vital rail hub, and disrupt communications. The crops were nearly ready to be harvested in the Shenandoah; drawing Union troops from the Val-

Battery G fought near the Dunker Church at Antietam, as the Confederates pushed the Second Corps out of the woods to the background (Library of Congress).

ley would allow the farmers to harvest them. In addition, the Army of Northern Virginia could get many needed recruits in Maryland. Politically, if the victory were decisive enough it would force an end to the war by threatening public sentiment in the North. There were critical congressional elections in November that Lee hoped to affect by having Democrats elected who were sympathetic to the Southern cause. Most important, the United Kingdom and France were on the verge of recognizing the Confederacy. One clear Southern victory in the North could permanently separate the South from the United States of America. Never were the chances of Union defeat and Confederate victory so great.[3]

Lincoln was shocked that the Confederates were so bold as to invade. He needed to counter the threat immediately. Within the Washington defenses were three Union armies. The president had to find a competent man to lead the forces and deal a death blow to Lee to stop the invasion, and end the war. After searching, he found his choices were limited. Of the senior corps commanders, only Edwin V. Sumner of the Second Corps had enough experience, but being in his sixties Sumner was too old for such an important command. Faced with little choice of leadership, the president placed George B. McClellan back in command of the Army of the Potomac. The news electrified the men in the ranks. The man who had made the magnificent army was once again back to lead his men to victory. McClellan quickly reorganized the army into seven corps, leaving two behind to guard Washington.

With the remaining forces under McClellan's command, the Army of the Potomac began marching on September 6 to the north and west to find Lee and destroy him. The Rhode Islanders in Battery G quickly joined in the campaign, leaving Alexandria and marching to Rockville, Maryland, where they remained in camp until the ninth as other units of the Second Corps caught up. Captain Owen and all the Second Corps artillery officers hurriedly held a council of war to insure their commands were ready. At Rockville, the artillerists performed a most distasteful act; they stole a cow from a farmer and ate it to supplement their rations. Foraging was officially prohibited by both armies, but most commanders turned a blind eye in exchange for some of the stolen property. On the morning of September 9, Battery G joined in the pursuit and marched northwest towards Frederick, Maryland, where they arrived on September 12. The Confederates believed that they would be seen as liberators in western Maryland; they were wrong, as it was the Army of the Potomac who received the honors. After a week of maneuvering in Maryland the time for battle had come.[4]

An amazing document was discovered on the twelfth when two Union soldiers found an order from Lee detailing his plans for the coming campaign. The letter was promptly taken to McClellan, who sat on the intelligence for two days before moving again to counter the threat. In the order, Lee divided the army into five divisions and detached a large portion of the army to capture a Union garrison at Harpers Ferry under Stonewall Jackson. This was necessary because, if the Confederates had to retreat back across the Potomac in a hurry, this large Union force would cut them off. The United States troops at Harpers Ferry were also directly astride Lee's proposed new lines of communication and supply for the Confederate army's continued thrust north into Pennsylvania. Meanwhile, D.H. Hill and his division would hold the South Mountain passes while Lee marched westward. The five portions would rendezvous near Sharpsburg, Maryland, on the banks of the Potomac.

McClellan pushed west from Frederick and attacked Hill on the afternoon of the fourteenth. In a decisive victory, the Federals cleared the mountains, but at a moderate loss to both sides. This was offset the next day at Harpers Ferry, where after a three-day siege 12,500 Union soldiers surrendered to Jackson. They were promptly paroled and sent north as Stonewall hurried north to Sharpsburg to Lee's aid; Jackson was surprised that the Army of the Potomac had traveled so quickly. The Confederate commander had yet to accomplish any of his plans in the campaign. Unable to maneuver and with his army starving, Lee knew that he had to engage the Federals. He brought the army to the small crossroads town of Sharpsburg.[5]

It was hoped this would be the Rebels' last stand. If McClellan managed to defeat the Army of Northern Virginia, they would have their backs

Lieutenant Otto L. Torslow was a veteran of the Swedish army. He was brave under fire, but was often drunk in the performance of his duties.

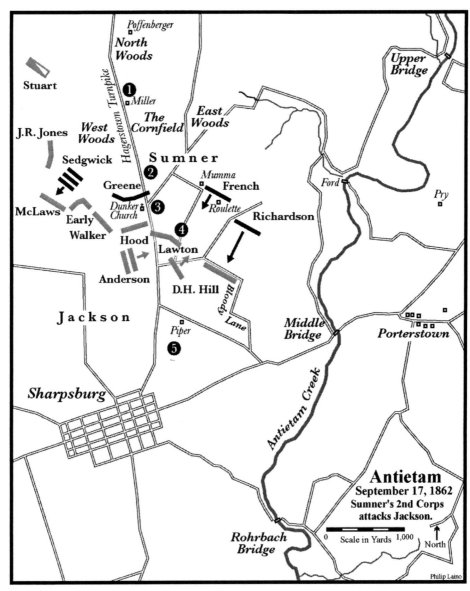

Poffenberger

**North
Woods**

Stuart

Miller

The   **East
Cornfield** **Woods**

J.R. Jones   West   Sumner
             Woods

Sedgwick

Greene   Mumma   French

McLaws   Dunker   Roulette
             Church

Early   Richardson
Walker   Hood

             Lawton

Anderson   D.H. Hill

Jackson   Piper

Sharpsburg

Antietam
September 17, 1862
**Sumner's 2nd Corps
attacks Jackson.**

0   Scale in Yards 1,000   North

Rohrbach
Bridge

Upper
Bridge

Ford

Pry

Middle
Bridge   Porterstown

Antietam Creek

Philip Laino

❶ Battery D, 1st Rhode Island advances with Hooker's 1st Corps. This first Federal assault fails.

❷ Battery A, 1st Rhode Island advances with Sedgwick. The 2nd Division of the 2nd Corps is mauled by McLaws.

❸ Battery G, 1st Rhode Island unlimbers near the Mumma farm and then is told to support Sedgwick. They deploy where Battery D had fought but as Sedgwick is routed, they withdraw back to the Mumma farm.

❹ Battery A, 1st Rhode Island has been withdrawn to a ridge north of Bloody Lane but runs out of ordinance. They are replaced with Battery G. After dueling with Confederate artillery, they then fire on Bloody Lane.

❺ Confederate artillery masses near the Piper house. Battery G starts a counterbattery duel with rebel guns.

to the Potomac and would be forced into defeat. Confederate units continued to swarm into Sharpsburg by the hour on the fifteenth and sixteenth as Lee placed his artillery and infantry on the hills to the north and east of the town. McClellan as usual did not wait to attack until most of his army was up. The First Corps crossed the Antietam in the late afternoon of the sixteenth, fighting a sharp skirmish north of town. Still campaigning with the Second Corps, Battery G marched through the small village of Boonsboro on the sixteenth and saw dead Confederates everywhere, casualties of the desperate fight at South Mountain. They arrived on the east banks of the Antietam at midnight and promptly crossed the creek at Pry's Ford, north of town. The men rested under the cannon, preparing for the battle sure to come at first light. Private Barber wrote, "Our men lay down to sleep in face of the enemy exspecting the morrow would bring a bloody battle that would anihalate the rebel army and drive them into Virginia." The noncommissioned officers checked that the rounds were properly packed in the chests as the horses were fed and watered. The battle was almost near.[6]

The bloodiest day in American history dawned as a dismal fog filled the hollows and a light rain subsided on September 17, 1862. The men flopped out of their blankets as the musicians sounded reveille and the troops prepared for a brief breakfast before the killing began. The pickets had been firing all night long as both sides formed their lines and began to march into the early morning darkness. James Barber recalled the opening moments: "Day came in pleasant. Our pickets began to skirmis with the enemy in front and was followed by the artillery and in short time became a general engagement the roar of Artillery and clashes of musketry and the crashin of shells nearly defend the ear all around." The battle began at 5:30 as long-range Federal artillery fire began hitting Confederate gun positions on Dunker Church Ridge. This strategic position was named after a small white

This wartime sketch shows Battery G engaged near the burning ruins of the Mumma Farm at Antietam.

church, on the Hagerstown Pike, of a peaceful religious sect known as the Dunkers. To counter the threat, Colonel Stephen Lee turned his battalion to the east and began to engage the Union position. Hopelessly outgunned, Colonel Lee retreated after many of his men were shot down. His words would go down in history to describe the artillery fighting at Antietam: "It was artillery hell."[7]

The first stage of the battle began as the First and Twelfth corps advanced into a wood-lot and a cornfield north of the Dunker Church. Assault and counterassault followed as the two forces collided in the cornfield. General Joseph Hooker, commanding the First Corps, was severely wounded and Joseph Mansfield of the Twelfth Corps was killed. With his death, the Union forces seemed to collapse, as thousands of Americans lay dead or wounded in the corn and a brigade of Texans and Alabamians from Hood's Division launched a fierce counterattack. Battery D of the First Rhode Island Light Artillery was heavily engaged in the early morning action, losing seven dead and double the amount wounded. The guns performed invaluable service, firing canister to keep the enemy from advancing into the crumbling Federal line. As the first Union attacks faltered, George Sears Greene, a native Rhode Islander serving in the Twelfth Corps, led his division into the fray and smashed through Jackson's lines, sending him into retreat. With this success, General Sumner ordered his Second Corps into the fight.[8]

Sumner pushed the infantry of the Second Corps across Pry's Ford a mile from the scene of the first fighting. He placed his corps so that the Second Division was in front, followed by the Third and the First. The old general did not wait for his entire corps to come onto line before he attacked. John Sedgwick hurried his Second Division forward. Through the smoke, the general followed Greene's Division into the fray. Sedgwick and Sumner galloped in the van together. Sumner's plan was for the three stacked brigades to march due west and after entering the West Woods wheel southward to roll up the Confederate line left to right. The general failed to deploy his brigades into a single long battle line; instead they marched in a column formation, one brigade behind the other. Advancing north to the support of Jackson near the Dunker Church was Lafayette McLaws, having arrived fresh on the field after the capture of Harpers Ferry only a few hours earlier. Marching into the West Woods, Sedgwick's Division was hit on three sides by McLaws. Within fifteen minutes the Second Division disintegrated; half of the force was left dead or wounded on the field. General Sedgwick himself received three severe wounds and was carried from the field. Battery A, also part of the Second Division, unlimbered and promptly began shelling the area near the Dunker Church to provide fire support to Sedgwick's assault. When the battle was over, a famous battle image was of dead Confederates around the Dunker Church. "In one spot a Rebel officer and twenty men lay near the wreck of a Battery. It is said Battery A 1st R.I. Artillery did this work," wrote Lieutenant Elisha Rhodes of the Second Rhode Island.[9]

Battery G had remained in their position from the night before near Pry's Ford. Now Major Frank Clarke, the chief of artillery on Sumner's staff, ordered Battery G into a position to support Sedgwick in the West Woods as the division fell apart. The battery galloped into action near the Mumma Farm, now ablaze after being set on fire by the Rebels so the Federals could not use it for cover. As the drivers crashed their whips and spurs into the horses, they faced a terrible ordeal. The six horses pulling each gun and caisson could often not be controlled by the three drivers, other than simply trying to make them go in the general direction that was ordered. Now, as the caissons came into the Mumma fields, dead and wounded men lay scattered throughout the meadow and there was no way to avoid them. Private Barber was sickened by the results: "Our Battery went galloping on to the disputed field riding on the dead both Union and Rebels as they lay on the field together." Owen's men were to take a position in a field to the right of the Dunker Church, near the Mumma Farm. A member of Battery G later remembered that, as his unit deployed into action, "Just in front of us a house was burning, and the fire and smoke, flashing of muskets, and whizzing of bullets, yells, of men, etc. was perfectly horrible."[10]

Unfortunately for Battery G there was hardly any room for the unit to safely place the guns. A battery in action required fourteen yards between guns so the horses could properly turn. Eventually Captain Owen found a small patch of ground near the Dunker Church, on the east side of the Hagerstown Pike, near where Battery D had fought earlier. Soon another problem arose. "We could not fire without doing injury to our own men," remembered Barber. The men in the Second Division continued to run for their lives all around Battery G. Lieutenant Otto Torslow saw the retreating troops. He summoned Bugler Thomas Mars to his side as the two galloped into the confused mass, trying to form the shattered force. Riding up and down the lines, Mars gave rallying calls on his bugle but to little avail; Sedgwick's men continued to retreat. For their actions, Lieutenant Torslow was mentioned in dispatches, while Mars was promoted to sergeant on October 5. The artillerists had just unlimbered the guns and were preparing for the first shot when Owen realized the hopelessness of the situation. Soon a brigade of South Carolinians was advancing steadily towards them. George Gaskell recalled the heroism of the Rebels as they pushed the Second Corps out of the woods while Battery A fired into their position: "Never in my life have I seen such valor as that displayed by the Southern forces who fought with despair driving us several times, but our artillery was too much for them." While the Rhode Islanders pushed back the Confederates, they inflicted casualties on Federals soldiers as well. As Sedgwick's men fell back, the Union cannoneers had no choice but to keep up their fire or the entire line would have collapsed. As a result some members of the division were killed by friendly fire.[11]

The officers of Battery G understood the hopelessness of their position at the Dunker Church; the other batteries had already retired as the Second Division broke apart. Although the cannoneers were eager to engage the Rebels, they would have to wait. Without support, Battery G limbered up and returned to an apple orchard near the Mumma Farm. It was a familiar scene to many of the men from western Rhode Island; the apple crop was ready for harvesting. Here the Rhode Islanders would remain, while the shells exploded overhead and the killing went on all around them. The north end of the line settled down as both sides prepared for the next round of combat, while Battery A limbered up and turned south.[12]

The battle now shifted a half mile to the south. A division of Confederates were hunkered down in a small country lane naturally depressed into the landscape after years of use. It provided superb cover for the defenders. This position was called the Sunken Road. The location was critical because it was directly on the path to Sharpsburg itself and Lee's line of retreat. It had to be defended or the Army of Northern Virginia would be annihilated. The North Carolinians and Alabamians in the road piled up the fence rails as they waited for the Union troops. Battery A unlimbered on a ridge north of the road and began to engage the Southern forces below. Some bold Confederates tried to take the battery as they emerged out of the road and began to fire into the ranks of the command. Battery A had already lost five guns at Bull Run and was not about to have it happen again. Now the cannoneers had to use rammers and other implements to protect the guns, but they managed to save them. Although severely wounded, Corporal Benjamin Child refused to leave the field and continued to sight his piece. For his heroism, he was awarded the Medal of Honor. Four men died and fifteen were wounded.[13]

It was now 9:45 and Battery G had remained at the still smoldering Mumma House waiting for orders. After being there for nearly two hours, Major Clarke ordered them into action again, to the relief of Battery A. Engaged since early in the morning, Battery A had fired an unbelievable 1,050 rounds of ammunition—every round in the chests. The Parrotts were so worn that the friction primers would not seat; the vents on the guns were gone. Unable to provide anymore use on the battlefield the shattered unit was pulled back as Battery G raced to the position; they were going to support the efforts at the Sunken Road.[14]

Captain Owen looked for a position to place Battery G atop the ridge Battery A had just vacated. First Sergeant Benjamin Kelley galloped at the head of the column, into the very midst of the Confederate fire. His horse was killed as the sergeant ran back to the command, and the sergeant was almost captured by the Confederate skirmish line. He quickly recovered from the fall and remounted to carry on his duties. The men had performed these complicated battery drills countless times before, but this was the first time under fire in combat. On the Peninsula, they had fired from stationary positions, only experiencing some return fire. Now the Rhode Islanders were earning their thirteen dollar per month pay. Lieutenant Torslow brought his caissons to the rear, but two of the axles on the vehicles broke. One of them was left on the field, as there was no way to repair it. The other five rumbled away as Torslow directed them to a position where they would still be available but safe from enemy fire. The section commanders began to identify the targets as the guns were quickly unlimbered and brought by hand to the front. The Twenty-Eighth Pennsylvania of the Twelfth Corps moved into a position behind the battery to give it support if needed.[15]

The target was identified as Read's Virginia Battery, a mile away near Sharpsburg, where they had been supporting McLaws' attack. Lieutenant Rhodes quickly pulled out his pocket watch; it was now 10:00 in the morning. Captain Owen ordered the guns sighted for four and a quarter degrees of elevation, while the Number Six Men set the fuzes on the shells for eight seconds in flight before exploding. Exactly as the manual instructed, the cannoneers loaded the piece. With a pull of his hand, the Number Four man in the First Detachment, the men from Westerly, fired his shot towards the battery; this was followed down the line by the other five guns. Captain Owen and Lieutenants Crawford Allen, William Rhodes, and Edward Sears watched as the rounds exploded on the target; they made minute corrections for each further shot fired. The men took their time, deliberately loading and sighting with accuracy; every round exploded on target "with good effect, as far as

Private Peter Riley of Cranston was severely wounded at Antietam.

I can tell," recollected Owen. This firing went on for twenty minutes as the Rhode Islanders continued to pound the position of the Virginians.[16]

William French's Third Division of the Second Corps was to have followed Sedgwick into the West Woods, but instead wheeled to the south, believing that the Second Division was there. They had begun their advance at 9:30, just as Sedgwick was being repulsed. The Third Division was a new unit, made up of troops who had been in the army for only several weeks; many of the men had been given only rudimentary drill, and some did not even know how to load their muskets. Now they marched, shoulder to shoulder in two ranks, into the muzzles of the enemy. The Confederates in the road could hear the Federals coming, but did not see them due to the ridge in the front of the Confederate position. Finally, the Stars and Stripes was seen coming through a cornfield to the front; then the troops appeared at the crest of the hill. French ordered his division to launch a bayonet charge directly on the road, head on: it was suicide. Seventy-five yards from the road, the Alabamians opened fire. Nearly every soldier in the front rank of the Third Division went down in the first volley. The New York, Ohio, Delaware, and Connecticut soldiers tried to return fire, but it was just too intense. Even veterans could not stand and face the immense amount of lead and steel flying through the air. The Federals had no choice but to flee. Around Battery G's position huge clouds of white smoke hung low over the ridge, obscuring the battlefield around them. The artillerists breathed in the sulfuric atmosphere as it burned their eyes and nostrils. Still the work continued.[17]

With Read's Virginia Battery driven away, Captain Owen began to search for another target; he ordered the guns trained on the infantry below as a quick change of position was needed to move to a better location to fire from. The drivers were preparing to limber up and move forward when a wave of Federal blue and zouave red came rushing by the Rhode Islanders. It was the retreating Third Division; furthermore, they were being pursued by some Confederates. The First Delaware that had been fighting to Battery G's left broke and raced for the rear, leaving the battery without any infantry support. Seeing a gap in the line General James Longstreet, in command of the Confederate right wing, ordered Colonel John Cooke to deploy the Twenty-Seventh North Carolina and Third Arkansas into the breach to attempt to threaten French's right. The two regiments advanced into action in an attempt to flank French and capture Battery G. With the North Carolina and Arkansas soldiers well within canister range, and no other Federals to help them, Owen ordered the Rhode Islanders to withdraw without engaging; he believed it was more prudent to fall back than to fight. As the last caisson departed the ridge overlooking the Sunken Road, the Rebels reached Battery G's position, almost capturing part of the unit. After retiring for 300 yards, Owen replaced his limbers for those of the caissons, which allowed him to resupply the ammunition for the guns. The captain then ordered his second in command to go in again.

The first section under Lieutenant Sears advanced to a position occupied by the few remaining troops in the Second Corps on the field. These soldiers retreated yet again as the Confederates pushed back the remaining men from French's Division. Captain Owen reported: "The infantry was unsteady on the right and broke the second time, and not deeming it prudent to risk even the section under such circumstances, I withdrew." With no support, Sears brought his section back to the rest of the battery. An aide from General Sumner then galloped up to the Rhode Islanders and ordered Battery G into position in the rear of the rallying Third Division, where they could still provide covering fire for the troops attacking the Sunken Road. The battery now entered the fray for the third time to engage the enemy.[18]

By 10:30 that bloody morning, the First Division, commanded by Israel "Fighting Dick" Richardson, advanced to the crest of the hill overlooking the road below. The lead unit was the famed Irish Brigade. Like the Third Division they were slaughtered, but they inflicted some damage onto the Confederates. The men stood the terrible volleys for nearly two hours. Colonel Francis Barlow of the Sixty-First New York saw a critical flaw in the defenses. The Rebels had not built up a substantial force to protect their flank as an entire division fled to the rear, thus exposing the vital center of the lane being held by a brigade of Alabamians. These men now fled the position after receiving conflicting orders. Barlow got into a perfect position to actually fire down the road. The Confederates did not know what hit them; they were taking fire from the front and flank and could not remain in the position. Due to the terrain of the Sunken Road, many could not climb out. Now they became caught, the same natural depression an inescapable death trap. Bodies began to pile up as the Federals pressed the attack. After the battle the road became known as Bloody Lane. Finally, after holding for nearly three hours, the remaining Confederates retreated towards Sharpsburg.[19]

General D.H. Hill, in command of the division previously holding the Sunken Road, rallied some men, but he had no reserves. At the same time, Richardson ordered the Union troops to re-form for one final assault. The only Confederates now on the field were several batteries of artillery, previously pushed back from the Dunker Church area. Now they massed at the Piper Farm and on the high ground immediately west of the Hagerstown Pike as over twenty guns fired into the Federals near the Bloody Lane, including the Washington Artillery of Louisiana. Among them was one commanded by General Longstreet, the second in command of the Army of Northern Virginia. He directed his staff as they fired the piece, trying to stem the Federal onslaught. General Richardson ordered his artillery to engage the Confederate positions. Battery G fired their rifles into the ranks of the Confederate artillery, again taking stock that each shot hit the target. This time, though, they were receiving well directed and aimed counter–battery fire. A New Yorker remembered the bombardment at the Bloody Lane as "a converging storm of iron that was fearful and incessant, merged into a tumultuous chorus that made the earth tremble."[20]

Four of the battery horses went down in the shelling. Several Rhode Islanders were hit as well, the first combat injuries in the command. After losing his stripes due to intoxication earlier in the year on the upper Potomac, Corporal William W. Potter had earned them again after the debacle at Fair Oaks. Now he stood directing the fire of his piece as he received a piece of shell fragment to the neck. Privates Joseph Smith and Manley Barber of Westerly were hit in quick succession. They were the first of the Westerly Boys to fall in combat, but unfortunately they would not be the last. Despite these casualties the men continued to work the guns exactly as they had been trained. The shells were landing around the Piper Farm, but were having no effect on the Confederates, who continued to fire rapidly to stem the Federal advance. Captain Owen was busy writing orders when a shell took the pen from his hands. Sergeant Allen Hoar was struck down as well. Another cannoneer lost his belt buckle and a Rhode Island button to the exploding pieces of iron. George Gaskell recalled, "Shell flew above, balls around and beneath me." The private and the small American flag he carried became a prime target. His horse was killed, and Gaskell had just about mounted again before that one was wounded. The flag itself was hit by the fire and had to be replaced after the battle. This was the worst fire these men had received thus far in the war.[21]

The most significant Union casualty was General Richardson, who was mortally wounded while directing the fire of a New Jersey battery. With his wounding went all hopes of the Union assault to break Lee's center. The Federal forces simply remained where they were. New division commander Winfield Scott Hancock took command for Richardson and received orders not to press forward, but to instead hold their line at all hazards. McClellan was fearful of a massive Confederate counterattack against his shattered right flank, north of town. In reality, there was only a thin gray line standing in the way of victory. In the ranks of Battery G, the men could see the Confederates running away as they continued to shell them. With the fight in this sector largely over, General French decided to pull Battery G off the line. There was a perceived threat that Confederate reinforcements would flank the Federals driving towards Sharpsburg. The battery moved back towards the Mumma Farm. This was much against Captain Owen's wishes; he wanted to stay and see the fight to a final end. Unlimbering, they threw two shots into the West Woods to make sure there were no more enemy forces present; the rounds missed the target. With this, Battery G went into position at the Roulette Farm, where the Second Corps was rallying and resting. For them the Battle of Antietam was over.[22]

After breaking through the line at Bloody Lane, but failing to take the initiative, the Federals again turned their attention south, this time to a small stone bridge across the Antietam. After three hours of trying to cross, Ambrose Burnside finally placed his corps across the Antietam. He already had sent Rhode Island General Isaac Peace Rodman south to ford the creek. Among the men under his command was the Fourth Rhode Island. After brushing aside some light resistance Burnside's men were rushing for Sharpsburg to again

A keen diarist, James Barber recorded the horrible sights he witnessed at Antietam (courtesy Providence Public Library, Special Collections [C. Fiske Harris Collection]).

cut off Lee's retreat. However, at the last critical moment Confederate reinforcements arrived on the field from Harpers Ferry. In the swirling hell of a forty-acre cornfield the Fourth Rhode Island lost half their strength against the Confederate veterans. Among the last to fall on this day was General Rodman, mortally wounded while he rallied his shattered division. The fighting ended at sundown. The Rhode Islanders at Antietam had taken part in state sponsored murder at the most extreme. Over 23,000 Americans had been killed, wounded or captured in the bloodiest single day in American history. Among the dead were forty-eight Rhode Islanders.[23]

Antietam had been the first real battle that Battery G was engaged in. They remained in the fight at Bloody Lane for forty on-and-off minutes and expended seventy-five rounds of ammunition. Seven horses were killed and five men were wounded. Only the injuries of Private Peter Riley of Cranston proved to be serious. He was discharged from the service in February of 1863. The other four men were back on duty within a week. Captain Owen praised the conduct of his men: "The officers and men behaved very well, and I cannot say to much of the conduct on the former." Private Gaskell added, "Our battery done much service and though obliged to retreat once came off with credit." As usual, the officers received the bulk of the compliments and rewards. One of their main complaints about the battle was the type of shells they were using, namely the Dyer. Owen complained that the ammunition did not take to the rifling of the barrel, which caused them to fly off the target. The problem was caused by the zinc sabot, which gripped into the rifling of the barrel and separated when fired, thus causing the Dyer rounds to miss their mark.[24]

Battery G had performed well in its first serious taste of combat. This was slightly tarnished after the war by the false statements of a Battery A veteran, and no member of Battery G ever attempted to rebuff his arguments. In his published war diary, Private Theodore Reichardt wrote of G's actions after relieving Battery A: "Battery G fired only a few rounds and left the position we held four hours and a half." Another Battery A veteran who complained about Battery G's performance was Corporal Amos M.C. Olney. He wrote, "We were relieved by a battery who only held their position about five minutes." Both men had seen Battery G in action only near the Dunker Church. The battery could not engage the Confederates because there was no infantry support. Immediately after Battery A pulled out of line to the north, Battery G went into action again at Bloody Lane. Battery G again relieved Tompkins' Battery at this location. Neither Reichardt nor Olney had been witness to the extensive combat at Bloody Lane because they left the field with their shattered command.[25]

The performance of the Rhode Island artillery in the battle was praised by all those who saw it. Batteries A, D, and G were all heavily engaged. The *Providence Journal* ran a small statement from the *New York Commercial*. It read, "Of light artillery there is a plentiful supply, and many of the volunteer batteries are equally famed to the famed Magruder's, Bragg's and Sherman's batteries of former days. Rhode Island furnishes the best light artillerymen."[26]

Even more of a compliment to the Rhode Island artillerists was an editorial printed in the *Boston Traveler*. Ever since Roger Williams was banished from Massachusetts in 1636 and founded Rhode Island, there had always been a sort of animosity among the two states, especially when it came to which was the best. The Bay State newspaper wrote:

> The different batteries from Maine, Massachusetts, and Rhode Island are the occasion of many favorable comments among military and naval men in Washington. It is due to Rhode Island to say that her artillerists appear the bear[ers] of the palm. The reason for this may be found in the fact that her batteries were among the first of the volunteer force in the

field, and consequently, they have had the most practice. As far as the truth of the statement is established, it is credible to your little neighbor. [27]

These statements were but two of the many praising the Rhode Island Light Artillery for their actions on the battlefield. At Antietam, they more than showed both friend and foe their capabilities in combat operations.

The battle was over, but thousands of wounded men still remained on the field, waiting transportation to hospitals. McClellan had held two divisions in reserve, thinking Lee outnumbered him. Many felt if they had been committed, the war would have been over. A tense stalemate ensued on the eighteenth, as unofficial truces were declared along the lines to carry in the wounded and bury the dead. Battery G remained in its position at the Roulette Farm, waiting for orders and tending to the casualties in their sector. For James Barber, it was worse than Fair Oaks: "The field was covered with the dead men and horses." All around the Rhode Islanders men had "fell like sheep at the slaughter." First Sergeant Benjamin Kelley recorded the following: "The enemy being driven back, we now hold the ground occupied by him in the engagement." For twelve hours, both sides had fought each other to a standstill. McClellan did not resume the fight on the eighteenth, but he planned to on September 19. During the night, Lee's battered army slipped quietly back across the Potomac. During the whole period after the battle, Battery G remained vigilant, waiting to be called on again. Sergeant Kelley wrote, "The enemy retreated towards the river + reported to have crossed, horses in harnesses, waiting further orders."[28]

The Confederates brought 45,000 men into Maryland and lost 30 percent of them between South Mountain and Antietam. In his diary, Private Albert D. Cordner best summarized the fighting at Antietam: "Commence the fight at daylight. First we drove them and then they drove us. Then we drove them back again. The fight lasted all day." George Gaskell called Antietam "the fearful battle of the 17th." Despite losing 3,000 more men than the Confederate forces, the Army of the Potomac had indeed defeated the Confederates. They held the field after the battle and sent the Army of Northern Virginia in retreat back across the Potomac. The *Providence Press* called the battle "a glorious victory." Abraham Lincoln seized upon the first major victory in the east, and five days after the battle the president issued the preliminary Emancipation Proclamation: after January 1, 1863, all slaves in states rebelling against the Union would be forever free. This permanently changed the objective of the war. There was no more threat of foreign influence coming in to help the Confederacy and now the conflict would not just be about preserving the Union.[29]

Battery G remained in position until the twentieth, when McClellan moved his army into an area known as Pleasant Valley, south of Sharpsburg. Here, instead of pursuing Lee, they would rest and recuperate after the horrendous battle. Lincoln was irate that the Federal commander did not pursue the enemy. Victory had been so close; now Lee was back in the Shenandoah. Battery G and the Second Corps were again sent to Harpers Ferry, recently vacated by the Confederates after their victory on September 15. Here the battery set up a permanent camp on Bolivar Heights, located west of the once thriving arms manufacturing town, now abandoned and inhabited by only some 100 people. Among the many sites the battery visited was the small building John Brown used as a fort during his raid in 1859. Some heard rumors they would remain at Harpers Ferry all winter, as it was rather late in the year to mount another serious campaign.

As the men settled into the camp, they felt very fortunate to have survived Antietam relatively unscathed. George Gaskell wrote, "If I ever fall, believe me I will die as a man and more too as one going to his rewards on high." Death was a constant threat of the

Civil War soldiers and they were always prepared to meet it. Besides their worry about the battle, a more pressing concern to the men was not having been paid since April. Gaskell also asked his sister for money and warm clothes for the coming of winter.

The view from the heights was stunning as the men gazed into the Blue Ridge. As the Second Corps camped around them the artillerists were shocked to see the reduced size of the infantry regiments. The Irish Brigade entered the Peninsula with nearly 3,000 men; now only 300 remained. Battery G at its full complement was half the size of an infantry brigade. The cannoneers prayed constantly for protection that they would not suffer the same fate as their comrades. The men were proud to style themselves as veterans and proud that all of the soldiers in Battery G had survived the Peninsula without much loss; unfortunately this aspect was about to undergo a sad change. The Pleasant Valley encampment would be far from pleasant.[30]

Each month the battery commander had to file his monthly return with the adjutant general's office in Providence. Captain Charles Owen processed what his battery had accomplished in the last thirty days. After leaving the Peninsula with new recruits, the battery had fought at Antietam, where seven horses were killed and five men wounded. The wave of desertion that had been prevalent in the first few months of the unit was nearly over for

the moment, though an occasional man did leave. Among them was Jacob Hagerdon, who had joined Battery G only on August 7 when the command was at Harrison's Landing. After fighting through Antietam he deserted on September 24. By the end of September, the captain began to receive chilling news that his orderly, Private Gaskell, had predicted. Many men in the battery, such as Albert Cordner and George Gaskell, still remained ill with dysentery and typhoid, illnesses caused from drinking the polluted water on the Peninsula. The worst cases had been transferred to hospitals in the North, while those less ill remained in camp.

The soldiers in the hospitals were on the verge of dying when they left the Peninsula. Now the sad returns were forwarded to Captain Owen and Battery G. By the end of the month nine soldiers in the battery had died of typhoid or

John G. Rathbun was one of the Westerly Boys and motivated his comrades through the war by the fiddle he brought from home (courtesy Kris VanDenBossche).

dysentery, most at hospitals in the north. Private Elijah Parsons of Providence was the most fortunate; he was permitted to die in his home state at Portsmouth Grove Hospital. But due to army red tape he could not be with his family in his last moments. Sergeant Jacob F. Kent was discharged, but died at home in Warwick in December. Eleven remained in the hospitals; half would never return to serve in the battery. Among these was Sergeant Henry Bowler, who had been ill since the Battle of Yorktown. In April, 140 Rhode Islanders had marched onto the Peninsula. Some died as a result of the disease they caught there, while many more remained ill for the rest of their lives. Remarkably, none of the Westerly Boys died as a result of the illness. Many were taken sick, but only two were discharged. Daniel Chapman a stonecutter, left his brother Thomas alone to his fate, while forty-year-old Nathaniel Niles, one of the oldest Westerly soldiers, finally received an honorable discharge and went back to farming, a broken wreck.[31]

While the men remained encamped at Harpers Ferry, President Lincoln visited the camp, pressing McClellan to move. The general refused, saying his troops needed rest. New regiments flooded into the vast camp of the Army of the Potomac. For the men from western and southern Rhode Island most important were the Twenty-First Connecticut and Seventh Rhode Island. Passes were frequently issued so the men could travel the short five mile distance to the Ninth Corps camps and visit friends, neighbors, and brothers. Although he was pleased to meet several neighbors in the Twenty-First, including his brother-in-law Henry Call, Private Gaskell was more concerned about his sick sister back home in Plainfield, Connecticut. She had a severe fever that would not break. He pleaded with his father to leave Smithfield and travel to Connecticut to take care of the children and comfort Mary. In addition, Gaskell was somewhat upset that Mary's husband had left his family to join the army. Albert Cordner was also pleased to visit the Twenty-First, recruited along the Connecticut–Rhode Island border. His brother Charles served as a member of Company G. Furthermore, his other friend, Peleg E. Peckham from Charlestown, went south as a sergeant in the Seventh Rhode Island.

Although many of the artillerists in Battery G were pleased to meet their friends and relatives in the new regiments, they looked on in disdain at their new clothing and boisterous attitudes about soldiering. Some of the old regiments had not been supplied with clothing since the Peninsula; the battery finally received an issue of pants in mid–October. Private Gaskell referred to the Seventh Michigan as "Battery G's favorite." It entered the Peninsula with full ranks of 1,000 men and after being slaughtered in the West Woods mustered only 120 men. Whenever Gaskell met one of the veterans he would firmly grasp his hand and say, "Yes, Comrade, we were on the Peninsula." Only ten months earlier the men of Battery G had been raw recruits as well. Now the new regiments would have to prove themselves in combat. They would not have long to wait.[32]

While new regiments were added to the army, changes at the senior levels of command were occurring as well. A major change in the command of the Second Corps occurred when General Sumner received a leave of absence to Washington, but left the command forever. The men were saddened to see the old warrior leave; he had organized the Second and had commanded it from the front every step of the way. Sumner would return to the Army of the Potomac as a wing commander in charge of the Second and Ninth Corps. He was replaced by Darius Couch, an experienced commander but the youngest officer to command a corps thus far.[33]

After six weeks of rest, McClellan finally decided to march. On the second campaign to take Richmond, he would take his 100,000 man army out from the Shenandoah and march south to Richmond via an overland route. Taking only the supplies in the wagons and what could be carried by the men, he would quickly outmarch Lee and capture the Confederate citadel: so was the plan. At Harpers Ferry, the artillerists continued to view the sights and swam in the Shenandoah River.

Private Gaskell worried constantly about his sister; he wanted to go home and take care of her. The orderly wanted to comfort her in Swahili, a language he had learned while sailing to Africa and that they used for private conversation together. Private Cordner was also concerned, about his brother in the Twenty-First Connecticut. Like many just adapting their bodies for service in the field, Charles Cordner was severely ill. At forty-two years of age, Private Michael Coffery of Battery G was an Irish immigrant living in Providence and was probably too old to have become a soldier. After being ill for months, he became the latest victim of the deadly typhoid, on October 18. He was interred with honors on Bolivar Heights, leaving a wife and seven children to mourn his death and carry on. For the funeral, Captain Owen authorized the use of one of the ordnance rifles; it fired three blanks cartridges in salute. Also on this day, John L. Rathbun died of the same illness at a hospital in Baltimore after being released from prison. In total a dozen men from Battery G died because of the typhoid and dysentery caused by poor food and water on the Peninsula.[34]

McClellan finally began his new campaign on October 27. The Second Corps was the first unit to march out of Pleasant Valley to the south. The rate of travel was horribly slow. For soldiers who in only a few months would march up to twenty miles in a day the pace was relaxing; they only marched five miles each day. Albert Cordner was pleased to be moving after remaining in camp for a month. "Had good time marched" was his diary entry on October 28. In addition, the men finally received some new clothing to replace that worn out on the Peninsula and at Antietam. President Lincoln was again aghast at the progress of the new campaign; McClellan was not moving fast enough to end the war. In one week, the Army of the Potomac had marched only seventeen miles into Virginia. Faced with no other choice, the president relieved the beloved general from his command for the final time on November 7.

General George B. McClellan had made the Army of the Potomac. Under his leadership they became an army, learning to maneuver and work as one. However, McClellan was not a field commander; overestimating Lee's strength and not being aggressive enough was his downfall. The men in Battery G were sad to see their general leave and cheered him as he gave one last review of the Second Corps. He was replaced with a man well known to all Rhode Islanders: Major General Ambrose Everett Burnside of Bristol. He had led the First Rhode Island Regiment at Bull Run and had then captured a large portion of the North Carolina coast for the Union. At Second Bull Run, his troops covered the withdrawal of the enemy, while they nearly made it to Sharpsburg during Antietam. The new commander promptly put his army on a fast-paced march to the Rappahannock River. Ahead for the Army of the Potomac lay more bloodshed, but most important for Battery G, a change.[35]

First Fredericksburg

Battery still engaged with the Rebels.
—First Sergeant Allen Hoar, December 13, 1862

With Burnside in command of the Army of the Potomac, the immense force set off on a rapid pace to Richmond. The season was already late to begin a new campaign, but with the army already on the march and Lee having not even moved out of the Shenandoah, Burnside decided to risk it. He would cross the Rappahannock River at Fredericksburg, outflanking the Army of Northern Virginia, and from there march directly to Richmond. Lincoln approved the plan and again Battery G was marching south.

General Burnside realized that his army was too large for himself alone to effectively command the massive force; indeed, he had already declined command of the Army of the Potomac twice. But upon being told that his rival Joseph Hooker would receive the command, he gave in. In order to facilitate easier control over the vast columns of men that marched south, Burnside established three "Grand Divisions" of two corps each. The Right Grand Division comprised the Second and Ninth Corps. Joseph Hooker commanded the Center Grand Division, comprising the Third and Fifth Corps, while the First and Sixth Corps comprised the Left Grand Division under William Franklin. The force was so large that they had to march on separate roads.[1]

General Sumner returned to command the Right Grand Division. The Second Corps and Battery G took the lead. The weather started to become cool as the men followed the Rappahannock from Warrenton on a direct course for Fredericksburg. Albert Cordner was pleased that his brother Charles was feeling better and had returned to duty in the Twenty-First Connecticut; he went to visit him on the nineteenth without a pass or permission. Captain Owen humiliated the private by making him carry a fence rail for two hours around camp as punishment. With the supply wagons stretched to the limit due to the fast pace of the campaign the men returned to foraging for their rations. On November 16 a turkey was found and enjoyed by the soldiers from southwestern Rhode Island.

On the seventeenth Battery G and the initial elements of the Union army marched into Falmouth, Virginia, in a driving rainstorm. The battery fired a few shells into Falmouth to insure it was safe for the army to move into the town; directly across the Rappahannock River was the city of Fredericksburg. The bridges in the area had already been destroyed in the first year of the war, so the Federals had no means of crossing other than fording the river, which Burnside deemed imprudent because his men might be cut off without supplies. The Rhode Island general was so successful that he had moved the army out from Warrenton without Lee even knowing of the action. Indeed the city was held only by one small Confederate brigade. Instead of ordering his men to ford the quarter-mile wide stream, Burnside decided to wait until pontoon bridges arrived from Washington. The delay would be fatal.[2]

A significant change for Battery G came on November 21. First Lieutenant Edward

Battery G took part in the December 11 bombardment of Fredericksburg.

Sears resigned his commission. Having been in the service for a year and a half, Sears decided to transfer to the United States Navy as a paymaster with the equivalent rank of major. Lieutenant William B. Rhodes now became the second in command as Second Lieutenants Crawford Allen and Otto Torslow both moved up in rank to receive the bar of a first lieutenant. Torslow's fancy officer's jacket had long since worn out, so he purchased two private's fatigue blouses from Quartermaster Sergeant William Westcott. Because of his family's stature and as a reward for his actions at Antietam, First Sergeant Benjamin E. Kelley was promoted to second lieutenant and took over Torslow's position as chief of the caissons. The officers brought the sections they had previously commanded to the new positions, while Torslow finally received command of the Center Section. These promotions echoed down the line, as Sergeant Allen Hoar became first sergeant. Having enlisted as a private, Hoar was a good soldier, rising to sergeant directly from private on June 9 when Sergeant Bogman lost his stripes; in addition he had been wounded at Antietam. Likewise, Corporal Nathaniel R. Chace of Westerly, another of the June 9 promotions, was made a sergeant, while Henry Sisson was promoted to corporal to replace Chace's vacancy. Now there would be a way to tell him apart from his twin brother, Charles. With the promotions taking place, the men did not notice a very real threat.[3]

With little to do, the men prepared for the upcoming winter. It became very apparent that they would be spending the entire winter here in camp if Burnside did not move. Instead of waiting for orders, the men took it upon themselves to build small, crude huts similar to log cabins, which were dug into the ground. The walls were built up to shoulder height, while roofs were constructed from the shelter tents. The red, clay-like Virginia mud that proved such a bother to the artillerymen served to chink the walls. Although small, cramped, and susceptible to leaking, they provided the men with a sound place to sleep. The soldiers decorated the huts to their liking and each one became a retreat from the world around them. The forest close to the encampment became decimated as all available timber was used for building the huts and a convenient source of firewood.

Unlike the infantrymen, who were only worried about their muskets, the drivers in

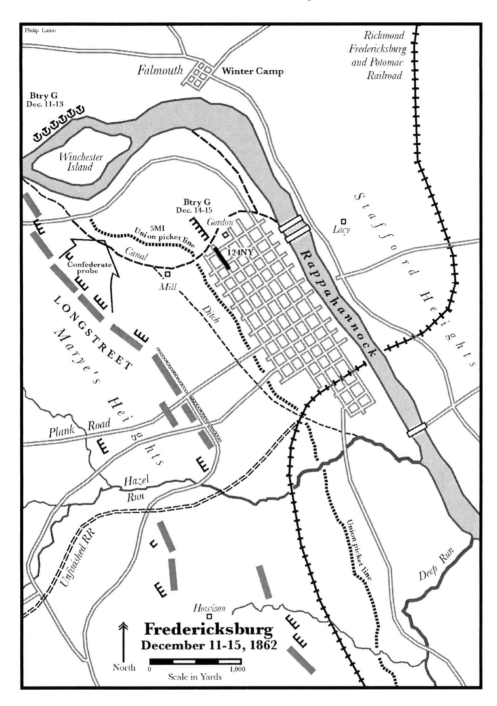

Philip Laino

Falmouth   **Winter Camp**

Richmond
Fredericksburg
and Potomac
Railroad

Btry G
Dec. 11-13

*Winchester
Island*

Btry G
Dec. 14-15

Gordon

5MI

Union picket line

Canal

124NY

Lacy

Stafford Heights

**Confederate
probe**

Mill

Ditch

Rappahannock

L O N G S T R E E T

Marye's Heights

Plank Road

*Hazel
Run*

Unfinished RR

Union picket line

Deep Run

Howison

Fredericksburg
December 11-15, 1862

North   0   1,000
Scale in Yards

Battery G had to constantly care for their horses. A large stable structure was being planned to house the battery horses, rather than tying them to trees all winter as had been done on the Potomac the winter before. By November 27 all was in order as the men prepared for their Thanksgiving meal. In Rhode Island, the families of the soldiers sat around enjoying traditional New England holiday fare, while the men were reduced to eating "hard bread, pork, and coffee." The survivors of the Chickahominy Fever had much to be thankful for and the entire battery was given a brief day of rest.[4]

While Burnside was waiting for his pontoon bridges so he could arrive to safely cross the river, the Army of Northern Virginia was not remaining idle. After losing over 12,000 men in the Maryland Campaign, Lee had rebuilt his army to nearly 70,000 men to fight against Burnside's 100,000 man force. Knowing that the Federals would have to cross at Fredericksburg, the Confederate commander set to build a series of impenetrable defensive points via a series of hills and swamps in the rear of the city. The Confederate line stretched for five miles and was anchored on Prospect Hill and Marye's Heights. On the Heights, Longstreet positioned two battalions of artillery, totaling twenty-four guns under Colonel E. Porter Alexander, a gifted artillerist. Among the batteries was the Washington Artillery of Louisiana, the same cannoneers Battery G faced at Antietam. The guns were placed in a murderous position to enfilade the length of the entire Federal line. In front of his position was Telegraph Road, which skirted the base of Marye's Heights. Years of use had eroded the road so it was now three feet below the base of the hill. It was reinforced in front by a four-foot high stone wall, allowing for a perfect defensive fire. Into this road was stationed a brigade of Georgians. Separating Marye's Heights and the city of Fredericksburg was a half-mile wide plain that the Federals had to cross in order to reach the hill. The Confederates built their lines so well that the plain could be covered from all angles and units could be maneuvered along the line as needed. Colonel Alexander said in reference to his defenses and the attackers, "Scarcely a chicken could live upon that field when we open up upon it." There was no other way to cross in front of Fredericksburg without a direct assault upon the hills and the fortifications. Each day the cannoneers could gaze across the river and see the Confederates preparing their defenses.[5]

As the new officers assumed their positions, Battery G limbered up from the camp and proceeded to the front on November 28. Opposite of Fredericksburg, on the Falmouth side of the river, was Stafford Heights, a strategic location from which the Union artillery could shell the city if need be. With the army arriving on the field daily, Burnside began to direct the artillery to Stafford Heights. Battery G took position on the extreme right of the Federal line, west of Falmouth on a rock outcropping over Winchester Island, a perfect place to enfilade the line. Immediately the privates began to build defensive shields for the guns called lunettes. By digging into the soil, the cannon would be placed in the pits and protected against counter–battery fire if it should be received. The downside was that there was less room to work around the guns.[6]

The weather continued to worsen as Burnside prepared for the assault. The pontoon bridges had still not arrived either. Now, instead of one lone Confederate brigade, the entire Army of Northern Virginia was across the river in Fredericksburg. On Stafford Heights the cannoneers finished the fortifications and, like the rest of the army, waited. The second of December marked the one-year anniversary of their muster in at the Benefit Street Arsenal. In that one year nearly a third of the original members of Battery G had died, deserted, or been discharged. Their places were filled with new comrades who remained loyal to the flag through all the defeat and disease the battery marched through. On December 7, the enlisted men were treated to a fine meal of potatoes and fresh beef and additional warm clothing was issued. Wood was brought in for the huts while final preparations for the battle were made. Finally, on December 10, the bridges arrived from Washington. With no other choice, Burnside ordered them placed across the Rappahannock. He ordered a direct assault on the city. At 10:00 that night, Battery G received their orders: they were going into action. Captain Owen placed his six three inch ordnance rifles into the defensive pits atop the hill, on the far right of the line. Private Barber wrote, "We took our position in Battery to give the rebs battle."[7]

On the morning of December 11, General Burnside called for engineers to build three bridges over the river. As the building parties engaged in their work, Confederate brigadier general William Barksdale and his Mississippians, who were holding the city proper, picked off the engineers as they built the bridges. Outraged at what the Confederates were doing, Burnside ordered his well-entrenched artillery to open fire and drive the Mississippians from the city. In total there were 140 Union guns in position. Captain Owen wrote, "The morning of the 11th dawned thick and foggy. I fired a few shot into the town; but, our ranges being very imperfect, and not being able to see the effect of the shot, owing to the foggy atmosphere, I ceased firing at that point." As a former member of the Providence Marine Corps of Artillery, Owen knew when to use his ammunition and not to waste it on frivolous targets.

The bombardment accomplished nothing; the Mississippians soon reappeared and continued the fight. A brigade of the Second Corps was then dispatched to drive them out, thus accomplishing the first amphibious landing under fire in American military history. Once in Fredericksburg, the soldiers began to fight block to block and house to house; the first large scale urban combat fought in the Civil War. As they were crossing the river, they came under fire from both infantry and artillery fire. Owen was ordered to engage again to provide covering fire for the Federal assault as they established a bridgehead in Fredericksburg. The artillerists were amazed at the power their guns was having on Fredericksburg; they had never engaged a target like this before. The city was largely flat, consisting of brick and masonry buildings. Private Barber recalled, "Our Battery commenced firing from the right of the line of Falmouth on the City we kept up fire until knight and the City was on fire in 7 places."[8]

At 4:00 the long-range Confederate guns on Marye's Heights tried to respond to the

Lieutenant William B. Rhodes brought a large amount of artillery knowledge to Battery G at the start of the war, almost died on the Peninsula, and later became a captain of his own battery (courtesy Phil DiMaria, Battery B 1st Rhode Island Light Artillery Inc.).

Federal fire, but at a range of 1,500 yards the shot and shell failed to inflict much damage. Private Cordner remembered "shot breaking on our battery." A piece of one of the few rounds to reach the position near Winchester Island hit Private Michael Callahan in the right knee, slightly injuring the young Irishman. One cannoneer became angry at this act and wrote, "We showed our appreciation of this ungentlemanly conduct by shelling them with so much vigor that they abandoned their guns." Battery G joined in a fierce twenty-minute counter barrage and stopped the Confederate fire, much as it had done at Antietam.[9]

After Barksdale's men were cleared from the city, the pontoon bridges were completed and the lead elements of the Union army crossed. The soldiers took mental note of the power the artillery bombardment had caused.

For the first time in the war the Army of the Potomac lost control. The soldiers broke into houses, pillaging and stealing all that was not bolted down. Large amounts of tobacco were found, while alcohol flowed freely. A private in Battery A wrote, "Soldiers could be seen, sitting on splendid furniture, mixing dough for flapjacks. Most of our Battery were cooking all night long." The reason for this destruction was in retaliation for the death and destruction on the battlefield suffered at the hands of the Confederates. For the first time the Union soldiers could show Southern civilians what war truly was. The artillery on Marye's Heights responded to the crossing but did not have much effect, except for lighting some houses on fire. Unlike the other guns which crossed with the infantry, Battery G remained behind in the defensive position ready to respond to any threat if need be. They remained there on the twelfth and thirteenth of December. In the streets of Fredericksburg the soldiers bedded down in the streets or in the many houses captured; for many of the men in blue it would be their last night on earth.[10]

The First Battle of Fredericksburg began on December 13, 1862, when the First and Sixth corps attacked Jackson's lines at Prospect Hill. They succeeded in breaching the position, but were repulsed when General William Franklin refused to send reinforcements to their aid. While this was occurring, Burnside planned for his main assault against Marye's Heights. The Second and Ninth corps were directed to attack up the long slope to reach the Confederates on the hill. In six separate waves, the Federals could not even make it to the stone wall. Several units, including the Seventh Rhode Island, made it to within fifty yards of the wall before the fire became so intense that they could advance no farther. The Confederate artillery had a supreme location to target all Union forces engaged on the field; indeed, it was their best day of the war. Combined with the infantry in Telegraph Road it was a perfect killing position; unlike Bloody Lane at Antietam, it could not be flanked. The Second Corps fought, as they did always, with great gallantry. Over half of General Winfield Scott Hancock's First Division became casualties, the most suffered by a single division for any battle of the war. During one pivotal moment, Battery B dashed onto the field to a position 150 yards from the road to engage the Confederates. They were there for fifteen minutes before retiring, having lost three killed and thirteen wounded, while encouraging the infantry to hold on, which was among an artillery battery's greatest duties.[11]

Across the Rappahannock, the men of Battery G could only imagine what was going on in the fields in front of Marye's Heights as there was nothing they could do to stop it. Many had relatives or neighbors in the attacking columns and had never seen an infantry unit from their state undergo what was happening in the Fourth, Seventh, and Twelfth Rhode Island regiments. James Barber borrowed a pair of field glasses from an officer and observed:

> The Potomac Army attacked the enemys works in the rear of the Town with his infantry and 12 pounds guns then the heavy roar and clashes of musketry commenced which nearly shook all around. General Sumner's Right Grand Division advance double quick on the enemys works under a galing fire from the rebels artillery which made numerous gaps in their ranks that was amended by the lines closing up and then again they rushed on like mad men till within a few hundred yards of their lines of works they would rise up out of their intrenchments and pour in fresh volles of musketry at short range with deadly effect.

Battery G took part in the battle by remaining across the river and occasionally firing a few shots towards Marye's Heights, but it was to little avail; no damage was done. The attacks continued fruitlessly until nightfall, when they were called off. Nearly 13,000 Union soldiers became casualties. Despite all of this, not one inch of ground was gained.[12]

The lines remained in place on December 14. Burnside wanted to personally lead another assault, but backed down at the final moment. The men in Battery G were spared the slaughter, but their time had come. At 6:30 that morning, Captain Owen received word to bring his battery to Colonel Alexander Hays at the Lacy House on Stafford Heights. Battery G, after replenishing their ammunition, would cross the river and take the place of several other batteries, which lost heavily in the fighting. Again, Captain Charles Morgan directed the Rhode Islanders into position. As they crossed the river on the pontoon bridge, Private Albert Cordner saw a wounded neighbor from Charlestown waiting evacuation to a hospital. Private Barber saw the damage to the town caused by the shelling: "Every house was riddled or torn to pieces by our shells and some of them was burnt to the ground."[13]

The battery was placed in the middle of Fredericksburg itself, behind a thin line of pickets. The position was located within the grounds of the Kenmore Plantation. Built in 1775 for George Washington's only sister, the Gordon House on the estate was now full of wounded Federals who were in the process of being evacuated and treated. Battery G had to hold this vital position so these soldiers could at least have some hope of recovery.

At least Battery G had some cover under a slight depression, but they were positioned right in the path of Richard Anderson's Rebel Division. Before leaving, Morgan left the battery with specific orders. Because Fredericksburg was filled with thousands of Union soldiers, many of them wounded, the rules of engagement were very specific. They could engage only Confederate artillery threatening the infantry. If the guns engaged Battery G, Captain Owen could not return fire. Owen further gave orders for his men not to talk throughout the fourteenth, not wanting to give away their concealed position.[14]

At dusk the Fifth Michigan was detached from the Third Corps and sent to reinforce the picket line, in addition to providing covering fire for the artillery. Captain Owen showed Major Edward T. Sherlock where to place his men. Two hours later, as his men quietly remained near the guns, Owen went out to inspect the infantry picket line, much as any good officer would do. He was aghast at the results:

> I found them only about 50 yards from the battery, and more than half had come in. Some new ones were soon stationed, but, being new troops, they were useless as pickets for night duty. About 11 P.M. I was aroused by the heavy picket firing directly in our front, and very near. Anticipating that our pickets would move in, I hastened out, and found nearly all the picket line had come in, and the Rebels were very close. I ordered up the reserves at once, and obtained a separate company for the picket duty during the remainder of the night; but we had no further trouble.[15]

The men remained wary that the Confederates would launch a night assault and capture the battery. Lieutenant Rhodes brought up the One Hundred and Twenty Fourth New York to assist if needed. The horses remained hooked to the limbers all night long, while the drivers nodded off in the saddle.[16]

During the night of the fourteenth the artillerists had to remain on guard duty in the streets. This caused many to come down with severe colds. Some took the opportunity to erect crude breastworks as a defense against the expected Rebel attack. Meanwhile the officers slept in the Gordon House on the Kenmore estate, described by William Rhodes as "a splendid brick house." Despite the many wounded, the officers still found room. In the middle of the night, the caissons brought in additional rounds of canister for the guns; this was done so that, if Battery G needed to cover a retreat, they had plenty of this lethal round. Some men volunteered to help bring in the casualties from the battlefield. While some cannoneers assisted with the wounded, others helped themselves to some of the few spoils not already taken from Fredericksburg. Private Cordner found a book and a new dress; he mailed them to his wife in Rhode Island.[17]

Finally, on the fifteenth, realizing he had been defeated, Burnside ordered a withdrawal and evacuation of Fredericksburg. Again defeat had come to Battery G. What had looked so promising after the Maryland Campaign, a final end to the war, was now out of the grasp of the powerful Army of the Potomac. The battle had been going on for three days. First Sergeant Allen Hoar recorded the same message in his orderly book for those three days: "Battery still engaged with the Rebels."[18]

At 11:00, the Union forces started their withdrawal, and at the same time the Confederate artillery began to fire against the retreating forces. Following their orders, Battery G began to return fire towards Marye's Heights. This gave up their covered position inside the swale, as the Confederate artillery began to hit near G's position. With this, Captain Owen ordered his men to cease fire per his orders. A battery horse was killed by the fire. Later in the afternoon, as the Union forces were completing their evacuation across the river, a Confederate patrol came down from the entrenchments and began to probe the thin Federal picket line. Approaching to within one hundred and fifty yards of the line, the Fifth Michigan and the battery saw the threat. A member of Battery G wrote, "When our infantry fell back the rebels came on with their battle flags. We gave them canister and with the support of the 5th Michigan, drove them back to the woods." A few salvos of canister from the guns and several volleys of musketry were enough to send the foe back to the safety of Marye's Heights. A New York officer added, "The action began immediately and lasted until after dark. The fire was directed against the two little breastworks." With the attack over, so was Battery G's mission; the retreat was successful. At 6:00 that night the captain instructed Lieutenant Rhodes to lead Battery G back across the Rappahannock and return to Falmouth. The Battle of First Fredericksburg was over.[19]

As the Federals pulled back across the river, the Confederates walked into a scene of destruction; much of the city was destroyed. Unlike their other battles, where the Union soldiers knew that they had been defeated by an aggressive enemy and not so much by bad generalship, Fredericksburg was a disaster. So many men perished and no position was taken or held. The blame by many was put on Ambrose Burnside for deciding to attack in the face of overwhelming odds. Unlike their other comrades, the Rhode Islanders thought it was not Burnside's fault, but rather that of General Henry Halleck, the commander in chief in Washington who many thought did not send the pontoon bridges in time. Private George Gaskell wrote, "Probably there is not another man who shares with Burnside, the affections of the people of Rhode Island. Every man in our camp speaks of him as if he were some relative, more than a mere successful military commander." The Army of the Potomac had been defeated by a force which three months earlier had barely been capable of retreating out of Maryland; now they seemed poised to fight on again. As the men looked back across the river at their foe, they were sickened to see many of the Confederates wearing the clothing they had stripped from the Union dead in front of Telegraph Road.[20]

In the Battle of First Fredericksburg, Battery G was very fortunate, as only one man was slightly wounded. The other Rhode Island units were not so lucky. Eighty soldiers died, while over 300 more were wounded trying to reach Marye's Heights. It was the single bloodiest day in the history of Rhode Island. The Seventh Regiment alone took 570 rifles into action and lost 220. In its long list of casualties, the *Providence Journal* erroneously reported a Private William Mason of Battery G as being killed in action; no such a member of the battery existed. Lieutenant Rhodes was pleased that Captain Owen was still alive, as he owed Rhodes $350. Although they had not taken any serious battle casualties, the campaign did have another sad chapter. On December 11, Private Jacob H. Salpaugh, a laborer and Irish immigrant from New York City, died of typhoid. He was buried in camp on December 16 with military honors. In addition, on this day three more men were discharged due to disability.[21]

Although across the river for little more then twenty-four hours, the men of Battery G had experienced the battle in all its horror. The battery expended 230 rounds of ammunition during five days of action, mostly case shot of the Hotchkiss pattern. Again, the commander complained about his ammunition. Owen wrote that the Dyer ammunition, similar to that used at Antietam, again flew off target, while the Hotchkiss shells burst in the barrel, creating a hazardous position for the cannoneers. This was the end of the Dyer projectile being used in the ordnance rifle. From now on only improved Hotchkiss solid, shell, and case would be used. The ammunition was often faulty; the soldiers of the battery were not. The captain wrote, "During the most trying circumstances they were perfectly calm and collected." These would become the last words Captain Owen would ever record about his battery.[22]

With the campaign to take Richmond over the moment, the artillerists in Battery G returned to their small huts near Falmouth and began to prepare for the winter. Some additional work was completed on the officers' huts to make them more comfortable, while guard, drill, and other routine aspects of soldier life began to become the norm again. Colonel Tompkins christened the new camp "Camp Pitcher," after Molly Pitcher. During the Revolution's Battle of Monmouth she had assisted her husband in loading a cannon.

Despite the fact that many hoped to pass a quiet winter, even in camp tragedies could happen. This became apparent on December 17. Each morning and night an officer had to supervise the drivers as they took the horses down to the river to drink. At 6:00 in the afternoon, it was Lieutenant Crawford Allen's duty. As Private Patrick Carrigan, an Irish immigrant, was inspecting his horse, he was kicked in the neck and instantly killed. His death rang throughout Battery G as a testament to how dangerous the light artillery service truly was.[23]

On December 20, Colonel Charles H. Tompkins visited the camp. He came to speak personally with Lieutenant Rhodes. Battery D had suffered severe casualties at Second Bull Run and Antietam and recently Captain Albert Monroe had been promoted to major, while only one officer remained on duty in the battery. A new captain had just been appointed, but the battery still needed more veteran officers. Tompkins asked Rhodes if he would transfer to Battery D. He was to help bring the command back together as an effective fighting force. The unit also contained a large contingent of men from Warwick, Rhodes' birthplace, residence, and the site of his militia service. The lieutenant consented and was given a week to complete his accounts before reporting to the new command. He would never return to Battery G. Lieutenant Allen heard of the commotion in camp and wanted to go with Rhodes, thinking promotion would follow him into another battery despite the fact that one month earlier he had been commissioned as a first lieutenant. Instead, he remained in Battery G and took over Rhodes' position as commander of the right section and second in command of the battery.[24]

On December 24, the men prepared for the Christmas holidays, thinking of their families at home, while the officers again enjoyed the benefits of their positions, feasting on a traditional holiday meal of turkey. The enlisted men as usual missed out. Albert Cordner wrote, "We never had no dinner for Christmas." That night Captain Charles D. Owen went to his trusted subordinate, Lieutenant Rhodes, and dropped a bombshell. He was going to resign the command of Battery G and return to Providence. Only twenty years old, Owen was already a veteran who had handled his battery well on the Peninsula and Antietam. Despite a credible battlefield performance, he had never gained the respect of his enlisted men. Now, after being in the field since June of 1861, he was going home to begin a business career, claiming "urgent family reasons." The captain told Rhodes not to mention the news to anyone, especially Crawford Allen, who was itching for a promotion to captain. Indeed, with Owen and Rhodes gone, Allen would become the de facto commander of Battery G until Governor Sprague could appoint a new commander. Captain Morgan, commander of the Second Corps artillery, was pleased to see Owen finally leave, and so were many of the soldiers in Battery G. Since the Peninsula, he had been considering turning in his commission, but waited until after the battles were over for the season. Morgan believed that Owen "lost interest in the battery." The resignation would also allow for the promotion of another Rhode Island officer to a captaincy. On December 26, Lieutenant Rhodes left Battery G for Battery D. Captain Owen followed two days later. With their two senior officers gone, the men could only predict who would command them next.[25]

An incompetent officer, Captain Horace S. Bloodgood's tenure as commander was disastrous (courtesy Phil DiMaria, Battery A, 1st Rhode Island Light Artillery Inc.).

By January 1, the situation at Falmouth was beginning to grow desperate for the Army of the Potomac. They were poorly supplied, fed, and had not been paid since McClellan commanded the army. Many were sick with typhoid, dysentery, or pneumonia, for which little could be done. The small huts and unsanitary conditions contributed immensely to the disease in the army. The recurrent illnesses many had contracted from the Chickahominy again appeared in Battery G's camp. Private Cordner had already fought off dysentery on the Peninsula; now he came down again with typhoid and rheumatism. Some days his condition was not so bad, while others he could barely walk. Cordner wrote that there was a "great deal of fever" in the battery. Musician William Lewis recounted the Falmouth encampment: "We have been encamped all winter in a miserable place where there is no shade what ever."[26]

Because the men had not been paid, they could not purchase any items to aid in their survival from the high priced sutlers, nor could the families of the poorer soldiers afford to help them. The Rhode Islanders in Battery G had to rely on their tattered government greatcoats and a fire to keep them warm. Some soldiers wrote letters to their families asking for aid, and one letter ended up in the *Providence Journal.* The anonymous soldier reported:

> The troops have returned to their old camps and are making themselves as comfortable as possible. We have few luxuries, but do not suffer much for many necessaries. The report that two men in this battery recently froze to death is entirely false; although if such stories will cause friends to send us mittens, socks, & c, I have no objection to their being circulated.

Despite the appeal, few items were sent to the battery as the struggle for survival continued. For some soldiers, especially those from western Rhode Island, it harked back to memories of a war eighty years earlier as they experienced what their ancestors went through at Valley Forge.[27]

Among those suffering was Private William O. Tabor. He was sent to Washington ill with typhoid on January 9. The soldier died of the disease on January 27, suffering to the end from the high fever and terrible conditions of the disease. His remains were returned to Richmond and added to the growing Wood River Cemetery; already six men from other Rhode Island units who had died of illness during the winter at Falmouth or who had been killed at Fredericksburg were buried there. His epitaph was one of many patriotic tomes for a young life sacrificed for the benefit of the nation: "His toils are passed, his work is done. He is fully blessed. He fought the fight, the victory won & entered into rest." Tabor's wife Phebe was devastated at the loss of her husband and only lived for two more years before joining him in a grave in Wood River. The artillerists in camp were more fortunate than the other troops; being concerned as they had to be only with the welfare of their horses and guns they could take better care of themselves. Indeed, the first week of the new year was spent exercising the horses and repairing the caissons. Although typhoid was a large factor in reducing the morale of the soldiers, the most important factor was that they knew they had been defeated soundly by the Confederates yet again.[28]

New Year's Day brought a dramatic change to what the war was being fought over: now, in addition to reuniting the country, slavery was going to be ended by force. After Antietam many in the battery had visited John Brown's small engine house at Harpers Ferry; now that cause was a national war aim for the United States. Many of the soldiers in Battery G had never seen blacks in Rhode Island; the several hundred freemen in the state lived primarily in Providence and Washington County where they worked the menial jobs no one else wanted.

The cause of abolition was a small one in Rhode Island; although some spoke out against slavery, most realized that the state could not support itself without the institu-

The Mud March was a severe test for Battery G.

tion. Although Rhode Island slave ships from Newport and Providence had already made their fortunes for families like the Browns in the eighteenth century, the human cargo that had been brought over on the Middle Passage continued to be of benefit to the smallest state, including for many of the men in Battery G. The economy of the state flourished because of slavery. The many mills that employed the soldiers processed slave-picked cotton and made rough cotton cloth for their clothing. Until new consumers could be found, along with sources of raw materials, many of the small mills in southern Rhode Island were hurting for a market for their products, causing a great strain on many families who depended on the small monthly pay of a Union volunteer.[29]

Once the battery arrived in the South, the men began to know blacks as a part of their daily life, encountering them everywhere they went. George Gaskell was one of the few cannoneers who had seen blacks before, as a sailor in his voyages to Africa. He had some respect for the slaves; in his opinion they had lost none of their African ways and they hounded Battery G trying to sell or barter their goods. His opinion was also shared by the many Irish in the battery. They feared that if freed, blacks would add to their competition for jobs. Albert Cordner viewed blacks as novelties who should carry on their current occupations but in the service of the Union army. On the Peninsula, he had frequently taken his meals at slaves' homes when he tired of hardtack and pork. Private James Barber stated he was "against the President." Nearly all of the men in Battery G were passive in their views of emancipation. They kept it to themselves, discussing it with their comrades and not letting it get in the way of their duty. President Lincoln had implemented the Emancipation Proclamation; now these artillerists found themselves fighting for the freedom of those held in bondage in the South, which was not the cause for which many had enlisted.[30]

While the cannoneers grumbled constantly about the weather, horrible food, no pay, and low morale, another, more pressing issue was on their minds. Lieutenant Edward Sears had resigned in November and had been replaced by the popular Benjamin Kelley. With William Rhodes' transfer to Battery D and the resignation of Captain Owen, the men in Battery G looked for another commander to lead them. Lieutenant Allen remained popular, but a solid combat leader was needed. The lieutenant himself tried to obtain the captaincy by having his father, who was a politician, use his power on Benefit Street. The men in the other Rhode Island batteries also became interested in the case. With two vacant officer positions in Battery G, they hoped one of their officers or sergeants would be promoted to fill the vacancies. Private William Barker of Battery A wrote, "Lieut G.L. Dwight left us this morning for Washington (perhaps Providence). He and Crawford Allen is fishing for the command of Battery G. Charles F. Mason of Battery H, I think will get it." Unfortunately, for the battery, it would not be one of these capable veteran officers.[31]

The fifth of January provided yet another change for Battery G. Another young man with the two bars of a captain set into a red field appeared in camp. His name was Horace Bloodgood, recently promoted to the command of Battery G from Battery B. Like Owen and Sears, he was from the Providence elite and a student at Brown when the war began. The captain was twenty-two years old and wore a large top hat around Providence. The men were formed into a line to meet the new commander. Captain Bloodgood addressed his battery with a short speech: "I have but little to say but you must do your duty. Men, I shall be a very easy captain, but if you don't obey we shall see what you will see." Lieutenant Allen then ordered the soldiers to give three cheers for the new officer; only a few men responded. Among Bloodgood's first orders was for one detachment to go on guard duty daily along the Rappahannock. This was new to the men, who were used to only policing the camp and taking care of the horses. Furthermore, Bloodgood upset the cannoneers by moving the sections around. The men retained the same horses and guns, but they changed positions in the battery line. In addition, Bloodgood was not pleased with the small huts and stable the men had built under Captain Owen's tenure, so he ordered them to be built again. All of this led to the men already feeling resentment for the new commander.[32]

Immediately upon taking command, Captain Bloodgood gave orders that were contrary to what the men in Battery G were used to experiencing in the army. Against army regulations, Bloodgood suspended the requirements which forced an officer to wake up every morning to attend to supervising the fatigue duties. Now a sergeant would be appointed as officer of the day, rather than the officers. He reiterated Owen's strict rules about maintaining a daily schedule, beginning at 5:30 each morning and ending with taps at 9:30 at night. In addition to these orders, the new commander issued another set of demanding orders. Under Owen, the men could wear whatever uniform they pleased; indeed, they often had to with the faulty supply systems. Now the soldiers were ordered to wear the regulation forage cap, dress jacket, and saber belt. Those who did not follow these directives would find punishment in the form of more duty being assigned. By ordering this, he added another burden to the men, as they had to carry two coats, while those who did not have a dress jacket had to draw it from the quartermaster.[33]

As Bloodgood arrived to take command of the battery, another soldier left. He was J. Russell Field, the former quartermaster sergeant who had disgraced himself by deserting his post during the Battle of Fair Oaks and was demoted to private a week later. Field was a merchant from Providence who had political connections through his business related affairs. Now those politicians used their influence to have the former sergeant transferred out of Battery G. Instead of assuming the same rank in another battery, Field was promoted to second lieutenant and given command of a section in Battery E. He would hold the rank for only two months, until he resigned on account of illness. When Field left, he also took former sergeant Charles H. Bogman with him; Bogman was another of the June 9, 1862, demotions. Bogman thrived in the battery; he would be wounded at Chancellorsville and survived until he was mustered out.[34]

On January 17, a review of the Second Corps was held by General Burnside. Many of the soldiers surrounding Battery G grudgingly went out to the review before the general who many in the Army of the Potomac felt had needlessly wasted so many lives at Fredericksburg. Indeed, Fredericksburg was a result of poor performances on the part of several key subordinates, rather than Burnside's fault. He was always seen poorly by the soldiers in the Army of the Potomac, despite having won a brilliant victory in early 1862 in North Carolina and contributing during the retreat of the Army of the Potomac from the Second Bull Run disaster. All that mattered to the cannoneers was that he was a Rhode Islander. The men looked and yearned for fresh leadership so they could take the field once more and end the Rebellion. Although defeated, the Union army was not broken; they simply needed a superb battlefield leader.

John Rhodes of the First Rhode Island Light Artillery said, "The open-eyed intelligence and quick insight into mechanical relations, which characterize the American Volunteer, and which make him, when properly led, the most formidable soldier of the world, render him also a very poor subject to fool with." In addition to leadership, something else was needed by these men who left home to defend their country: many soldiers had not been paid in over six months, contributing to the ever declining morale of the army. While they waited for the paymaster, the men in Battery G heard the rumors for another campaign and promptly began preparing their horses and equipment for another expedition. With pressure from Washington, Burnside decided to mount another major campaign on January 20, 1863.[35]

The Army of the Potomac would advance up the Rappahannock, and march around Lee's flank on the road to Richmond. The general issued orders for the army to commence the offensive on January 21. The rain began on the twentieth and continued for three days. Private James A. Barber described the weather the first day: "The day comes in with a cold rain storm wit the wind blowing a gale from the East. It was fearfully dark and the rain was falling in torrents." The Army of the Potomac did not advance very far, going only four miles on the first day. Battery G limbered up and marched out of Falmouth to the exact location on Stafford Heights where they had been the previous December. This placed them in position to repulse any Confederate counterattack as the enemy followed the Federals up the river. Each yard the cannons were pulled, they became hopelessly stuck in the mud. At 2:00 in the morning on the twenty-first, the orders were rescinded and Battery G joined in the main assault, marching towards the United States Ford on the Rapidan River. Horses and men became covered in the red mud of Virginia that was a foot deep, more in most places. A member of the Fourth Rhode Island described it: "Virginia mud had this peculiarity; that when wet it assumes a paste like consistency, and sticks to the feet like glue." It took fourteen hours to march five miles, at which point the battery simply had to stop. Even more than on the Peninsula, the drivers had to utilize their sharp spurs and whips as the cannoneers pushed the tons of iron and wood through the mire; it was worse than the march through the Chickahominy Swamp.[36]

A barrel of whiskey was produced to help the men carry on as they prepared to bed down for the night after deploying the guns to cover the ford. The tarps on the top of every limber were thrown over the pieces and caissons as the weary men crawled in for a few hours' rest. The soldiers tried to dry their clothes by the small fires but they could not, nor could many of them sleep. Rumors flew through the army of entire battalions being swallowed in the mixture. Instead of a proud force wearing blue uniforms, the Federal soldiers turned yellow in the mud. This was a standard New England Nor'easter that the artillerists felt with fury: all were miserable. Many thought it would never end. By the twenty-second, the situation in Battery G was desperate. Private Barber wrote, "The mud was the worst of any of our mooves since this army was first organized. The roads was filled with teams stuck in the mud and the troops was wallowing along in the darkness."

On January 23, a cold and even more demoralized Battery G stumbled into its old camp at Falmouth, as the campaign was finally over. James Barber remembered it as "the most disappointing and disgraceful movement that has ever taken place in this army." This was Burnside's second chance and he lost it. The general was a superb division and corps commander when acting under little or no authority from Washington. He was not part of the Washington political machine and could not work under the orders being given to him. Burnside resigned on January 26 and was given a command in the western theatre.[37]

Even in this winter of discontent, the State of Rhode Island remained concerned about her soldiers serving at the front. In December and again in January a delegation of doctors and concerned citizens was sent to visit the wounded and sick soldiers in the hospitals around Washington. In total, 408 Rhode Islanders were found. One of the delegations was led by Charlotte Dailey, a nurse from Providence. She discovered that the soldiers did not complain about the inadequate care they received; they simply wanted to see the Union preserved. Most of the artillerymen that she located had been injured by horses. In total, five men from Battery G were in the Washington area hospitals. Among them was the still wounded Private Peter Riley, who was hit at Antietam. Silas R. Ripley was also among the ill. He deserted from the hospital in January, but returned to Battery G in May.[38]

General Joseph Hooker was appointed as the next commander of the Army of the Potomac, the third in one year's time. A native of Massachusetts, he was a West Pointer and a Mexican War veteran who had led the early morning drive towards the Dunker Church at Antietam, in addition to having distinguished himself on the Peninsula. Almost overnight Hooker began to establish reforms to improve the morale of the soldiers under his command. The first was to have the entire army paid off. He ordered that soft bread and onions be issued rather than hardtack, while men who had shown bravery on the battlefield would be rewarded with a ten day furlough at their homes. Among those rewarded was George Gaskell, who hastened to Plainfield to be with his sick sister. Sanitation conditions in camp improved and the mail was received in camp faster. Although Hooker's reforms did have a positive effect, some petty crimes still occurred in Battery G. Corporal Edward Mann was convicted of drunkenness on duty and was sentenced to carry a twenty-five pound log around camp for a day; the corporal was very fortunate to save his stripes.[39]

The remainder of February and into March was spent performing picket duty along the Rappahannock. The men could look over and see the Confederates preparing earthworks as the two sides occasionally exchanged in conversation. A sad duty was performed on February 12 when the artillerists assisted several agents from Rhode Island in the retrieval of the remains of some Rhode Island soldiers killed at Fredericksburg. It was judged "one of the most disgraceful affairs that ever befell the Union Army" by Private Barber when he recalled the battle. Another disgrace for Battery G came when Private James McCardle deserted and was captured trying to leave camp. He was court martialed and confined to camp for a month, but he was not dismissed from the service.[40]

The desertion and discipline problems in Battery G climaxed on February 16, 1863, when Private Jesse Young was brought before a panel of eight Second Corps officers, including a lieutenant colonel, four captains, and three first lieutenants, all from infantry regiments. Indeed, the court also tried three other men in the same time period. Young had deserted in the face of the enemy on May 27, 1862, as Battery G marched towards Fair Oaks. He managed to supply himself with a pair of grey trousers and returned to Providence onboard a merchant ship. Young was apprehended in the city on November 7 and was returned to Virginia escorted by Sergeant Henry H. Bowler, who received a discharge and returned home with a twenty-five dollar bounty for apprehending the deserter. Young was confined to camp as the army waited for winter to come to begin the proceedings; he was employed in grooming horses. Finally, in mid–February the trial commenced. The charges were read to Private Young, who pleaded not guilty to deserting in the face of the enemy, and despite offers of representation, chose to represent himself.[41]

The prosecution, led by Captain Richard L. Thompson of New York, first called Lieutenant Otto L. Torslow, to whose section Young belonged. The lieutenant testified that the private was a shirker: "He always claims to be sick, is an old man, and not very active." Although desertion was a serious crime, Young's case was even viler; it was done in the presence of the enemy, on the eve of battle. Sergeant James Chase repeated Torslow's comments, while adding he had been guarding the prisoner since November, which duty often took him away from his pressing duties as a detachment commander. In interviewing both men, Thompson wanted to know if Private Young had been paid and went over the hill after receiving his money, but like all of the cannoneers, he had yet to see any money and went home with empty pockets.

Young then offered his only defense by calling Sergeant Gilbert Westcott, a friend. The sergeant testified that Young was a good soldier, and had, even while under arrest, volunteered for duty. During the Battle of Fredericksburg, he served in the critical Number Three position on Westcott's gun. The sergeant further offered that Young had done his duty since returning to Rhode Island. With his friend's testimony complete, the private told Lieutenant Colonel Francis Sawyer that he had rested and was ready to accept his fate.

The panel of eight officers retired to deliver the verdict. Young was guilty of deserting his post in the presence of the enemy and was sentenced "to be shot to death at such time and place the commanding general shall designate." Despite this harsh sentence, two thirds of the officers recommended clemency and forwarded the case to President Lincoln. Because desertion was not yet a serious factor in the armies, no one had yet to be executed for the crime. Death sentences for such offenses as desertion or sleeping on post were simply meant as a deterrent; the men knew they would not be shot. As Second Corps commander, Major General Darius Couch concurred with the panel and commuted the sentence, claiming that the judge advocate used improper methods and the trial was too hasty. Furthermore, Sergeant Westcott's testimony had saved the private, as Couch believed that he had performed his duty under fire at Fredericksburg and had made up his time. The soldier was released back to his battery without spending one day in prison. Private Young served honorably until he was mustered out in December of 1864.[42]

On March 3, two steamers arrived from Rhode Island carrying supplies for the relief of the soldiers. Two days later brought another of the army reviews. Because they were assigned to the reserve of the Second Corps, Battery G was always the last unit to parade. General Hooker saw the event and was pleased at the conduct of the Rhode Island artillery. The sixth brought two citizens from Westerly who delivered even more supplies to the men from their town. They spent the night in camp, departing in the morning. After spending the evening in a small, cramped hut the men could rightfully say that they had experienced a little of the life the Westerly boys had been encountering for over a year. A week later was St. Patrick's Day, which was celebrated by the many Irish in Battery G, with their fellow countrymen in the Irish Brigade, with horse racing and the usual drunken revelry. The non–Irish in the battery celebrated as well by playing horseshoes and the new game of baseball.[43]

Battery G had been weakened to the point that they now needed infantrymen to come to the unit to help man the guns. Volunteers were asked for from the Second Corps and eight men were assigned to the battery. This contingent was followed two weeks later by an additional eight men. Twelve of them came from the Twelfth New Jersey Volunteers.

They were integrated into the different detachments as needed. Nearly all of the detached men were assigned as drivers, thus allowing the trained artillerists to work the guns.

Hooker's most important morale booster came on March 21, when he issued orders designating a badge for each corps in the Army of the Potomac in order to set it apart from the other corps. The idea originated as a means to distinguish men who had straggled and make them easier to return to their units, but soon took on a more symbolic meaning as the men sewed the different shaped badges to their hats or jackets. The three divisions in each corps all had a separate color. The colors were red, white, and blue for the first, second, and third divisions respectively. Each design was different; the First had a circle, while the Eleventh wore a crescent. The Second Corps proudly displayed a trefoil. These simple woolen items were cherished by the men as service to the corps they belonged to.[44]

An ugly April Fool's Day joke was played when the Second Corps batteries received notice to instantly harness up and prepare for action as the Confederates were nearby. General Oliver O. Howard was only testing the readiness of the men under his command. The weather was starting to grow warmer, while the rain and mud, which had plagued the army at Falmouth, was subsiding. Battery G was very fortunate this winter. Many of the other Rhode Island regiments encamped there lost heavily due to disease. Battery G lost only three men in December and Private Tabor, who died in January. Compared to what had occurred to Battery G on the Peninsula, the winter of 1863 was comparatively healthy.

As the warm weather began again and the disease and privation started to subside, the men knew something was coming. Drills began daily again as the men practiced the sharp movements which the light artillery was known for. In March, Sergeant James E. Chase had received a commission to replace Lieutenant Rhodes and was finally mustered into the service. Coming up from the ranks, he quickly became adept at leading his section in the drills and represented, along with Lieutenant Kelley, a change in the Rhode Island Light Artillery. Governor Sprague had been placed in the United States Senate, and James Y. Smith took over his position. No longer was the governor looking for political favor when he commissioned officers. Enlisted men who proved themselves in the field received the commissions rather than political appointees from Providence.[45]

Although constant drilling did occur, some off duty distractions were always present. On April 4, John G. Rathbun of Westerly received a fiddle from home and entertained the battery "with merry glee." On April 8, Sergeant Thomas F. Mars, who had won his stripes for heroism at Antietam, was reduced back to musician for "gross neglect of his duties." His friend George Gaskell claimed that it was "unjustified." Despite losing his rank, Mars maintained his dignity. Instead of deserting, he returned to playing his bugle. Many of the Battery G soldiers did not follow Bugler Mars' example. As April began to wind down, the last batch of furloughs was given out. Lieutenant Kelley was among the fortunate ones; he had not been home since 1861.[46]

Captain Bloodgood's tenure in command of Battery G had been disastrous. He was constantly ill and failed to complete the necessary paperwork to the Rhode Island adjutant general's office. Indeed, Bloodgood had been ill since joining the service in August of 1861; a surgeon told him he should resign and go home after being in the field for a week. His promotion to the battery was due solely to a political move; Bloodgood was not an effective officer and did nothing to lead or inspire his men at the time they needed it the most. Plagued with rheumatism and dysentery, he tendered his resignation on April 20, 1863, and returned home to continue a career as a merchant. Lieutenant Crawford Allen took command of the battery for the second time in four months, and the men again waited for another leader.[47]

Battery G experienced a major change at Falmouth. It lost several officers for better or worse. The men survived the privation at the camp, as they had done on the Peninsula with vigor. A new commander for the Army of the Potomac brought new ideas to boost the soldiers' morale and also conceived another plan of attack, while the president issued a new war aim. In late April, the vast Federal force readied itself to move once more and Battery G, First Rhode Island Light Artillery, prepared to gallop into artillery hell.

8

The Death Warrant

I worked on the pieces the rest of the day but never had death stare me in the face so as it did. 4 men was shot down on the piece i was on i expected my turn to come next.
—Musician William H. Lewis, May 21, 1863

A brutal winter and ineffective leadership had dulled the razor sharp edge Battery G had forged in the 1862 campaigns. Now, still encamped at Falmouth, Virginia, the battered but still brave Rhode Islanders continued with a soldier's long held tradition: waiting. As Captain Bloodgood left for Providence, orders again came from army headquarters, filtering down from the Second Corps to Artillery Brigade headquarters. After spending four months reequipping and reorganizing the Army of the Potomac, Joseph Hooker had assembled the largest army ever to take the field on the American continent. His plan was simple, yet complex. Hooker would take the bulk of the army and march to the United States Ford where it would advance across the Rapidan on the defensive to allow Lee to attack them. In this manner the Army of the Potomac would not have to undergo the same blood-letting it had seen at Fredericksburg in December. A smaller force—commanded by John Sedgwick, now recovered from his Antietam wounds and commanding the Sixth Corps—would remain at Fredericksburg along with the Second Division of the Second Corps. They would assault Marye's Heights and then march to Hooker as the combined force united to deliver the final blow to the Confederacy. The Army of the Potomac left the Falmouth Camp on April 26, 1863, to begin yet another campaign to take Richmond.[1]

The prospect of being engaged in a battle raised the spirits of many in Battery G. After surviving the drudgery of camp life at Falmouth, they now prepared to take part in the engagement. On the twenty-eighth, orders came for Battery G to support the crossing of the Rappahannock north of Falmouth. Battery B was originally assigned to the duty, but could not go because their Napoleons did not have the range of G's ordnance rifles. When orders came to the command, the battery was in no condition to move. Stillman Budlong of Battery B recorded the following: "The officers of Battery G got drunk and the Gen would not let them go." Battery A was sent in their place. New battery horses had been issued in late April and were still in the process of being broken in. Among those who received a new mount was William H. Lewis, one of the two musicians in the command. He wrote, "I am riding all the time i have got one of the pritty horses there is in the Battery he is white as snow." Lewis also armed himself with a brace of pistols and a new sword, while viewing his mother's image daily. The bugler recorded, "I am a savage looking chap." Although he had lost his rank for cowardice on the Peninsula, Lewis was sure to more than make up for it in the contest ahead.[2]

After marching up the Rappahannock, the Army of the Potomac arrived and dug in around a large house in a place called Chancellorsville, some ten miles west of Fredericksburg. Hooker received reports that Lee had left the city and was rapidly approaching the Union forces. Now Hooker knew that he had lost the advantage, as he was unable to maneuver in the dense undergrowth of a forest known as the Wilderness west of Chancellorsville. The terrain was covered with interspersed woods with occasional large meadows. This made things very difficult for infantry, but it was even more difficult for artillery to move. Hooker's army continued to entrench and watch for the Rebels.

With the Federal initiative lost, Robert E. Lee was ready to risk the largest gamble of his military career. Prior to the start of the campaign, nearly a third of the Army of Northern Virginia had been sent to Suffolk, Virginia, to block a Union force advancing up the Peninsula. Now Lee further divided his forces, into three parts. Jubal Early would block Sedgwick at Fredericksburg while Lee took two divisions to monitor Hooker's front. Thomas "Stonewall" Jackson would command the bulk of the army as they conducted a twelve-mile march to the west before striking the flank of the Army of the Potomac. Oliver O. Howard, a former Second Corps division commander, now led the Eleventh Corps, which was on the extreme left of Hooker's line. Against orders Howard failed to entrench, thinking no Confederates would dare to attack him near the Wilderness: he was wrong. Lee planned for an attack on May 2, 1863.[3]

Almost as planned, the Confederate forces conducted the flank march magnificently and rolled up Howard's flank, sending it reeling in retreat towards Chancellorsville. Lee also directed the attack against the Federal center with his smaller force. Hooker tried to get word to Sedgwick to cross the river and attack, but the telegraph lines were cut. Lee's daring plan worked brilliantly. The Union forces retreated under the constant Confederate attacks. At Hazel Grove, near Chancellorsville, Lieutenant John Knight Bucklyn of Battery E stayed by his section in the midst of the onslaught. The Rhode Islanders fired every round in the chests and remained in position until the Confederates were within twenty-

A veteran officer, Captain George W. Adams came to Battery G at a critical moment and led it through the rest of the war.

five yards of the position before they pulled one gun out by prolong; one was sacrificed to the enemy because there were no more horses. Lieutenant Bucklyn's actions earned him the Medal of Honor.

A cannon shot screeched into the front porch of Chancellor house, incapacitating General Hooker. The Confederates kept on advancing as the Federals tried to hold the line. Valor ran high on both sides; as midnight approached, Third Corps commander Daniel Sickles ordered a bayonet charge in the darkness. By this time, the Confederate assault had begun to lose momentum; the Rebels conducted the twelve-mile march and went right into the fight. Now Jackson rode ahead of his troops, searching for a location to pierce the Federal line. Instead, his own men believed his party to be Union cavalry and fired a volley. Stonewall Jackson was hit and died a week later of pneumonia; the Confederacy lost one its greatest commanders and gave the Federals an advantage on the battlefield.[4]

Waiting had become the one thing Battery G was exposed to throughout its service. Now they waited again to go into action. The days before the battle had been very unpleasant as another rainstorm struck the camp. "It seems heaven was against us," recorded George Gaskell. The storm cleared on April 30 as Battery G moved back to the lunettes they had built the previous winter. Gaskell borrowed a pair of field glasses from an officer and looked across the river to see the Confederates again preparing their entrenchments. An Alabama artillery officer deserted and swam across the river to the Federal lines, claiming he was tired of starving for the Confederacy. The men knew that unlike previous engagements they would be engaged significantly in this battle. Although defeated in the 1862 campaigns, the cannoneers had not lost their esprit de corps. Private Gaskell wrote, "But now while waiting for the battle to commence unknowing its termination I must say that I am with all spirit bound to the utmost to prosecute the war and fight it out to the last. May God be with us." As the artillerists patiently waited to be joined in battle, another article they were waiting for arrived in camp.[5]

As the Union forces were fighting at Chancellorsville, a third man wearing the rank of a captain appeared in camp on May 2. Unlike his other two predecessors, this officer was twenty-nine and was a tried and true combat veteran. His name was George William Adams. Like Bloodgood, he had been promoted from a lieutenancy in Battery B, but unlike the prior captain, he had excelled on the battlefield. Captain Adams was born into a wealthy merchant family in 1834; several of his ancestors had fought in the Revolution, and his grandfather had been a congressman from Massachusetts. Adams was educated in the schools of Providence before entering Brown in 1851. At the University, like many students he took a profound interest in

Lieutenant T. Fred Brown of Battery B beat Captain Adams' men, but then his cannoneers watched in horror as Battery G was destroyed (courtesy Kris VanDenBossche).

military matters and enlisted as a private in the Providence Marine Corps of Artillery. It was here that he learned the art of gunnery that would make him such a deadly factor on the battlefield. He dropped out of Brown in 1854 and opened a mercantile business in Providence. He was married in 1860, but his wife died only a few months later. Adams went to England to pursue further business, but was in Baltimore on April 19, 1861, when the Sixth Massachusetts was fired upon in the streets. He quickly returned home to Rhode Island seeking a commission. He was rebuffed so he traveled to New York and tried to join the navy; again he was turned back. Finally, an opportunity came in June when Adams enlisted in Tompkins' First Battery as a private. Promotion to first lieutenant came on August 13 as he was given command of a section in Battery B.[6]

The lieutenant led with distinction at Ball's Bluff, on the Peninsula, and at Fredericksburg. At the latter battle, it was Adams who took his section close to Telegraph Road to engage the enemy. With these qualifications, Adams was advanced to the captaincy of Battery G. Like most officers of his time, however, he was very fond of drinking and gambling when off duty. On the Peninsula, this became a bit of a problem, as Adams and Bloodgood frequently played cards and drank whiskey rather than attending to their men. Corporal David B. Patterson of Battery B claimed, "George Adams is not the man he was 6 months ago." In addition, on the Peninsula Adams had developed a reputation of being a strict disciplinarian; when the popular first sergeant of Battery B failed to carry out his duties, the lieutenant saw that he was reduced to the ranks. He also targeted those of higher rank. When Captain Thomas Vaughn of Battery B kept a prostitute in his tent by calling her his sister, Adams and Bloodgood saw it as a breach of army regulations. They wrote to Governor Sprague, who forced Vaughn to resign his commission. Despite this, Captain Adams remained a popular officer and took command of his new battery at the most critical moment in their history.[7]

The Second Division was assigned to support, but not take part in, the actual assault upon Marye's Heights unless called for. Most of the Sixth Corps Artillery would fight further down the slopes of Marye's Heights near Prospect Hill, while the two Rhode Island batteries would be out in the open to engage the enemy near the stone wall. Like Battery G, the Second Division was going into action for the first time under veteran officers new to positions of higher command. Brigadier General John Gibbon came to command the division after leading the famed Iron Brigade in the summer of 1862. In addition, several new regiments and commanders would be bloodied for the first time. Furthermore, in February Colonel Charles Tompkins had been relieved

Bugler Thomas F. Mars helped to rally the line at Antietam and was killed at Marye's Heights.

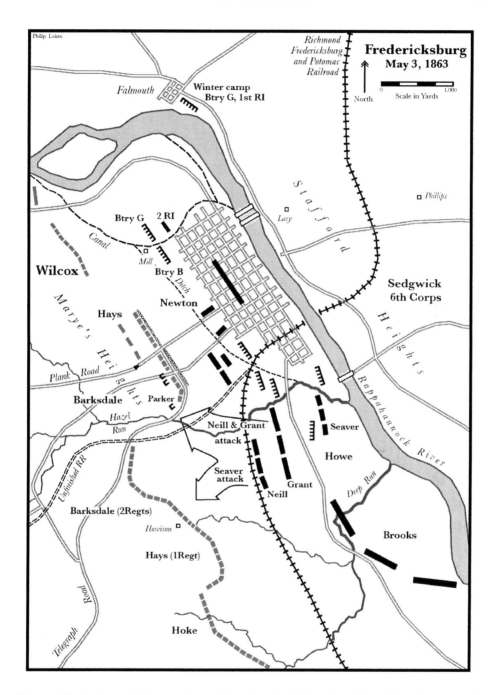

of duty with the Second Corps and transferred to the Sixth when Sedgwick took command; the general wanted a superb artillerist he could trust.[8]

The cannoneers spent the night of May 2 busily working in the limber chests. Corporals ensured that all of the rounds and friction primers were in their proper places, while the men ate a small meal. The drivers again hooked up the horses, keeping them in harness all night in the event that sudden orders to move were received. The men finally loaded their personal equipment on the limbers and lay down for a short rest. For Battery G, the scene was very reminiscent of the night before the Battle of Antietam.[9]

Finally, at midnight on May 3, the telegraph lines were restored and Hooker ordered Sedgwick to assault Marye's Heights. The Union forces had to break through the defenses at the Telegraph Road to link up with the beleaguered forces frantically digging in around Chancellorsville. Unlike in December, the Second and Sixth corps had a chance at breaching the wall. Only two Mississippi regiments were in the road proper, while two batteries of the Washington Artillery and a section of Parker's Virginia Battery were on the crest of Marye's Heights. It would be the third time in the war that Battery G would face these distinguished cannoneers in gray. Five months earlier these same guns had been responsible for killing or injuring nearly 400 Rhode Islanders.[10]

At thirty minutes past midnight, musicians Thomas F. Mars and William Lewis began blowing reveille as the drivers and cannoneers awoke and prepared to leave the camp for the front. The sounds startled many of the sleeping privates. "Our men were sleeping peacibly all knight with knothing disturbing the quiet of the camp until the shrill bugles voice aroused us from sleep," recorded Private James Barber. By 1:30 in the morning, Battery G, in tandem with Battery B, left the defenses on Stafford Heights and prepared to deploy down on the banks of the Rappahannock. The engineers again built the pontoon bridges across the river; this time they received only one volley from Barksdale's Mississippians as they hastily evacuated the city and retreated back to Marye's Heights. In his first act as captain, Adams ordered two shells lobbed into the city to insure that there were no Rebels

present. The bridges were quickly laid down. After the Second Corps infantry was across, Battery G led the column. A staff officer from General Gibbon directed Captain Adams to cross immediately with his command to support the infantry. As they left Battery B, the men cheered and yelled "good-bye." The men in G were pleased that they were going into action first; this would be only their second real engagement and they were given the honor of starting it.[11]

There were two roads that Battery G could have taken to get to the bridge, one very short and steep; the other was rather long and less dangerous. Adams chose the second one for his command. As the battery made it down to the pontoon bridge, Lieutenant T. Fred Brown of Battery B promptly saluted Captain Adams, repeating the compliment of "good-bye" as Battery B crossed first. It was then Battery G's turn. The cannons and caissons crossed the pontoon bridge single file; almost immediately, they attracted the attention of the Con-

Originally a member of the First Rhode Island Infantry, Benjamin E. Kelley joined Battery G, was promoted from the ranks, and died in his first battle as an officer.

federate guns on Marye's Heights. Battery B was already engaging the enemy with their Napoleons, but General Gibbon ordered Lieutenant Brown to bring his command to the left and closer to Marye's Heights.[12]

General Sedgwick had personally given the orders for the two Rhode Island batteries under his command to go into battery in an advanced and hazardous position close to the enemy's lines. They were going to provide vital covering fire as the Sixth Corps formed up for the assault on Marye's Heights. The two units would serve as a distraction to draw the Confederate fire from the hill. Sedgwick knew the mettle of Colonel Tompkins and the men under his command. They would not let him down. Unfortunately for the Rhode Islanders of Battery G, General Sedgwick had just signed their death warrants.

It was now ten o'clock on the morning of May 3, 1863. As Captain Adams deployed Battery G, they were only 300 yards from their position during the first battle. At the same time, five hundred miles away in Rhode Island, many people were going to Sunday worship in the numerous small white-washed clapboard churches representing the many Baptist faiths in western and southern Rhode Island, while in Providence the upper class went to their Episcopal services and the Irish went to the masses at the newly established Providence Catholic Diocese. Little could these wives, mothers, and daughters know that their husbands, brothers, and sons in Battery G were about to experience hell on earth.

Before Battery G could move into a field, they had to cross another small bridge over a canal. A shell landed directly in the middle of one of the caissons as it was midway across the bridge; with a thunderous roar, the caisson exploded and was sent to the bottom of the canal. None of the drivers were injured as they hurried to clear the bridge for the rest of the battery. Finally, Battery G took up position to the right of Battery B. Captain Adams' Rhode Islanders galloped into position a scant 600 yards from the enemy, well within range of the command's six three-inch ordnance rifles, but too close to the enemy's guns. The Second Rhode Island Infantry moved up to support both batteries.[13]

The battery was not even unlimbered and they were receiving a severe pounding from the artillery on Marye's Heights. The two ten pounder Parrotts of Parker's Virginia Battery on the far left of the heights had a perfect position to enfilade and shell the Rhode Island line as their commander called for case shot. James Barber remembered, "The enemy seeing our mooves opened a heavy fire on us." The first round exploded in the midst of the horses on the Westerly gun as the drivers positioned the cannon. Privates Charles H. Lawrence, William F. Mulligan, and John K. Johnson were instantly killed, along with the six horses. The Westerly cannoneers had no time to mourn as they detached the limber and cannon and moved it by hand to the front. In the rest of the battery, the cannons were finally unlimbered and began to engage the enemy.

The three section commanders identified the targets as the Virginia guns on the left side of the ridge, as they were the ones firing down on Battery G and had a clear field of fire into the infantry as well. On top of the heights, the Confederate cannoneers were protected by the same lunettes the Rhode Islanders had built across the river. Unlike their foe, Battery G was out in the open. Private Gaskell recalled the horrors of the opening engagement: "There was the most hellish fire upon us possible. We had not so much as a bush to cover us." The Second Rhode Island lay down in the rear of Battery G and could do nothing to stop the carnage being inflicted on their brothers; the cannoneers had to stand and load the guns in the midst of the storm of iron. Lieutenant Elisha Rhodes remembered: "The Rebels had a plunging fire from the hills." Another shell struck near the right section, decapitating Lieutenant Torslow's horse and slightly injuring the Swede; almost at the same instant, another fragment hit Lieutenant Allen in the wrist. The horrible effects of case shot were now being seen as large fragments and small musket balls rained down over the Rhode Islanders' position. There was no place to run. Another fragment tore a gash into the face of Westerly's Private Samuel C. Mitchell.[14]

Rhode Islanders were being shot down all around as the cannoneers of Battery G continued to load and fire the guns in the struggle. Bugler Lewis was mounted on his snow-white horse when it was shot down; one of the projectiles also carried away a piece of his boot. Although dismounted, Lewis never lost his mettle. He recorded, "I worked on the pieces the rest of the day but never had death stare me in the face so as it did. 4 men was shot down on the piece i was on i expected my turn to come next." Lewis' position as bugler was taken over by musician Thomas F. Mars, who went down with a mortal wound to the side while playing his commands next to the captain. Remarkably, Adams survived the ordeal unscathed. The men in the First Detachment from Westerly were receiving the brunt of the Confederate fire, as their gun was closest to the enemy. Private Johnson had already been killed; now more men from the small southwestern Rhode Island community went down.

Privates George, Ira, and Nathaniel Austin were all brothers from Westerly who had each joined Battery G at a different date. Now they stood together working the number one gun cannon. A piece of case exploded overhead, hitting George Austin. The thirty-three-year-old soldier hit the ground with a minie ball wedge in his leg, while a piece of the case had ripped across his face, causing instant blindness in the right eye. The same shot hit the other two Austin brothers as well. The wounds of George and Nathaniel, the youngest brother, were too severe and they were discharged a month after the battle, while

Battery G was responsible for inflicting this damage to Parker's Virginia Battery during the Battle of Marye's Heights (Library of Congress).

Ira Austin survived until he was mustered out. Private Barber became the next Westerly soldier to go down. He wrote of the battle: "The Rebel Guns were belching forth their Thunder firing their death dealing missels into our Battery killing or wounding some of the men with nearly every shot."[15]

The men in gray continued to pound the Rhode Islanders as Private Daniel Hoxsie of Richmond went down with the first wound he would receive in the war. The officers of Battery G looked through their field glasses and viewed the rounds as they landed atop Marye's Heights; the three section commanders believed it was having no effect. The situation was much different. In an artillery duel between Captain George Adams' Rhode Islanders and Lieutenant Thompson Brown's Virginians, the men in gray were gaining the upper hand, but the cannoneers in blue were putting up a fight as well. Brown had initially received orders to ignore the Federal artillery and save his limited ammunition for the infantry attack sure to come; the Rhode Islanders in the open proved too tempting a target.

Because of the terrain, the two Parrotts had an advantage over the six ordnance rifles of Battery G, but the Rhode Islanders had better ammunition and tactics, concentrating their fire on one lunette at a time. Captain Adams thrived in combat and was more than showing it as he continued to lead and inspire his men in the struggle. The gunners accurately sighted the pieces and one round landed in one of Brown's lunettes; the gun was dismounted, but was quickly back in action. A member of Parker's Battery described the fire from the Rhode Island artillerists as "a tempest of cannon shot." While Battery G was not having any luck hitting the visible targets on the front of Marye's Heights, the results were far different on the opposite side of the slope. Despite being wounded, James Barber stayed on the field and watched as "our guns answered them with deadly effect plunging nearly every shot into the heart of the Rebel works." The area thundered with constant explosions as the rounds over flew the top of the ridge and landed amidst the parked limbers and horses. Five Virginians were wounded, two limbers destroyed, and a dozen horses were killed. Despite this destruction, Lieutenant Thompson Brown was having his revenge on Battery G.[16]

The soldiers of Rhode Island's Battery G had been trained well. They could easily have abandoned the guns and run for cover, but they did not. They chose to stay and fight on against overwhelming odds. The officers and sergeants continued to bark commands as the drivers sat erect in their saddles, waiting to move if called for. The cannoneers continued to perform their ballet of loading the bloodstained, red hot, smoking cannons. As soon as one comrade was shot down, another instantly stepped in to replace him. There was no time to drag the wounded or dead to the rear, the rifles had to be served as fast as possible. The clouds of white smoke, the noise and the terrible smell of burnt gunpowder were enough to drive one to insanity, as it caused deafness and blindness among the men. On the limbers, the Number Six Men cut their fuzes well, hoping they would hit their targets. The debris of battle littered the ground as shell fragments, shredded canteens, haversacks, gun carriages, and horses were ripped apart. It truly was an image from hell that few of the men could ever have imagined; now they were in the center of it.

Throughout the ranks of the battery, men and horses were being shot down at a continuous rate. Private Joseph W. Sunderland of South Kingstown was hit in the head by a piece of case. He was evacuated to a hospital in Washington where he lingered for eleven months; he was never discharged and sent home. Finally, in April of 1864, Sunderland succumbed to the wounds suffered this day. Another soldier to meet a later demise was Private Patrick Brennan, an Irishman from North Providence. He was wounded in the leg and survived long enough to receive a discharge and return home. However, he as well would die of his wounds the following April. Although wounded, Lieutenant Allen remained by Captain Adams' side, helping him to give words of encouragement to the men and personally sighting the cannons, taking the task over for some disabled noncommissioned officers. At the same time, a small band of men from Westerly continuous to cluster around their number one gun, which was already glowing red from continued firing. A shell exploded near the trail, severely wounding Corporal Alexander Sisson, as his twin brother, Charles, a cannoneer, watched.[17]

The Second Rhode Island had been positioned in front of Batteries B and G, as they supported them in the event of an infantry assault. The men lay prone on the ground, occasionally looking to the rear at the destruction being wrought on their friends and neighbors. Much as the men of Battery G had been helpless to those assaulting Marye's Heights in December of 1862, now there was nothing the soldiers of the Second could do for Battery G. Among those watching was Sergeant Patrick Lyons of South Kingstown. He saw the destruction being wrought on his fellow soldiers from Washington County:

> Our position was entirely exposed and subject to an enfilading fire from several of the enemy's batteries, which were strongly fortified on Marye's Heights, and consequently the batteries at least suffered, especially the 8th on our right which lost 22 men and so many horses that they had to haul off their guns by hand. The captain of the crippled battery was fairly beside himself with rage & did some good execution.

All watched as the man with a rough beard and two bars on his shoulders worked his battery for all it was worth in the face of a determined foe. Captain Adams' leadership was awe inspiring to all who observed it.[18]

Lieutenant Benjamin E. Kelley was in his position in the center of the battery, directing the fire of his section for the first time. In an instant, a shell ended the officer's short battlefield career. The missile exploded, killing Kelley's horse and inflicting a horrible wound to Kelley's thigh. He was quickly recovered by the men and taken to the rear under a fusillade of enemy fire. Lieutenant James Chase rode to the fallen lieutenant's position and continued to direct the fire of the center section.[19]

For thirty-five minutes Battery G remained in the open field, losing men and horses at an almost equal rate. The experience of combat at Antietam was nothing compared to what these men were facing now. Throughout the engagement the gunners had to be very cautious of their elevation and the time in flight for the shells being sent into Marye's Heights; this was because of the thousands of Sixth Corps infantry that lay down in front of the battery, waiting to make the charge. As the shells continued to burst, another disgraceful event occurred in the battery. "The men behaved very well only some 3 or 4 of them run off the field and secreted themselves behind the banks of the river until the fighting was over," recollected Private Barber.[20]

As Battery G withdrew from the field, the cannoneers in gray on top of Marye's Heights began cheering. They were pleased to have driven back a battery, but they braced for the infantry assault that was sure to come. Battery G's nemesis, Lieutenant Thompson Brown, recalled the engagement and wrote, "I opened upon a battery in their rear. A spirited duel took pace lasting to the period of thirty minutes, when the enemy withdrew badly crippled." Although Brown had inflicted the damage on the Rhode Islanders, their loss was about to be avenged even greater on the Virginians.[21]

Despite taking many casualties, Battery G was having a good effect as a morale booster to the infantry. Private Wilbur Fisk of the Second Vermont was among those waiting to go forward. He remembered: "Our batteries played over our heads and helped us all they could. The air seemed to be full of hissing shot and bursting shell. The roar was terrific and it required men of nerve to stand it." Captain Adams' Rhode Islanders had stood it for over a half hour. It now became very apparent to the captain that his battery was losing its momentum. With a large portion of the command already down, he galloped to General John Gibbon to ask permission to change positions. Finally, the general relented and Battery G left the hell they had just fought through. With so many horses dead or injured, the cannoneers attached the prolong ropes to the trails of the cannon and dragged them to a position to properly support Sedgwick's assault on Marye's Heights. Here Battery G again came into position, changing it twice to support the infantry charge; they fired an additional sixty-five rounds without suffering any loss.[22]

While they had been waiting to go in, many soldiers had a gut-wrenching feeling that they were going to experience the same events that had befallen the Federals five months earlier; the Sixth Corps had been spared the bloodletting on Marye's Heights. As the Thirty-Seventh Massachusetts was preparing to go forward, they saw Battery G retire. James L. Bowen remembered, "The Union batteries have been playing with dreadful energy upon the Confederate entrenchments, but the Washington Artillery on the heights holds on defiantly." Lieutenant Charles Brewster of the Tenth Massachusetts added, "Amid the roar of Artillery our Battery poured their fire at the force on top and rifle pits and stone walls on the sides of the roads. Never was a calm waked up so fearfully on a quiet Sabboth morn before. The boys never faltered or wavered a particle." Many of the soldiers saw the Confederate artillery slacken their fire as Battery G withdrew and believed the Rhode Islanders had accomplished their mission in silencing the guns. In reality, the Mississippians, Louisianans and Virginians were holding their fire for the infantry attack sure to come.[23]

Formed into a compact body four ranks deep, the Third Division began their advance at the same time Battery G was being withdrawn. Immediately the Confederate artillery and the Mississippians in the road began to target the Federals. It was nearly the same result as in December; hundreds of Union soldiers went down in the barrage, but still they kept advancing. The Seventh Massachusetts led the assault from the left of the field, the same place where three Rhode Island regiments had charged during the first battle. Forty yards from Telegraph Road the Confederates fired a devastating volley, which struck down many of the Bay Staters; still they kept on going. The officers cried out, "Forward men, we shan't get this close again." Finally, the Federals surged over Telegraph Road as the Mississippians retreated up the slopes of Marye's Heights.[24]

Within fifteen minutes, the Sixth Corps had advanced over the killing ground and secured the wall. The Sixth Maine charged up the Heights and captured the cannon from the Washington Artillery and Parker's Battery as the artillerists abandoned their pieces and ran for their lives. The Mainers captured nearly all of Brown's men and their two Parrotts, which had been responsible for the near destruction of Battery G. Lieutenant Brown claimed the Sixth Maine had captured "the best battery in the Confederacy." With Marye's Heights captured, General Sedgwick ordered Gibbon and the Second Division to return to Falmouth as the Sixth Corps turned west to link up with Hooker.[25]

The artificers had remained at Falmouth to care for the materiel left behind in the camp. Now they moved to the pontoon bridges to assist in the evacuation of the wounded. Welcome C. Tucker was waiting to cross the bridge when he saw two men from the battery carrying a stretcher back across the river. Lying in agony upon it was John D. Wells, a private from Westerly who was a caisson driver; he was Tucker's friend. Wells was hit in the face and hip by the shell fire and was coughing up blood at an exorbitant rate. The blood covered Wells' face to the extent that Tucker could not identify his friend except by the driver's whip he still grasped. Private Wells was sent to a hospital in Washington, but he would never serve in Battery G again. William Lewis was among those who cared for the wounded. He recalled the aftermath: "I saw many a poor wounded man beaing carried on stretchers with there bible + parents pictures lying on there breasts."[26]

Once Marye's Heights was taken and secured, Battery G and the rest of Gibbon's Second Division received orders to return to Stafford Heights in a reserve position. The dead and wounded were collected as the battery finally left the city. As he briefly returned to the field to carry out the duty, Private Gaskell heard a faint voice call out his name as he turned away; it was the mortally wounded bugler Mars. Gaskell promptly dismounted and attended to his friend. Mars was hit by pieces of shell in his thigh and chest. Gaskell and another private helped Mars to a barn serving as a field hospital. The bugler asked Gaskell to take his watch and to write his wife and father. Private Gaskell did as instructed and bade farewell to "my comrade and only true friend." Despite losing his sergeant's rank, Mars always remained cheery and ready to do his duty. Bugler Thomas F. Mars was sent to a hospital in Washington where he died of his wounds on May 9.[27]

Private George D. Austin of Westerly served with his two brothers; they were all wounded at Marye's Heights (courtesy Kris VanDenBossche).

The severely wounded Lieutenant Kelley was quickly brought back across the river to the Lacy House on Stafford Heights, where he was placed in a comfortable position. Dr. John Merrill of Westerly, familiar to many of the men from that small corner of Rhode Island and now the surgeon of the Second Corps Artillery Brigade, examined Kelley, along with Dr. J. Franklin Dyer of Massachusetts. The thigh wound was mortal. Kelley remained conscious and uttered no regrets about his fate. He calmly asked to be placed in a room alone, where he quietly prayed. Lieutenant Benjamin Eddy Kelley died twelve hours after receiving his wounds. At age twenty-two, he became the first officer to die in combat from the First Rhode Island Light Artillery Regiment. Musician Lewis called him "1 of the best leutanats." By the following morning, every officer of the five Rhode Island batteries on the field knew of the death of their brother. Lieutenant Kelley's remains were sent home, where he was buried with full military honors at Swan Point Cemetery in Providence. Rhode Island's secretary of state, John Russell Bartlett, eulogized the young officer: "His record is noble and brilliant, and the testimony of his comrades bears witness to his unshirking devotion to his duty at all times—to his bravery in every hour of danger." Kelley's mother had lost everything. Her husband and daughter had died shortly before the war, and now her only son was dead, killed while doing his duty.[28]

While the officers mourned the loss of Lieutenant Kelley, the enlisted men began to hear the rumors that Battery G had been destroyed in the shelling. It was so bad that Battery A was pulled off the line near Chancellorsville and marched back towards Fredericksburg to take their place in the Second Division, Second Corps, line. Battery A was no stranger to heavy fighting, having fought hard at Bull Run, Glendale, and Antietam. This time, however, the soldiers did not know how many of their brother artillerymen had been lost; but they knew the toll had been heavy. Private Thomas Aldrich of Battery A wrote, "Battery G was badly cut up."[29]

Second Lieutenant James E. Chase was one of several enlisted men who became commissioned officers in Battery G (courtesy Phil DiMaria, Battery B 1st Rhode Island Light Artillery Inc.).

The town of Westerly was particularly hard hit by the men serving in the First Detachment. The *Narragansett Weekly* reported the following: "The Westerly Boys in Battery G suffered their share in the battles near Fredericksburg." Nearly every member of the gun detachment was injured. Nine men were wounded, and Private John K. Johnson was killed in action. He was buried in Falmouth, but after the war was removed to a new National Cemetery on Marye's Heights. Half of those wounded were either discharged or transferred to the Veterans Reserve Corps. This new unit was composed of soldiers still able to bear arms and perform garrison duty who could no longer fight in the field. Those who had serious injuries were promptly sent to the surgeons; those slightly wounded remained in camp. First Sergeant Hoar performed his duties by recording the names of those killed or wounded and directing the injured to the hospitals. The aftermath of the battle was quite a shock to the Rhode Islanders, who had been under a heavy fire only once before, at Antietam. For many it was strange to no longer see familiar faces that only that morning had been alive and well, before the battery was plunged into combat.[30]

Lieutenant Kelley's loss was a severe one for Battery G, but the enlisted men lost more heavily. Until this point in the war, no Rhode Island battery had ever taken the amount of casualties Battery G did this day. Seven soldiers were dead or dying; among them were two detached from the infantry, while twenty more were wounded in some form. In total, twenty-seven Rhode Islanders were hit by the cannonading. Furthermore, twenty-five horses had died and many more were injured. As he was engaged in the battle, Bugler Lewis' estranged father visited the Falmouth camp, wearing a lieutenant's uniform. The senior Lewis made a fool of himself, as he was presented as a lieutenant but had never seen a day of service in his life. "I am sorrie to see he has taken up his old ways," said his son. The fake Lieutenant Lewis wrote of his son's bravery in the battle to the *Providence Journal,* reporting the losses in the engagement. This caused much confusion between the adjutant general and Captain Adams, as there was no lieutenant by the name of Lewis in Battery G. Bugler Lewis became upset that his father visited the camp, but he had more pressing duties to attend to in the battery.[31]

The enlisted men could gain a small solace in knowing that they had performed extremely well in the face of the terrible fire and had earned the praise of their commanders. Some men did develop contempt for General Sedgwick; they felt he needlessly sacrificed Battery G to divert attention from the infantry attacking the Heights. One private wrote that the battery was "worse than a wreck" after the engagement. Battery G was defeated, but not whipped. They had simply been rendered hors de combat by a well entrenched foe. In the aftermath of the artillery duel, Private Gaskell developed dark thoughts about the Union cause. In eighteen months of war, Battery G had never experienced a clear-cut, decisive Union victory. Gaskell wrote, "Let me say that I believe we cannot conquer the South."[32]

As the Sixth Corps cleared Fredericksburg and marched west along the Orange Turnpike, they were met by a fierce Confederate counterattack near Salem's Church. With his remaining three divisions, Lee directed his attention to defeating Sedgwick and stopping him from linking up with Hooker. The Second Rhode Island followed their corps and suffered heavy losses as they saved the Fifteenth New Jersey regiment from destruction in a set of woods near the church. After several hours of fierce attacks, Sedgwick was forced to vacate the field by evening and retreated in haste towards Bank's Ford on the Rappahannock. Here the Sixth Corps dug in, waiting for orders from Hooker. The Battle of Salem's Church, combined with the resumption of the attacks against the Army of the Potomac's main body at Chancellorsville, led May 3, 1863, to become the second bloodiest day of the Civil War. The Sixth Corps lines remained in place May 4 and 5. During both days, the Confederates launched constant attacks against the entrenched Federals. Only because of Colonel Tompkins' well-organized and well-placed gun line was the enemy kept at bay.[33]

The Confederates managed to cut the Sixth off from the rest of the Federal army and isolate it near the Rappahannock, but could not press the advantage by destroying the force. After returning to camp on May 3, Battery G was again ordered to the very familiar location on Stafford Heights to fire into Fredericksburg if needed. Finally, on May 5 they got their chance as Jubal Early's Rebels circled around Sedgwick's flank and recaptured Fredericksburg. The battery engaged the targets as they appeared in the town. A heavy thunderstorm fell as the men gave up after firing a few more shells into the city. On May 6 Joseph Hooker gave the orders for the Army of the Potomac to abandon the campaign. On the seventh, Battery G limbered up from its camp at Falmouth and traveled to the lower pontoon bridge site on the Rappahannock. Here Captain Adams received orders to arrange his guns to keep Early from advancing on Sedgwick as he retreated across Banks' Ford. The captain hid the caissons in a brush thicket so they would not be spotted. The mission was successful and the battery was not called into action. The Battle of Chancellorsville was over; it was another Federal defeat and a brilliant Confederate victory.[34]

After losing two commanders in four months, the new captain had to prove himself to the men: this he did. Corporal Edward Adams wrote of Captain Adams' performance on the battlefield: "Although coming to the Battery at an unfavorable time, Captain Adams showed himself to be equal to any emergency, by his skillful handling of the Battery, and his coolness during the trying ordeal through which the Battery passed on the 3d of May.

Capt. Adams led the Battery in the hottest of the fight, and by his bravery won not only the confidence, but high esteem of the men." Private Barber added, "The men like him very well for he is kind towards the men of this company."[35]

Captain Charles D. Owen was very similar to George B. McClellan; he created Battery G and trained the men how to be artillerists. Unlike McClellan however, he was not a field commander. His performances on the Peninsula, at Antietam, and at Fredericksburg were credible, but did not truly show what Battery G was capable of. In addition, Owen did nothing to inspire the men under his command. He did little to curb the intoxication that plagued the battery, and his actions on the Peninsula made enemies of many of his men. Horace Bloodgood's four months as captain were a disaster; he accomplished nothing to improve the men's sinking morale after Fredericksburg and the Mud March. In his first battle, Captain Adams proved he was the opposite of the two former captains; he was a combat leader. The captain had arrived only hours before the second major battle in Battery G's history and had acquitted himself quite well on the field. The battery lost severely in the contest, but never faltered in carrying out its assignment. Under the command of Captain George Adams Battery G would fight the rest of the war.

In addition to acquitting himself on the battlefield, Captain Adams was prompt to write to General Mauran in Providence; indeed, the adjutant general had not heard any news of Battery G's actions since December, when Captain Owen last wrote. Adams forwarded a list of the men he lost in the battle. Furthermore, he had to report to the commander of the Twelfth New Jersey the fate of three men from that regiment in Battery G who were killed or wounded at Marye's Heights. Of the sixteen detached infantry serving in the battery, two were killed in action and two others were wounded. Although Lieutenant Kelley had just died and his body was still in the process of being returned to Rhode Island, Adams knew that another subaltern was needed immediately.

Despite being in command of the battery for two only days, the captain knew the man for the task: First Sergeant Allen Hoar. Like Kelley, Hoar had entered the service as a private, albeit in Battery G, and rose rapidly to sergeant. Captain Adams wrote, "I would respectfully recommend for promotion Sergt Hoar of this Battery who behaved with great coolness and bravery, and should like to have him assigned to this battery." The captain's request was accepted and Hoar became the third lieutenant to be promoted from the ranks into his old battery. This system had a positive impact on the men, as they could clearly see the results of good behavior versus having an unsoldierly bearing and being intoxicated while on duty. Even if a man could not receive a promotion the good behavior was rewarded by being relieved of some of the less pleasant duties or being given additional rations. While Hoar gained a pair of shoulder straps, Sergeant Nathaniel Chace, one of the Westerly Boys, gained a diamond and became the new first sergeant. The promotions echoed down the line as Alexander B. Sisson and Daniel Hoxsie, both wounded in battle, were promoted to sergeant and corporal, respectively, of the First Detachment. The men from Westerly did not look on disdain at Hoxsie being promoted to their gun as he was a neighbor from Richmond.[36]

The Army of the Potomac returned to their old camps near Falmouth, where they again became a defeated force under timid Union leadership. General camp duties again became routine for the artillery. Captain Adams began to reorganize the battery after their ordeal at Marye's Heights. He had to know the whereabouts of the wounded, while additional horses were received and reports had to be forwarded to Washington and Providence chronicling the losses in men and materiel. Furthermore, a new gun carriage and caisson were needed to replace those destroyed at Marye's Heights. He also rearranged some of the noncommissioned officers and also placed a large amount of responsibility on George L. Gaskell who was ordered to take charge of all cooking for the battery.

Although there was always a steady stream of men leaving and returning to the battery, some returned after extended absences. Privates Nathan Champlin and Silas R. Ripley both deserted in January and now returned to the unit in May, after the battle. Private Champlin had good reason to return; his brother Samuel had been wounded in the battle. Another loss for the battery was that of Lieutenant Allen, who was promoted to adjutant of the First Rhode Island Light Artillery Regiment and reported to Colonel Tompkins at Sixth Corps Artillery Brigade Headquarters for duty. He was replaced by Lieutenant Otto Torslow as second in command of the battery; if anything happened to Captain Adams, the Swedish immigrant stood at the verge of commanding a battery.[37]

With the losses in action and by disease, and the attachment of men to other duties, Captain Adams had present only three officers and seventy-one enlisted men fit for duty. By the end of May, eleven men remained in the hospital recovering from wounds, while twenty were sick from disease and other causes. Furthermore, with the losses in horses, only 102 of them were present in the command. Although these casualties did present some problem, Captain Adams promptly reorganized the command by drilling frequently in the school of the detachment, section, and piece. The wooden carriages were washed, and the leather was oiled, ensuring all was in order for the next campaign.[38]

During Hooker's army wide reforms, General Henry Hunt had pleaded with him to realign the organization of the Army of the Potomac's light artillery. Hooker refused and many saw his failure at Chancellorsville as a result of not having a stratified artillery command structure. Indeed, all could see what Tompkins had done at Bank's Ford; the Sixth Corps batteries saved the infantry from being crushed and swept into the Rapidan. Finally, after the defeat, Hooker took his chief of artillery's advice and re-formed the artillery.

The general discontinued attaching individual batteries to brigades and divisions, and created one brigade of five to ten batteries for each infantry corps. They would be able to fight with any part of the corps as needed. The batteries were divided so there was a proper ratio of Napoleons, Parrotts, and ordnance rifles present with a corps to provide different firepower as needed. The main problem was that the senior artillery commander in the brigade took command; he often ranked no higher then a captain. Furthermore there were no staffs and the officers had to be drawn from the batteries, reducing the units. In 1862 the War Department began to forbid the mustering of officers ranking higher than captain in the artillery; after this, most states simply sent independent batteries to the front. With no chance for higher promotion, many competent artillerists such as John Gibbon, George Getty, and Alexander Hays were forced to transfer to the infantry so they could find higher rank.[39]

Rhode Island was fortunate to retain a full regiment of light artillery throughout the war, thus creating some sense of a regimental structure. Despite this, however, the commanders continued to report directly to Providence. At Gettysburg only three field grade officers, including Colonel Tompkins, would hold the proper rank in command of the brigades, numbering over 700 men each. This presented some serious command and control problems on the battlefield. The officers had practically no staff to assist them, except perhaps one or two detached lieutenants, which left the batteries without their subalterns. Despite this, the noncommissioned officers stepped up and filled in the critical gaps.

General Henry Hunt was still relegated to the position of a staff officer, but he supervised ensuring that each gun in the Army of the Potomac had 200 rounds present in the limbers and a further two hundred in the trains. The Artillery Reserve was expanded to over one hundred pieces. These batteries could be divided as needed and dispersed throughout the entire army; it consisted of one Regular and four volunteer brigades. The artillery was the neglected branch of the army, despite the service they had rendered in the war to date. It was always lacking in manpower, horses, and the proper equipment. This did not stop them, however, from becoming the crack branch of the United States Army.[40]

This realignment of the Federal artillery would be of great service in the next few months. The early war distinction between Regulars and Volunteers had largely disappeared. There were still some volunteer batteries not up to par, but in all of their reports, the generals always praised two organizations for gallantry and success on the battlefield: the Regulars and Rhode Island batteries. Of the seventy-five batteries in the Army of the Potomac, five were composed of Rhode Islanders: Batteries A, B, C, E, and G. Battery D served in the western theatre, while F remained in North Carolina, and Battery H served in the defenses around Washington. Furthermore the scattering of the command was not only limited to the batteries, but the senior officers as well. Regulations forbade the combining of batteries from the same regiment; if a brigade took heavy casualties it would prove disastrous for that state. Colonel Tompkins and his brother John, recently promoted to major, and the regimental staff remained on duty at Sixth Corps Artillery Brigade headquarters. J. Albert Monroe, the lieutenant colonel, commanded an artillery training camp in Washington, while the second major remained in Providence, forwarding recruits to the batteries in the field. The wide distribution of the regiment led one veteran to compare it to a "Geography Class."[41]

On May 12, Battery G received some unexpected news; they were relieved of duty with the Second Corps. With the expiration of the enlistments of many nine-month and two-year New York regiments, the Army of the Potomac was losing nearly twenty thousand more men, in addition to those lost at Chancellorsville. Without much need for additional artillery within the Second Corps, four batteries were sent to the Artillery Reserve. This was an army-wide reserve that could be used as needed, by sending individual batteries or brigades to other parts of the line. The men in Battery G were losing an identity as members of the Second Corps, although they were still allowed to wear the trefoil upon their hats for the time being.[42]

In addition to transferring out of the Second Corps, fourteen men left Battery G as well. These were the detached infantrymen who had joined G. Eight men had been part of the original contingent who joined in March, while eight more were attached in April. They did not go with Battery G because they could not be readily transferred back to their parent organization if needed. Instead, they were sent to Battery A. Their loss was severely felt, as the command was critically short of privates. Captain Adams moved his command to their new camp at Reserve Headquarters, near the headquarters of the Army of the Potomac itself. Here the Rhode Islanders would be under the watchful eye of General Henry J. Hunt, the chief of artillery who had organized the brilliant gun line at Malvern Hill.[43]

Many were pleased to have moved from the dreary conditions at Falmouth to a new shady camp at Belle Plain, some three miles away. At the new encampment, Adams, like his predecessors, had to issue orders to properly direct his soldiers. The men had to learn to salute their officers and to appear at headquarters properly dressed. The United States Army was unique among forces at the time: a soldier could simply walk up to a commissioned officer and talk to him and vent his complaints. This was because in the American system officers came from the ranks and the same social backgrounds; they were the same as the men they commanded. This led to tighter unit cohesion on the battlefield and persuaded the soldiers to accept the orders as valid. The orders were not coming from an aristocrat, but rather a fellow statesman, who had to return home to face the public if that order had fatal consequences. In the officer ranks of Battery G were Second Lieutenants James Chase and Allen Hoar, both of whom entered the service as enlisted soldiers and were now commissioned officers. Although the men could once have called these officers by their first names, the two were now commissioned and were responsible for those under their command. By 1863 the problems of the officer elite, which had largely plagued the First Rhode Island Light Artillery in the early stages of the war, were mostly gone, as nearly all the lieutenants were promoted from the ranks.[44]

With the loss of fourteen attached infantrymen and those who fell at Fredericksburg, Battery G was severely reduced; it needed more soldiers, but could not gain them from their native state. On May 13, the same day the attached infantry departed, new soldiers arrived in camp to replace them. Unlike the infantry, they were trained artillerists in the

form of thirty-one enlisted men from the Tenth New York Battery. After serving in the Artillery Reserve for a year, all of the officers in the battery resigned because the command did not see any combat. Finally, at Chancellorsville the battery was engaged as part of the Third Corps; they were cut up as Jackson struck their line. This reduced the Tenth New York below the minimum acceptable numbers for a battery. The cannoneers were thus ordered to be transferred to other artillery commands that needed men. The soldiers refused and nearly mutinied; they had to be escorted to Battery G's camp under guard, where they settled in peacefully. These men also brought a welcome relief to the battery: additional horses and artillery equipment. Captain Adams satisfied his new recruits by placing them together in one section, under their own noncommissioned officers.[45]

The burden of general camp duties continued to be placed upon the men. A few new horses were again issued and broken in while the men prepared to pack for the upcoming summer campaign. Although the men were

Being assigned to the battery staff allowed George L. Gaskell the ability to know of the inner workings of Battery G (USAMHI).

used to it, the government issued clothing only lasted several months, which required a constant supply to be kept on hand by the quartermaster sergeant. Many of the artillerists became adept at sewing in order to repair their uniforms as they were without benefit of mothers and wives. The noncommissioned officers supervised the men in mechanical maneuvers as they stripped down the carriages, greased up all moving parts, and put them back together. During an inspection of the battery, General Hunt complimented Captain Adams for "keeping the battery in good order."[46]

It was a very quiet time for the soldiers; they knew something was brewing in the west, but were not quite sure what it was. Picket duty was performed occasionally along the river. The men tired of the poor leadership they were forced to serve under. Although not an effective field commander, McClellan knew how to inspire his men and had made the Army of the Potomac. Hooker had attempted to do the same thing after the debacle at Fredericksburg, but Chancellorsville erased whatever small transformations he did effect; only the corps badges survived. Private Gaskell was among those displeased with the commanding general. He blamed Hooker for the losses of Battery G at Marye's Heights and wished he would resign: "The men have not the confidence in him they had for McClellan, nor ever will." Ever since McClellan had been removed from command the previous fall, the majority of the soldiers in the Army of the Potomac wished he would return. In addition to reporting the usual unpleasantness in the command structure, the private heard a rumor that Battery G was going to be transferred back to the Peninsula. On the sixth of June Bugler Lewis wrote, "We expect to move shortly some where i dont know where." These rumors proved true, but in a totally opposite direction: north.[47]

Gettysburg

*We brought our guns to bear on the Rebel wagon train scattering them
in every direction driving their rear guard through the village of Fairfield.*
—Private James A. Barber, July 5, 1863

With the freshness of his victory at Chancellorsville, Robert E. Lee decided on yet another fateful course of action. He would again invade the North, this time hoping to fulfill the plans set forth in the summer of 1862 of bringing the war to Pennsylvania and attempting to gain European support. Using the Shenandoah Valley to cover their movements, the lead elements of the Army of Northern Virginia quietly slipped out of the camps near Fredericksburg and marched north on June 8. Once he knew Lee had moved, Hooker set the Army of the Potomac in motion to find and destroy the Army of Northern Virginia.

On the morning of June 12, the familiar sounding of Boots and Saddles was again heard in camp as the men packed up, drew three days' rations, and again prepared to march north to defend the Union itself. Private Barber wrote, "This created a great excitement about where the Army was going but we all believed the Army was going to fall back on Washington." As their camp was directly on the river, the Confederate rear guard still occupying Fredericksburg could view the artillery encampment. They fired several long-range projectiles near Battery G's camp as they pulled out; the men watched the rounds fly harmlessly overhead. The day before, the First, Third, and Eleventh Corps had moved out. The Second, Fifth, Twelfth, and the Artillery Reserve marched this day, while the Sixth brought up the rear. Each day the artillerist observed enemy cavalry scouting their movements. William Lewis felt as though the Federals were retreating rather than advancing, as they marched north instead of traveling south to Richmond. The officers and men in Battery G followed the reserve; marching or driving as the case may be at the high rate Hooker placed his army in order to find and destroy the Army of Northern Virginia.[1]

Battery G had been part of the Artillery Reserve for only a month when surprising orders were again received by Captain Adams, on June 18. The Sixth Corps Artillery Brigade was among those units forced to give up several batteries to the reserve when two dozen infantry regiments were mustered out. With 16,000 men, the Sixth Corps was the largest in the army. Commanded by John Sedgwick it was well led and disciplined and was comprised largely of veteran regiments from all over the North, with New Yorkers and Pennsylvanians accounting for over half the command. The artillery brigade was now commanded by Colonel Charles Tompkins, who was among the most capable artillerists in the army and had followed Sedgwick to the Sixth. When it became apparent that two of the Rhode Island batteries were sitting idle in the reserve, Tompkins suggested Sedgwick request their transfer to his brigade. Consequently, the request was made and Batteries C and G now became part of the Sixth Corps Artillery Brigade; here they would remain throughout the rest of the war. The two Rhode Island units joined six other batteries, including two from New York, three of Regulars, and the First Massachusetts, a direct descendent of the battery trained by the Providence Marine Corps of Artillery in the 1850s. The soldiers in Battery G traded their trefoils for the red Greek cross of the Sixth, which was now displayed on their hats with the letter "G."[2]

Battery G was not unknown to General Sedgwick; the two had served together since the Second Corps was formed in early 1862. Captain Adams also was familiar with the general, having served in Battery B. An incident, though, on the Peninsula at the Fair Oaks camp the previous summer had seriously damaged their relationship. One night, after drinking heavily and playing cards, Adams was quite intoxicated. He grabbed a driver's whip and promptly began whipping a battery horse for a long time, all the while being under the influence. After some time had passed in this manner, someone grabbed Adams off his feet in the darkness: it was General John Sedgwick himself. The general blasted Adams for being drunk on duty and for beating the poor horse. If Sedgwick ever caught Adams performing the same behavior again he said he would "throwe his boots to him."

Although on somewhat unsteady ground with the general before, Adams had won back his reputation with him at Marye's Heights. Now Captain Adams and the Rhode Island battery he commanded prepared to follow their new corps north to victory or defeat. This would take place at a small crossroads town named Gettysburg.[3]

As the rear guard of the entire Army of the Potomac, the Sixth Corps was the last in the column of march. The rapid pace soon brought Battery G to Fairfax Courthouse, on June 25, where they received orders to abandon most of their personal baggage. Although a battery could carry additional material, Colonel Tompkins did not want the extra weight putting strain on the carriages. So he ordered all cannoneers to only bring one blanket, a piece of shelter tent, a blouse, a jacket, two pair of drawers, three pair of socks, one pair of boots, and a forage cap. The drivers were allowed to use a greatcoat instead of a blanket, as it folded over the saddle. Other than the Rhode Islanders, the men in the Artillery Brigade were largely

Private Simon W. Creamer was one of many detached infantrymen to serve in the battery. He was killed at Gettysburg serving in Battery A (USAMHI).

disgusted with Tompkins. As the commander of the Providence Marine Corps of Artillery, the colonel was obsessed with having all of his cannoneers remembering all the parts of the cannon by the proper name, such as the cascable, nave, fellow, and trunion. (Sergeant John W. Chase of the First Massachusetts Battery decided on an interesting name for Colonel Tompkins, "the great Critter.") With this reduction complete, Battery G and the Sixth Corps Artillery Brigade again struggled northwards. On one occasion, a group of soldiers from the Second Rhode Island saw General Hooker ride by them and they yelled out: "Pull the Chancellorsville Murderer off that horse." Private Daniel A. Handy of Providence would best describe the campaign: "They marched us like dogs."[4]

The Potomac was crossed on the twenty-sixth as the cannoneers shouted, "Farewell Old Virginia." On June 28, General Joseph Hooker had had enough of the Lincoln administration. He pleaded with the War Department to order him to withdraw the garrison from the crucial Harpers Ferry junction where many supply and transportation lines met. The commander wanted these men to bolster his army as the Federal forces did not have a large numerical superiority over Lee. Lincoln refused and Hooker resigned on June 28. He was replaced by George Gordon Meade, a Pennsylvanian who had performed well at Antietam and again at Fredericksburg, where his division became the only troops to pierce the Confederate line. Meade was not the type of leader McClellan was, being referred to as "an old snapping turtle" by his men. He was, however, the veteran officer the country now needed. He continued to direct the Army of the Potomac on a march north to Pennsylvania; this time they would be fighting the Confederates on true Northern soil.[5]

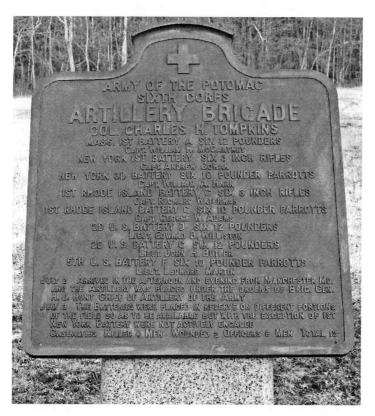

Remarkably, they continued on. Through the intense heat, dust, and flies the Sixth Corps marched forward at an unbelievable pace. In the vanguard was Battery G as they led the corps artillery on the march. With yet another new commander, the Army of the Potomac was on its way to destiny. Somewhere to the north, the Army of Northern Virginia had already been foraging in Pennsylvania for nearly two weeks. With a firm idea of where the Confederates were, Meade hurried his forces along for battle. As the need to

This marker at Gettysburg is the only battlefield tribute to Battery G.

find the Rebels increased, so too did the rate of march for the Sixth Corps. As the last command in line they were a full day's march behind the rest of the army. Sedgwick pressed his men forward into the blazing heat of late June. In three days the battery marched sixty-one miles. Men died along the side of the road from heatstroke but nothing could be done to save them; the Sixth Corps had to keep marching to reinforce the Army of the Potomac. The straggling was so great that the corps was spread out over five miles.[6]

The situation was much the same in Battery G; only the officers, sergeants and drivers were mounted, allowing the cannoneers to join in the misery of the infantry. The rations issued to the men did nothing to give the vital energy needed to sustain themselves on the march. A Rhode Islander described them: "Raw salt pork and wormy biscuits were eaten with relish. The clothing was in a state not to be described." The women of Maryland passed out buckets of ripe cherries to the soldiers as they marched by. In addition, pails of rye whiskey were given out to keep the weary men moving onward. Many had far too much and they simply stumbled out of the column to be rounded up by the provost guard; the Greek cross on each man's cap let them know which corps they belonged to. Each night the men threw themselves on the ground, utterly exhausted at the rate of march; but they knew that this battle would decide the fate of the country.

Meade had dispatched his cavalry to the north and west in an effort to locate the main body of the Confederate army. It was one of these patrols that located a small Rebel force near Gettysburg, Pennsylvania, on the thirtieth of June. The stage was set for the bloodiest battle in American history.[7]

The Battle of Gettysburg began on July 1, 1863, when a single division of Union cavalry held off two Confederate corps for three hours before the Army of the Potomac's First and Eleventh corps arrived on the fields north and west of town. In pitched battle all day, the Federals suffered massive casualties and were forced back through the town itself. Here they began occupying a series of ridges and hills south of Gettysburg. By nightfall on the first, additional forces were on the field and the Federal line begun to take the shape of a fishhook, based at Culp's Hill and extending down Cemetery Hill and Cemetery Ridge. As more units arrived on the field, they filed into position until the line extended almost three miles. The Confederates occupied the heights to the north and west along Seminary Ridge as both sides brought up reinforcements to continue the sanguinary battle on the second of July.[8]

With the battle underway, General Meade ordered all of his commanders to rush their forces to Gettysburg with all possible speed. He did not know the strength of the Confederate army, and, like McClellan, feared the Federals were outnumbered. With these orders General Sedgwick again ordered the Sixth Corps to march with haste. At 8:00, only an hour after bedding down for the night on July 1, Sedgwick ordered the corps awake and moving. Captain Adams wrote, "Broke camp at 8 P.M. After a march of 5 miles, entered the Westminster and Gettysburg Turnpike, and continued rapidly through the night." The orders did not dampen the men's spirits; they knew the fate of the country lay in their hands. It was a cool, calm night, and the stars provided ample light to guide their path. Private Barber remembered, "Our Battery mooved rapidly." Although assigned to the Sixth Corps Artillery Brigade, Battery G marched as part of the Third Division and was to support them in the event of battle. The Third had recently changed commanders, and was now led by General Frank Wheaton of Providence, a former colonel of the Second Rhode Island. This regiment was also in the division as part of a Massachusetts brigade.[9]

After a late start on the morning of the second, the Confederate forces advanced down to the southern portion of the Union line and began to attack what they thought was unoccupied terrain. Instead, they ran into the Army of the Potomac. In places with names such as Little Round Top, Devil's Den, Wheatfield, Peach Orchard, Slaughter Pen, and Valley of Death, Rebel soldiers hurled themselves against the Union defenders. Batteries B and E of the First Rhode Island Light Artillery were overrun by the Confederate attacks: both units lost heavily. Second Lieutenant Benjamin Freeborn was a former sergeant in Battery G. Despite being severely wounded, he was the last officer remaining in Battery E and brought off what was left of the shattered command. The Federal forces were again pushed back but managed to hold the line against determined assaults. These men were United States soldiers. Now they stood in Pennsylvania defending their country against an invading force. Indeed, the majority of Union soldiers at Gettysburg were Pennsylvanians fighting for their own state. The engagement lasted until dark. When it was over, neither side had gained a clear advantage, as the Union forces still held the high ground and the Confederates had only captured some rocks and woodlots.[10]

Because of the need to arrive on the field, General Sedgwick ordered that only three halts of five minute be given to the men. The cannoneers of Battery G approached Gettysburg with apprehension; they could only imagine what was occurring ahead of them. All day long, the men had seen the smoke and heard the battle in the distance while hundreds of wounded were carried to trains in Maryland to be transported to Washington. Private Barber remembered, "Very soone we could discover the bursting of shells and the sharp crackling of musketry that began to tell us that our men was engaged desperately with the rebs."

At 4:00 the lead elements of the Third Division, Sixth Corps, arrived on the field near Little Round Top, but elements of the Fifth Corps were already engaged and the Rhode Islanders, Bay Staters, and Vermonters who composed the lead element were not called for. Battery G was with them as they arrived on the field in time to make a difference. The battles still raged along the southern portion of the line, but the Sixth Corps units were ordered to hold themselves in reserve, ready to reinforce any breakthrough along the line. Barber remembered, "A sharp cannonading in our front and lasted some time when the rebels made a charge on our lines and desperate fighting with the Infantry began and was keep up till darkness." The corps had marched an unbelievable thirty-seven miles in one day. The men were exhausted but promptly obeyed orders to hold themselves in readiness to go into action. But no orders ever came. During the evening, General Sedgwick's wagons appeared and his headquarters was erected one hundred yards from Battery G's position.[11]

At night the attacks again shifted north to Culp's Hill, where a single New York brigade under George Sears Greene of Warwick held back the Confederates. For the second night in a row no sleep was gained. On the night of July 2, Colonel Tompkins visited each battery commander, instructing them to keep their men alert and awake in the event the enemy attacked at night and the batteries were needed: no action came. During the night as well, General Sedgwick strengthened his end of the line in the event action came on the following morning. The Third Division filed into a large gap left by the First Division, Second Corps, while a brigade of the First Division connected with it on the right and anchored on the Fifth Corps to their left on Little Round Top. The Fifth Maine came onto line and advanced into the Valley of Death as pickets, but to also provide support to Battery G if they were called to act. During the night, both sides exchanged occasional picket fire, and all settled down for what they knew was coming on the third. The Confederates had thrown everything into battle and almost gained victory. This led Lee to make the ultimate decision.[12]

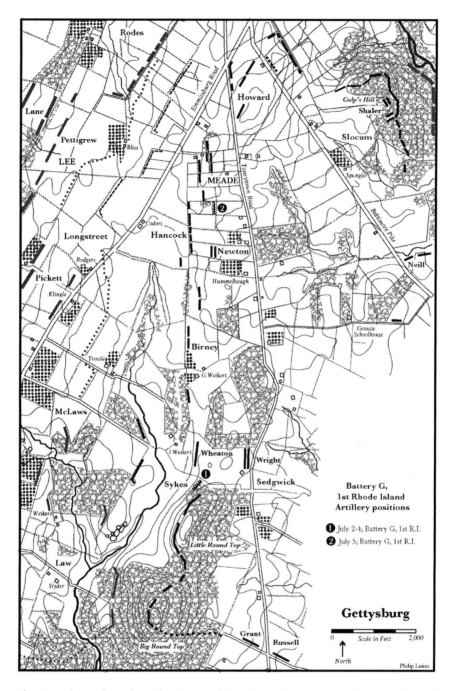

Battery G,
1st Rhode Island
Artillery positions

❶ July 2-4; Battery G, 1st R.I.
❷ July 5; Battery G, 1st R.I.

Gettysburg

0   Scale in Feet   2,000

North

Philip Laino

After two days of combat, the Army of Northern Virginia was almost to the point of having a decisive victory on Northern soil. Unable to defeat the Union forces on both flanks, the Confederates would launch a direct attack against the center of the Federal force on Cemetery Ridge. It was almost the same plan as Fredericksburg: march a mile over open ground, uphill to attack a well entrenched force backed by artillery. Lee was confident that his infantry could make it. He ordered three divisions into position, while 150 guns prepared for a massive bombardment to drive off the Union defenders. At 1:00, when all was in position, the Confederate artillery opened up. The objective was a small clump of trees on Cemetery Ridge, which would be a guide point for the three divisions to coordinate the assault. Holding this position was the Second Corps, Battery G's old command.

Throughout the war the cannoneers in gray would always suffer from faulty fuzes, poor ammunition, and poor tactics, which more than proved true this day. Many of the rounds overflew the Second Corps Artillery Brigade on Cemetery Ridge, or the fuzes did not work. Located on the ridge, on either side of the clump of trees, were Batteries A and B, First Rhode Island Light Artillery. These two units were in the eye of the hurricane, as they received the brunt of the Confederate fire. While the Second Corps infantry hugged a stone wall for protection, the Rhode Islanders stood upright and continued to work the guns. In the engagement a cannon from Battery B was hit by three shells, killing three members of the detachment and disabling the gun, as the remaining cannoneers discovered when they tried to place a round in the muzzle and it became stuck. Indeed, Battery B suffered forty-five casualties, including nine dead. This far surpassed Battery G's loss at Marye's Heights. In the ranks of Battery A was Private Simon W. Creamer. He was a German immigrant, detached from the Twelfth New Jersey and had recently been transferred from Battery G. Creamer was decapitated by a Confederate shell while driving a team of horses.[13]

At the height of the fury, an aide from General Meade found Colonel Tompkins and directed him to inspect the artillery line. Tompkins did as ordered, bringing up fresh batteries and additional ammunition and sending his Sixth Corps batteries into position. Major Thomas W. Osborn, who had been commanding the Eleventh Corps Batteries on Cemetery Hill, was preparing to withdraw his shattered command, which was low on ammunition and manpower after being engaged for three days straight. Meade directed Tompkins to place his four batteries of Napoleons on the hill; only the Third New York made it before the orders were countermanded. The remaining units waited on the Taneytown Road for orders. Because they were already in line supporting the Third Division, Battery G was not called upon. Indeed, if the attacks of the previous day had been renewed they would have been in the center of the fury, but they found a safe position near their brothers of the Second Rhode Island, which had received orders to support the efforts near Meade's headquarters and was marching north.[14]

Battery G was assigned to a position near the base of Little Round Top, in support of Rittenhouse's Battery D, Fifth United States Artillery, atop the summit. They remained here all day on July 3, without firing a shot. The shells continued to explode in the air near the Rhode Islanders, but the men were safe. They attributed their safety to the large rocks which surrounded Battery G's and the Fifth Maine's position; the thick granite boulders shielded the men as they held their position against the storm of iron. The real target was Rittenhouse's Battery, which was inflicting severe damage on the Confederate positions from Little Round Top.[15]

Finally, after two hours of the incessant bombardment, the Confederate guns relented, and the three divisions crossed the mile of open ground in the attack popularly known as Pickett's Charge. The results were the same as First Fredericksburg, except this time it was the Confederates' turn; the Second Corps infantry and artillery blasted the Rebel columns. Only a handful of the 12,000 men who made the charge ever penetrated the line atop Cemetery Ridge: they were easily repulsed. General Henry Hunt and the Federal artillery were one of the main contributing factors to the battle as they manned the cannon and fired with precision. Hunt's doctrine of constant training and keeping large amounts of ammunition on hand worked exactly as planned. The Army of the Potomac had won its first decisive victory. As the Confederates retreated, the Federal soldiers began shouting, "Fredericksburg, Fredericksburg."[16]

The Sixth Corps was not engaged in any of the main fighting at Gettysburg, rather units were sent to places as needed. Of the batteries, only the First New York saw any real combat, replacing Battery B during the height of the Confederate assault. After the charge, Battery C replaced Battery A in its position. The following day after the battle they attended to the unpleasant duty of burying their fellow Rhode Island artillerymen in shallow graves; the dead were buried in their red Rhode Island blankets. Battery G took no part in any of the fighting. Captain Adams recorded the following: "Moved forward from position of last night toward the front and center; formed sections, and halted on the right of Hazlett's battery. Remained in reserve during the day. Toward night moved to the rear 1 mile and encamped." Independence Day was also spent here. During the day, both sides remained in position, with only minor picket firing occurring. Although he was not engaged in the battle, Private James A. Barber noted as follows: "This day is a day to bee long remembered by all those that witnessed this great slaughter of life on the Battle Field of Gettysburg."[17]

The Battle of Gettysburg was the bloodiest engagement ever fought on the North American continent. Lee suffered 28,000 casualties to Meade's 23,000; over 51,000 Americans fell in three days of fighting. When the carnage was over, twenty Rhode Island artillerists were dead and eighty others were wounded; the losses came from only three batteries. Gettysburg was the costliest battle in the regiment's history, but it furthered the myth and glory that the First Rhode Island Light Artillery attained during the war. The cannon of Battery B, hit during the great bombardment, became the first relic of the war as soldiers gathered around to see the damage inflicted. The battle was the first decisive Union victory in the east. Indeed, the Army of Northern Virginia would never be the same and would never again mount a major invasion of the North. The Army of the Potomac could not savor the victory, though. The Sixth Corps was ordered to pursue Lee on July 5 in the midst of a pouring rainstorm that pelted them worse than the Confederate shells.[18]

Awaking at 3:00 in the morning on the fifth, Battery G was harnessed up at 4:00 and moved to Cemetery Ridge to relieve the First New York Battery as they went to the rear and reequipped after fighting on the third. When the rolls were called, Private Hazard Watson was nowhere to be found; he had deserted in the face of the enemy. Watson later returned to the battery and was discharged in December for disability. Arriving atop the ridge, the men were met with the worst destruction that many had ever seen after a battle; human bodies, dead horses, and tons of materiel littered the ground. Although the artillerists did not experience the fury of combat, they continued to be drenched by the rain. The guns were unlimbered and placed in battery, but there were no Confederates present except for the dead. The Rebels had begun their long retreat back to Virginia in the early morning hours of July 5.[19]

Late in the morning, as the rain continued, General Meade ordered Sedgwick and his Sixth Corps to pursue. Lee was severely hindered by a seventeen-mile long wagon train filled with wounded Confederate soldiers and plunder. Private James Barber wrote, "We marched on cautiously over the fields covered with the rebels dead and every house and barn was filled with their wounded they was not able to carry away in their hasty retreat." As the Union soldiers proceeded west over land heavily scarred by the dead of the first day of fighting west of Gettysburg along Seminary Ridge, the Pennsylvania farmers rushed out of their houses to thank the Sixth Corps soldiers for liberating them from the Rebels who had stole everything they owned. In addition, the Confederates had established numerous hospitals and abandoned many of the wounded unable to make the journey along the

Fairfield Road; the Sixth Corps captured 250 of them. The road itself was one of the main retreat routes of the Army of Northern Virginia, who had churned up the hardpacked earth bed. Combined with the torrents of rain, there was nearly a foot of mud on the road; for the pursuing Federals it was starting to resemble the Mud March all over again.

Around 1:00 in the afternoon Cowan's Battery fired a few shots at a South Carolina hospital about two miles west of town, striking the camp and forcing the Confederates into surrender. One surgeon was aghast that the artillery did not respect the yellow hospital flag he was flying. The soldiers from both sides exchanged pleasantries as the Sixth Corps men told the Carolinians that they were the ones who had taken Marye's Heights. The Confederates reacted promptly by reminding them that they had driven them back at Salem's Church. Colonel Horatio Rogers lost control of his Second Rhode Island Volunteers as the men began throwing amputated limbs in the air for sport. As Sedgwick marched his command down the Fairfield Road and each hospital or band was captured, he dispatched a battalion to hold them until the provost could relieve them, so the column of march changed frequently.[20]

At six o'clock, after marching the short distance of six miles, they found a portion of the train east of the small village of Fairfield. The town was the convergent point of the Fairfield and Cashtown roads, which led directly into the Cumberland Valley and safety for the thousands of wounded in the wagons. The Confederate doctors had set up a field hospital, and three troops of the Thirty-Fifth Virginia Cavalry and some artillery protected the encampment. Furthermore, Jubal Early's Confederate division, who were acting as Lee's rear guard, had blocked a critical pass through the South Mountain Range at Jack's Mountain west of Fairfield. It was only 100 yards wide and heavily defended, as it controlled Lee's main escape route back to Virginia and the safety of the Potomac. The Rebels had to hold the gap long enough for the wagon train to move through, which was bogged down as they entered the village of Fairfield because of the two roads converging. Of even more concern for Early at the time being was blocking the junction of the Cashtown and Fairfield roads to prevent the Federals from capturing the train; it was vital for all the wagons to make it back to Virginia in order for the Confederate army to be able to survive. General Sedgwick had orders from Meade not to bring on a general engagement, but to simply probe the enemy positions. The remainder of the Army of the Potomac was taking other roads in the pursuit of Lee; the Sixth

"Uncle" John Sedgwick of Connecticut commanded the Sixth Corps (Library of Congress).

Corps was alone and unsupported five miles from the nearest support. Uncle John determined it too strong to assault, but sent in skirmishers.[21]

The Thirty-Fifth Virginia reported the advancing Federals to Early, and he prepared his defense, while the Sixth Corps deployed into a line of battle. Early instantly galloped through Fairfield, revolver drawn, trying in vain to get his wagons into the safety of the valley. He too did not want a large fight and only decided to commit enough strength to cover the withdrawal. Early dispatched three guns from the Louisiana Guard Artillery to block the intersection and turned to John B. Gordon for assistance. Gordon sent in the Twenty-Sixth Georgia to block the Fairfield road a half mile east of the village and hold the Federals back as the rest of the Confederates moved the wagons along as fast as they could be sent through the junction towards the heavy entrenchments on Jack's Mountain. General Early described the measures he took to hold back the Federals: "When the advance of the pursuing column of the enemy appeared on a hill to my rear with a battery of artillery supported by infantry, and I opened with shell on it."[22]

The Louisianans instantly targeted the Vermont Brigade, which led the column. In the meantime, the First Division swung from a column into a half-mile long line and prepared to advance. Sedgwick passed the orders for Colonel Tompkins to get his artillery into action to counter the bombardment. Tompkins rode to his brigade and called for the Third New York and Adams' Battery G. The New Yorkers and Rhode Islanders instantly obeyed and they galloped pass the Vermonters onto the right side of the Fairfield road and unlimbered in a wheatfield on Granite Hill, a commanding hill which overlooked the fields of Fairfield; the town was a mile away.[23]

Captain Adams positioned Battery G and they began firing at the Georgians and Louisianans. He had seen the Twenty-Sixth deploy into a woodlot on the south side of the road and began to shell the area as the Georgians prepared to give battle. The Thirty-First Georgia was doing its part to help untangle the mess at the intersection at Fairfield while watching the fight unfold before them. Captain William Harrison of the Thirty-First recalled, "The guns were run into battery and for half an hour they vigorously shelled the woods." Private William H. Moore of Harn's Battery was among those on the north slope of Granite Hill lending his part to the fight. The New Yorker recalled, "For a while we had a lively time of it." Colonel Edmund N. Atkinson, commander of the Twenty-Sixth, realized that the threat was not in the road; he could not hold the position with the small regiment. Instead, the Federals were advancing on his right flank through a woodlot. Atkinson ordered a right oblique as the Georgians entered the woods to confront the threat.

Apparently, Captain Adams and his men did not see the movement in the smoke of the battlefield, as they continued to shell the area surrounding the road instead of the woods south of the Fairfield road, even though no enemy force was still there. This caused many Confederates to begin laughing, as they thought the Federals were wasting their ammunition on an enemy that was not present. Eventually Adams saw his mistake and ordered the ordnance rifles turned on a better target: the Confederate wagon train. He would let the infantry fight it out. The corporals quickly adjusted their elevation screws and began targeting the wagons bogged down in the gap. Even in this uncivil war humanity still existed, and the hospital was not targeted. The bombardment was making life miserable for the Confederates. Captain Harrison wrote that the Federals were "annoying us with their artillery from nearly every hilltop as usual." As usual, the Rhode Islanders were becoming very pleased with their part in the fight. Private James Barber wrote, "We brought our guns to bear on the Rebel wagon train scattering them in every direction driving their rear guard through the village of Fairfield."[24]

The Louisiana Guard Artillery targeted the Sixth Corps troops with their ten pounder Parrotts, but the rounds flew harmlessly overhead, failing to explode. Battery G was not about to have another losing duel with Rebel artillerists and instantly brought their guns to bear on the any visible Confederate target. On Jack's Mountain, several high ranking Confederate officers, including Richard Ewell, the corps commander, watched the battle unfold below. The two Federal batteries saw them and begin to fire against their position. After two rounds exploded nearby, the general moved farther to the rear to insure the wagons continued moving. The horrible weather did not have any effect upon the way the cannons were operated. Even in the precipitation, the friction primers went off as not only the rain fell but iron as well from Adams' Battery. Adjutant George Bicknell of the Fifth Maine watched the two batteries on Granite Hill and thought they were giving the Confederates a "parting token" as they retreated back to Virginia.[25]

Private Fisk of Vermont watched the bombardment: "Our batteries sent back shells enough to pay them and leave a heavy balance in our favor." The Vermonters deployed for battle as well, but spent five minutes dressing their line as they moved up to support the batteries. The New Jersey Brigade of the Sixth Corps held the extreme left of the corps'

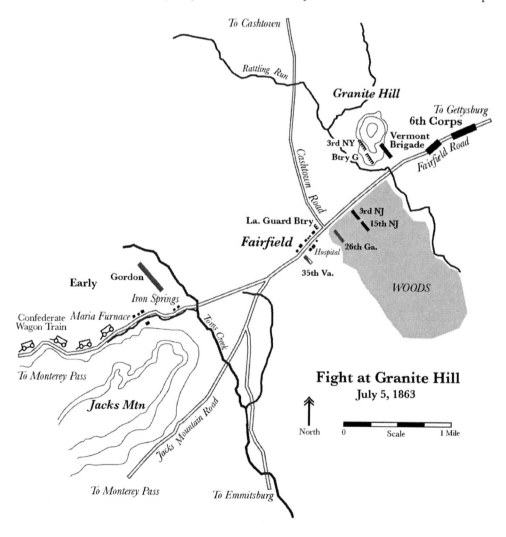

Fight at Granite Hill
July 5, 1863

line and was deployed into line as General Alfred T.A. Torbert received orders to send in skirmishers. Torbert selected the Third New Jersey and two companies of the Fifteenth New Jersey, which were sent in to contend with the Georgians in the woods. An elderly couple lived in the woodlot and became scared to death as they realized their peaceful set of woods was about to become a battlefield; they hid inside as the battle enveloped them.[26]

The Jersey regiments fixed bayonets, as muskets would not work in the downpour, and charged into the Twenty-Sixth. In the thick undergrowth, combined with the sulfuric smoke of the battle, the rain caused the line to come apart. Officers became separated from their commands as the men pressed forward into the woods, towards Fairfield itself. With a bayonet charge they drove off the Georgians, back towards Fairfield and eventually towards Jack's Mountain; the Southerners had done their duty and sacrificed themselves to save the wagon train. When the smoke cleared two members of the Twenty-Sixth were dead and eleven were wounded; six of them were captured by the Federals. One member of the Third New Jersey was killed. Alanson Haines of the Fifteenth New Jersey recalled the fight: "With a cheer they ran down the hill, deploying as they came. The whole swept forward, driving the enemy from the woods and across the field beyond. There was considerable firing, but our casualties were not numerous. We drove the enemy back a mile." Because of the tight quarters, and with darkness growing, Lieutenant Colonel Edward L. Campbell ordered his battalion to halt after clearing the road and woods. They would return back towards the First Division's line to avoid a protracted battle. Under the cover of supporting artillery, the two New Jersey regiments were able to clear the field of enemy infantry at a minimal loss.[27]

When the Thirty-Fifth Virginia Cavalry had reported to Early that the Federals were approaching, he had galloped through the streets of Fairfield, trying in vain to implore the wagons to move. The fire from Battery G and the Third New York was doing exactly what the Confederate general had wished: "The enemy's battery replied to mine, and Fairfield was soon cleared of wagons, as the teamsters and wagon masters found it more convenient to comply with this inducement to travel than my orders and solicitations." The

John S. Babcock of Westerly was twice wounded in action—at Marye's Heights and Cedar Creek—and captured after Gettysburg. Unlike many of the Westerly Boys, he survived to be mustered out (Kris VanDenBossche).

artillery had again proved to be invaluable on the field; they drove the Confederates away, out of range and sight over the mountains. In the brief engagement one Union soldier was killed and two were wounded; the total Confederate casualties were never recorded, as they continued to retreat. The fire from the guns and the charge of the Third and Fifteenth New Jersey had its effect and resulted in "taking prisoners, killing a number of their horses, and wounding some of their men," according to Private Barber. The battery expended a total of 162 rounds before the wagons were gone; they engaged for an hour. Battery G "helped to hasten his journey back to Virginia by a vigorous application of shot and shell," as Corporal Edward Adams recalled.[28]

Although it had only lasted an hour, the fight at Granite Hill had proved what well-directed artillery fire could accomplish. Except for the actions of the Third and Fifteenth New Jersey, the outcome of the battle was the result of the artillery. They had accurately shelled an enemy wagon train and driven the retreating and demoralized Confederates even farther back to Virginia. Sedgwick had orders not to bring on a large engagement, thus missing a golden opportunity to capture a large portion of the Confederate wagon train. Early had put up a spirited resistance, and managed to hold out long enough for the wagons to make it over South Mountain. Battery G had been transferred to the Sixth Corps only three weeks earlier. At Fairfield they showed their fighting spirit, which had been forged on the fields of Antietam and Marye's Heights, to their new corps. It was almost dark as Sedgwick decided to rest his tired soldiers; the men simply went to sleep on the wet ground beside the guns, exhausted and glad they had survived another engagement. The Gettysburg Campaign was over in Pennsylvania; now the fight would shift to Maryland.[29]

Pushing on through the rain, the Artillery Brigade of the Sixth Corps pursued Lee for four days straight; the men did not sleep, as they continued marching. The shoes on the horses wore down to nothing, and the men became "played out." On the night of July 7, Battery G experienced its most harrowing adventure during the Gettysburg Campaign. Sedgwick was pushing his men hard through the Catoctin Mountains to cut off Lee before he reached the Potomac. The rain had contributed to conditions similar to those on the Mud March. The general pressed Colonel Tompkins to get his artillery brigade up and over the peak of a hill so the men could establish camp and have a few hours of rest. Because of the steep terrain, the night, and the rain, the batteries were going nowhere. Sedgwick rode into the mass of confusion and for the first and only time lost his temper against Tompkins and his artillery. Colonel Charles Wainwright of the First Corps Artillery Brigade watched; later he wrote, "Uncle John was mad." Sedgwick barked for the colonel to get his guns through no matter what. Tompkins countered that the road was not serviceable and soon found another. He ordered the batteries to turn around and begin on the easier road, but few of the commands, including Battery G, heard the orders to change direction. The men and horses were just too far gone to work anymore. Finally at 3:00 on the morning of the eighth, with the assistance of some of Sedgwick's staff, Tompkins had his brigade on the correct road.[30]

On July 9, George Gaskell hastily wrote a note to his sister while riding his horse; he had hardly been out of the saddle for nearly two weeks. Gaskell was very happy to still be alive and prayed that he would survive what many thought would be the final battle of the war in several days: "You will probably not hear from me in some time as I am constantly in the saddle." To compound the problem for the artillerists, they had to deal with "impassible roads" as they marched through Maryland. Finally, the Army of Northern Virginia entrenched along the banks of the Potomac, waiting for the river to subside before crossing. The entire army was brought up, but Meade did not order the attack. Battery G went into line of battle on July 12 at Funkstown, Maryland, on the banks of the Potomac.[31]

Because it was night, orders were given not to open fire. The battery remained in position there for two days. Meade received much criticism for not vigorously attacking his foe, but the Army of the Potomac was exhausted after the long campaign to Pennsylvania and back. It was not capable of mounting another serious offensive for some time. The soldiers were very upset about not attacking; many felt the war could have been over. Sergeant John Chase of the First Massachusetts Battery wrote, "I believe we could just about settled the thing right here but I suppose that is the last thing a good many of our damn poor apologys for officers want to see for then there occupation gone and they will have to retire to there [their] former obscurity." Lee slipped across the Potomac and back into Virginia on the night of July 13. Instead of crossing the river to pursue immediately, Battery G was sent to Hagerstown for three days of rest.[32]

With the Gettysburg Campaign over, the United States had won a decisive victory over the Confederacy. Meade was applauded as a hero for his victory, but lambasted by others for not pursuing. On July 16, the Rhode Island General Assembly passed a special vote of thanks for the Rhode Island soldiers engaged in the war for their continued service to the state and for "maintaining her honor, enhancing her reputation, and illustrating her history anew, by their courage, loyalty, patriotism, and valor." None of this, though, affected the artillerists in Battery G, who continued to slog on through the mud at the front.[33]

After a brief rest at Hagerstown, Battery G recrossed the Potomac River on July 19 and began the pursuit again, this time in Virginia. Lee fled into the Shenandoah Valley, so the Army of the Potomac set a course of march for Warrenton. From there they could recuperate and refit, while protecting Washington and watching the Army of Northern Virginia. The weather was the hottest that many of these men had ever known, the temperature topping over one hundred degrees daily. The supply lines had been cut, so the men were reduced to eating handfuls of blackberries, which contributed to the spread of dysentery in the battery. To further fatigue the men, the battery officers pushed them on all night. Sergeant Chase of Massachusetts continued to vent his frustration against the colonel: "Colonel Tompkins who may be a very smart officer but I dont see it." Apparently General Sedgwick saw it, although he lost his temper on July 7 when Tompkins had trouble in the Catoctins; the colonel had provided the general with months of solid artillery leadership. Sedgwick nominated Tompkins for promotion to full brigadier general; indeed, the colonel was the senior artillery colonel in the army and the senior Rhode Island colonel as well, having gained his rank in September of 1861. No promotion ever came.[34]

While their colonel failed to gain his star, the men of Battery G failed to gain glory as well. Except for one letter from the Peninsula and a brief account of what happened to them at Marye's Heights, the *Providence Journal* carried no news from the command. The reason for this was simple; most of the battery was recruited in the hinterland of Rhode Island. The small space available for soldiers' letters would go towards letters from soldiers who had friends in Providence. Despite this the papers remained the only source of news from home, besides the letters from loved ones, which came sporadically to the command. A set of articles printed in July of 1863 irritated not only Battery G, but nearly every other Rhode Island soldier who suffered through the long months of campaigning. The Twelfth Rhode Island returned home in late July after serving for nine months. They gained much praise from the Providence papers for their actions at Fredericksburg and subsequent marches into Kentucky. In reality, the Twelfth was a poor regiment that broke and ran right after it entered combat at Fredericksburg. The soldiers in Battery G looked on in disdain at the papers for not carrying their story. For nine months the *Narragansett Weekly* ran the column length letters of a soldier-correspondent from Westerly. Meanwhile the Westerly Boys of Battery G were allocated only four small lines to tell of their bloodbath at Marye's Heights. Albert Cordner wrote several letters to the paper, but none were ever printed. Private Gaskell lamented, "How little do the 9 mos. Men of a soldiers life. However, they get the credit the bounties and the glory. We have what—a Grave—."[35]

The battery horses continued to give concern to the drivers. They simply gave out and died along the side of the road; in Battery G fourteen died during the march from Gettysburg. In order to insure that the guns and caissons had the requisite number of horses the noncommissioned officers and battery staff were dismounted and their horses assigned to the detachments. Furthermore, the men's clothing looked like rags instead of blue uniforms. They had been resupplied at the start of the Gettysburg Campaign, but the shoddy, poorly made items simply fell apart. Some men, like Bugler William H. Lewis, wore superior garments custom made in Providence that lasted far longer than army issued material.

Apparently not pleased with his already elaborate musician's jacket, Lewis added even more color. He sewed fine gold thread into the garment, and broke army regulations by cutting the collar down and the bottom of the coat so it only had eleven buttons. The jacket did have a certain appeal to the young women that he met on the march as he entertained them with his fiddle: "I have got a pretty southern damsel as ever you saw. I till you the read tape on my jacket draws the gals rite to me." For many of the younger, unmarried men in the battery, fraternizing with the local women offered a distraction from the arduous duty they performed every day. Even though they were seen as the enemy, they were treated in a civilized manner. In July of 1863, the original enlisted men in Battery G were halfway through their three years enlistment. Despite all of the death and destruction he had witnessed, George Gaskell still had hope, the motto of the state where these men hailed from. He wrote, "Somehow I believe I shall live through it."[36]

In July, the deserting resumed, with five men leaving the battery; furthermore six severely wounded men remained in the hospitals still recovering from wounds suffered at Marye's Heights. It took several months for the army to complete its "red tape" and give the injured soldiers a discharge so they could return home; many died waiting for it to come. With the large number of attached men from the Tenth New York Battery, the command had

Corporal George W. Cole of Coventry was discharged because of disability, but later became a captain in the Fourteenth Rhode Island Heavy Artillery.

112 enlisted men able to perform their duties, while thirty-five were absent, the majority of them sick on account of the weather and poor rations. Sergeant Charles Jennings received a promotion that kept him permanently detached from the battery until the end of the war. He became the ordnance sergeant at Sixth Corps Artillery Brigade headquarters. Sergeant Jennings was responsible for maintaining all the guns in the brigade and insuring that a constant supply of ammunition was always at hand.

An interesting occurrence happened on July 24 when Battery G finally arrived in Warrenton. Corporal Charles Conners and Privates George Lavender, Duncan Patterson, and John S. Babcock, the latter from Westerly, were all captured by a raiding party of John Mosby's Confederate rangers, who terrorized this part of Virginia. Mosby's columns appeared out of the middle of nowhere and ambushed the train. They were captured as they drove a slow-moving mule wagon for the artillery brigade. Babcock and Patterson were released from prison in October, while Conners and Lavender were held until the end of 1864; remarkably they managed to survive the ordeal. These were the only casualties Battery G suffered during the sanguinary Pennsylvania Campaign.[37]

In order that the Army of the Potomac might be able to regain some of the strength that it lost at Gettysburg, Meade ordered the army to go into camp near Warrenton to protect the capital as a buffer to Lee's forces.

10

Winter at Brandy

Why don't you court marshal me.
—First Lieutenant Otto L. Torslow, October 20, 1863

With the Gettysburg Campaign over and Battery G marching south towards Warrenton, a major event was occurring in Providence. This was the first ever draft held in the country. Rhode Island, as were most states, was forced to draft men to fill its quota of soldiers. Now in July of 1863 she had to raise 3,469 recruits. The small state simply had no more American citizens men willing to go into the service. Instead, immigrants, criminals, and deserters arrived in Providence to receive the large bounties being offered; many never served and instead deserted. The majority of these soldiers were bound for two new regiments, instead of filling up the depleted regiments and batteries at the front. As Battery G was the second to last battery, they only received the last of the recruits. Many of the Rhode Islanders paid the three hundred dollar commutation fee to avoid service, or joined several days before the draft was issued to collect the 400 dollar bounty being offered. Remarkably, there was no rioting in Providence over the draft, as was common in many other northern states, although there was much grumbling. The soldiers joined peaceably, never showed up, or deserted when they got the first chance. In Westerly eighty men were called to serve, but all decided to pay up or find a substitute instead of joining their neighbors in the battery.

In all, Battery G received sixteen of these soldiers to fill its vacant ranks. Nearly all of them were residents of other states, serving as substitutes for drafted men. Lieutenant James Chase and Privates Lafayette Nichols, George Simmons, and James W. Walworth were sent to a camp near New Haven, Connecticut, to train the recruits for several weeks before bringing them south for Battery G at Warrenton and to insure they did not desert on the journey. They arrived in camp on August 16, bringing the number of enlisted men to 130, the most since the command arrived on the Peninsula. Their escort did not prevent seven of these men from deserting between July and October of 1863. Those that remained became good soldiers. Some, like Simeon Starboard, would pay the ultimate sacrifice.[1]

While the battery remained at Warrenton, the weather maintained a high temperature and humidity, something very unnerving to the Rhode Islanders, brought up in the climate of the northeast. The campaign had a severe impact on the men's health as well. Even the officers were not spared; Lieutenant Torslow was ill for most of August and September. On August 10, Stable Sergeant William B. Wilbur, an artificer from Providence, died of disease in his tent. As the men set up a permanent camp, they were allowed to leave it to explore the local area. Private Gaskell visited an Episcopal church one day and was amazed to see Southern women dressed in mourning regalia on one side of the church, while soldiers of the Sixth Corps crowded into the other side. The minister preached "strength and deliverance" against the Federal soldiers, while both sides listened attentively.

Each evening the private spent at the house of a local woman, listening to a young girl play the piano as he sang Confederate patriotic songs. This was the exception, not the rule. The Southerners hated the Sixth Corps soldiers. "They look upon us as a God forsaken, thieving, speculating inventing parcel of Yankee robbers. They will have to find that there is the best and purest of blood in the veins of our rank and file," wrote Gaskell. Furthermore, the private noticed a marked difference between the women of Maryland and Virginia. In the former state, they always welcomed the men in Battery G and provided them with food and smiles, while in the latter the men were cursed and scorned.[2]

While the men enjoyed the social life around Warrenton, the noncommissioned officers prepared for an important task. As the recruits assembled in Battery G's encampment, they were trained in the manual of the piece and began to learn the duties of an artillerist. The duties at the camp near Warrenton remained pleasant as somewhat better rations began to filter down to the battery, although not always in plentiful supply. Unlike during the Peninsula Campaign and throughout 1862, the soldiers continued to be paid every two to three months. Many of the men, such as William Lewis, who sent home nearly every cent to his abandoned mother, gave up at least part of their pay for their families.

In the battery, there always seemed to be a constant need for noncommissioned officers; they were never available in plentiful numbers, as men were discharged or lost their stripes. On the seventh, two privates were promoted to corporal, including Westerly's James Barber. Unfortunately for the young soldier he was forced to transfer from the First Detachment because Corporals Henry Chace and Daniel Hoxsie were the gunner and chief of caisson respectively. Instead, Barber found himself as the chief of caisson for the Third Detachment. Lieutenant Torslow remained a unique character in the battery. He was mostly intoxicated while on duty, and on September 9 he fell from his horse and was badly injured.

As the recruits continued to learn their role in the army, they brought many problems to the command. Many brought their large cash bounties south as they had no other place to store it. On the eleventh, Privates Patrick O'Brien and James Carroll, both substitutes, were caught stealing from another new soldier. They were chained together for three days and placed on bread and water. On the same day, one of the recruits became intoxicated and began firing his revolver into the air. This startled the entire camp, as they were not expecting it and thought an attack was imminent.[3]

By the middle of September, the battery was ready for a change, which came on the sixteenth as the Sixth Corps moved from Warrenton to Culpeper, where they remained until October 2. The camp of the battery was in a ravine, a poor place for the men and horses. One night it rained so much that the camp was totally destroyed and this caused Adams to "swear like hell about the Batry being in such condition." After regaining his composure, the captain properly instructed the men how to build a camp and received permission from Colonel Tompkins to move out of the ravine to a new camp. This would not be for long, as Boots and Saddles was again raised on the second of October and Battery G was again moving.[4]

Once more Lee had stolen the initiative, and he was advancing at a rapid pace towards Washington. Since, after Gettysburg, the rations had been cut—as the supply trains were hit frequently by the Confederate irregulars—the men took relish in ears of corn, foraged from local fields and roasted over a fire. Although rations arrived for the men, forage was not always to be found for the horses. Captain Adams personally led detachments of eight men armed with revolvers into the countryside weekly with two of the battery wagons to search for provisions. On one occasion, they found a calf, which was promptly turned into a hearty New England beef stew. Bugler Lewis called it "a bully meal." The arming of the men on these patrols was necessary, as Mosby's Rangers were constantly on the prowl and Battery G had already tangled with them on the march from Gettysburg.[5]

While the men in Battery G struggled to survive in Virginia, life went on in Rhode Island. The farmers continued to till the rocky soil, and the textile mills continued to make cloth. This time their clients were not women wanting to make dresses, but the United States government needing fabric to cloth its ragged soldiers. In Westerly, the many mills continued to produce but suffered heavily when the skilled workers went to war; instead women and blacks took their places in the factories. A group of concerned citizens formed a committee to collect funds and supplies for the needy soldiers from Westerly, many of whom served in Battery G. Items such as mittens, blankets, and drawers would be needed in the winter months ahead. The organization also helped the soldiers' families by supplying them with firewood for the winter. Due to the political machine, however, little of the money collected went to those who needed it; most of the funds went into Republican coffers in the town. Occasionally though, the politicians would give back to the soldiers by allotting relief money to their families, as the small government wages could not support a soldier with a wife or children. These efforts were but a few of those organized in Rhode Island to help the soldiers. Although they did provide some comforts, the relief societies could not stop the one problem constantly occurring in Battery G.[6]

Private Henry Seamans (left) is joined by Bugler William H. Lewis (seated) and his brother Theodore during their veteran furlough to Providence in the winter of 1864 (Connecticut State Library).

Whiskey was strictly forbidden by army regulations. Despite this, it continued to seep into the command and afflict the soldiers in Battery G. There were two Privates Patrick O'Brien in the battery. One of them was an Irish immigrant who joined in March of 1862, while a younger man of the same name was a substitute. The second Private O'Brien became so intoxicated on October 18 that he violently assaulted Captain Adams. The captain had to hit O'Brien over the head eight times with a club before he was subdued. Adams then ordered the drunk to be given the most common form of punishment in the light artillery. Each caisson had a spare wheel attached to its rear. It presented an easy and unique means of tying the offender by his limbs to the wheel. Punishment in the Civil War was meant to not only humiliate and punish the offender, but to show others the consequences as well. Although many of the men in the command took part in the excessive intoxication, others did not. William Lewis and Henry Seamans formed a pact between them not to drink. Lewis' mother continued to worry he would give in to temptation while in the army. The young musician replied, "There is no one in this world that despise liquors any more then i do it has no temptations for me. God knows that I have had example enough before me to know the folly of it." With yet another alcohol related incident over, the two armies were again in motion.[7]

In October, Meade prepared to strike back at Lee. Instead, it was the Rebels who stole the initiative yet again. The Confederates made a mad dash for Washington, hoping to get between the capital and the Army of the Potomac. In order to protect his left flank, Meade sent the Sixth Corps to the west. The orders came on October 5. The destination was to be Cedar Mountain, site of a brutal clash in August of 1862. Battery G followed their corps in the movement. On the eleventh, a large enemy force was observed marching around their flank. In response, the First and Sixth corps pulled back to Culpeper. Knowing that Meade was threatened, General Sedgwick ordered a hasty march back towards the main body of the Army of the Potomac. Meade brought the Army of the Potomac into line of battle near the twice contested field of Bull Run, but the Confederates did not give battle. It rained the night of October 13 and the Sixth Corps marched as quickly as possible to the relief of their fellow soldiers. The artillery in particular had a difficult time, as recorded by George T. Stevens of the Seventy-Seventh New York: "Drivers cursing, cannon rattling, soldiers singing, and shouting, horses racing and all that sublime confusion which can never be see except in a hasty but well directed retreat of a vast army." The Sixth was not retiring, but simply redeploying to counter the threat; in one day they marched thirty miles.

On the fourteenth, a large Confederate force struck the rear of the Second Corps near Bristoe Station, but was beaten back with heavy losses. The soldiers in the Sixth Corps heard the firing in the distance, but did not make it into the fight. Battery G stopped at Centreville and remained there all day before moving towards Chantilly. The conditions were starting to become the same as the previous fall when the battery marched from Harpers Ferry to Falmouth—continuous rain. As a reminder of the infamous Mud March, the roads became impassible for the guns, leaving the privates to push them along. The men received their thick overcoats from Washington that had been sent there before the Gettysburg Campaign. Bugler Lewis was fortunate to be mounted and able to carry on with his peculiar duties. The months of hard riding had left his hips and back sore, making him unable to play some days. He wrote of the journey from Bristoe: "A verry long march through mud & rain it has been very cold." The young man continued to suffer from intermittent illness from the Chickahominy swamp, while the poor food he ate did not help it. In addition, Lewis' rubber coat had been lost; he asked his mother to send another. With the Bristoe Campaign over, Meade brought his entire army south again to camp, pondering his next move.[8]

At 7:00 on the night of October 20, Battery G was marching to a new camp near Warrenton after leaving New Baltimore. It was a dark night as Private Gaskell led the column. As he was proceeding at a slow and cautious pace, Captain Adams galloped up to check on his progress and noticed that First Lieutenant Otto L. Torslow was not at his post; his right section led the column. First Sergeant Chace was instantly dispatched to find Torslow. The officer was at the rear of the column trying to hurry up a caisson that had dropped a tarp used to cover the cannon while in camp. The drivers had not noticed that the tarp had fallen off, and the caisson fell out of line to retrieve it. Sergeant Chace delivered the captain's message and Torslow abandoned the mission, ordering his men to move on as he rode to find the captain. As Adams found the lieutenant, he politely asked "Why were you away from your section, sir?" The captain also pressed as to why a noncommissioned officer had not been dispatched to see the caisson along, instead of the battery's second in command. The lieutenant fired back, swearing at Adams in a violent manner, claiming Adams would have censured him either way—whether Torslow or a sergeant had been there. Finally he yelled out, "Why don't you court marshal me." Adams then said, "You know what I want." To this the disgruntled officer fired back, interrupting in mid sentence: "I don't care what you want." Captain Adams obliged and instantly declared Torslow under arrest, stripping him of his sword and command. That night the lieutenant took his frustration out on his horse by whipping the poor beast much as Adams had done on the Peninsula. This time it was the captain who stopped it.[9]

Lieutenant Torslow was charged with violating the Sixth Article of War: "behaved himself with contempt or disrespect towards his commanding officer. He shall be punished according to the nature of his offense, by the judgment of a court martial." A brigade court martial was held on October 28 to try the officer, who pleaded not guilty. To avoid prejudice, no Rhode Island officer served as a member, while Captain Adams excused himself, as he had filed the charges and was to testify against Torslow. Captain William T. Harn of the Third New York Battery presided. This was not the first time Adams had brought charges against Torslow. In August he wrote to Colonel Tompkins requesting Torslow be dismissed from the service for being intoxicated on duty and absenting himself from his command. Tompkins returned the letter, stating there was not enough evidence to support such an act.[10]

Captain Adams was the first witness for the government. Oddly speaking in the third person he stated that his subordinate "did use disrespectful and contemptuous language and in a violent and ill temperate manner in the presence of enlisted men toward Captain George W. Adams." In his statement, Adams also mentioned Torslow's other problems in the battery. Furthermore, the captain took note that his lieutenant was a Swede by birth. Adams said, "He has been neglectful in his duties as chief of section and orderly officer since about the middle of August last." Torslow had remained on the sick list most of the time, and had not attended to his men.

As he was always near the commanding officer, musician William H. Lewis swore that Torslow acted in a violent manner and used harsh language against Adams; indeed, Lewis was only three yards away when the incident occurred. Lewis said, "He was quite angry." He also spoke of the horse whipping as evidence of Torslow's anger. Privates George Gaskell and James Taft also testified as they were at the head of the column. Adams called only men in to testify who had been with in proximity to the conversation that night. Gaskell saw Torslow ride to the rear and thought nothing of it, as he continued to lead the column. The private did hear the conversation occur, though, as the two officers rode together back to the head of the column. As usual, he supported the side of his captain. Most important to Torslow's case was the testimony of Private Taft, who like Torslow was an immigrant. The Irishman said, "I did not notice Mr. Torslow particularly and I could not say if he was excited or not. I heard no sharp words used at all." After the testimony, the government rested, and Lieutenant Torslow presented his defense.[11]

After explaining the case of the missing tarp, the Swede told the court, "I thought it my duty to stay by the caisson to get it up with the Battery." Torslow testified that he had never said the words that the three witnesses had testified to, and the only reason he was absent from duty was after falling off of his horse. He offered, "I am a professional soldier, and take pride in my position and I was never before accused of ungentlemanly conduct or neglect of duty." He presented evidence of his service in the Swedish army and said he had never shirked from duty. Two letters from Captain John G. Hazard of Battery B and Captain Charles H. Morgan of the Second Corps staff were also introduced as proof of his bravery. Morgan wrote, "I regard him as one of the most capable officers I have met in the volunteer force in his arm of the service." Captain Hazard spoke of Torslow's "coolness, bravery, and judgment" at Antietam. It did not take long for the panel to reach their verdict. The officers agreed with the two captains and found Torslow not guilty. The lieutenant remained off duty through the end of November, however, recovering from his injury. For the meantime, Captain Adams would have to put up with his unruly subordinate, while transferring a large amount of responsibility to subalterns and enlisted men he could trust.[12]

With the unpleasantness of Torslow's court martial over, Adams finally received some good news to tell his men. The captain read a proclamation from Governor James Smith of Rhode Island. Because Battery G had enlisted in December of 1861, the original men's enlistments were due to expire in 1864. The United States government feared that they would lose tens of thousands of disciplined and well-trained volunteers, so they offered an unbelievable reenlistment bonus. If the original soldiers in Battery G returned to the army, they would receive a $400 bounty from the United States, and $300 from the State of Rhode Island. Furthermore, they could officially call themselves veterans by wearing a special stripe on their jackets. The greatest incentive was a thirty-five day furlough home. Because of the staggered enlistments of the men in March and August of 1862 there was no fear that the battery would run out of men and be forced to consolidate with another battery.

After much debate, twenty-eight of the original enlisted men who had gone south in 1861 reenlisted by December 1. Among them was Bugler Lewis. He was determined to see the war to an end, and looked forward to receiving the large bounties being offered to give to his mother. Despite this, he remained ill and in the saddle constantly, attending to his stressful duties. Although he vowed to stay in the army, Lewis was looking forward to returning to Providence after the war: "When i get home i am going to work some kind of business and go to school nights." In addition, he received a large clothing shipment from his mother; the extra items were placed in Captain Adams' personal wagon. For many of the artillerists, they would not have long to see their small state again.[13]

November passed quietly for the Rhode Islanders in Battery G. The weather remained moderate: it had yet to snow. This part of Virginia was like a desert; the soldiers had to go farther and farther from camp each day to get wood and forage. Quail became a popular food as the cannoneers placed snares around the camp to catch the birds. Although absent on staff duty since after Marye's Heights, Lieutenant Crawford Allen was promoted to the vacant captaincy of Battery H and was replaced by Elmer Corthell, recently recovered from a severe wound suffered at Gettysburg. Like the first officers, he was a student at Brown University when the war began. Instead of seeking a commission, he enlisted as a private in Battery A. The *Providence Journal* reported: "Lieut C. was a student at Brown University, a candidate for the ministry, but enlisted as a private, received promotion, and has reenlisted." Corthell had fought well with Battery F as a sergeant in North Carolina, which earned him a commission and a transfer back to Battery A. His actions at Gettysburg earned him the bar of a first lieutenant and assignment to Battery G. While the captain welcomed a new officer to his command, he had to deal with another, constant problem as well. The deserting and insubordination that always plagued the battery continued; twenty-one enlisted men were absent without leave, while only three were sick.[14]

As the command marched near Culpeper again, Private Gaskell took notice of the poor, suffering women as he wrote to his still ill sister: "What few women I have seen appear like specters dressed in black with pale, hungry, never smiling faces. Do our North women ever dream what these of the South are suffering. Do they think of the thousands raised in ease and luxury young and old alike who are now stripped of clothing and the simplest necessities of life." The people of Rhode Island had no idea of what this war truly was, except that they saw the never ending return of soldiers maimed for life and those who died in the service of their country. "Do they ever think of the gallant boys who have laid for hours in agony on the field, whom perhaps their folly and inconstancy had driven from home to die alone."[15]

The men of Battery G viewed women in many different lights, much as they did blacks. Nearly a third of the men, like Albert Cordner, were married and many had children. The younger men, like William Lewis, used their off duty time to flirt with the local women; for some the only woman in their lives was still mother, who received much of their pay. Other artillerists continued to receive letters from sweethearts at home, and some of them would be married after the war. George Gaskell received letters throughout the war from Mary and Ellen Shepard, from back home in Plainfield, among others who considered it their patriotic duty to write to a soldier. The orderly even went so far as to write his friend Reuben Bliss, a discharged soldier, not to marry. Eventually Gaskell became tired of receiving the letters, as he confessed to his sister Mary:

> I have seen incidents which would almost have cause me to curse women forever. They need not accuse the soldiers of inconstancy. Let the young women show her lover that she has a mind which can comprehend something beside ribbons and photographs and if *he is* a man there will be no danger of "tumbling out." I don't want a wife, and I won't in future be mean enough to correspond with a single woman who may think that I fancy her. Young women of today who are not immensely rich nor angels of beauty: will find that they must not treat men like playthings of an hour if they may to secure them for husbands. A man like Bliss, who faced death in every form on the Peninsula is not going home to be toyed with by a girl who has neither beauty, education, nor money. Would I. I think not. But I've said enough on this subject. Both sexes have their faults.

The women of the South were uniquely different from those in the North and presented the changing face of warfare when the soldiers were dealing with civilians, instead of just an opposing army. They gave the Rhode Islanders a place to rest in their off duty time, but the artillerists still had to remember these women were the enemy. The war changed all those who fought through it. Private Gaskell would eventually change his stance, marry, and raise a family.[16]

When not serving as Captain Adams' primary musician, William Lewis was proving to have other skills necessary for service in the army. He was proving to be an excellent forager, finding hams and corn for the officers' meals; he was allowed to eat the excess. During a review of Battery G on the twentieth, the musician stole the show as he played

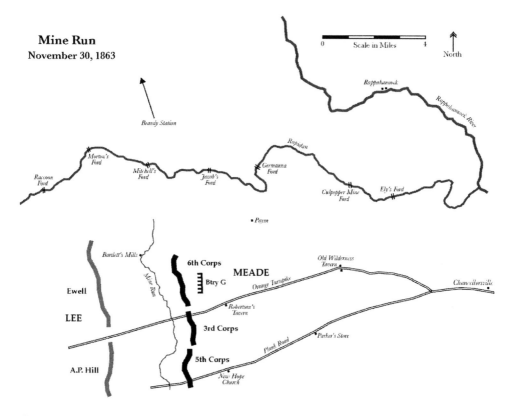

Mine Run
November 30, 1863

the commands before General Sedgwick in his fancy dress jacket. He wrote, "The captain said that i looked the best of any bugler there he think a great deal of me." Adams also extended his liberal benefits to good soldiers by giving Lewis additional privileges: "i can go and come just as i like." The four months of camp duty had partially rebuilt the Army of the Potomac; now the time had come to strike.[17]

Finally, at the end of November, Meade decided to launch another campaign. He allowed the army to rest on Thanksgiving before commencing on November 27. In Battery G, the men feared the results of the campaign. "The enemy have all the advantage of position, every foot of ground beyond the Rapidan will be red with blood: but; if we accomplish the object—Gordonsville—it will do much towards closing the struggle," recorded Private Gaskell. The men awoke at 2:00 on the morning of the twenty-seventh as Bugler Lewis blew reveille; within a short time the command was underway. Before marching, Captain Adams read a special order informing his men of the victory at Chattanooga, Tennessee, several days earlier. This simple message raised their spirits as they again started south through the cold weather. The Army of the Potomac marched for Mine Run, west of Fredericksburg, where the Army of Northern Virginia was lurking. Like the previous year it was too late in the season to begin a campaign. Every day it continued to rain as the tired cannoneers strained their muscles to keep the battery moving; they simply refused to abandon the guns by the side of the road.[18]

After several days of indecisive minor skirmishing Lee drew the Army of Northern Virginia up against the banks of Mine Run. It had taken the battery from 1:00 A.M. on the twenty-eighth until eight on the morning of November 30 to reach its position. During the march the men had to ford the freezing Rapidan River and pass over the Payne's Farm battlefield, where the Third Corps had been heavily engaged on November 28. With the Confederates in such a daunting position, Captain Adams knew that his Rhode Islanders would be needed quickly as they marched down the Orange Turnpike to join in the rest of the Sixth Corps on the right flank of the Army of the Potomac.[19]

As soon as they arrived on the field, Colonel Tompkins directed Battery G into position near Robertson's Tavern; directly across from them, across Mine Run and waiting in a woodlot, were the Confederates. Adams instantly ordered his men to take the shovels and axes off the caissons and begin throwing up entrenchments. The cannoneers struggled to clear part of a thicket to their front which obstructed the field of fire. Instantly the battery came under fire; fortunately, only one man was hit, the injury just a small flesh wound, and the unidentified private never went to the hospital.

That same morning, Meade planned to assault the impregnable line; it would be murder for the Union soldiers attacking it. At 8:30, General Sedgwick ordered the Sixth Corps artillery, including Battery G, to begin a preparatory bombardment. Corporal Barber was there, serving with the Westerly Boys: "Our Battery opened fire followed by the enemy with the large 20 pdr Parrotts Guns and a brisk little Artillery dewel was kept up for a hour and the rebels finding our fire to effective on their lines ceased firing." The unit shelled the Confederate line, expanding 111 rounds of ammunition. The preparatory bombardment was having some effect, as recorded by one of Colonel Martin McMahon of General Sedgwick's staff: "Sedgwick opened fire with all his batteries at the hour indicated. The enemy replied with spirit, but in such a manner as to continue the view that his line at this point was not strongly held. The fire of the batteries prevented anything looking to reinforcement of the enemy's position, which was in our left front." The return fire also struck Battery G's position and damaged the axle of one of the cannon, rendering it inoperable during the action. After the short bombardment Adams ordered his men to cease firing, as the infantry prepared to assault at 9:00 A.M. He quickly rescinded the order and the men resumed.[20]

The Sixth Corps was the general reserve for the entire army. The soldiers could look out across the field and realize what they were walking into: it was Fredericksburg all over again. An anxious New Yorker, waiting to charge, recorded as the Sixth Corps artillery continued its barrage, "The artillery has kept up a constant roar in almost vain attempts to shells the rebs out of the woods." At the designated hour, no orders arrived from head-

The encampment of the Sixth Corps Artillery Brigade at Brandy Station during the winter of 1864 (Library of Congress).

quarters. Another hour went by, still no orders. General Sedgwick received an urgent message from Meade: "Suspend the attack until further orders." Some artillery firing had continued as the battery commanders tried to soften up the Confederate defenses as Colonel Tompkins galloped along the line ordering them to cease fire, which was met with the same response from the Rebel positions. Corporal Barber recalled, "The Genl. finding the rebs had damed up a stream and the water was to deep for our men to ford the weather was so could for wounded men the charge was postponed." The soldiers in the Army of the Potomac realized that Meade had lost his nerve; he saved many lives by not ordering an attack.[21]

Nearly 1,500 Union soldiers became casualties in the brief campaign, while some men froze to death at night. The forage for the horses ran out on the first, forcing the men to find food for their mounts. At 4:00 that morning Adams ordered his men to limber up as they began to withdraw back to the Rapidan. On December 2, the Army of the Potomac abandoned the Mine Run Campaign, and Battery G completed their second year in the army. The battery fell back twenty-eight miles over two days, crossing the freezing Rapidan along the way. By the sixth day of December, the entire army had arrived back at Brandy Station. It was here that Battery G would make its encampment the winter of 1864, along the banks of Hazel Run. Brandy Station presented Meade with a good location; he was safely across the Rapidan River and could still protect Washington.[22]

Private George L. Gaskell continued to work hard as the orderly to Captain Adams, in addition to serving as the guidon bearer, battery clerk, and chief cook. This work did not go unnoticed. His two years of duty were rewarded with a commission as a second lieutenant in the Fourteenth Rhode Island Heavy Artillery. This was a black regiment in the final processes of being outfitted in Rhode Island; already two battalions were serving in Louisiana. Although a Rhode Island unit, only Companies A and B were composed of the state's small free black population; nearly every other soldier was from New York, Kentucky, or Tennessee who had been transported to an island in Narragansett Bay for training. The captains and lieutenants were mostly former enlisted men in different Rhode Island regiments who had proven themselves in their respective stations and were worthy of promotion to officer rank but could not receive it in their own regiments. Despite his reservations about blacks, this represented Gaskell's only chance for the promotion he had been craving. Though commissioned by the state, the officers still had to pass a rigid examination in Washington before General Silas Casey, a native of North Kingstown. Private Gaskell was wary about taking the commission. He only had a year left to serve of his three-year enlistment; he also feared he would not pass the test. He wrote, "I am proud of the offer. Still I mean to show that I fight for Country and not money." As an officer, Gaskell would receive over one hundred dollars per month instead of thirteen. Furthermore, an acquaintance Corporal George W. Cole, who had been discharged from Battery G because of a Peninsula related illness, returned to the Fourteenth as a captain. Private Gaskell accepted the commission and passed the test. In January 1864, he left Battery G and traveled to the swamps of Louisiana to join his regiment.[23]

The Sixth Corps was encamped on the plantation of John Minor Botts, a prominent Virginia Unionist. The men began the winter at Brandy Station much as they had done the winter before at Falmouth. Wood was gathered to build the small huts while a corral protected the horses. Instead of cutting a large portion of the timber, the drivers in Battery G simply gathered the fence rails from local farmers to build the stable with. Prior to the war, Botts had claimed 600 miles of split rail fence on his property. A week into the winter camp there was none left; he was reimbursed for the loss. The Sixth Corps encampment was named Camp Sedgwick, in honor of their commander. The ninth of December brought yet another batch of recruits to Battery G. Unlike others, these men were all trained soldiers. Under a special provision, Rhode Island infantrymen were allowed to transfer from their regiments into the First Rhode Island Light Artillery to raise the numbers in the batteries: nine were sent to Battery G. All of these men came from the Second Rhode Island; most of them were draftees or substitutes from July of 1863 who found the infantry service disagreeable and decided to transfer on their own. Private Thomas Byrnes was an Irishman who had performed well in the infantry, rising to the rank of sergeant. Like Lieutenant Edward Sears, he took a demotion, this time to private, to join Battery G. Their arrival added even more permanent men to the battery's role. As Westerly's First Sergeant Chace called the roll that day, he had even more disparaging news to report to Captain Adams. While nine men had been added to the roll, two were gone. Privates James Carroll and William Osmond of Providence both deserted during the course of the day and were never seen again in the Army of the Potomac.[24]

While Battery G added strength to the unit, the Sixth Corps lost one man on the eighteenth. He was a bounty jumper who had been caught deserting. Rather than simply jail time, the sentence was death, much as it had been for Jesse Young. This time there was no pardon and President Lincoln upheld the sentence. At high noon the entire corps formed in a three sided square for the execution. The prisoner was brought in on a wagon containing his own coffin and was given time to pray. Meanwhile a firing party from his regiment stood by to carry out the sentence. Finally, it was time and the detail fired the volley, breaking the still Virginia air. Each man in the Sixth Corps was then forced to walk by the scene to see the results for themselves. This was thought to have a positive effect on the army, but it did not deter desertion, especially in Adams' Battery. With the frightful event over, the men of Battery G returned to camp hoping for a quiet winter.[25]

On December 26, the original members who reenlisted received the best Christmas present many ever were given. Captain Adams announced that those who had reenlisted would receive their thirty-five day furloughs after the New Year. In addition to the original members who reenlisted, thirty-two other members of Battery G who had joined in March and August of 1862 "went in for three years more." Their reenlistment, coupled with the substitutes and detached men, would insure Battery G would not face the humiliation of being combined with another battery. Twenty men did not reenlist. Captain Adams was authorized to grant them a special bonus of one hundred dollars for reenlisting for an additional year, but none of the men took it. Before leaving for home, the men were paid the 100 dollar bounty promised to them when they enlisted in 1861. Neighboring Battery C was not so fortunate; they led the regiment in total losses to date and only thirty of the soldiers reenlisted. With their service over in August these men would be without a home. While the original members returned home, the remainder of the battery resumed the general duties of camp life. As promised, on New Year's Day the first group of men left Brandy Station for Providence; the artillerists went home in staggered increments to insure that men were always present.[26]

The year 1863 was the critical turning point of the war. With the Union victories at Gettysburg and Vicksburg, it appeared as though the Federals would finally prevail. The men of Battery G remembered 1863 as the year that brought emancipation, two new captains, a bloodbath, an epic march North, and several court martials, as well as the usual set of deserters and substitutes. Private James Barber of Westerly had seen both triumph and defeat during the year, but the war was still not over. He could best sum up 1863: "Another year has passed in sad lamentation and numerous battles have been fought during this seasons campaign and but little advantage has been gained over the enemies of this country."[27]

The winter passed very quietly for the battery. Other than a thick, pasty mud that covered the camp it was quite pleasant. Christmas was celebrated in camp with a barrel of whiskey purchased for the enlisted men by Captain Adams. Although the substance had plagued Battery G since the beginning, it was a tradition of Adams to donate a cask of an intoxicating beverage to his command for Christmas; in Battery B the men drank beer. Camp life was quite enjoyable as the men recalled the past year's experiences. Corporal James Barber called it "pleasant days." The rations were good and the mail always got to camp. Furthermore the disease which had plagued Battery G in 1862 largely subsided; except for occasional colds, illness was virtually nonexistent. Daily inspections, dress parade, and taking the carriages apart and placing them back together occupied most of the time. Two nights a week First Lieutenant Elmer Corthell held meetings in his hut for the non-commissioned officers. Here the lieutenant went over the drill books night after night, studying advanced tactics in gunnery, many of which were not in the books. Lieutenant Corthell had risen in rank from private to lieutenant and knew how to properly handle his guns in combat. In addition, he was a good teacher; when the men went away they were better trained in use of the guns.[28]

The men continued to go on their furloughs in squads of four or five. Before leaving camp, many drew a new mounted services jacket. The bright red piping was sure to impress relatives or sweethearts, far more than the rags the battery was sometimes forced to wear. The Westerly Boys enjoyed their time at home, while also spending some of their bounty money. Nearly to a man they visited John Schofield's photographic studio in downtown to have their images taken. Wearing their uniforms and leaning against a chair, the proud men from southwestern Rhode Island enjoyed a brief moment of rest in a hellish storm. The men were on an honor system to return to Battery G when their thirty-five days were over, and nearly all of the men did. Five of them did not. Four of these were native Rhode Islanders who had enlisted in 1861 but deserted while at home. The fifth man, William Dawson, was an attached recruit from the Tenth New York Battery.[29]

Lieutenant Elmer L. Corthell established a school of instruction for the noncommissioned officers and was promoted for gallantry at Cedar Creek.

As the furloughs of the men expired and they did not return, Captain Adams ordered them reported as deserters; a five dollar bounty was offered for bringing one to a provost marshal in Providence. Private Patrick Brown was among those who overstayed his return home. He had good reason, as he was severely ill with a disease he had contracted in the service and was unable to move. Still, the soldier had purchased a ticket back to

New York to rejoin the army. As he was lying in bed sick, a party of men broke into his house and arrested him. They brought the bewildered soldier to the provost office in Providence as the posse collected a bounty for capturing a supposed deserter. Brown was returned to Brandy Station under guard to face the charges. He told the truth, that he was sick, and produced the ticket. Adams believed the private and dropped the charge of desertion. Corporal James Barber was another soldier who arrived late from his furlough. Arriving in camp on March 17, he feared he would be punished for being four days late, the reason being there was no transport from Washington to Brandy Station. Much to his relief Captain Adams was on his furlough in Providence at the time and Barber was free.[30]

At the Brandy Station camp, the men in Battery G began to perform their first assignment at regular guard duty. Each day, a lieutenant, sergeant, corporal, and nine privates were assigned to the duty. Armed with their revolvers or sabers, the men were on duty for eight-hour shifts, with three on each rotation. They had to watch the horses and gun line to make sure no one tampered with either. Furthermore, they were responsible for watching any prisoners held in the guardhouse. These duties were monotonous until the night of March 7. That night Corporal Benjamin Tennant and Privates Patrick Breman and Patrick O'Brien were under arrest for being drunk on duty. During the night, a member of the battery slipped past the guard and released the three men. They were apprehended in the camp the following morning. Captain Adams was furious that someone committed the act, but even more so that the guard was not watching the small building. The captain personally offered a twenty-five dollar reward for the arrest of the perpetrator, but he was never found. After that night, the number of privates in the guard was doubled to prevent such an incident from happening again.[31]

One day William Lewis received a letter from his mother, who needed false teeth; he promptly obliged with the necessary funds. In late March, Colonel Tompkins organized some training for his brigade; each battery got to fire several shots across Hazel Run to test their accuracy and precession. This was only the second time Battery G had managed to accomplish this since their tour of duty on the Potomac. Many of the Sixth Corps soldiers went down and viewed the performance. Sergeant John Hartwell of New York called it a "noisy & busy time." The training had its effect as each battery tested out their guns for correctness but also as a means of gentlemanly competition to see which unit was the most accurate; that honor went to the First Massachusetts Battery.[32]

As the first signs of spring began to appear so too did another com-

Major General Horatio Wright replaced the beloved "Uncle" John Sedgwick, gaining Battery G's favor and granting Captain Adams permission to charge at Petersburg (Library of Congress).

mander for the Army of the Potomac. Imported from the West to end the war in the East was the recently promoted Lieutenant General Ulysses S. Grant. He was well known throughout the entire country; for two years he had been winning victory after victory in the western theatre of the war, including opening the Mississippi River at Vicksburg on July 4, 1863. Now Lincoln called him east to take command of all Union armies and finally end the war. Grant placed himself in a position to supervise the Army of the Potomac, although George Meade was still the de facto commander. Grant would direct him where to go, ordering Meade to follow Lee to the death. On April 18, he arrived in the camp of the Sixth Corps at Brandy Station and was treated to a review of the entire corps, including Battery G, which proudly marched by their new commander. The battery was issued new white gloves to perform the impressive light artillery movements before the general. Corporal Barber called it "a splendid appearance."

On April 24, two privates in the battery were baptized in Hazel Run. Because of its unique combination of Catholics from Providence and the many different types of Baptist faiths found in the western reaches of Rhode Island, Battery G truly represented Roger Williams' "lively experiment" of religious freedom begun in 1636. Chaplain John D. Beugless of the Second Rhode Island, a Freewill Baptist minister from Warwick, conducted the ceremony. The men wore their uniforms, but were given white robes for the baptism. Hundreds of Union soldiers watched the scene as the men underwent this rite of passage. When it was over, they prayed at a specially constructed church at the Second's camp.[33]

The winter of 1864 was a productive one for Battery G. Sixty men reenlisted as veterans, while only one of the soldiers died of the disease which had plagued the battery for so long. The paymaster visited on schedule, and on April 16 he delivered the first $150 installment of the veteran's bounty. The twenty-seventh of April brought yet another ten attached soldiers to Battery G. These men were from the Fourth New York Heavy Artillery, four companies of which were assigned to the Sixth Corps Artillery Brigade to guard the supply wagons and perform other duties, thus relieving the light artillerymen employed in these areas so they could return to duty with their batteries. The Fourth New York was originally assigned to the defenses of Washington, to man the heavy guns and forts surrounding the city, but it was transferred to the field in the spring of 1863. With their assignment to Battery G, a third of the 119 privates in the command were detached from New York regiments. Although men were constantly in the process of moving into and out of Battery G, three men left for good with a transfer to the United States Navy. Among them was the constantly intoxicated Private Patrick O'Brien.[34]

On April 30, Quartermaster Sergeant William B. Westcott received a commission as a second lieutenant and transferred to Battery H. He was replaced by Sergeant William W. Potter. Despite the earlier incidents of drunkenness, Potter still showed his mettle and was appointed until a sergeant could fill the position. He never officially was mustered in as the quartermaster sergeant, receiving an additional stripe and pay. The same day he was promoted, Potter instigated a thorough inspection of the battery, making sure all was in order and no equipment was needed before the campaign began. Sergeant Albert C. Gray, a detached man from the Tenth New York Battery was one of the last in the battery to receive a furlough, as the other soldiers were allowed to have theirs first. After reading in the New York papers that a new campaign was immanent, Gray arrived back at Brandy Station on April 29, ten days before he was due in. The time had come once more.[35]

11

Overland to Richmond

On the 12th battery opened at 5 A.M.; continued firing until 3 P.M.
—Captain George W. Adams, May 12, 1864

Throughout the winter of 1864, the officers and men of Battery G had prepared for combat. Remembering the carnage of Marye's Heights and the unpleasantness of Otto Torslow's court martial, Captain Adams had trained his command all winter long, with additional training in gunnery being provided by Lieutenant Corthell. With the refreshment of their winter furloughs, the soldiers were prepared as a new commander issued them orders to follow Lee to the death. The first of May brought orders to reduce the baggage load once more, and all that was unneeded was sent home or thrown away.

May brought yet another new officer to Battery G to replace James Chase, recently promoted to Battery B. The replacement was Second Lieutenant Charles V. Scott of Providence. The lieutenant was twenty years old and had worked at a screw factory in Providence before the war. Totally devoted to his widowed mother, Amanda, he gave her all of his pay when he was employed as a machinist and continued to support her fully while in the army. For Scott this promotion took nearly three years to reach him. At First Bull Run he was responsible for saving the only gun of Battery A to escape the battle. He further distinguished himself on the Potomac River by swimming into Virginia to conduct reconnaissance missions. In addition, Scott had been among the hundreds of Rhode Islanders wounded at Fredericksburg. At the time of the promotion, Scott was serving as a sergeant. Governor James Y. Smith had finally received word of his actions at Bull Run and promoted him to second lieutenant. Scott received command of the center section.[1]

After months of waiting, the orders from Grant finally came on the morning of May 3: the Sixth Corps was to leave Brandy Station at four in the morning the following day. The soldiers in Battery G prepared for the move by making sure there were fifty rounds in each limber chest, the harnesses were oiled, and each bolt and fellow was secure on the carriages. Corporal Barber was among those waiting: "Things is all ready and we are to moove in the morning." At 6:00 on the morning of May 4, as the rolls were called, two Irishmen, Privates Patrick Brennan and John Burke, were found to have deserted that night. With red Greek crosses on their hats, Battery G, First Rhode Island Light Artillery, left Brandy Station for the last great campaign of the Civil War. Ahead for the command lay agony, carnage, and glory.[2]

General Grant directed the army out of the winter camps on yet another campaign south. Grant was now the commander of all the Federal armies, but he stayed with the Army of the Potomac. His plan for battle was almost identical to that of the previous commanders of the main army in the East; the army would constantly maneuver around Lee's flank, thus avoiding direct contact at all possible hazards, while moving in to capture Richmond. Standing in the way was Robert E. Lee and the 70,000 veterans that comprised the Army of Northern Virginia. Although the force had suffered massive casualties, including

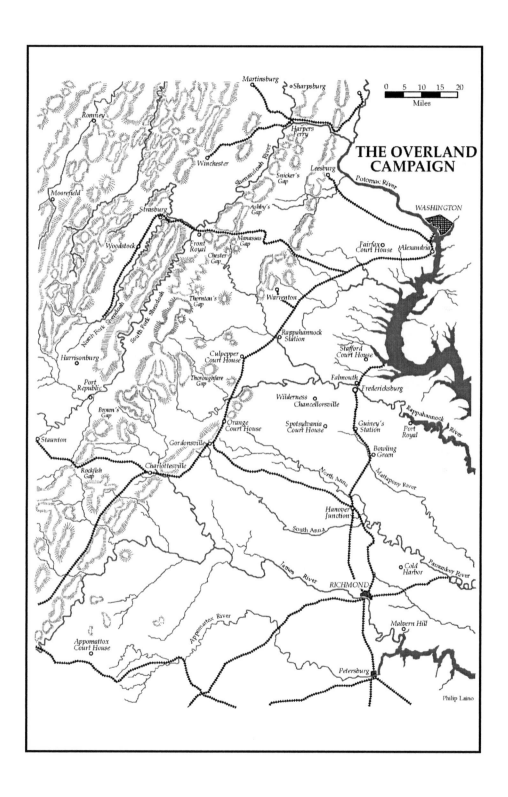

THE OVERLAND
CAMPAIGN

Philip Laino

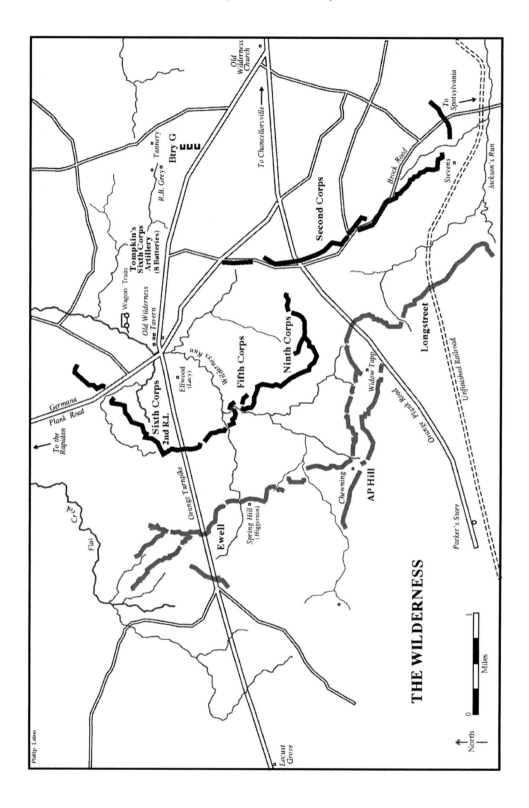

THE WILDERNESS

many formidable commanders, the Confederate army again prepared to fight with the same zeal that had carried them through three years of war.

The Army of the Potomac had changed radically over the winter. At Gettysburg there were seven corps present; now only three comprised the army, while the Ninth and Cavalry Corps were attached. Because the First and Third corps had been split up between the Second and Fifth to make up for losses at Gettysburg, the Sixth only received two brigades to join its third division. In total, the Army of the Potomac mustered 125,000 men, while 23,500 of these were in the Sixth Corps; it was the smallest in the army. Many of the famed veteran regiments, including the Second Rhode Island, were mere skeletons of their former selves, having only one hundred original members and the rest being drafted men or raw recruits.[3]

Colonel Tompkins now commanded nine batteries in his brigade. It was a largely Yankee outfit: one battery from Maine and Massachusetts, two from New York, one of Regulars, and a battalion of the Fourth New York Heavy Artillery to guard the trains and provide support to the batteries in the field. Most important to Tompkins were three batteries of his own regiment. Batteries C and G of the First Rhode Island Light Artillery had been part of the brigade since before Gettysburg. With the Third Corps disbanded, Battery E was transferred to the brigade. The battery was under the command of Captain William B. Rhodes, a former lieutenant in Battery G. Although the Federals had a large numerical advantage, there was always the perceived fear they were outnumbered.[4]

After fording the Rapidan River, the Overland Campaign began almost immediately on the morning of May 5, when Union scouts from the Fifth Corps located a large enemy force. Moving west along the old Chancellorsville battlefield, the Army of the Potomac found the Confederates in the thick undergrowth of a forest called the Wilderness. The Sixth Corps infantry was in the thick of the fight. The Second Rhode Island, part of the Second Division, was engaged in a bloodbath as the division tried to hold the critical junction of the Brock road and Orange Turnpike to prevent the enemy from smashing through the center of Grant's line. Somehow, the Rhode Islanders, Pennsylvanians, and Vermonters held on for two days, but at a terrible cost: half the division went down. In two days of hellish fighting, Northerners and Southerners fought each other to a standstill in a see-saw action. There was little use of cavalry or artillery; the dense woodlots, combined with relatively tight open fields, made it impossible for the mounted commands to move in the forest. The woods caught on fire as the two forces exchanged point-blank musket fire in a swirling mass of confusion.[5]

At 5:00 on the morning of the fifth, Colonel Charles Tompkins and his Sixth Corps Artillery Brigade followed Sedgwick into the fight, but were of no use in the battle. Tompkins brought his nine batteries down the Germanna Plank Road to the Wilderness Tavern. From this central location, all of the supply wagons and artillery were located until called for. Tompkins deployed Battery G a mile to the east of the tavern, near the farm of Robert B. Grey, to defend the Orange Turnpike in the event the Confederates flanked the position and attacked from the rear. Captain Adams deployed the six guns along the road, waiting to be used if called for; but no orders ever came. The men simply sat alongside the road, listening to the battle rage around them. Corporal Barber heard "the sharp crackling of rifles close in our front and this told us the enemy was near."

Battery G spent the sixth of May guarding prisoners with the Fourth New York. As some Fifth Corps troops ran by the battery in disorder, the prisoners began cheering, as the Rebels held the upper hand. Several used the confusion to try to escape; they were quickly shot down by the pistols of the noncommissioned officers. The thick masses of Fed-

eral and Confederate forces simply hurled themselves at each other until Rebel reinforcements arrived on May 6, repulsing the Army of the Potomac. After two days of indescrib-
able combat, no ground was gained by either side: it was a draw. The Army of the Potomac
lost 18,000 to Lee's 9,000.[6]

With the carnage of the Wilderness over, Grant decided on a fateful course. After
being defeated in battle, every commander of the Army of the Potomac had returned to
Washington demoralized and defeated. The new commander made a critical decision; he
would not turn back, but would keep on marching south. The men cheered, knowing that
this commander was not going to let them down. Silently, on the night of May 8, the Sixth
Corps pulled out of the Wilderness and marched south. The soldiers passed the Chancellorsville battlefield; it had been a year since Battery G's own bloodbath at Marye's Heights.
After suffering 20,000 casualties in the opening stages of the campaign, Grant decided to
march onward to a small crossroads village called Spotsylvania.[7]

Ever quick to move, Lee brought his army into the area first, as it was on the road
leading directly to Richmond. Here the Army of Northern Virginia built a series of impenetrable defenses. Deep trenches were constructed to completely shield the defenders. They
were reinforced with earth, branches, logs, and sharpened sticks. Into the entrenchments,
Lee placed his infantry and artillery, creating a position that was even more defensible than
the line that was at Marye's Heights. The main position was placed around the high ground
near the McCool House. The Rebels continued to build the defensive position, which took
the shape of an inverted letter "u." The works were brilliantly built; the Confederate high
command firmly believed that they would not be broken and built a further series of

The Battle of Spotsylvania was remembered as one of the worst of the war. Here the Sixth Corps
assaults the Mule Shoe as the artillery supports.

defenses in the rear to retreat to in the event there was a breakthrough. The attacking Federals named the position the Mule Shoe salient.

While Lee dug in around Spotsylvania, Grant ordered an assault to test the defenses on May 9, which was easily beaten back. He would wait until more Federals arrived from the Wilderness. As Battery G traveled via the Brock Road, they passed a large field hospital where the artillerists could view the horrors of battlefield surgery being performed. The Sixth Corps was the first Federal unit to arrive at Spotsylvania; instantly they came under fire. Sharpshooters posted in the trees became annoying, hitting some of the soldiers and sending others to the rear, as they could not stand the sporadic fire. These sharpshooters were considered little more then murderers.[8]

Major General John Sedgwick and Colonel Charles Tompkins arrived on the field with the lead elements of the corps and promptly began making plans to place the Sixth Corps artillery. Battery G and the First Massachusetts moved up to their place in the First Division line and unlimbered, prepared for action. After watching a group of men retreat from the sniper fire Sedgwick said, "They could not hit an elephant at that distance." No sooner had the general spoken the words when he was shot through the eye. Colonel Tompkins was at his side; he caught Sedgwick as he fell and beckoned for a stretcher bearer, but it was too late.

The men in Battery G saw Sedgwick being carried away, but the officers would not say what happened to him. In his diary, James Barber simply wrote, "Genl. Sedgwick was killed today by a sharpshooter." Of the thousands of men General Sedgwick had commanded in a career spanning over thirty years, none had served under him longer than Colonel Tompkins and Battery G. His loss was felt severely. Although some believed he had needlessly sacrificed the battery at Marye's Heights, Sedgwick had always performed his duty with ardor and was viewed as a father figure by his men. Now "Uncle John," as the soldiers called their beloved commander, was dead at age fifty-one. Grant considered his loss worth that of a division. General Sedgwick's body was returned to Cornwall, Connecticut, where for decades afterwards Sixth Corps veterans would visit; the monument was surmounted by a large Greek cross. With the senior corps commander dead, General Grant selected Horatio Wright, commanding the Sixth Corps' First Division. Wright was well known to the Rhode Islanders, as they had been transferred from acting with the Third Division the previous winter and were now in the First. General David Russell moved to command the division.[9]

On the ninth, Colonel Emory Upton, commanding a brigade in the First Division, Sixth Corps, brought his plan to Wright and Grant's attention. By massing a large force of infantry in column, they could smash through the enemy's line without firing a shot, then deploy in the works and start fighting. This had already worked brilliantly for the Sixth Corps at Marye's Heights. The idea had great promise and Grant gave his consent; Upton picked twelve regiments and prepared them for the assault, which came on May 10. Upton's Assault was a success; the regiments crashed through the Confederates defenses, captured hundreds of prisoners, and almost made it, but no reinforcements were brought up. The Federals abandoned the works and took their prisoners to the rear; Upton was rewarded with an on-the-spot promotion to general. During the charge, Battery G moved onto the Brock Road and went into battery in the rear of the Vermont Brigade. Although the rest of the Sixth Corps artillery was heavily engaged in the battle, Battery G was not. The cannoneers began to fear that they would never see any fighting in the battles, leading Corporal Barber to write. "Our batry has not fired a single shot at the enemy." All this was about to change.[10]

The initial success of Upton's Assault on May 10 was followed with the same idea and plan on May 12. Early in the morning, Major General Winfield S. Hancock and the 15,000 soldiers of the Second Corps broke through the Confederate defenses around the Mule Shoe, capturing an entire division; the pouring rain and the absence of Confederate artillery were large factors, as it was a formidable position with these defenses in place. Battery B, First Rhode Island Light Artillery, charged along with the infantry, firing point blank blasts of double canister right into the position to drive the Confederates from their works. The shattered Southern forces retreated to another line of entrenchments a half mile in the rear of the Mule Shoe and began to fortify them again. The Second Corps charged again, and for twenty hours in the pouring rain, both sides killed and wounded each other with clubs, swords, and bayonets. It was the most insane, nonstop fighting the world had ever witnessed.[11]

At the Mule Shoe, it was attack and counterattack as both sides retreated and advanced constantly. Bodies became so compacted in the narrow works that there was barely room to stand; after the battle, the fortifications were simply collapsed on top of them. As the Second Corps fought on, Grant ordered the rest of the Army of the Potomac into action to support them. At 5:00 in the morning, some Sixth Corps units fell back in disarray as Colonel Tompkins galloped along the lines shouting out orders for his batteries to open fire. Within thirty seconds, Battery G was sending shells screeching into the Confederate positions a half mile away. Corporal James Barber wrote, "Our men stood by their little guns as shell after shell came whistling close overhead. The artillery nearly shook the earth where it stood and the screeching of the murderous projectiles seemed as if the work had begun." Although the farthest Sixth Corps unit from the apex of the assault, the Rhode Islanders could still keep their presence known to the enemy. The combined fire of nearly 100 cannon was having some effect: "Their fire soon become so week they did but little harm to our men and horses."[12]

The situation was very similar to that of the previous July at Granite Hill. The rain prevented much of the infantry from firing their muskets. The artillery had no problem, as the primers fired their small flame into the flannel powder bags, causing the explosion as the round left the tube. The mountains of smoke, combined with the torrents of rain and the groaning of thousands of wounded Americans in the moonscape of Spotsylvania, led to an unbelievable scene that the Rhode Islanders in Battery G continued to fight through.

For the entire day, as both the Confederates and rain pounded away at the Sixth Corps, Battery G kept up a steady fire, occasionally having to

A cigar maker from Providence, Private Thomas Wilson spent most of the war on Colonel Tompkins' staff (courtesy Phil DiMaria, Battery B 1st Rhode Island Light Artillery Inc.).

elevate the guns to prevent friendly fire as the Federals advanced. In the storm of both metal and rain, a calm wind blew for just a brief moment, which allowed Captain Adams and the section commanders to finally see their targets across the meadow in the Confederate entrenchments. Instantly the officers of all the Sixth Corps batteries called for case as they began pounding the target, seeing the first real results of the day. In the midst of controlling his section in combat for the first time, Lieutenant Scott was calm and reserved, while urging his men to do their utmost—the primary traits of an officer. Just as the batteries were finding their mark, a young staff officer from General Wright came galloping up to the line with some terrible news. The Vermont Brigade had seized the works to their front and were piling in; the shots were killing Union soldiers. The officers instantly ordered a stop, but not before a sobering event. The First Massachusetts Battery failed to halt in time and a shot accidentally killed two men in the Second Rhode Island, which held its position near the Mule Shoe, in the midst of a fusillade of lead. The begrimed men in blue and red let out a cheer as they saw their brothers make a breech in the line. It was only for an instant, as the Confederates instantly counterattacked and the Federals continued to blaze away as well.[13]

For Battery G the battle and slaughter continued, even as the chiefs of caissons reported that the limbers needed to be changed frequently. Every round of solid shot, case, and shell was used—all the ammunition except for canister, which could not be brought into effect because it was a short range round. The fire was very effective on the enemy, as nearly every shot hit the entrenchments. The smoke and the rain obscured the entire field as the cannoneers fired in the direction of the fighting near the Mule Shoe. "Our Battery kept up its fire all day and night," recorded Corporal Barber. When the ammunition in the limbers and caissons was expended, the men turned to the enemy for supplies. Hancock's success had captured forty-two cannon and tons of ammunition. Barber wrote, "Our men brought off the Guns and caissons after they had been shattered nearly to pieces by bullets and none was fit for service."[14]

The cannoneers scurried around trying to find three-inch ammunition for the use of the six cannon. Several cases of the Hotchkiss rounds, especially made for the ordnance rifle, were located among the debris of the battlefield, allowing the battery to go back into the fight. James Barber was horrified at the scenes he saw inside the Confederate works: "Our battery fired away all its ammunition we had and planted our missels in the rebel lines making great havoc in their ranks and dismounting their artillery cutting down the trees and destroying their works." At high noon, the soaking wet artillerists begrudgingly limbered up and moved to a position near the center of the line to properly support the actions at the Mule Shoe, where they continued the barrage; neither side would budge from the Mule Shoe, despite the tons of ordnance being used. In total, Battery G expended 873 rounds of ammunition, the most ever fired by the command in a single engagement. Colonel Tompkins called May 12, 1864, "the hard fight." As the rain pressed on, a surprising sight passed Battery G in the form of Battery H, First Rhode Island Light Artillery. This was the last battery in the regiment and had recently been released from the Washington defenses to serve at the front. As the storm continued, the Rhode Islanders briefly met to exchange pleasantries as Battery H marched to join the Ninth Corps on the right of the line. Finally, the battery stopped firing at 3:00 and the men retired to the rear to eat, but, more important, to sleep. The fatigue of ten hours of nonstop combat had taken its toll; the cannoneers were exhausted. Corporal Edward P. Adams recounted, "Used up five and half tons of iron and did not lose a single man or horse."[15]

Remarkably, the casualties had been almost nonexistent in Battery G; the story was

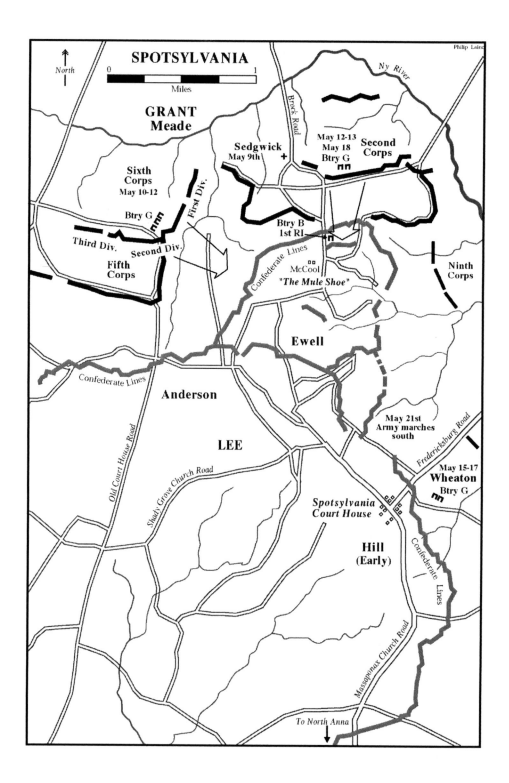

Philip Laino

SPOTSYLVANIA

North

0   Miles   1

GRANT
Meade

Ny River

Brock Road

Sedgwick
May 9th

May 12-13
May 18
Btry G

Second
Corps

Sixth
Corps
May 10-12

Btry G

First Div.

Third Div.   Second Div.

Fifth
Corps

Btry B
1st RI

Confederate Lines

McCool
"The Mule Shoe"

Ninth
Corps

Ewell

Confederate Lines

Anderson

May 21st
Army marches
south

Fredericksburg Road

LEE

Old Court House Road

Shady Grove Church Road

May 15-17
Wheaton
Btry G

Spotsylvania
Court House

Confederate Lines

Hill
(Early)

Massaponax Church Road

To North Anna

far different for the Sixth Corps infantry. Only one soldier was wounded—in the head by a shell fragment. This was Private Duncan Patterson, on detached duty from the Tenth New York Battery. In 1863, the unfortunate soldier had been captured by Mosby's Rangers following the Gettysburg Campaign. His wound now was slight, and he soon returned to duty. In circumstances very similar to that of Private John L. Rathbun two years earlier at Fair Oaks, Private James Callahan was captured. He was a young weaver from Pawtucket who was transferred from the Second Rhode Island. The private became separated from the battery during the day and was captured by a Confederate patrol. Callahan was sent to the infamous Andersonville prison in Georgia, where he died of dysentery in July; he was one of three Battery G soldiers who died from the effects of Confederate imprisonment. For the first and only time, none of the men from southwestern Rhode Island were among the injured.[16]

That night the soldiers rested on the battlefield, as the fury still raged around them. Corporal Barber was among the exhausted Rhode Islanders: "Our men was played nearly out all covered in mud and the grime of the powder." Fires were forbidden, as they would draw enemy fire, but the men in Battery G built them anyway to dry out their soaking wool uniforms; soon fires were appearing in other camps as both sides rested briefly in the midst of so much destruction.[17]

On May 14, Captain Adams' Rhode Islanders moved yet again, to the far right of the line, near the Ninth Corps positions. The Sixth was brought up to try attacking this portion of the line; Battery G was not called into action. Even so, yet another casualty occurred. Private George D. Fenner had been sent to Washington sick in 1863. There he had recovered, but instead of returning to Battery G, he found himself in Company I, Second United States Infantry. Now as the Fifth Corps attacked on the thirteenth, Private Fenner was killed in action.

Battery G's constant companion since Marye's Heights had been the Second Rhode Island Regiment. Now nearly half the regiment was gone. "There will be sad hearts in R.I. when the news reaches home," wrote Lieutenant Elisha Rhodes. The battles of the Wilderness and Spotsylvania were taking their toll, especially on Company E from Washington County. The company had sustained almost 50 percent casualties. On the fifteenth, the battery moved yet again, this time into a thick woodlot near the Myer Farm to support General Frank Wheaton's brigade; but they remained in reserve until the seventeenth. During this week-long period the battery engaged sporadically, firing into the thick woods and entrenchments only if an enemy could be observed.[18]

The seventeenth of May represented a sad day, but it did not involve the loss of a comrade. The field artillery had required little use in the campaign to date. Therefore, Grant directed the majority of the batteries to return to Washington, as infantry was needed more than the artillery. General Henry Hunt, still serving as the chief of artillery for the Army of the Potomac, intervened. To save the artillery, which Hunt had labored for over two years to perfect and turn into a superb battlefield instrument, several proposals were passed on to Grant that would make it possible to save the guns, and still have artillery within the Army of the Potomac. Hunt asked Grant to let him send part of the Artillery Reserve back and disperse the rest to the corps artillery brigades. In addition, Hunt would reduce each battery by one section—two guns. The fourth lieutenant in a battery was almost always on detached service, leaving a sergeant to command. Now the problem would be eradicated, as Battery G turned in two of the three-inch ordnance rifles that had served the command so well to date. The two caissons which normally followed the guns were retained so more ammunition could be retained for the battery.

Captain George Adams commanded the battery, while First Lieutenant Elmer L.

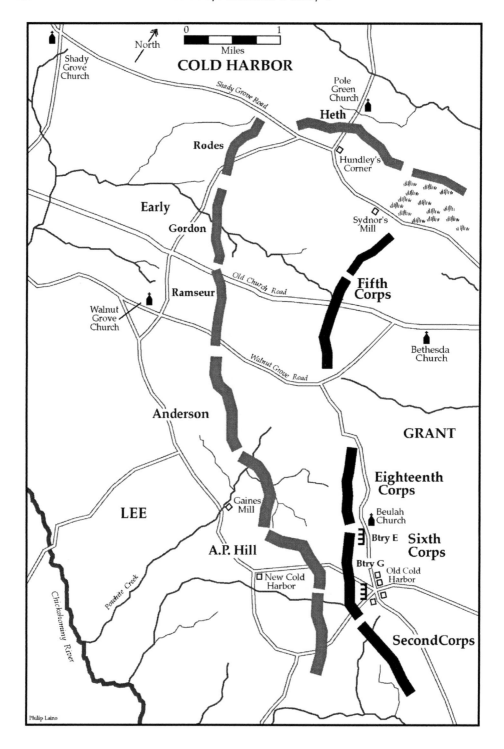

Corthell commanded the right section and Second Lieutenant Charles V. Scott the left. Lieutenant Frank G. Waterman was new to the battery, having recently been promoted from Battery D. Now he moved to command the caissons and baggage train. Lieutenant Otto Torslow remained ill. Allen Hoar had been promoted at the start of the campaign to serve on Colonel Tompkins' staff and would gain the bar of a first lieutenant with a transfer to Battery H on the seventeenth.[19]

At midnight on May 18, Battery G countermarched back to its May 12 position as Grant ordered another head-on assault to end the struggle. The plan was to break through again and totally defeat the Confederate force. It was much the same as on the twelfth, attack and counterattack; but Lee still remained. Again, Adams' Rhode Islanders only fired sporadically. Finally, on May 21, Grant decided the Army of the Potomac was done with the bloody battle at Spotsylvania. His army had again lost heavily, over 21,000 men, but again Grant decided to press on.[20]

Every day there was a battle as the Army of the Potomac pushed further south. On May 23, Battery G and the Sixth Corps in general were spared from the slaughter at another engagement along the banks of the North Anna River. The Army of Northern Virginia was fighting for its very survival at the hands of an unrelenting enemy commander. Barricading every river crossing, they inflicted thousands of casualties on the Federals. The Rebels were only prolonging the inevitable; there was in effect no stopping the Federal onslaught. Each day the Providence papers printed the long casualties lists that the regiments were suffering. Sergeant Charles E. Perkins of the Second Rhode Island wrote, "We have had a very hard time of it. The worst we have ever seen." Despite suffering tens of thousands of casualties, the Federal commander did not back down, proclaiming, "I intend to fight along this line, if it takes all summer."[21]

As Grant pushed on, so did Battery G. The Rhode Islanders continued to follow the Sixth Corps, bringing up its rear as they crossed the Pamunky River. Lee countered with every maneuver he could think of to try to block the massive Union force. Although the Army of Northern Virginia had taken thousands of irreplaceable casualties, hundreds continued to reinforce Lee's main line, coming forward from rear echelon positions. In one month the Federals had suffered 50,000 casualties. Unlike the Confederates, the Army of the Potomac could somewhat afford to take such massive casualties, but not for long, as manpower and public sentiment ran out. Grant directed that the heavy artillery regiments protecting Washington be removed from the fortifications, given muskets, and sent into the field as infantry. Most of these regiments mustered over 1,500 men, making them larger than an infantry brigade. What neither side could replace was competent leaders, such as John Sedgwick and Alexander Hays, who were being shot down every day. The Confederate commander knew that if Federals managed to cross the James River, the only option for him would be to lay siege to Richmond, a move that would ultimately end in a Confederate defeat.

With enough forces now at his disposal, Lee set out to make final effort to try to defeat the Federals. He chose Cold Harbor, named after a small tavern nearby. His men took whatever entrenching tools that were available and began to build another set of impenetrable defenses. Digging down into the yellow clay-like soil, the men constructed trenches to provide immense protective covering for the Rebel defenders. The trenches were reinforced on top by notched logs to protect the soldiers' heads. In addition, the trenches were built back at right angles so that all of the line could be covered. As was the case at Spotsylvania, Lee built his lines along the main route leading to the Federal objective: Richmond. Faced with little room to maneuver, Grant ordered another head-on assault.[22]

This area was well known to the few members of the Army of the Potomac still alive in the ranks who had embarked on the Peninsula Campaign exactly two years earlier; they were fighting on the same ground. Indeed, the bodies and debris of the previous campaigns could be seen all around. The Chickahominy River also wound through the Cold Harbor area. It was this river that had killed more of the soldiers in Battery G than the shells at Marye's Heights. While their first taste of combat at Fair Oaks had sickened many of the veterans from Battery G, the officers and men were now long used to such sights, and indeed, they were so frequent that few took the time to record them, and even fewer had the time to write about the progress of the campaign.[23]

The weather was absolutely brutal and the Confederates howled all night long to keep the Union forces on edge. Rations again became scant when the supply lines were cut; this time the men subsisted on dried corn found in abandoned cribs when the inhabitants fled the advancing armies. Upon arriving at Cold Harbor, the Federals promptly began building trenches of their own. Two battles were fought on the first two days of June; the Federal forces were repulsed with ease. Battery G moved into position as Captain Adams and First Sergeant Chace went over the rolls for their monthly return; not one soldier had deserted during the campaign in May.[24]

On the second of June, Battery G moved into the trench system with the Sixth Corps in a "thick forest." The cannoneers promptly began reinforcing the rough trenches by digging and throwing up the dirt so the guns would be protected against enemy fire, as had been done in front of Fredericksburg. On June 3, Grant ordered an assault of the entire Confederate line; if the Army of the Potomac broke through the war would be over. The Federal advance went awry from the start; commands which should have been in position in time to advance did not, while the Union soldiers simply threw themselves at the defenses, only to be thrown back. The new heavy artillery regiments were slaughtered, as the veterans stayed behind and the new units went forward. The results were not surprising. Many soldiers saw it as murder: 7,000 men became casualties in the assaults, nearly all of them going down within the first ten minutes.[25]

Severely wounded twice in action, Sergeant Alexander B. Sisson of Westerly served with his twin brother, Charles, a private (courtesy Kris VanDenBossche).

Battery G remained in its

position, as sharpshooters, posted in trees around the Sixth Corps position became a problem all day, much as they had been at Spotsylvania. They kept the cannoneers pinned down, unable to perform their duties. This forced the artillerists to hide behind trees, or hug the ground for protection. Finally, the section commanders had enough and Battery G opened fire into the trees opposite. The power of the guns was felt as the bolts and shells knocked down the trees to prevent the Confederates from returning fire; 159 rounds were used on this day. Most of the Rebel fire hitting the position simply annoyed the Rhode Islanders, as it passed harmlessly overhead. Corporal James Barber recalled, "The minnie balls rained upon us for some time."

Some rounds did find their mark, however. Lieutenant Scott received a severe wound to the shoulder; he was evacuated to Washington and then spent two months at home, recovering in Providence. Although seriously wounded, Scott was able to return home in time to take part in the return celebrations for Battery A, his original command. In his one month as a section commander in Battery G, Scott had proven himself a fine officer who knew how to inspire and lead men, while also being a deadly effective combat leader. He would be missed throughout the rest of the summer campaigns. Corporal Daniel Hoxsie of Richmond (who had previously been wounded at Marye's Heights) was shot in the head; he returned to duty, along with Private James H. Horton, who received a slight wound.[26]

The attacks on June 3 accomplished nothing. For the rest of his life Grant would regret ordering the attack: "No advantage was gained to compensate for the heavy loss we sustained." Yet again, the men retired to rest beside the guns on the night of the third. Rations became nonexistent, and the artillerists faced a dreadful sight around them. As Corporal Barber recorded, "The stench from the dead made the air very uncomfortable." Over the next three days the battery was under fire most of the time, occasionally exchanging fire, while doing everything humanly possible to keep their heads down. On June 10, after remaining in position for a week, Battery G again limbered up and turned south. Two days later the command bid farewell to seven more comrades. A small contingent of men detached to the battery from the Fourth New York Heavy Artillery was returned to the unit to make up for losses suffered in the campaign so far.[27]

Battery G crossed the James River on the sixteenth, after camping at Charles City Cross Roads for two days; it was here that the command had started the desperate march to Harrison's Landing. Corporal James Barber recalled the stories he learned as a child about John Smith and Pocahontas; the site of the legend was near where the battery now passed "through long dark columns of men." The river was spanned by an 1,800 foot pontoon bridge, an engineering marvel. On the far side of the river,

Second Lieutenant Frank G. Waterman was transferred to Battery G during the middle of the Overland Campaign but spent much of the Valley Campaign sick in Washington.

the men could see the city of Petersburg. Confederate General Pierre Beauregard had built thirty miles of defenses to protect Richmond and Petersburg. Like the other series of trenches, they were impenetrable and were now heavily defended by the entire Army of Northern Virginia.

Just as in his previous assaults, Grant sent his entire army forward, on June 16 and again over the next two days, only to be repulsed with severe losses. The Army of the Potomac managed to capture some of the trenches. Stubborn Confederate defenses and courage defeated the timidness on the part of several Federal commanders who had already seen the results of such charges at Cold Harbor. Battery G arrived at the outskirts of Petersburg on the nineteenth and moved to a "green shady grove." Battery C of the Sixth Corps was already shelling the line as Adams' Battery moved in. Richmond was so close that the church bells and steeples could clearly be seen, again. After two years of maneuvering north of here, Battery G had finally returned. They had not been this close to Richmond since Fair Oaks in 1862. Unlike the Peninsula Campaign, the Federals suffered over 60,000 casualties to get near the enemy citadel this time.[28]

Immediately the artillerist removed the shovels, axes, and picks on the caissons and helped to build up the Union defenses. "Our whole army is heaving up a line of fortifications," wrote Corporal Barber. The Sixth Corps was thrown on the left of the line, while the batteries were placed in a position 3,000 yards from the enemy positions, at the extreme range of an ordnance rifle. The Confederates kept up a constant bombardment, but fired harmlessly over the Rhode Islanders' position. The soil was extremely dry, allowing the strange Virginia earth to cling to the soldiers, turning their blue uniforms a dingy yellow. The artillerists threw up their shelter tents to ward off the harsh rays of the sun, as they baked in the trenches. Water and whiskey became prized commodities as the soldiers had to travel several miles to find both. The horses suffered as usual, often being deprived of many needs; but like the soldiers, they somehow continued to carry on. After four days of bloody assaults, Grant decided that he would lay siege to the city. For the Confederacy, the end had begun.[29]

Finally, on the nineteenth, Battery G was brought up to help support the attacks. It was deadly work fighting in the trenches before Petersburg. Sharpshooters again kept the command pinned down, but no one was hit. The horses had been removed and sent behind

The cannoneers quickly learned to adapt themselves to fighting in the trenches before Petersburg.

the lines, as the guns of Battery G were put into position, being served by three officers and 129 enlisted men. The limbers and caissons were also taken to the rear, as the ammunition chests had been removed and stacked near the guns so the rounds could be easily grasped in the heat of combat. On the twenty-first, Captain Adams saw a group of Confederate engineers directly in front of the battery, throwing up some fortifications. He quickly called the men to their posts and ordered the ordnance rifles set for maximum elevation as the Rhode Islanders prepared to send the foe their compliments. Corporal Barber wrote of what happened next:

> We opened fire on the rebels working party planting our shells in their midsts tearing up the earth and causing great havoc among them the men drove their working party off and then the rebels got mad and opened their guns on us those that could reach us was 2 20 pdr Parrotts they fired several shells closely over the heads of our cannoneers. Our battery has made splendid shots at the Rebel works.

In their first three days in the trenches, Battery G expended 149 rounds. However, the long range and deep entrenchments made any fire from field guns negligible.

On June 22, a slight change of position was in order, as the Sixth Corps moved farther west and Battery G followed. Arriving in position the cannoneers opened fire as the gunners sighted the pieces with precision. Despite the accurate shooting, a far more pressing issue was on everyone's minds: the murderous sun that beat down constantly and the absence of water in the dry conditions. What little water that was found was often given to the horses before the men to prevent them from suffering in the extreme heat, and as they were considered more important sometimes than the men. For men and animals used to a cooler climate, it was brutal.[30]

While they remained in action most of the time, cautiously keeping aware of the Confederates in their front, the cannoneers did have a few moments of relaxation during lulls in the fighting. They took the time off as usual to visit friends and relatives in neighboring regiments and the Rhode Islanders saw the grim carnage of the spring fighting. For the first time during the three years of war, Colonel Tompkins' entire First Rhode Island Light Artillery Regiment was on the field in one location, albeit in four different corps. Battery D had recently returned from the western theatre, while a new unit many of the men had never seen was present in the Eighteenth Corps. This was in the form of Battery F, which had spent the majority of the war in North Carolina, only engaging in the occasional battle. Now the officers and men flocked to the other batteries to view comrades they had not seen since leaving Providence. Battery F had a special relationship with Battery G, as their excess men had formed the nucleus of Battery G; not many of these men remained on duty, however.[31]

With Battery G busily entrenching before Petersburg, Captain George W. Adams was again occupied with an unpleasant duty in the command. When the reenlisted soldiers returned to Providence in the early months of 1864 on their furloughs, five of them deserted. Two of these soldiers, George Wilson and Daniel C. Stevens, were arrested in Providence in April. Colonel Tompkins ordered these two deserters in his regiment to be tried by court martial for desertion. The paperwork was filed for the trial, but the start of the Overland Campaign had prevented it. The two prisoners were sent south under guard and arrived back at the Army of the Potomac on June 14. Now that the army was stationary at Petersburg, the officers of the Sixth Corps Artillery Brigade could gather together and try the two criminals.[32]

Both trials were held on June 28, before a board of six artillery officers; four of them were Rhode Islanders. Among the jury was Captain Adams. Since taking command of the battery, Adams had faced desertion and intoxication of soldiers on numerous occasions. Now it was going to be dealt with severely. The two privates were charged with overstaying their veteran furloughs; both Stevens and Wilson pled not guilty. Private Wilson was tried first. Captain Richard Waterman, the commander of Battery C, First Rhode Island Light Artillery, was the president. First Sergeant Nathaniel R. Chace was called to the tent as the only witness. Chace stated that he knew the prisoner as a member of Battery G and produced the necessary regimental books showing that the furlough was for thirty-five days and that Wilson had overstayed it. When the private did not arrive back at Brandy Station on February 1, Captain Adams ordered him considered absent without leave; this was changed four days later to desertion. Private Wilson offered no defense and the officers retired for several minutes to deliberate. The verdict was unanimous: guilty. Private George Wilson was ordered to forfeit ten dollars per month for a year for his crime.[33]

Later that day Private Daniel Stevens was brought in and charged with the same crime. Unlike Wilson, Stevens admitted to deserting, but not to doing it knowingly. Again First Sergeant Chace testified for the prosecution, claiming "his conduct has always been good." Furthermore the sergeant discussed Stevens' willingness to always perform his duty. Captain Adams was then sworn in. He testified to never punishing Stevens for any petty crimes, while telling of his heroism as a driver during the Battle of Marye's Heights. These men were good soldiers, cited for bravery under fire, but they had to be punished as a deterrent to others. Unlike Wilson, Stevens offered a defense, but it was useless. Despite Adams and Chace's testimony on his behalf, Private Stevens was punished even more severely. He had to surrender twelve dollars a month for a year. This was a severe tax on the private's pay, which had recently been raised to sixteen dollars per month. Instead of being sent to the Rip Raps or Dry Tortugas prisons, the men returned to duty in the battery.[34]

While the court martial was occurring, Battery G lost a staple that had been present since the beginning. This was First Lieutenant Otto L. Torslow. The last of the original officers when the battery was mustered in, Torslow had remained on duty through three separate captains, only rising in rank once. He was the senior lieutenant in the regiment, but he had no hope of promotion. The lieutenant was a brave officer and had tried in vain to rally the troops at Antietam. His alcoholism led to many periods of being drunk on duty, and his bad temper contributed to his court martial in 1863. Now he obtained a medical certificate, claiming he was suffering from an "inguinal hernia." What the discharge certificate did not read was that the injury was caused by falling from a horse while intoxicated. This paper was enough, and Torslow took his leave, receiving an honorable discharge. Officially, he resigned and was medically discharged from the service, but the enlisted men saw it differently. Corporal Barber, who served in his section recorded, "He could not agree with our officers."[35]

As the two armies probed each other and continued to build a vast series of fortifications, death was always present; so much as lifting a head above the works could bring an instant dispatch of lead. On the twenty-ninth of June, Battery G completed an all night march to Ream's Station, south of their position on the Weldon Railroad, near the North Carolina border. It was believed that a large Confederate force was traveling from North Carolina to reinforce the Confederates at Petersburg and would attack the Federals from the rear. The Sixth Corps was dispatched to the area to meet the threat, but the Confederates never appeared, and Battery G was back on the Petersburg lines on the night of the thirtieth to resume their deadly duties. As Grant tried to gain the initiative and capture Petersburg, something else was brewing along the trenches occupied by the Army of Northern Virginia. Lee also planned on continuing the struggle by ordering one more invasion of the North. Battery G would soon find itself heading into familiar territory.[36]

Into the Valley

Battery G soon made it uncomfortable for the Rebels that they ceased firing.
—Captain Elisha Hunt Rhodes, July 18, 1864

With his army pinned downed in trench warfare, Robert E. Lee again prepared to steal the initiative as the two armies engaged in a death struggle around Petersburg. With the majority of the troops in the Washington defenses removed to join the Army of the Potomac, Lee felt the Confederates could make an attack down the Shenandoah Valley, and threaten and even possibly capture the United States capital. With the supply lines being stretched daily, this campaign would be the Confederates' last chance to win the war. Lee tapped Jubal Early; his sole remaining senior commander, who would march Jackson's former command down their former stomping grounds in the Valley. Time was essential. Early had to reach Washington before Federal reinforcements made it to the city. The main Confederate contingent was already in the southern part of the Shenandoah, having defeated a Federal attack earlier in the month at Lynchburg. Since May, there had been a constant struggle for control of the Valley. Finally, every Union army had been driven from the field. Early's force marched on June 19. By the first of July, the army was at Harpers Ferry and invaded the North for the third time during the war. The force was detained here for four days by a dogged Federal resistance.[1]

Finally, Grant knew of the Confederates' movements and dispatched the Sixth Corps to reinforce Washington, as they were nearest the railhead; even though mustering only 12,000 men, they were the largest in the Army of the Potomac. Originally, Grant had ordered the Sixth Corps commander, Horatio Wright, to only take his infantry, leaving the artillery behind. Wright pleaded with his superior to have his batteries present; victory or defeat could lie in their hands. Grant relented and the artillery was released. With these orders, Battery G was again heading north. They did so with reduced ranks. There were only three officers and 120 enlisted men on duty. Ten men were absent sick or wounded, including Lieutenant Scott, while only three soldiers were absent without leave. Corporal James Barber had become ill in late June and was sent to a hospital in Washington; he was not excused from duty, as every available man in the city was given a rifle to fight off the Confederate invasion.[2]

At 9:00 on the night of July 9, the Sixth Corps Artillery Brigade received orders to move to the City Point docks immediately; within an hour and a half, the batteries were on their way to counter the threat. Colonel Tompkins had already left with the lead elements of the corps, so Captain James McKnight of the Fifth United States Artillery was placed in temporary command. Before the batteries were allowed to board the vessels he quickly rushed through the ordnance depot at City Point, rounding up every available artillerist that could be found. McKnight did not know what he faced to the north, and wanted as many men in his batteries as could be mustered. Sixty men were found and sent to the Sixth Corps Artillery Brigade. Because of the hastiness of the situation, Captain

Adams did not have time to record their names. Most of them were sent back after the emergency was over. Battery G embarked on the eleventh of July and hurried north.[3]

On July 9, Early was at Frederick, Maryland. Here General Lewis Wallace put together a ragged line of militia and the Third Division of the Sixth Corps to try to slow the advancing Rebels. Wallace had been defeated at the Battle of Monocacy. His defeat bought precious time for the Sixth Corps to arrive in Washington, as the remaining two divisions sped up the Chesapeake in an all night rush up the bay. The greatly needed reinforcements arrived in Alexandria on July 12 and quickly disembarked. Battery G dashed through the streets of the city along with the rest of the Sixth Corps as they hurried to the forts north of the city. The citizens lined the streets, instantly recognizing the Greek crosses on the men's hats, and they shouted out, "It's the old Sixth Corps. Those are the men who took Marye's Heights." Even local Maryland slaves knew what the Greek cross represented, for behind it marched men who knew no fear. Some dropped to their knees as the Artillery Brigade marched by, believing Jubilee had come in the form of men in short red jackets and thick Yankee accents.[4]

Only a few hours later the Confederate force arrived within the gates of Washington itself. General Wright had delivered his men in time to make a difference as they marched to reinforce the forts north of the city. A sharp skirmish erupted at Fort Stevens as the Sixth Corps repulsed the Confederate attack; President Lincoln became the only sitting president to ever be under enemy fire. For Battery G the mad rush from Petersburg had been for naught. They were held in reserve and were not engaged at all. Indeed, none of the artillery was called for, as the infantry slugged it out. Finally at dusk, the Rebels broke off the assault and began their withdrawal. Even though not successful, they had made a point. If Early had attacked only a few hours earlier, he would have been successful. "Early was late," one Rhode Islander recorded.[5]

Elisha Hunt Rhodes of the Second Rhode Island was one of many Federal infantrymen who felt the welcome effect of Battery G's firepower (USAMHI).

After being defeated, the Confederate force retreated towards Virginia as a stunned Lincoln ordered that the Confederacy be destroyed. With some wait on the morning of July 13, Corporal Augustus Buell of the Fifth United States Artillery noticed another in a long series of feuds between the Rhode Islanders of Batteries C and G and the First Massachusetts Battery. This time it was settled with a boxing match; but before

it could be finished, orders came to move out. The cannoneers decided they would settle their differences on
the fields of battle sure to come. Twenty-four hours
after arriving in Washington, Battery G left Fort Stevens
and hurried after the Confederates. Before the Sixth
Corps Artillery Brigade departed, Colonel Tompkins
reduced his forces, as the guns were desperately needed
at Petersburg. Of the nine batteries in the brigade, three
were sent back; among them were Captain William B.
Rhodes and Battery E. In addition, Tompkins divided
his brigade so each infantry division would have one
smoothbore and one rifle battery assigned to it. Battery
G now marched as part of the Third Division, Sixth
Corps.[6]

With the Confederates in full retreat towards the
Potomac, the Sixth Corps marched to Leesburg to cut
them off. This area was intimately familiar to the original members of Battery G, as they had served here in
the early part of 1862, when they were raw recruits. Now
as a veteran battery, they marched south again trying
to defeat the enemy. On the fifteenth, a small portion
of Early's force was detected near Poolesville, Maryland, racing to Virginia, only ten miles away. The Sixteenth Pennsylvania Cavalry was ordered to charge into
the rear guard and drive them into the Potomac. They
were to be supported by a section from Battery G. Captain Adams ordered Lieutenant Corthell's right section
to engage. The charge was successful, as the Confederates ran for their lives, while a Baltimore battery
engaged the force. Lieutenant Corthell promptly unlim-

Captain Adams knew how to effectively use the Hotchkiss shell from
his guns.

bered his section and fired twenty-seven rounds, clearing the town and driving away any
remaining Confederates. When it was over, the last Rebel invasion of the North was finally
finished. Battery G had had the satisfaction of finally driving the enemy from Northern
soil.[7]

In his eight months in the battery, Corthell had risen to Adams' expectations and
more; he held extra sessions to train the noncommissioned officers and easily moved into
the position of second in command after the resignation of Otto Torslow. The *Providence
Journal* reported the promotion: "Captain Adams thinks very highly of Lieutenant Corthell,
and certainly he deserves praise. Being the only commissioned officer in the battery with
the captain much has fallen to him to perform, which has been faithfully done." Now as
Battery G marched back towards the Potomac Corthell was the only lieutenant on duty.
For unknown reasons Lieutenants Freeborn and Waterman remained in Washington during the pursuit, while Scott remained in Providence recovering from his Cold Harbor
wound. The officers would remain on detached duty for the rest of the campaign, granting Adams only one subaltern for the time being. This allowed the senior sergeants a brief
opportunity to command a section and experience the difference between shoulder straps
and stripes.[8]

Battery G was ordered to remain behind as the rear guard as most of the Sixth Corps

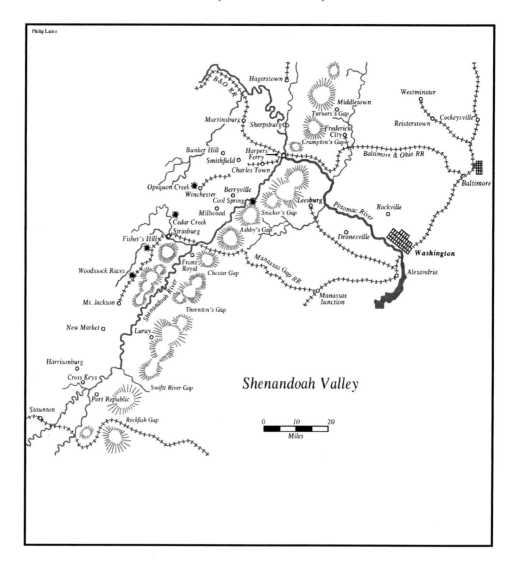

Shenandoah Valley

moved ahead and crossed the Potomac on the sixteenth; Adams' Battery crossed the following day. They were back in Virginia after a five-day foray in to Maryland. Meanwhile, General Horatio Wright pressed his men hard and ordered the Sixth Corps into the Shenandoah Valley. On the eighteenth, Battery G and the One Hundred and Twenty-First New York passed through Purcellville and Snicker's Gap as the Sixth Corps continued on with its mission to find the Rebel army. The march was not without its problems; "moved by a very rough rocky road," recorded a Vermonter in the Sixth Corps. On the afternoon of July 18, the Confederates were located on the west bank of the Shenandoah River.[9]

   Jubal Early had positioned his forces on the right and left of a farm named Cool Spring; here they commanded a vital ford. Early hoped for a rearguard action as his forces withdrew in the face of superior numbers. This was exactly what he had done a year earlier at Granite Hill, after Gettysburg. At 3:00 in the afternoon, the First Division of the Eighth Corps under Colonel John Thoburn forded the Shenandoah River and came under immense small arms and artillery fire as they tried to establish a bridgehead. They soon

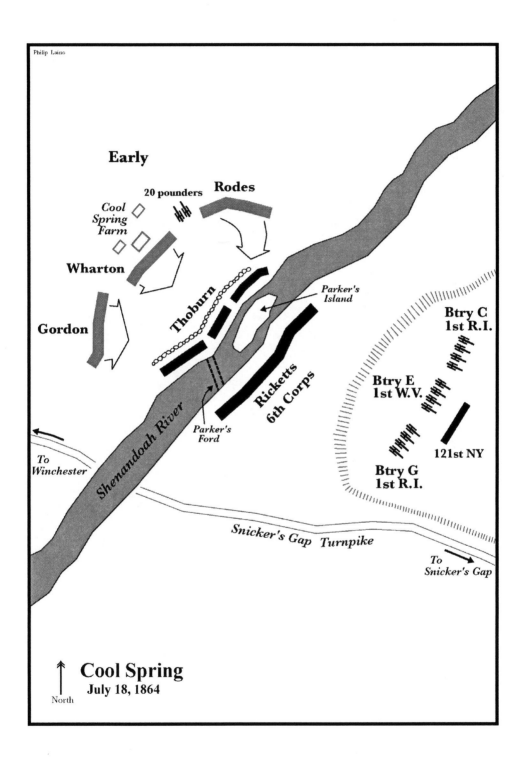

Philip Laino

Early

Rodes

20 pounders

Cool
Spring
Farm

Wharton

Thoburn

Parker's
Island

Btry C
1st R.I.

Gordon

Btry E
1st W.V.

Ricketts
6th Corps

121st NY

Parker's
Ford

Shenandoah River

Btry G
1st R.I.

To
Winchester

Snicker's Gap Turnpike

To
Snicker's Gap

Cool Spring
July 18, 1864

North

became pinned down, unable to advance or retreat as two Confederates divisions bore down upon them. Without any other support, Thoburn's men built a barricade behind a stone wall and kept looking to the east, waiting for reinforcements to arrive.

At 6:00, as the Federal line seemed to be crumbling, the men searched for support that finally appeared in the form of the Sixth Corps. General Wright did not want to bring on a large battle; instead, he only sent General James B. Ricketts' Division to the east bank of the Shenandoah to lay down a covering fire as Robert Rodes' Division approached to within 100 yards of the thin blue line. As this was occurring, Rebel artillery from the Monroe Artillery began to shell the advancing Federals with a pair of twenty pounder Parrotts. Like General Sedgwick had done in the past, Wright turned to a man who could be counted on in a moment of crisis: Colonel Charles Tompkins.[10]

Immediately Tompkins took command of the situation and knew what needed to be done. There was a large, wide open hill overlooking the ford where Battery E of the First West Virginia Light Artillery had already been stationed with their four Napoleons. The Rhode Island colonel knew it was the perfect position to place his guns and called for his two favorite batteries. It was difficult work getting the guns up the ridge, but time was of the essence; and with the Confederates almost right on top of Thoburn's men, there was no time to waste. The Rhode Islanders and some New Yorkers strained every muscle in their bodies to get the four ten pounder Parrotts of Battery C to the right of the crest and the four ordnance rifles of Battery G to the left of the Virginians. The men did not hesitate and quickly brought the guns into action. Captain Adams realized that he had to be extremely careful. With the enemy only five hundred yards away and firing over the head of friendly infantry, his number six men would have to be precise in the cutting of the fuzes. Meanwhile the gunners would have to take steady aim to insure their targets wore gray and not blue. Finally, all was in order as Adams barked out the command to open fire.[11]

The Sixth Corps correspondent of the *Washington Chronicle* described what happened next:

> At this critical moment, Adams' Rhode Island Battery came into position on an eminence overlooking the valley below. They immediately opened upon the enemy with shot and shell from three inch rifled guns, creating great havoc among them. The range was very accurate, and each shell burst in their midst. The enemy finding the damage to their infantry so great, attempted to silence the battery by firing upon them with twenty pound Parrotts, which however lasted, but a moment, as they in turn were fired upon and forced to cease. The scene was a most exciting one; generals, colonels and others were standing near, and high compliments were passed on to this battery by General Russell and others. The writer of this met this command at Fort Stevens; and having, some experience in military matters could not fail to admire their soldierly appearance, and felt assured that if and opportunity occurred during the campaign, they would distinguish themselves.[12]

The cannonade from the heavy Parrott rifles had no effect on Battery G. The rounds flew harmlessly overhead, landing in the ranks of the New Yorkers posted to the battery's rear. Among Thoburn's regiments was the Eighteenth Connecticut, recruited along the Rhode Island border. Now down to sixty men, they finally received the miracle they had been praying for. As Chaplain William C. Walker wrote, "A rebel battery opened upon the Union force with some effect, and would have done great harm if it had not been checkmated by a battery of the Sixth Corps, which by a well directed shot blew up a rebel caisson."

The actions of Battery G were becoming a scene of great interest to all who knew of it. A Vermont officer on General Ricketts' staff wrote, "Batteries were at once placed in position and the Enemy were shelled + their advance checked."

Other Sixth Corps soldiers watched the spectacle occurring on the banks of the Shenandoah River. Captain Elisha Rhodes of the Second Rhode Island recalled, "Battery G soon made it uncomfortable for the Rebels that they ceased firing." General Wright dispatched the Thirty-Seventh Massachusetts and the Second Rhode Island to the support of the Third Division. These two regiments had recently been armed with the new seven shot Spencer repeating rifle. This added even more support to keeping the Confederates away from the stone wall and the remaining Union survivors. Despite this added firepower, the Bay Staters were still amazed at the support coming from their rear: Adams' Rhode Island Battery. James L. Bowen wrote, "They were punished by the Union batteries on the opposite hills."[13]

The firepower of the three-inch ordnance rifles of Battery G and the ten pounder Parrotts of Battery C were having their effect on General Rodes' Division on the opposite side of the Shenandoah River. The earlier problems the battery had with the Dyer and Hotchkiss ammunition, at Antietam and First Fredericksburg, had largely disappeared as the ammunition worked exactly as it was supposed to. Each round of Hotchkiss shell and case was fired precisely and timed to perfection to burst in the midst of the Confederates. Corporal Edward Adams remembered it as "a most destructive fire." A member of the Fourth North Carolina, on the receiving end, described the bombardment as "a deadly fire into our ranks with impunity." Although the cannonade was having its effect, the closeness was worrying some Federal commanders on the west bank of the river. Lieutenant Colonel Thomas F. Wildes from the One Hundred and Sixteenth Ohio observed, "The lines were so close to each other that some damage to our own men was caused by shells from our batteries. But they kept the rebels discretely under cover." Sergeant John Hartwell of New York wrote, "Our batteries made terrible havock of the enemys line & forced them to seek cover under hills & stonewalls."[14]

As night came on, the artillery on both sides, including Battery G, continued the barrage; the only light being the muzzle flashes of the cannon, which allowed the Gunners to focus in on their targets. With the artillery and darkness as their allies, the surviving Federals successfully crossed the river. Early had hoped for another Ball's Bluff, where the Federals would be destroyed as they crossed the river. That battle in October of 1861, which involved Battery B, was a distinct embarrassment to the Union cause in the wake of Bull Run. However, now was not 1861 and two Rhode Island

General Frank Wheaton was a native Rhode Islander who commanded the division in the Sixth Corps to which Battery G was assigned (Library of Congress).

batteries would not let it occur again as they continued their work into the darkness. Finally, at 9:00, the Battle of Cool Spring was over. It was a draw; Early escaped, and Wright did not pursue. In the engagement, Battery G fired a total of 134 rounds. Federal casualties were 422 to 397 Confederates. In the aftermath of the battle, Chaplain Alanson Haines of the Fifteenth New Jersey attended to the dead and wounded and observed the following in reference to the Union casualties: "Losses were four hundred men, and those of the enemy must have been also large, as they were exposed to our batteries, and the next day were observed burying their slain."[15]

For Battery G, the Battle of Cool Spring was a supreme victory. The artillerists were able to use their guns effectively as an offensive weapon to help the beleaguered Union forces from being overwhelmed by a vastly superior foe. This enabled the Union to hold on until darkness allowed their escape. Indeed, one historian of the battle argued that without the artillery support, the Federals would have been driven into the Shenandoah. Relating to Battery G's role, he wrote, "George W. Adams' Battery G went into position on an eminence behind the ford and soon it began to find the mark just at the right moment."[16]

Wright bivouacked the Sixth Corps along the Blue Ridge on the night of the eighteenth, but during the night, a Confederate battery reappeared and shelled the line, causing it to be moved in the middle of the night. As they were after many of their engagements, the Rhode Islanders were exhausted. In forty-eight hours, Battery G had marched over sixty miles. The hard packed macadam roads in Maryland and the Shenandoah contributed to the misery of the cannoneers as their own worn shoes and those of the horses wore completely out. "The men were plaid out as ever," recalled a member of the Second Rhode Island.[17]

With the engagement over, Battery G continued on the march in pursuit of Early, but saw no further action. The local inhabitants were largely all Unionists, but, even so, chickens and turkeys were still foraged by the hungry soldiers. Unlike other Federal soldiers, the artillerists in the Sixth Corps always left enough food for the citizens to have so they could still live. Finally, after several days of skirmishing near Leesburg, Early was believed to have retreated back up the Shenandoah and thence on his way to reinforce Lee. In light of this occurrence, Grant ordered the Sixth Corps back to Petersburg. The command had no sooner arrived near Washington than the Confederates reappeared and destroyed the town of Chambersburg, Pennsylvania, in retaliation for Union-led destruction on the Valley. The Sixth Corps was again ordered west and then south, where they marched and rendezvoused near Harpers Ferry, West Virginia. Battery G had last visited the area after Antietam, camping for a month on Bolivar Heights. Captain Adams moved the command two miles west of Harpers Ferry to Hallstown, a small community that guarded the roads to Charles Town and Sharpsburg. On August 7, a stocky little general named Philip H. Sheridan arrived in camp. He had already made a name for himself out west and in his command of the Army of the Potomac's Cavalry Corps. Now Sheridan took command in the Valley and had a combined force of 40,000 soldiers from the Sixth, Eighth, Nineteenth, and Cavalry corps.[18]

Battery G remained at Harpers Ferry throughout August. Lieutenant Charles V. Scott returned to the unit on August 21 after recovering from his Cold Harbor wound. He also arrived to a brevet promotion to first lieutenant in recognition of his activities during the Overland Campaign. Furthermore, the three men who had been reported as deserters returned to the battery from Washington. The number of horses continued to be of concern; only eighty-eight were present. When this occurred, some teams could only hook up four of the mounts to each gun or caisson. Captain George Adams spent August 23 in his tent, writing a report to Colonel Tompkins that chronicled Battery G's actions from Brandy Station to Harpers Ferry, via the Wilderness, Spotsylvania, Petersburg, and Cool Spring. Casualties had been light, but the nonstop, fast paced campaign had taken its toll on men, horses, and equipment. Now the artillerists waited in the calm, before the storm began again.[19]

Sheridan was taking time to insure that all the troops were in order and all the supplies and other necessities were in place before the campaign began; he would not make the mistakes of his predecessors. With George Gaskell out of Battery G, Bugler William Lewis continued to serve as Captain Adams' orderly. With the months of successful foraging under his belt, Lewis felt as though he would be promoted to corporal once more and requested that his mother send his chevrons back to the battery. Unfortunately, Lewis was more valuable as a musician than as a gunner and no promotion ever came.[20]

The battery was severely weakened on September 7, when the twenty-eight men from the Tenth New York Battery were discharged from Battery G and returned to reform a new Sixth New York Battery. For nearly fifteen months, they had served and fought as Rhode Islanders. While losing many members, one welcome reinforcement arrived on the eighth: Corporal James Barber. After recovering from an illness in Washington, and surviving Early's Raid, he was finally well enough to return to camp. Barber was warmly greeted by his comrades and by Captain Adams, in particular, who was pleased to have a good gunner back in command of his number three gun. The following day the New Yorkers left for Washington. Barber's comments rang true for many about the men from the Tenth: "We were very sorry to part with them." On the same day, Battery G left Harpers Ferry and moved to an advance camp near Clifton, Virginia.[21]

The reduced numbers again affected the command; many heard rumors that Batteries C and G would be "consolidated together on the account of both being short of men." Again one hundred dollars was offered to the remaining men who had not reenlisted. In only a few months their time would be up. The only men to take the offer were two brothers from Charlestown, Corporal Peleg D. Tucker and his brother Welcome. Both men had enlisted in March of 1862, so they had three more months to serve after the men were mustered out in December. Now they would serve until the end

Corporal James A. Barber was one of many Westerly men in the battery and one of seven soldiers awarded the Medal of Honor (courtesy Midge A. Frazel).

of the war. Captain Adams failed to record that the men had reenlisted. This would cause a problem when both brothers went to collect their bounty when they were discharged; there was no record of it with the Rhode Island paymaster general. After completing a great deal of paperwork, and going through their congressman, the Tucker brothers finally received their money in 1866.

Now, with only 102 officers and men, Battery G prepared for action once more.[22]

13

Bloody Autumn

Our guns belched forth their thunder, firing heavy charges
of canister in the midst of the advancing Rebels.
—Corporal James A. Barber, October 19, 1864

Throughout August of 1864, Philip Sheridan had bided his time, collecting men and supplies at Harpers Ferry. Each week he would send out patrols, and each week they would be sent reeling back to the Potomac. The soldiers thought of it as a comical event and called it "Harpers Weekly," after the newspaper of the period. The little general thought if he was too zealous it would cost Lincoln the upcoming election; much was riding on his decisions. Finally, in early September, General Grant had had enough and traveled from the Petersburg front to meet with his subordinate at Harpers Ferry. The meeting was a success and the two generals formulated the plan of attack. As he left, Grant left Sheridan with a simple order: Go In.[1]

Nearly two months after entering the Shenandoah Valley, all was finally in order at 2:00 on the morning of September 19 as the Army of the Valley marched south towards Winchester along the Berryville Pike, where the Confederates waited along Opequon Creek. The cavalry had been engaged since early in the morning as General Horatio Wright hurried the Sixth Corps along. The Second and Third divisions were thrown into the fight at 11:30. The First Division was initially held in reserve as the other two attacked. The Confederates instantly counterattacked and drove the Eighth and Nineteenth corps away, threatening the flank of the Sixth; for nearly three hours the two sides ebbed and flowed and finally came to a standstill.[2]

The infantrymen with Greek crosses on their hats laid on the ground as they faced a horrific barrage of bullets and shells as the Confederates tried desperately to press forward. The Confederate artillery fired sporadically at the Federal line. As he waited with Battery G to go in, Corporal Barber later remembered that "the fire from the Rebel Batteries became very annoying." The infantry kept looking over their shoulders, waiting for support. Wright knew that it was too early in the engagement to send in the First Division, so he ordered Colonel Charles Tompkins to deploy several batteries into the fray at 2:30. That morning Sheridan had told Tompkins he wanted to "see some dead horses before night," in other terms, to sacrifice his batteries if necessary to win the battle.[3]

Tompkins saw a point of advantage on the right of the Sixth Corps line and sent in the Fifth Maine and First New York on the right of the pike. The colonel then returned to his column and sent in Battery G and the First Massachusetts Battery. Captain Adams obeyed as the battery dashed into an open field on the left side of the Berryville Turnpike. Promptly unlimbering, the Rhode Islanders kept up a galling fire of shell and canister, depending on the target, engaging the Confederates near Winchester. Again the artillery became the morale booster that the Federal infantry needed to see and feel to hold on. Lieutenant Colonel Aldace Walker of the Vermont Brigade wrote, "The batteries were nearer

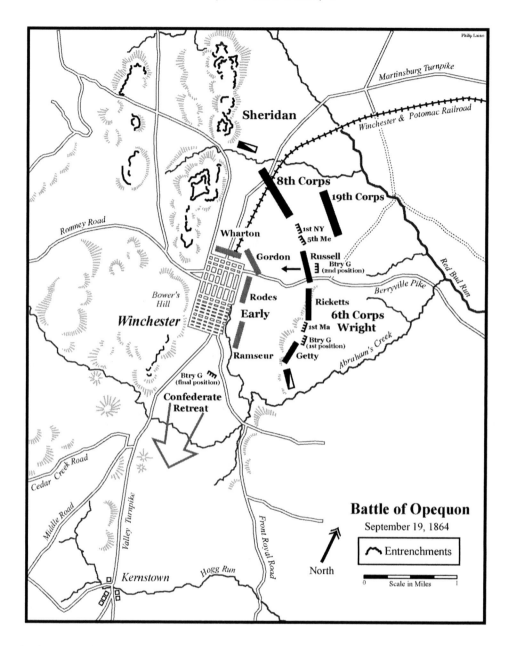

Philip Laino

Battle of Opequon

September 19, 1864

⌢ Entrenchments

North

0   Scale in Miles   1

the front that day than we had ever seen before." Through the tremendous smoke to their front, Cox's Brigade of North Carolinians started to approach the two batteries, intent on capturing them. Seeing the threat, Captain William H. McCartney ordered his men to prepare to limber up and retire to escape the threat. Adams' Battery was going nowhere, and the Bay Staters blocked the Rhode Islanders from engaging the enemy.[4]

In the confusion of the battle, Captain McCartney regained his composure and redeployed the First Massachusetts. To his left, Captain George Adams knew what was coming. He calmly barked out the command for canister as the Number Seven men pulled the round out of the chest and passed it to Number Five, who then ran it to Number Two.

The four Rhode Island guns waited for the opportune moment to engage. At four hundred yards, Adams gave the command to open fire and the Rhode Islanders and Bay Staters blasted the deadly rounds as the Carolinians advanced closer; still Battery G stood fast. Adams made the crucial command decision to stay in position, even at the risk of losing the guns. The decision was the right one, as Battery G's fire "checked the enemy."[5]

Private Thomas J. Watkins was a member of Cox's Brigade. He remembered the attack against Battery G:

> We ran against a rock fense in a piece of woods defended by a yankee line and a masked battery. That opened on us. There General R.E. Rodes was killed by a piece of shell. The most of the guns of this battery were was loaded with grape and canister doing some damage to our unprotected lines; the writer found a large oak stump that was sound and he took position behind this making as safe a protection as our would need.[6]

The limber chests only held ten rounds of canister, but more was constantly brought up from the caissons. Corporal Barber described the attack: "We opened such a murderous fire on the Rebels that the battery soon drove them from their position."[7]

Battery G performed its assigned task and repulsed the Carolinians, who pulled back towards Winchester. With this accomplished, Colonel Tompkins galloped up from the right of the line and redeployed Battery G onto the right side of the Berryville Pike, now eight hundred yards from the enemy, as shell and case became the primary weapons of choice. Again, with the First Massachusetts Battery, the two commands worked in tandem to destroy the Virginia Amherst Artillery that had tried to enfilade the Second Division. By this time in the war, the Confederate artillery had become not much of a factor on the battlefield as they low on ammunition, horses, and guns. Still it presented a nuisance as Sheridan prepared to deliver the final blow. The fire became very effective, as the Rhode Islanders sighted the guns with precision. The results were seen immediately.[8]

One of the members of the Amherst Battery was Henry E. Berkley. He wrote about the destruction the Bay Staters and Rhode Islanders were inflicting on his command:

> At one time came a Yankee shell which struck the middle horse of my limber right between the eyes, and bursting took off the middle horses head, cut off the hind legs of the saddle horse in front of him and the front legs of the horse behind him, cut out the pole of the limber in two places, and passed through the limber box, which fortunately was nearly empty.

Two limbers were blown up, in addition to killing the eight horses

General Lewis Addison Grant commanded the Vermont Brigade, which finally rescued Battery G from its fiery ordeal at Cedar Creek (USAMHI).

that pulled them and some of the drivers. These were just a few of the 462 rounds fired this day.[9]

After the battle, however, as the Federals cleared the field of debris, many would be sickened by the results of the precision shelling. Private Frank M. Finn of the Thirty-Eighth Massachusetts wrote, "The dead were horrible dead. It seemed as if the majority had received their death from shells. Most of the bodies were mangled beyond recognition. Our artillery, borne across the plateau to its farthest verge, did a work so terrible, that to witness it was sickening." The artillery accomplished the vital task of holding the Confederates back while the corps commanders made final preparations for the counterassault.[10]

The time was now 3:00; it was time for the First Division of the Sixth Corps to go in. General Wright recorded the movement: "The First Division moved admirably on the enemy, and the batteries with canister opened upon them with murderous effect, the two driving them back in much disorder. This was the turning point in the conflict." General Robert Rodes, a Confederate division commander, was trying to push his men forward when he was struck down by a shell fired from a Sixth Corps gun. The movement of the First Division was followed by simultaneous blows from the rest of the Sixth Corps, in addition to the Eighth and Nineteenth; the entire Confederate line began to crumble. The Federals charged strait into the Rebels, driving them from Winchester and down the Valley Pike towards Fisher's Hill. Early tried to position some artillery to cover his retreat, but they were met by the First Massachusetts and Rhode Island Batteries C and G, which again drove them back in disarray. Eventually the exhausted Federals became too tired to pursue; when the Confederates were out of range, Adams ordered the men to cease firing.

The Battle of Opequon was a decisive Federal victory, but did come at some cost. Five thousand of Sheridan's men became casualties, to 4,000 Confederates; it was the bloodiest battle ever fought in the Shenandoah. General David A. Russell, who commanded the Sixth Corps' First Division, was killed by a shell and was replaced by General Frank Wheaton. The men in Battery G had served under Wheaton's command occasionally since Gettysburg; now he was their full-time divi-

Although demoted on the Peninsula, Musician William H. Lewis was a born soldier, displaying valor at Marye's Heights and Cedar Creek, where he paid the ultimate sacrifice saving a gun (Connecticut State Library).

sion commander. General Wright praised his artillerists for the action, including Colonel Tompkins and Captain Adams. They had held back the enemy long enough for the First Division to make its charge. The general wrote, "The artillery of this corps alone expended eighteen army wagon-loads of ammunition, and all with good effect upon the results of the conflict. All of my batteries were effectively engaged." With the battle over, Battery G helped to guard 500 captured prisoners as they slept in the eastern environs of Winchester; cheered General Sheridan all night long. Early was not entirely defeated; instead he fled south, further up the Valley.[11]

With Winchester firmly secured, Sheridan had an invasion point and supply base to launch attacks further up the Valley. On the twentieth, the Rhode Islanders saw a familiar site as Battery D, First Rhode Island Light Artillery, passed them on the road as part of the Nineteenth Corps. After retreating south from Winchester, the Confederate forces dug in along Fisher's Hill, overlooking the Shenandoah and controlling the Valley Turnpike. With overwhelming numbers, Sheridan ordered the army to attack the entrenched enemy on the hill. The Sixth Corps hurried from their camp south of Winchester into action, dashing thirteen miles without a stop. This was nothing, however, compared to the march the summer before to Gettysburg. Again Battery G marched all night. Early had sworn that he would hold the fortified hill against a Federal attack; it was the "Gibraltar of the Shenandoah." If Fisher's Hill fell it would spell doom for Early's army. On September 22, the second battle for possession of the Shenandoah Valley was to be fought: Battery G would be in the eye of the storm.[12]

Sheridan had his army in place early on the morning of September 22, as the cavalry scouted the positions to look for a weakness. Although Early's men had built substantial earthworks, backed by artillery, the right flank was in the air. At 4:00, with all in position, Sheridan ordered the assault. The massed Confederate artillery opened fire on the Federals as they came onto line. This momentarily stunned the Second Division of the Sixth Corps, but George Getty quickly took control of the situation and pressed forward into the fire. Instantly General Sheridan rode to Colonel Tompkins and ordered him to deploy his five batteries to counter the threat. The twenty guns, including those of Battery G, unlimbered and soon began "pouring shot and shell into their works with marvellous rapidity and accuracy." Generals Horatio Wright and George Getty also joined in the spectacle as the cannoneers performed their choreographed steps to operate the guns. Sheridan and Tompkins remained by the batteries, observing as each round hit its target.[13]

Battery G's old companions, the Vermont Brigade, deployed into line and supported the Sixth Corps guns; a few shells landed in the ranks, but not enough to cause alarm. Soon the Rebel artillery was driven from the field. As the bombardment was kept up, Sheridan could see the Confederates running away and instantly ordered the Eighth Corps into action to flank the hill. As the first units of the Eighth made their advance, yet another Confederate battery opened fire from the right of the hill, into the ranks of the Sixth Corps artillery. Wilbur Fisk, a soldier in the Second Vermont recalled what happened next:

> Immediately Gen. Sheridan had every piece trained on this new position. God pity them now. Their destruction is inevitable. The artillery fired with remarkable precision. Although the Rebels were so far off that you could not distinguish a man from a mule with the naked eye, they would burst the shells over their works every time and scattering the deadly fragments right among them. Scarcely a shot was thrown away, and yet it took them less time to sight their pieces than an ordinary hunter would take in aiming his rifle at a woodchuck.[14]

Battery G played a crucial role in each part of the battle, as the ordnance rifles fired round after round into the Confederate ranks. The Rhode Islanders were using case shot, a favorite round for this type of operation. When fired, the shell exploded overhead. It not only rained down large pieces of iron, but up to one hundred small lead balls as well. Soon this battery as well was fleeing from the scene of battle. Corporal Barber recalled the role of his battery: "We silenced their thunder." The Rhode Islanders were able to use their ordnance rifles as an offensive weapon. By countering the threat at long range, they provided pinpoint firepower to neutralize a large threat to the entire Federal line, which permitted the infantry to go forward and face only the Rebel infantry, which was the next target.[15]

With all three divisions of the Sixth Corps and those of the Nineteenth Corps on line, and the Confederate artillery out of commission, they attacked the hillside as the Eighth and Cavalry corps flanked from the left. After this victory, Captain Adams brought Battery G forward with the Third Division as they pushed up the hill. Each time a target appeared, the four rifles were fired. Again, Corporal Barber was at his post directing the fire of the number three gun. He wrote, "Our guns was turned on the strong point held by the Rebels and our rifle guns planted the shell and case shot in the Rebels works so lively we drove the Rebel infantry nearly all out."[16]

After a brief struggle, the Sixth Corps gained the heights; again Early was sent flying up the Shenandoah. As the Confederates retreated, Battery G kept up a "hot fire" with case shot until they were out of range, again fleeing further south into the formidable Shenandoah. Union losses were five hundred, the Confederates nearly 1,300. Furthermore, the Federal forces captured twenty guns. Battery G lost two horses killed and the 218 rounds that were fired. They contributed immensely to the Federal success of the attack. The battery provided long range supporting fire for the Sixth Corps infantry during the assault; this was the new practice, to use artillery as an offensive weapon, not just for use in defense or as a morale booster. Artillery had covered the advance of the Sixth Corps up the slopes of the hill. The Confederates continued to run before the powerful force Sheridan commanded. A Massachusetts artillerist wrote, "Early has left us and I think he has done some damn tall traveling."[17]

Following the Battle of Fisher's Hill, the Sixth Corps continued up the Valley to Harrisonburg. For sixty miles, there was a running battle as Sheridan marched his army hard against the retreating foe. The Confederates simply threw away much of their equipment, which was picked up by the advancing Federals; the pursuit became known as the "Woodstock Races." In the front of the column were Battery G and the First New York Battery. Each time an enemy force was located, the guns were unlimbered and a few rounds thrown towards their position. Corporal Barber was there as he con-

Although he served in Battery G for only six months, Lieutenant Charles V. Scott was twice promoted for gallantry and died trying to save a gun from capture.

stantly sighted his number three gun: "Our Battery galloped on after them untill we come up with them and then open fire until they was out of range and then chase them again which was fun for us and death for them." Occasionally the Confederates would counter and attempt to stop the Rhode Islanders. The results were the same every time: "Our Battery fired a few rounds of case shot in among the brave rebel artillerymen and they got out of the way."[18]

Finally Early fled from sight and the Federals arrived at Harrisonburg. Here they camped until the sixth of October, being engaged only in foraging duties and some slight skirmishes with Confederate cavalry. The horse problems continued to persist, so Lieutenant Scott was dispatched to Washington on September 27 to retrieve mounts. All of the Morgans, which William Rhodes had so tenderly cared for during the long journey from Vermont to Rhode Island and then further south, were dead. These noble comrades had seen much harder service than the cannoneers, experiencing even greater privation, and still had given the last full measure trying to pull the guns out of the Virginia mud. In Washington, Scott's mission was unsuccessful and no further mounts were received.[19]

Because the cannoneers did not always receive their full complement of supplies from Harpers Ferry, they took ample opportunity to forage through the countryside. This was in regard to Sheridan's orders to make the Shenandoah Valley a wasteland and prevent it from feeding the Confederacy. Everything that was of military value or that could be eaten was foraged. Private Horace Tanner of Hopkinton recorded, "I have helped myself to anything I have found in the enemies country without liberty or license and all the rest of the boys have done the same. We have consumed or destroyed everything we have come in contact with in the line of subsistence for man or beast." This ardent foraging combined with the two victories at Opequon and Fisher's Hill humbled the local populace, as the southerners could see firsthand that the Confederacy was on the verge of defeat.[20]

The men took the time at Harrisonburg to travel through the countryside and collect food; on one occasion, 118 sheep were taken. On the thirtieth, one of these missions nearly ended in disaster for the command. A section of Battery D was on horseback, foraging some twenty miles from camp, when they were attacked by a small force of Confederate cavalry that was repulsed with ease. As the sun started to set, the lieutenant in command of the detail brought his men and prisoners back towards Harrisonburg. In an instant, a party of armed men appeared in front of them. The soldiers in Battery D thought it was more Confederate cavalry, as the darkness concealed what uniform was being worn. The weary cannoneers did not engage. It was a fateful decision that prevented a horrible friendly fire incident, for the men riding into the darkness were a foraging party from Battery G, commanded by Lieutenant Elmer Corthell.[21]

On the second of October, the battery received much needed additional ammunition that had been expended at the two battles, while the guns and vehicles were greased and readied once more. As this was occurring, Sheridan firmly believed that he had dealt the death blows to Early's army in September and thus ordered his forces to pull back down the valley towards Cedar Creek. He further believed that the Sixth Corps was no longer needed, so he issued orders for them to prepare to return to Petersburg for the second time. When the commander heard that Early might have been reinforced, he canceled the orders and gave directions for the Army of the Valley to dig in along the banks of Cedar Creek as Sheridan left for a conference in Washington; Battery G arrived on October 14. The weather started to turn cold in the valley as Battery G erected a semipermanent camp near the Belle Grove plantation. The shelter tents were pitched, as the generals believed that the Confederates had withdrawn.[22]

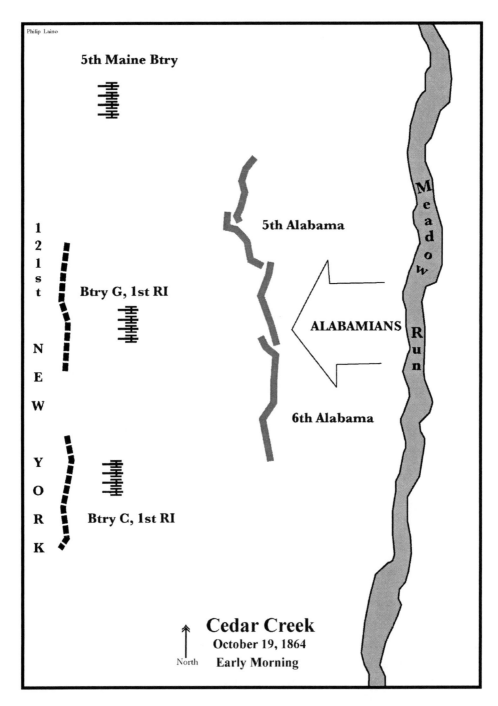

Philip Laino

5th Maine Btry

121st NEW YORK

Btry G, 1st RI

Btry C, 1st RI

5th Alabama

ALABAMIANS

6th Alabama

Meadow Run

Cedar Creek
October 19, 1864
North   **Early Morning**

As the Army of the Valley remained camped along Cedar Creek, Jubal Early prepared his forces for one last battle to determine the fate of the Shenandoah. For several days, he had been observing the encampment from Massanutten Mountain, looming over the plain that the army was camped upon. The Rhode Islanders sensed that something was occurring around them, as strange-looking farmers viewed their movements daily. The officers

Battery G was the subject of a "rough and tumble fight" between the attacking Alabamians and the defending New Yorkers and Vermonters.

tried to calm the men, telling them that the Rebels were not going to attack again. The weather briefly warmed, reviving the soldier's spirits. Captain Adams ordered the men to maintain their equipment in preparedness to move, but no orders came. As the quiet of camp life continued, Early gathered all available Confederate forces for battle. He would attack in the early morning hours of October 19, believing that, with Sheridan gone, the Union would not fight as well. In addition, the early hour of attack would allow the Confederates to attack and conquer before a successful counterattack could be organized.

Before leaving for the conference, Sheridan had posted the army with the Sixth Corps on the right flank, followed by the Nineteenth, and then the Eighth on the left. The cavalry was posted on the flanks of the corps. A small stream called Meadow Run ran through the encampment; the Sixth Corps was on the left bank. The Third Division held the left, followed by the Second, with Wheaton's First holding the right of the line. In order to protect the camp, Colonel Tompkins placed three of his three rifled batteries on the east of the line directly to the right of Belle Grove. Battery C, First Rhode Island, held the right of the line with Adams; Battery G was in the center and the Fifth Maine Battery on the left. The One Hundred and Twenty-First New York, which had supported the Rhode Islanders at Mine Run and Cool Spring, were detached from the First Division and assigned to support the artillery.[23]

The night of October 18 was very mild for that time of year in the valley. A thick ground fog filled the hollows and camouflaged everything, much like the night before Antietam. The sky was clear, with a bright moon and stars. The Confederates had stealthily marched all night, even as they forded freezing Cedar Creek. Finally, at 5:40 the enemy was in position on the left flank of the army, the Eighth Corps line. A few Union soldiers were partially awake, getting the fires started and preparing for another boring day of camp duty. The Confederates managed to acquire Federal clothing and snuck in close to the picket line and killed the soldiers assigned to this duty without firing a shot. Corporal James Barber of Battery G was sleeping with his pard in his shelter tent; he heard some annoying firing to the south and thought it was only some inexperienced recruits firing at a noise they heard in the woods. All of a sudden, a heavy crash of musketry echoed through the still morning air that let the experienced combat veteran know that an attack was imminent. Barber hastily packed up his equipment and ran to his number three gun.

The Rebel yell rang out as Joseph Kershaw's Division smashed into the Eighth. The half-sleeping and half-dressed soldiers heard the firing and shouting as they ran for their lives from the resistance. They did not put up a fight, but continued running. Only a small band of alert Vermonters put up a desperate fight. The attack shifted to the left and the Confederates attacked the Nineteenth Corps. A dozen artillerists from Battery D went down, as half the battery was quickly captured. Into the ranks of the Sixth Corps ran thousands of Federal soldiers. Some men did not stop running until they reached Winchester, some eighteen miles away. "They appeared to be scared out of their senses," remembered Corporal Barber.[24]

The musketry awakened the rest of the artillerists as the battery commanders in the Sixth Corps Artillery Brigade ordered all of their wagons, forges, and other noncombat vehicles to the rear immediately. Throughout the encampment, the buglers were blowing Boots and Saddles as the men quickly arose. Immediately the rolls were called to insure all were present as the men quickly packed up their belongings, throwing them on the caissons. It remained foggy as the Confederate infantry screamed towards the camp. John Pegram's Division flanked the position from the right, as Stephen Ramseur's Division hit the Sixth Corps camp on the left side of Meadow Run. The few remaining Federals from the Eighth and Nineteenth corps tried to stem the Rebel onslaught, but it was to little avail, as they fired several shots and then ran. This opened the way for the Confederates to hit the Sixth Corps artillery, which was in the process of getting organized.[25]

The Confederates crossed Meadow Brook and saw the guns directly in front of them. Colonel Tompkins galloped through the camp trying to get his men to their posts, all the while seeing what was coming towards him. He ordered Captain Adams and Lieutenant Jacob Lamb, commanding Batteries G and C respectively, to hold their position at all costs as the rest of the Sixth Corps was organized. The Rhode Islanders were to sacrifice themselves to the enemy to buy the precious time needed to prevent a total rout of the Army of the Valley. Before doing so, they had to move the guns

Sergeant George W. Flagg was typical of the gruff, no-nonsense Vermonters who depended on Battery G for support and returned the compliment at Cedar Creek by trying to save the guns (USAMHI).

out of the depression they were camped in, so they could be brought to bear on higher ground to the rear. General Ramseur saw the artillery to his front as well, and directed Cullen Battle's Alabama Brigade to attack. Lieutenant Colonel Edwin Hobson of the Fifth Alabama wrote about the scene:

> I soon got permission to attack the battery that was playing upon us. Upon giving the order to the brigade to storm and take the battery the men bounded forward with a yell and in a few moments they were in the midst of the artillery calling upon the Yankees to surrender and when failing to do so cutting them down with their swords or shooting them down. We

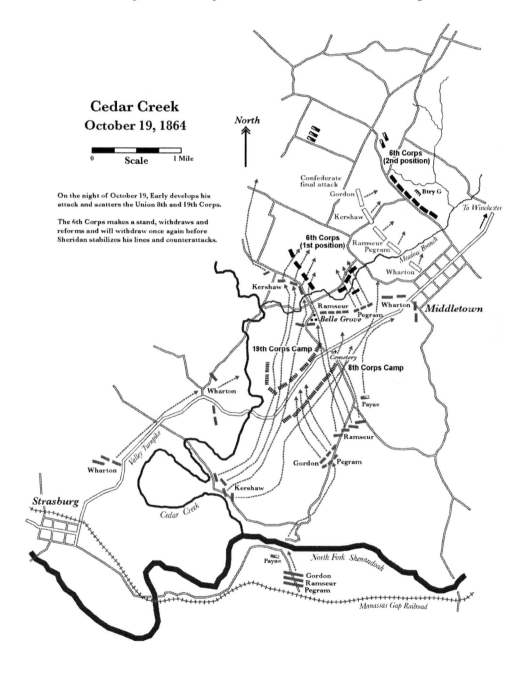

then captured six pieces of arty. The enemy defended manfully this battery & yielded possession of it to us only after the 5th Ala & portion of the 6th Ala Rgt were answering the guns.

As the Rebels stormed in among the guns and caissons, men in short red trimmed jackets scrambled to their positions.[26]

Musician William H. Lewis was among the members of Battery G already at his post, galloping on his horse and issuing calls on the bugle for the drivers to mount and begin moving. Despite losing his rank on the Peninsula, the nineteen-year-old soldier had never lost his battlefield prowess, serving with a gun detachment at Marye's Heights and as an ardent forager. In the instant between life and death, Lewis made the ultimate decision. He could have galloped to the rear or continued blowing commands, but he would have none of it. Now he seized the moment and knew what needed to be done. Lewis leaped from his own mount onto the lead team of one of the pairs of horses that were already harnessed up and began to get the gun moving, all the while the elaborate gold trim on his coat shimmering among the campfires. Only a moment later, an Alabaman leveled his musket and pulled the trigger. Bugler Lewis fell off his horse to the ground, shot through the chest; two comrades grabbed him and raced for the rear. Although severely wounded, Lewis "saved the gun from being captured." One piece was moving to the right and safety, three more needed to follow.[27]

The scene in the artillery park was unbelievable; horses and artillerists were being shot down at an immense rate as they tried to move the guns. The fog, coupled with the Rebel yell and the flashes of musketry, was terrifying. Surgeon George T. Stevens of the Seventy-Seventh New York recorded, "They rushed our lines with those wild, exultant yells, the terror of which can never be conceived by those who have not heard them on the field." Private Charles G. Gardner of Battery G was detached to Sixth Corps Artillery Brigade Headquarters. He was trying desperately to evacuate the medical wagons of the brigade when he was killed in the melee. Lieutenant John Knight Bucklyn of Colonel Tompkins' staff galloped through the camps transferring orders to get the batteries moving. The lieutenant rode through a hurricane of lead as the Alabamians fired volley after volley into the camp. In the middle of their field of fire was Battery G. Corporal Barber was among the first to join in the fight. As he looked into the fog, he saw "advancing Rebels who came rushing onto our Battery yelling like the devil and firing as they come."[28]

Private James McDonald of Providence was mortally wounded by a shot through the lung. Another man with the same name, but from Richmond, was also wounded in the leg. James Matthewson received a disfiguring wound to the face. The minie balls splintered the gun carriages and some made the distinct and frightening sound of hitting bone. To Corporal Barber, the projectiles sounded like hailstones "and the air seemed to be full of them." Finally, Lieutenant Bucklyn's horse was shot down and he carried on the mission on foot to get the guns moving. Private Thomas Harper, a Canadian immigrant from Providence, was hit but still ran for his life. The Confederates now took possession of the entire encampment, getting between the guns and the shelter tents still standing; they fired at anything that moved. Panicked men continued to stream past Battery G; the drivers and cannoneers remained by their places as the Confederates roared in. Adams had trained his men well; they did not run, but tried in every way to save their guns from the enemy. Battle's Alabamians and another brigade of Georgians were soon almost on top of the battery. Corporal Henry E. Chace, of Westerly, the brother of First Sergeant Nathaniel Chace was killed at his post.[29]

In the tight, compact area of the artillery brigade's encampment, the soldiers in Battery G were receiving tremendous fire. A few of the artillerists tried to form a skirmish line and return fire with their revolvers, but it accomplished nothing as the Alabamians continued to fire at the Rhode Islanders. Most soon abandoned this plan and ran back to their guns, trying in vain to get them moving. The Westerly Boys in the First Detachment were again suffering severely. Sergeant Alexander Sisson and his twin brother, Charles, were both hit, while John S. Babcock was seriously wounded in the legs as he helped to evacuate their gun. Private Edward Forrest lost his nerve and skedaddled to the rear; he would rejoin the command the following day. While the enlisted men were trying to perform their duty, the officers were not sitting idly by. As Lieutenant Charles V. Scott ran to his section, the young officer was shot in the left knee and right thigh. Despite being in excruciating pain, Scott's men helped to carry him to a waiting wagon for treatment before returning to the guns.[30]

While the horses were being shot down all around him, Captain Adams and two men were trying to get one of the guns moving—three Rhode Islanders trying to push a ton of iron and wood. The *Providence Journal* called the act one of "unsurpassed bravery." The Confederates had already killed all the horses on the gun. Now Corporal Daniel Hoxsie, recently recovered from his Cold Harbor wound, was shot in the leg as he worked at Adams' side; this was the third wound he had received so far in the war. Also wounded was the unidentified private. Other Rhode Islanders were quickly on the scene and rescued their two comrades, leaving the gun to the enemy. Hoxsie would languish in a hospital in Washington and would not be discharged until the following August. Finally, Colonel Tompkins himself dismounted and tried to push the gun out of harms' way with one of his captains. The colonel received a wound to the arm that took him out of active field service for the rest of the war. Tompkins would be rewarded with a brevet of brigadier general for his services in the Shenandoah Campaign. Privates Nathaniel and Samuel Champlin were brothers from Westerly; now they were both shot trying to save their battery.[31]

With no other support, Captain Adams was forced to abandon two guns and two caissons on the field to the Confederates as he ran to join the remaining one piece already moving on, the only one to have its horses, which had been saved by William Lewis. The captain left just in time, as the Confederates were "up nearly to the muzzles of our guns." The worst fear of a cannoneer had been realized. Battery G had lost two of its guns to the enemy. While Adams had been struggling to save one gun, another had been noticed by some of his cannoneers, who were in the process of preparing to drag it off the field. The men were fortunate to save two of their pieces from the grasp of the enemy. Captain Hazard Stevens, a transplanted Rhode Islander on General Wright's staff, wrote, "Only by great bravery and steadiness was any of the artillery saved. Every man seemed to be doing his best, and more acts of courage and desperation have seldom been scene." As the Rhode Islanders left, three of their comrades remained behind severely wounded; they were promptly taken prisoner by the Confederates.[32]

The full force of two Confederate divisions was directed against the Sixth Corps encampments. "The firing became very hot," recorded Corporal Barber, who continued to fight on with his detachment. Yet another Westerly soldier went down; Private William C. Douglass became the latest fatality in Battery G. The One Hundred and Twenty-First New York of the Sixth Corps had been on the firing line, trying in vain to hold back the Rebels. Now they obliqued to the left and charged towards the artillery to lend support. Forming a line near the two Rhode Island batteries, they managed to hold the Confederates at bay long enough for the artillerists to finally get the other gun moving. The Rebels tried to make one last effort to take the guns, but the New Yorkers fired a murderous volley as the second cannon was pulled out by hand. Private John D. Ingraham recalled, "We poured it into them wicked, which checked them for a while." Some of the infantry threw down their muskets and helped the Rhode Islanders pull their gun out of the cauldron. So many horses were dead that this was the only way to withdraw. The One Hundred and Twenty-First suffered heavy losses, but managed to hold out long enough to cover the withdrawal. As the guns were withdrawn, clumps of dead and wounded New Yorkers, Alabamians, and Rhode Islanders were left among the wreckage of the camp. Colonel Tompkins recalled, "The guns were not deserted by their gunners, but were heroically worked and defended until nearly every man fell at his post."[33]

Once Captain Adams was positive that there was no Federal infantry to the front of his guns, he gave the order for canister as Battery G began to fight back against the onslaught. The section wheeled to the right and helped to stem the flow of the Sixth Corps to the rear. Instantly the Alabamians began to be mowed down and they evaporated into a pink mist; still, those left kept advancing. With Scott down and Lieutenants Frank Waterman and Benjamin Freeborn still in Washington, Elmer Corthell took command of the section, again fighting with vigor. As usual, Adams came alive amid the incessant firing, leading his men with vigor as they began to fight the enemy. The remnants of Lamb's Battery C of Rhode Island joined in the fight to Battery G's left as the Vermont Brigade launched a desperate charge to their right to save McKnight's Battery of the Fifth United States Artillery. What was left of Penrose's New Jersey Brigade supported the efforts to cover Battery G's withdrawal, all the while pulling back under an unbearable fire. The results of the canister were seen immediately. "Our guns belched forth their thunder, firing heavy charges of canister in the midst of the advancing Rebels," recorded Corporal Barber. To their front the men watched as their fire tore huge gaps into the advancing lines, knocking down a Rebel color bearer; still the enemy kept on advancing.[34]

First Lieutenant Charles A. Brown was given a commission to serve in Battery G, but he never did because he was taken prisoner (courtesy Phil DiMaria, Battery B 1st Rhode Island Light Artillery Inc.).

Even the Confederates who were trying to capture Battery G could not believe the bravery being shown by the Rhode Islanders in devotion to their guns and each other. Although the cannoneers and drivers continued to be shot like fish in a barrel, they would not yield their ordnance rifles, which had served them on every battlefield since the Peninsula. Benjamin F. Cobb was a member of the Tenth Georgia, which had joined the Fifth and Sixth Alabama in the mad rush to take the Sixth Corps artillery. Private Cobb remembered:

The order was furnished and we marched up a hill about one hundred yards with a battery shelling us from the time we struck their picket line at the creek. But they did us very little damage until we got to the top of the hill. I remarked to Lt. Hentron, who was marching by my side, saying look out we are going to catch it and just at that time the whole line opened fire on us. That really done us more damage than all the balance of the days fighting. Killed and wounded scores of our boys. But that was all the licks they got at us, there we gave a Rebel yell and ran right in on them and scattered them like chaff before the wind.

The Rhode Islanders continued to fight on against the odds and in the next blast of canister severely wounded Cobb and Hentron as they made one last attempt to get to the two guns.[35]

Although the battery had suffered heavily, they were making their presence known to the Confederates who had attacked them. Colonel Hobson of Alabama wrote, "The brigade was exposed to withering and accurate shelling from a battery of the enemy distant about three hundreds yards and obliquely to the left. The men behaved with unequalled calmness while those shells were rapidly thinning their ranks." Battery G put up a heroic fight as they withdrew. Firing as they pulled back, using a large rope connected to the limber to pull the guns backwards, they helped to cover the withdrawal of the Sixth Corps. At the same time, Private George W. Bowen received a mortal wound. To their front, the artillerists could see the other two guns that were abandoned, but many in the ranks yelled out, "We will retake those guns before night." Much to the horror of the soldiers in the Sixth Corps, not only had the Confederates captured the guns, but they were swarming over them, readying the pieces to fire on their rightful owners. The two ordnance rifles of Battery G were then turned on the battery itself by the enemy. Private William H. Burton had already been wounded at Marye's Heights; now he was hit again.[36]

Battery G was not the only Sixth Corps battery to suffer terribly; most had lost many of their horses and could only pull two guns out, while leaving many men behind to the enemy. The pieces were not given up without a fight, as Federal infantrymen fought against overwhelming odds to save them. The guns were considered living things by the men, part of the family that comprised the United States Army. They would simply not be cast to the enemy. As Battery M, Fifth United States Artillery, was drawn back by hand, Corporal Augustus Buell looked in the distance and saw the overwhelming fight against the Rhode Islanders. He wrote that Battery G "got into a hot place and was made the subject of a regular rough-and-tumble between Upton's Brigade and a strong force of the enemy. The Rebels got into the battery once, but were driven out of it. Then their second line took it again. They got away, but nearly all their men and horses were killed or disabled." The fighting continued as the boys from Rhode Island were being slaughtered, all the while obeying their colonel's orders.[37]

Under the tremendous firepower being thrown against the Sixth Corps, few of the infantrymen who had been fighting alongside Battery G remained on the field; they had either been killed or had run away. In the meanwhile, the Rhode Islanders had continued their mission to save their two remaining ordnance rifles. A small force of Jerseyans that had been providing covering fire broke and ran to the rear. The situation was now more than desperate for Captain Adams; a third of his men were down and there was only a few rounds left in the chests. All of a sudden, through the white, sulphuric smoke of battle, the Rhode Islanders saw a most welcome sight. It was a brigade of men with white Greek crosses and sprigs of evergreen in their hats; it could mean only one thing. These men were from the Vermont Brigade, which Battery G had supported on several occasions. The Green Mountain Boys held firm, ready to repay the services rendered by the artillerymen. Now they stood on a hill with leveled Enfield muskets ready to blast away at the advancing foe as soon as Battery G was clear from their field of fire. The brave Rhode Islanders had done their duty; they had stymied the flow of retreat, but at a huge price. Now they were under the protection of a solid wall of Sixth Corps infantry. General Wheaton witnessed Battery G's stand and wrote, "I never saw a battery more ably and desperately fought."[38]

For two hours, the Sixth Corps put up a heroic fight, grudgingly trading ground as they delayed the Confederates. Battery G withdrew a mile and a half under fire. Unlike the other two corps, which simply fled and panicked, the Sixth was standing and exchanging volleys with the Rebels. Finally, for no apparent reason, Early halted; he stopped the attack, satisfied he had driven the enemy from the field. His subordinates pleaded with him to renew the initiative; the Federals were running and they would continue if pushed. Early negated as his men plundered the encampment. General Horatio Wright took the lull to regain the initiative and rearm his soldiers. Although wounded, Colonel Tompkins returned to the field and ordered the batteries to change ammunition chests for the struggle ahead, replacing the chests on the limbers as the horses were moved from the caissons to the gun limbers.

At 10:30 that morning, General Sheridan galloped from Winchester and re-formed his forces. Most of the army was re-forming a mile and half to the rear, while only two divisions of mixed troops continued to exchange long-range volleys with the Confederates. Sheridan took his time to rally his men, preparing them to deliver the deathblow to Early's army. After the battle, many wearers of the Greek cross would be shocked to see that Sheridan received all the credit for the battle. If General Wright had not taken matters into his own hands and fought a defensive battle in the morning with the Sixth Corps, the Federals would have been driven out of the Shenandoah. Although Wright had done his duty to halt the Confederates, the Army of the Valley was nearly shattered and required the electrifying leadership of Sheridan to re-form and strike.[39]

At 3:00, all was in order as the Federals counterattacked. The Sixth Corps and the cavalry smashed into Early's thin line as the Confederates retreated in disarray. The artillery acted much as it had at Fisher's Hill, working with the infantry to drive back the enemy on the front line. Although they had been slaughtered in the early morning fight, Battery G again went into combat for twenty minutes with its two guns, using the case shot that remained in the limber chests, shelling the fleeing Rebels and their wagon train that had become bogged down on the Valley Pike. Captain Stevens wrote, "Adams' G Battery maintained a rapid and effective fire until the enemy gave way." By dusk it was the Confederates who were running; they had been engaged all day and were exhausted. At a cost of 6,000 men, the battle was won. The fierce counterattack won the day and an unbelievable victory for the Union cause.[40]

When the battle finally was over, the exhausted survivors of the Sixth Corps Artillery Brigade simply wanted to eat a meal and go to sleep. No sooner had this happened that they were aroused by the bugle. The Federal cavalry had captured forty-eight artillery pieces from the Confederates; Sheridan wanted them removed from the field immediately. In Battery G, the men were anxious to perform the duty, as they finally retook the two guns lost in the struggle. The cannoneers worked all night to drag in the pieces and recover wounded comrades. The Sixth Corps soldiers looked on in disdain at the Eighth and Nineteenth corps; only the Sixth had put up significant resistance. As they cleared the field of the guns, the artillerists were sickened. Even though the Confederates retreated, they stripped the dead of their clothing and equipment, leaving a ghastly scene on the battlefield. The fallen of Battery G were spared such a fate. That night the men in Battery G lay down to sleep in their old camp. Some things would never be the same. Many comrades who had served for nearly three years never returned to duty, or found a soldier's grave. Corporal James Barber wrote, "This has been a day which shall live in history and one long to be remembered by those who took part in this engagement."[41]

The Sixth Corps Artillery Brigade suffered heavily. In total, 130 artillerists were hit; a third of the brigade. Two thirds of the horses were dead. The scene was sobering to even the most battle-hardened veteran. After surviving the carnage of Antietam, Gettysburg, and the Overland Campaign, one Regular confessed, "All the batteries of the Sixth Corps suffered heavily." Of the losses, nearly half were Rhode Islanders; Battery G had the highest amount of casualties in the brigade. The pride of the cannoneers was shaken; there were twenty-four pieces in camp, of which seven were captured and later retaken. That night General Wright rode up to the shattered command and personally thanked Captain Adams and his battery for their performance in the battle, claiming they had saved many lives by their fighting retreat. Another officer summed up Battery G's performance by stating they had "rendered effective service."[42]

Musician Lewis was carried to a field hospital by his two comrades, one of them Henry Seamans, his best friend, who had remained by his side throughout the war. A surgeon examined the gruesome wound and declared it mortal. Privates Seamans, Francis Baker, and Edwin Henshaw ignored their duties with Battery G to attend to Lewis. A small picture of his mother and a pocket Bible proved to be his solace as the bugler quietly prayed; he knew the wound was fatal. Lewis remained conscious throughout the ordeal, denying whiskey or stimulant to keep the promise that he made to his mother not to drink. He directed Seamans to send the remainder of his bounty home to his mother and brothers, so Lewis' estranged father would not receive any of it. Bugler William H. Lewis died of wounds received at the Battle of Cedar Creek on October 21, 1864. The funds were forwarded home, along with his elaborately trimmed musician's jacket. Lewis' body was buried by his friends in a small cemetery near the battlefield, overlooking the scene of the carnage below. In a letter of condolence to his mother, Henry Seamans told her, "All the men that are left out of our Battery feel deeply with you and Mrs. Lewis no heart can tell you how bad I feel. The last words he said to me was these tell my Dear Mother if my wound shall prove to be fatal that I died an Honor to my Coun-

Lieutenant Andrew MacMillan was assigned to Battery G from Battery C but resigned shortly after being released from prison (USAMHI).

try." Lewis had taught his friend how to play the bugle, and now Henry Seamans was promoted and took his comrade's place as Battery G's musician.[43]

The officers and men of Adams' Battery obeyed Colonel Tompkins' orders to stay and
fight; the cost, however, was almost more than could be borne by one small command from
the smallest state. Battery G had suffered the second highest loss for a Rhode Island battery in the war; only ninety officers and men had been engaged in the battle. Of these, nine
soldiers were killed or mortally wounded, while twenty-three were wounded and survived.
Of the wounded, three men were captured and taken to Richmond as prisoners of war.
Among the dying was Private Simeon Starboard, a substitute, who unlike many others
remained in the service and died like a soldier. Starboard had only recently returned from
being sick in Washington, where he still owed the sutlers sixteen dollars. The men in Westerly's First Detachment again lost the most; two were killed and seven were wounded. One
of the injured from the town was Private Samuel W. Place, who had been hit in the lower
right leg. The surgeons had no choice but to amputate and try to save his life before gan-
grene set in. The operation was successful and Place survived; he was fortunate, as nearly
half of all amputation victims died afterwards.[44]

Four of the wounded in the battery had been hit at both Marye's Heights and now at
Cedar Creek. As much a part of the battery as the cannoneers and drivers, another group
of battery members suffered horrendous losses: forty-five horses died. Battery G lost one
third of its strength at Cedar Creek, almost unheard of for an artillery battery. There was
no rest for the artillerists the day after the battle; following a brief meal, the battery went
back to the battlefield and performed the solemn task of burying the four men who were
killed in action. With this completed the battery received additional ammunition to replace
that expended in the battle.[45]

As usual, the people of Rhode Island had only a fleeting glance of what happened to
Battery G at Cedar Creek. The *Providence Journal* presented a small paragraph about Captain Adams' attempt to evacuate the cannon on October 24. Three days later the paper
printed the standard casualty list, forwarded by a member of the command. The people of
Rhode Island had long since been used to such gruesome news, and it did not faze them;
at least it was not Fredericksburg, where seventy-five Rhode Island sons were lost in one
day of combat. Private Thomas L. Stillman of Westerly wrote two letters to the local *Narragansett Weekly*. One headline was "Rhode Island Battery G appears to have had warm
work in the battle of Cedar Creek." The second was a listing of the many casualties the
battery had suffered, with a special emphasis on the majority from southwestern Rhode
Island.

It had been nearly three years since the detachment visited Westerly on its recruiting
mission and taken over twenty of the local boys to Providence. Now the citizens read about
many of them receiving their wounds on a faraway battlefield. The general lack of cover-
age of the battle was not only of concern to the Rhode Islanders, but to all of the soldiers
who fought through it. A Massachusetts soldier in the Sixth Corps soldier wrote, "We have
no Newspapers to blow for this corps."[46]

In Westerly, the way of life had continued much the same throughout the war, except
that most of the young men in the town were gone. With the war going on, the town
became a hub of commerce and transportation as the many mills produced the rough
kersey cloth for the pants and blankets being worn by the cannoneers. The many local
farms as well had continued to produce food for the Union war effort. Now, after yet
another harvest, the third since Battery G left, two of Westerly's bravest sons were never
coming home. Corporal Henry Chace and Private William C. Douglass had both just been

killed in the Battle of Cedar Creek. Unlike most Westerly soldiers who died in the conflict, their bodies were left in the South and not returned to River Bend or a cemetery on their own property. Like John K. Johnson had been after Marye's Heights, these two latest Westerly Boys to give their lives were forgotten; no memorial service was ever held. Poor Yankee farmers and mill workers, their families could not afford to have the remains of their sons brought home.

The bloodbath that the Westerly Boys had gone through would be forgotten by many in the town after the headlines had disappeared, but the scars carried by the survivors would always be present, both physically and mentally. The only solace that Archibald Chace could take was a letter, relating to his son Henry, from Captain Adams that stated, "He performed his duty faithfully, and was loved by everyone." Old Farmer Chace could take pride in the fact that his surviving son, Nathaniel Ray, had not only survived the engagement, but had earned a rare battlefield promotion and was on his way to join Battery B.[47]

Unlike other fields of battle where Rhode Island artillerymen fought and died, there was never a memorial erected at Cedar Creek. Rather the forgotten words of Colonel Charles Tompkins stand in a thick piece of blue Westerly granite: "The conduct of officers and men was gallant in the extreme and it merits the hearty commendation of all who witnessed it. Rhode Island has just cause to be proud of such soldiers."[48]

Promotion was swift to come for the officers of Battery G in recognition of the services performed in the action. Two days after the battle, Lieutenant Elmer Corthell was promoted to the vacant captaincy of Battery D. These soldiers as well were recovering from the shock of being overrun. He was replaced by First Lieutenant Charles A. Brown of Battery B. Brown had distinguished himself at Gettysburg and Spotsylvania, where his section actually charged the Mule Shoe salient and fired canister point blank into the faces of the Confederates. Unfortunately, the officer never reported to Battery G; he was captured a week after Spotsylvania and brought to a prison camp in North Carolina. Brown eventually escaped, but was discharged from the service when he arrived back at Union lines. Instead of Brown, Second Lieutenant Benjamin Freeborn of Battery E was promoted and transferred. For Freeborn, the promotion to first lieutenant brought him back to the battery he had originally enlisted in. First Sergeant Nathaniel R. Chace, who had just lost his brother, was promoted to second lieutenant and assigned to Battery B. One of the many Westerly men in the battery, Chace had enlisted as a private and now became an officer after years of hard work. Marcus Streeter, a vet-

First Lieutenant Jacob H. Lamb was the only Newport soldier in Battery G. He served for three months until becoming captain of Battery E.

eran sergeant, was promoted to fill the vacant place of Chace. He would have his work cut out for him.[49]

Also rewarded was Captain George Adams. General Wheaton was amazed at Adams' handling of his battery at Cedar Creek, and wrote several letters calling for his promotion: "In my opinion he has few superiors in the service, and his admirable battery has been so skillfully and gallantly handled in battle." General Wright added, "Captain Adams is not only thoroughly competent to discharge the duties of an advanced grade, but had claims for promotion earned on many a hard-fought field, and I am only discharging my duty in commending him." The two letters were forwarded to Sheridan's headquarters; the little general apparently had heard of Adams' actions, as he affixed his own endorsement before sending them to Secretary of War Edward Stanton. The secretary acted upon the recommendations and Adams received a brevet of major in November. Although these officers received the promotions, it was the actions of the noncommissioned officers and privates that caused them to be made.[50]

Throughout the Valley Campaign, Colonel Charles Tompkins' Sixth Corps Artillery Brigade had provided the vital firepower needed to support the infantry of the corps. Before serving in the Valley, the corps had been butchered during the spring fighting at the Wilderness, Spotsylvania, and Cold Harbor. This had severely reduced the strength of the Sixth. The force that General Horatio Wright took with him from Petersburg was not the same corps that "Uncle" John Sedgwick had made and commanded. Because of the small numbers, much of the infantry force in the Shenandoah Valley was composed of draftees and recruits who had never seen combat before. Tompkins was fortunate that all of his batteries were composed of hardened combat veterans who had seen years of service. They tipped the balance at Cool Spring, Opequon, Fisher's Hill, and Cedar Creek. When the infantry buckled and could not hold, it was the firepower of the Napoleons, ordnance rifles, and Parrotts that won the day for the Army of the Valley.

On the twenty-seventh, thirty men from the Ninth New York Heavy Artillery arrived in camp to fill the places of the men lost at Cedar Creek. These foot cannoneers arrived with rifle-muskets in hand, which were placed away as they fell in on the guns to learn light artillery drill. Corporal Barber took note of the quietness of the area now that the enemy was finally gone. Although the Confederates had left, another enemy returned in the form of intoxicating beverages; three men were tied to a caisson for intoxication on the twenty-eighth. On the following day, any slight received in the past was overshadowed by another vote of thanks by the Rhode Island General Assembly, which singled out Battery G for its actions at the battle.

On November 2, new equipment was issued to the men to replace what was lost at Cedar Creek. Among the new pieces given out were sabers and belts to all the enlisted men, and pistols were given to the noncommissioned officers. With Sergeant Chace promoted to lieutenant, Sergeant Marcus M. Streeter was promoted to first sergeant. As they did after Marye's Heights, the artillerists needed a respite, but remained alert that Early should strike again.[51]

The three battles in the Shenandoah—Opequon, Fisher's Hill, and Cedar Creek—combined with William Tecumseh Sherman's capture of Atlanta, were the final victories President Lincoln needed to gain the support of the country for his reelection. More important for the men of the Union army, he would continue to serve as the commander in chief. His opponent was George B. McClellan, the first commander of the Army of the Potomac. Many Rhode Island soldiers wrote to their local newspapers, urging their fellow citizens to vote for Lincoln. The country had much to decide; Lincoln would carry the war out to the end, while McClellan would compromise and end it, thus saving their lives. The *Providence Journal* had never been polite to McClellan, carrying little news of his operations. The paper went so far as to call Rhode Island soldiers "failures," should McClellan be elected. The remedy to this was simple: "The men who believe that the soldiers of Rhode Island are not failures will express their sentiments when they vote for Lincoln." The political pundits had their say; it was now up to the people of the United States, including the men of Battery G, to help decide the fate of the United States.

The men of Rhode Island cast their votes for the same person they had elected in 1860. The vote in Westerly was typical and not surprising, 332 for Lincoln and 120 for McClellan. For the first time the soldiers would be allowed to vote from the field. In Battery G the artillerists had much to debate. They had seen McClellan bungle the Peninsula Campaign as the battery waited only ten miles from Richmond for three weeks. The result was the death of more Battery G soldiers than the Confederates had killed at Cedar Creek. On the other hand, they knew Lincoln would not let them lose.

Even if the cannoneers had wanted to vote for McClellan, they could not have, because the Rhode Island Democratic Party failed to supply any ballots to the Rhode Island forces in the valley. Even though there were no ballots, the men still did not want McClellan in office. In Adams' Battery only fifteen native Rhode Island soldiers over twenty-one could be found eligible to vote. Among them was James Barber, who voted in his first presidential election. Although he had not supported Lincoln's political policy towards emancipation, Barber was sure that Lincoln was the only man who could reunite the United States. These fifteen men were unanimous in who they wanted to remain as the president: Abraham Lincoln.[52]

After being defeated at Cedar Creek, Early was relieved of command, while most of the surviving members of the Confederate forces returned to Petersburg; only a small cavalry remnant remained. Several small skirmishes were fought, but the Shenandoah Valley Campaign of 1864 was over. It was not without triumph and tragedy for the officers and men of Battery G. Corporal Barber wrote, "Our Banner with glory and our enemys is near exhausted having been beated in every battlefield during this campaign." On November 9, the Sixth Corps left the scene of battle at Cedar Creek and moved down the Shenandoah to Kernstown, the site of two battles and a new supply depot for Sheridan's Army. Here the Sixth Corps would rest for a month before returning to the front.

Sutlers or contractors providing goods to the army at outrageous prices appeared in camp to peddle their wares. Many of the soldiers in Battery G had lost everything at Cedar Creek, as the Confederates looted the camp; the quartermasters and the supply wagons could not always keep the men well outfitted. The sutlers sold shirts for fourteen dollars, nearly a month's pay for articles that cost the government one dollar. The men remained occupied building entrenchments and digging in; although the Confederates had been defeated, Cedar Creek was not going to happen again. The horse problem continued to persist as several died of "glanders" disease and replacements had yet to be made for those lost in battle. A miserable, cold rain, occasionally turning to snow, pelted the Rhode Islanders daily as they did what soldiers always do, wait.[53]

On November 26, the artillerists were treated to a traditional New England Thanksgiving dinner; cooked turkeys were transported from Providence, one being given to every three men. This was the first meal of the kind the men were to enjoy since leaving their native state. Unlike under Captain Owen's tenure, the officers did not steal the food for themselves. However when the turkeys arrived in camp they were rotted; the men foraged the barren countryside for a meal. After surviving the hellish fighting at Cedar Creek, the remaining soldiers in Battery G had much to be thankful for. Each day they were reminded of the effects of the battle, as many of the artillerist, were dead or remained wounded in the hospitals. Among the comrades remembered was William Lewis. "It seems so lonsome without Billy. He will never be forgotten in our Battery every day there is some one talking about him," recorded Private Seamans to Lewis' inconsolable mother. The private sent Mrs. Lewis her son's effects, and visited his grave often.[54]

After Sergeant Sisson was wounded at Cedar Creek, Sergeant George F. Russell took command of the small remnant of the Westerly detachment. Now, on December 2, he was officially promoted to quartermaster sergeant as he replaced William Potter, who had been serving unofficially in the position since April. Potter took over Russell's detachment. The fifth of December brought an odd visitor to camp; this was the combat artist James Taylor, who visited Battery G's encampment at Kernstown.

The men used their small shelter tents to protect themselves from the cold blasts of an early Virginia winter; there was already snow on the ground, and it fell daily. Expecting to remain in the position all winter, some men added chimneys and made the crude huts they had been used to living in during winter encampments. A section of the battery was constantly posted on the Valley Turnpike, insuring that no Confederates surprised the camp as they had done at Cedar Creek. Taylor introduced himself to Captain Adams, who allowed him to sketch the camp. The artist was surprised that the men had not cut down an old oak tree, which could have provided much fuel for the cold nights. But the Rhode Islanders respected its age. Even more interesting was the crude stables the drivers had erected to protect the horses, a symbol of their Yankee ingenuity.[55]

After remaining in the Shenandoah Valley for five months, Grant ordered the Sixth Corps back to the Petersburg lines. Battery G was not going with their parent organization however; they had more pressing business to attend to in Washington.

14

Consolidation

What is the regard to having men for the Battery.
—First Lieutenant Jacob Lamb, December 18, 1864

The Shenandoah Valley Campaign was the greatest test Battery G had ever faced in their three years in the Union army. At each battle, from Cool Spring to Cedar Creek, the Rhode Islanders had proven themselves on the field by their skilled handling of the guns. Now Captain George Adams' Rhode Islanders were going to Washington for a much needed rest; but what was more important they were to refill its vacant ranks. On December 9, Battery G finally left the Valley and proceeded to Camp Barry. This was an artillery training camp located south of the city, under the command of Lieutenant Colonel J. Albert Monroe of the First Rhode Island Light Artillery. The men were sent into barracks, and they set about to repair the guns, receive new horses, and prepare for duty once more.[1]

Because the battery had been mauled at Cedar Creek, additional soldiers were needed. Battery C had been mustered out of the service in September; now only some sixty odd veterans and recruits remained, and even this skeletal command was reduced by severe losses in the Valley Campaign. With this in mind, the War Department issued orders for the consolidation of Batteries C and G. This had already worked well in August when Batteries A and B of the Second Corps formed into a new Battery B. Because the original Battery C was already mustered out, the new command would still be called Battery G. Corporal Barber was pleased to have the men from Battery C in his unit: "The news was very well received to have the brave boys of C in our company."[2]

While the men from the decimated ranks of Battery G were happy, the soldiers in the other battery were not so pleased. The cannoneers from Battery C felt as though the men from G should be consolidated with them, as they were the senior command. Others, such as Horace Tanner, were unaware that such a momentous occasion was even occurring. Lieutenant Jacob Lamb, who commanded the remnant of Battery C, launched a last ditch campaign with the adjutant general's office in Providence, trying to get recruits for the battery. Lamb pleaded with a senior aide de camp to the governor to press him for recruits: "What is the regard to having men for the Battery. If I do not take some steps at one the Bat will be consolidated with Baty. G." Four days after the letter was written, the War Department issued the nail to the coffin that was once a proud Rhode Island Battery. There would be no compromise; the two batteries would be united.[3]

Battery C was drawn largely from northern Rhode Island. This command was the fourth battery to leave Rhode Island and had seen some of the fiercest fighting in the Union army. In addition, they had also suffered one of the greatest overall losses for an artillery battery in the Army of the Potomac. Battery C had largely distinguished itself on the Peninsula in 1862 as part of the Fifth Corps, covering the retreat during the Seven Days Battles. At Gaines Mill, the battery was overrun and three pieces were taken. Four days later at Malvern Hill, they were the subject of friendly fire that inflicted many casualties. They had

Billy Lewis still rests in the soil of Virginia, along with five other Battery G soldiers, at the National Cemetery in Winchester.

further fought at Antietam, Fredericksburg, and Chancellorsville before they were transferred to the Sixth Corps. Here their combat record largely mirrored that of Battery G, including the brutal contests at Opequon and Cedar Creek. With so few artillerists on duty in both batteries, the only logical conclusion was to combine the two understrength units into one large one. One last draft was occurring in Rhode Island, but all of the recruits were being sent to the Second and Seventh regiments, which had been slaughtered during the Overland Campaign.[4]

In preparation for combining the two commands, Captain Adams had to make some slight adjustments. He had enough vacancies that none of Battery G's officers would be mustered out. However, there would be too many noncommissioned officers. With several of those in Battery C receiving their warrants before the men in G they were senior. Adams was forced to issue Orders 49 reducing Sergeant Alexander Sisson and Corporal Daniel Hoxsie to the ranks. The captain wrote, "This reduction is caused by the exergencies of the service and not through any fault of Sergt. Sisson or Corp. Hoxsie." Both soldiers had been severely wounded at Cedar Creek and it was doubtful they would be returning to the battery. In addition, Corporal Peleg Tucker voluntarily took a reduction to artificer; he was still paid the same amount of money each month and used his carpentry skills to repair the wooden equipment in the battery.

Of all the detachments in the battery, few were more unique than the first, comprising men from the same town. The three years of campaigning and Cedar Creek had effectively ended the all Westerly detachment; hardly any of the original twenty-one from the town were left. Corporal Barber was among them, and even he bore the scars of battle wounds. Only one of the men from Battery C, Maurice Sullivan, was from Westerly. With their leaders gone, the Westerly detachment was officially disbanded. Its members and the survivors from Charlestown, Richmond, and Hopkinton were integrated into rest of the battery.[5]

Among the new Battery G soldiers was Charles H. Rice. A farmer from the small hamlet of Hopkins Hollow in southwestern Coventry, Rice had joined Battery C in August of 1862 to fight alongside his brother William, who had gone to war in 1861. William Rice had decided not to reenlist and went back to Hopkins Hollow, while Charles would muster on in Battery G until he was discharged. Unfortunately the homecoming of the Rice brothers would be premature, as Charles carried home the disease that would kill him in 1868; it was acquired while serving his country.[6]

The men spent Christmas touring the city, while the officers hurriedly finished the paperwork. Battery C would officially cease to exist as a combat unit, and all of its records had to be made in duplicate and then forwarded to Providence and Washington. Finally, on December 29, sixty-four veterans from Battery C arrived in camp. Captain Adams promptly greeted the men by reading their names off and telling them of their duty in his battery. In order to allow the Rhode Islanders to fully integrate into his command, Adams allowed all of the noncommissioned officers to remain and gave them their choice in selecting which detachment they wanted to serve with. Furthermore, the privates not only named which detachment they wanted to be assigned to, but also what numbered position that they wanted to serve in. Some men became defiant and still referred to themselves as

Lieutenant Reuben H. Rich was transferred from Battery C and was wounded during the storming of Petersburg (USAMHI).

serving in Battery C, even though it no longer existed. Despite this defiance to orders, the men settled in peacefully and boosted Battery G's ranks. The new cannoneers and drivers provided a welcome relief and would add even more luster to Battery G in the months ahead.[7]

With the consolidation complete, Battery G had an aggregate of 214 officers and men in the new command; this included some thirty men attached from the Ninth New York Heavy Artillery who were returned to Petersburg and their unit on New Year's Day.

Battery C was represented by Lieutenants Jacob Lamb, Reuben H. Rich, and Andrew MacMillan. Like Lieutenant Charles Brown, MacMillan was being held as a prisoner of war; he would resign when he was released. Reuben Rich's war had been remarkably similar to Captain Adams' service. Like Adams, he had been a member of the Providence Marine Corps of Artillery and had enlisted in the First Battery as a private, then joined Battery C as a corporal and was steadily promoted. Rich as well had been severely wounded in the right leg at Cedar Creek, but unlike other members of the command he was harboring some dark news from home. His wife had committed adultery and "consorted with persons of lewd & bad character." Lieutenant Rich had already begun divorce proceedings from the field and they would be finalized when he returned home.[8]

Battery G's second in command, First Lieutenant Freeborn, was sent on detached duty to the Sixth Corps Artillery Brigade. Lieutenant Lamb became the de facto second in command of the battery. The oldest combat officer in the regiment, Lamb was a former Regular who had fought in Mexico. Settling in Newport after that war, he became a merchant and in 1861 enlisted as a sergeant in Battery E, along with his twelve-year-old son. Like all of the other officers in the command, Jacob Lamb had risen from the ranks to an officer's commission. A member of the Vermont Brigade who had watched him command Battery C during the rout at Fisher's Hill called him "a gray-haired Rhode Islander."[9]

Because a large number of men from both batteries were still absent, suffering from wounds, there were 166 enlisted men present for duty. This was the largest number of men Battery G had ever had in its ranks. The large force was reduced slightly on December 18, when the three years' enlistment of eleven original battery members expired. They were paid off and returned home to Rhode Island after having served their country for three years and seeing the war almost to the end.[10]

While sixty-four men reported to camp for duty with Battery G, two men did not. First Sergeant John B. Peck and Quartermaster Sergeant Christopher Carpenter of Battery C tried to justify their rank with the War Department; indeed, they were senior to the men in Battery G. Despite this, Adams refused to allow their muster in, and the two men would not take a reduction in rank. Lieutenant Lamb had tried to save Sergeant Peck from losing his rank by requesting his promotion to second lieutenant and transfer to another battery for actions at Cedar Creek; there was only one opening in the regiment and it went to Nathaniel Chace. For the time being, the two sergeants would remain in the army with pay, but without a unit to serve in.[11]

As the two batteries effected their consolidation in Washington, another chapter in the history of Battery G was ending in Providence. After resigning his commission in June, Lieutenant Otto L. Torslow returned to Rhode Island to establish a mercantile business, the same job as the other men who had commanded Battery G. Still having friends he could count on in the Rhode Island General Assembly, Torslow soon began to play up his wounds from Marye's Heights. They were slight and the officer did not have to go to the hospital in May of 1863. Now he began to complain that the wounds were proving to be mortal and he would die any day. He had applied for a pension but had still not received it. The Republicans, who controlled the general assembly, passed a resolution in January calling for the state treasurer to pay Torslow one hundred and seventy-five dollars "as a gratuity for his faithful services, and in consideration that he now lies, without relatives in this country, suffering under a grievous and probably fatal wound, without means of support." This was an insult to the many other immigrants in Battery G, namely the Irish, who never received additional money for the injuries they suffered in the service and carried on without complaining. Lieutenant Torslow collected his money and resumed work in Providence.[12]

While politics were being hammered out on Smith Hill, two mothers who had been affected by the Shenandoah Campaign mourned their losses in the Olneyville section of Providence. Amanda Scott had yet to hear any news on the fate of her son, Lieutenant Scott, who still lay in agony in a hospital near Winchester. In a house down the road, Jane B. Lewis had already received the news in October that no mother ever wants to hear. Her son, William Lewis, was killed at age nineteen years.

Although Jane Lewis still had three sons, the loss of Billy, as he was called, affected her deeply. She desperately wanted to bring her son's body home, or at the very least visit the grave. Henry Seamans talked her out of both, as it would cost her a great deal of money she needed for her family, and the area where he was buried was still haunted by guerillas. The musician assured the grieving mother that he had been "buried as good as if at home." Mrs. Lewis' strong Christian faith kept her going; her sister, Irene P. Williams, one of Bugler Lewis' aunts, composed a short poem about his life and death:

> I speak of one who left this state
> When his country's voice come
> How sad, and mournful was his fate
> He died far, far, from home.

While nobly fighting on the field,
A deadly missile from the foe
Pierced through his sides, there was nought to shield
The tidings to his home brought woe.

When far from home and those he loved
What must his thoughts have been,
Perchance with fancys eye he roved
For the streets at home again.

Fond mother, look beyond the grave
Your son is now in heaven,
Eternal life he there will gave
By God's own hand its given.

Rest loved one rest, though here on earth,
Mother, and brothers mourn thy loss
From scenes of war you're gone we trust;
Where gold is never mixed with dust.

Unable to ever see her son again, Jane Lewis took comfort in the fact that he died doing his duty and was missed tremendously by his comrades in Battery G. Private Seamans wrote, "God would not took your son from this wicked world if he had not thought best. Billy is far more happier ware he is now that he would be in this world." The young soldier did as requested by his friend and sent home to Olneyville over four hundred dollars in bounty money and back pay that was owed to Bugler Lewis; Lewis' mother did not have long to wait until she began receiving a mother's pension in January.[13]

Back in Washington, each day at Camp Barry the artillerists arose and after breakfast began hours of drill. This was to insure that the original members, transferred Battery C soldiers, drafted men, substitutes, and detached infantry all understood the movements of the battery. It was very similar to the scene of some three years earlier when Battery G arrived in Maryland to learn the same process for the first time. Throughout the entire ordeal, Captain Adams was very strict when it came to orders, paying attention that every detail and every move was done in accordance to the manual. In January a correspondent from the *Washington Chronicle* visited Camp Barry and was quite pleased to view Adams, who, unlike many other officers, took a direct role in the leadership and training of his men: "His whole soul is in his profession and though a strict disciplinarian, he is loved and respected by his command. He has striven to make soldiers of his men, and the fact is admitted he has succeeded."

With the city nearby, the alcohol problems that had plagued the battery for so long continued to persist; Captain Adams simply tied the offenders to a caisson wheel. This discipline was very necessary and had, unlike in other units, prevented Battery G from coming apart at Cedar Creek. Although a merchant by training, Adams defined the role of a citizen-soldier: to leave everything behind to go to fight for one's country. He had risen through the ranks from private and transformed a disorderly gaggle of Rhode Islanders into one of the premier batteries in the United States Army. During one day of drill, Buglers Henry Seamans and Francis C. Baker, both new to this trade, blew Boots and Saddles, the artillery call to assemble and be ready to move. It only took a half hour for the entire battery to fall in, pack up, harness the horses, and begin moving. A newspaper correspondent watching wrote, "Battery G is not surpassed by any battery in the service, and has a record for hard fighting that the state may well be proud of." The constant drilling would prove invaluable in several months.[14]

After receiving two severe wounds in the legs at Cedar Creek, Lieutenant Charles V. Scott spent three miserable months in a crowded field hospital at Winchester. His left leg was amputated, and there was some hope that he could recover. Indeed, on December 9, Sergeant George Russell visited Scott and reported back to Battery G that "he was doing well." But on January 21, 1865, the young officer died of infection caused by the amputation. Instead of being sent home to recover, the army red tape had prevented him from dying in his home at Portsmouth Grove. On February 1, he was posthumously promoted to brevet captain for "gallant and meritorious services at Cedar Creek." Before the advent of medals, brevets were given as additional rank increases to cite bravery, but carried no extra pay. Brevet Captain Charles V. Scott was the highest ranking officer in the First Rhode Island Light Artillery Regiment to lose his life during the war. Unlike the other members of the battery who fell at Cedar Creek, Scott's body was returned to Providence for burial; his mother, Amanda, received his back wages of $227.46. Mrs. Scott was left destitute; her sole provider was gone.

After Marye's Heights, the body of Lieutenant Benjamin Kelley was buried at the exclusive Swan Point Cemetery with full military honors and members of the state hierarchy attending. When Scott's body came home, it was given a simple Episcopal service and was buried in the middle class Grace Church Cemetery in South Providence. No military honors or heroic speeches were delivered; even the Rhode Island Militia did not parade. It was strictly a private affair. The difference between the two officers was stark. Kelley's family were members of the Providence political elite; a commission came easily to him after a year as first sergeant. Scott was a member of the working class, making screws in Providence before the war. He had enlisted as a private and earned his commission at Bull Run and it took almost three years to reach him. In her pitiful condition, Amanda Scott could not even provide for her son in death; he was buried without a grave marker. Lieutenant Scott died a forgotten officer. No notice of his death was carried in the Providence papers, and he never made a postwar listing of deceased officers.[15]

With the consolidation completed, Battery G received a new complement of four three-inch ordnance rifles to replace the four worn guns first issued to the battery in 1862, and which had seen service through the Peninsula, Antietam, the battles of Fredericksburg, Gettysburg, Mine Run, and Spotsylvania, and the Valley Campaign. The integration of the men into the battery was over, while drill and general camp duties were the order of the day as the men prepared to leave Camp Barry and return to the front. Finally, on February 20, after nearly three months in camp, the orders were received. The artillerists from Rhode Island were returning to the front at Petersburg.

"The Forlorn Hope"

*This detachment was of great service in the operations subsequent to the
assault in turning the captured guns upon the enemy's columns and works.*
—Major General Horatio Wright, April 4, 1865

Two and a half months in Washington had produced a new Battery G. With their consolidation and retraining, the command was ready for any task placed before it. Now they would show that to both friend and foe alike as they were reassigned to the Sixth Corps Artillery Brigade, now in position before Petersburg. As the battery returned to the front, things were different. There were no more brave men like Charles Scott and William Lewis, or the others from the New York, Rhode Island, and Regular Batteries who had fallen in the Valley. Gone too was the one man who had made Battery G and the Rhode Island Artillery all that it was: Colonel Charles H. Tompkins. His wound was too severe for him to return to the front and he was given a desk job. In his three years in command of the regiment, Tompkins' training had more than paid off on every battlefield the Rhode Islanders had unlimbered on. Now they were going back to his former command, but without their brave colonel to lead them.

After a four day voyage and march from Camp Barry, Battery G arrived at Petersburg on February 24. The command moved into an extensive line of trenches that the Union troops had been preparing since the Sixth Corps had left the preceding July. The weather remained extremely cold, with frozen earthworks. The battery took position near Fort Fisher, the largest earthen fort at Petersburg, recently completed by the Seventh Rhode Island. With Colonel Tompkins still recovering from his wounds received at Cedar Creek, Brevet Major and Captain George Adams took command of the Sixth Corps Artillery Brigade until Major Andrew Cowan returned from detached duty. Grant's plan all winter had been to constantly push west in an attempt to outflank Lee. In this he succeeded by stretching the lines to thirty-seven miles around Petersburg and Richmond. The Sixth Corps moved to the extreme left of the Federal line, recently vacated by the Ninth Corps. While other soldiers had to live in bombproofs, shelters dug into the ground to offer safety from artillery fire, the men in the Sixth Corps simply built huts or erected their shelter tents. Petersburg had changed radically since Battery G was last present in July of 1864. During the Shenandoah Campaign the battery had been assigned to provide fire for the Third Division of the Sixth Corps. Now back at Petersburg they were transferred back to General Wheaton's First Division, which had played such an important role with them at Cedar Creek. The cannoneers positioned the four new ordnance rifles in the fort, and the horses were corralled in the rear.[1]

As Battery G returned to the front, changes were again taking place in the unit. The effects of the Battle of Cedar Creek continued to be felt daily in the battery. Of the twenty-three men who had been hit and survived the brutal struggle, eighteen of them remained in hospitals around Washington recovering from wounds, with ten more suffering from

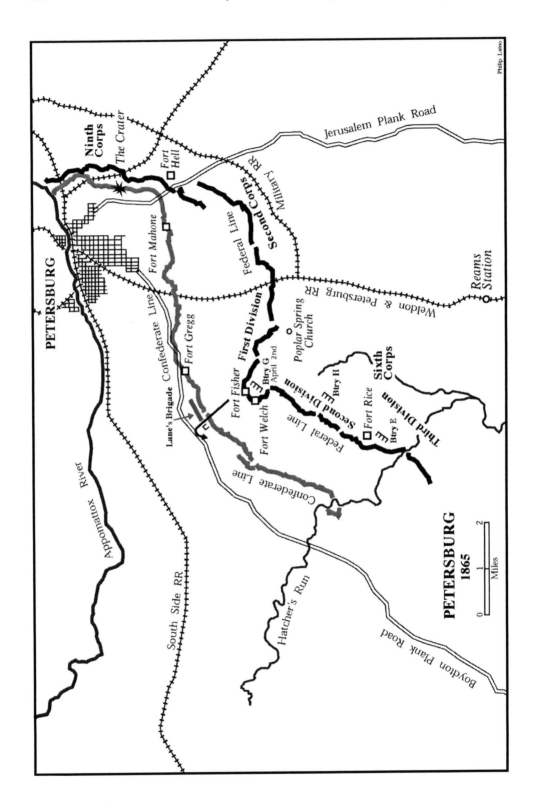

illness. Several artillerists remained at Camp Barry on detached duty. As usual, five men were absent without leave. Furthermore, three members of Battery G were very close to the command, but far away at the same time. These were the three men who had been captured at Cedar Creek and were being held prisoner in Richmond. One of them was Private Albert C. Durfee of Foster. He suffered daily from a debilitating lung ailment caused by his yet to heal gunshot wound and the dank conditions of the prison. Among those not with the battery was the recently transferred Second Lieutenant Andrew C. MacMillan. The lieutenant was also absent as a prisoner of war, having been captured the previous September, immediately after the Battle of Opequon. When he was finally released, however, he was a supernumerary officer and was mustered out of the service.[2]

The winter of 1865, like that at Brandy Station, passed very quietly for Battery G. Both cannoneers and drivers strengthened the works by digging into the frozen soil of Virginia, chopping down trees and constructing abatis, sharpened sticks to act as the first line of defense for the soldiers at the front. This building kept the men occupied as they waited for action. The four cannon were kept in the parapets of Fort Fisher. The men simply performed manual labor or drilled to pass the idle moments; off duty time was spent gambling or writing. Although the enemy never appeared during the day, they came frequently at night but in a far different manner than they had previously.

Because of the harsh conditions in the trenches before Petersburg, hundreds of Confederates deserted to the Union lines. They were encouraged by promises of a bounty and food. Circulars were given to the pickets to throw into the trenches to inspire the Rebel soldiers to leave their cause. The Confederates in the front of Battery G did not engage the battery that frequently and no opportunities came to return fire. With over 2,000 yards between them, the entrenchments separating the two sides were the farthest apart of any on the line. On the right, at the Ninth Corps encampment, the lines were so close that men could be heard in an ordinary whisper; but near Hatcher's Run things were different. Shots were exchanged infrequently as the two sides were often more concerned about surviving the elements than each other.[3]

Vermont Captain Charles Gould's order to "take the guns" allowed Battery G's deed of valor to be performed (USAMHI).

On the third of March, Battery G again said farewell to ten more comrades whose time was up; among those who went home was Albert Cordner. To make matters even worse, six attached men were transferred to Battery E. They had been detached from their parent units for some time, but instead of returning there they had reenlisted in the First Rhode Island Light Artillery. Now they were sent to Battery E to rebuild the strength of that unit. To replace them, ten men were drafted from the Fourth Maine Battery. Captain Adams asked the State of Rhode Island to forward twenty-two recruits to Battery G: none came. Despite the men who were recently transferred from Battery C, Adams was concerned that he only had ninety-seven men on duty.[4]

The large Irish contingent in Battery G again celebrated Saint Patrick's Day on March 17. This time it was extra violent, as some soldiers became terribly intoxicated and fell off their horses, resulting in some injury. The Confederates saw the celebration and fired, but stopped once they knew what it was. Although there had been prejudices against them early in the war, the Irish had proven themselves on the battlefield and in the battery. On March 22, Sergeant Edward G. Sullivan became the last Battery G soldier to die of the disease that had constantly plagued the unit. He was interred with military honors in the Sixth Corps Artillery Brigade cemetery. With little relief, the men continued with their duty, waiting for the end to come.[5]

On March 25, Lee decided to launch one last offensive. The Army of Northern Virginia would attempt to break out of the Petersburg defenses and march south to North Carolina to link up with another large Confederate force and carry on the fight. In order to force his way out, Lee dispatched a large force to attack and capture Fort Stedman on the Federal right; this distraction would allow the Confederate force to slip away. The assault went as planned in the early hours of the twenty-fifth as the Rebels struck the fortification and pushed back the Pennsylvanian defenders. Almost immediately, the Confederate cannoneers facing the Sixth Corps began to fire their guns to keep the Federals on the left from reinforcing the attack on the right. The Pennsylvanians counterattacked and soon drove back the enemy. In Fort Fisher, the men in Battery G and the Third Vermont Battery instantly answered and began sending shells into the Confederate works to prevent an enemy force from attacking their sector of the line. This was at the extreme distance for the guns, but the artillerists provided covering fire for a vital mission. Seeing an opportunity, the Vermont Brigade of the Sixth Corps went in and captured an advance portion of the Confederate entrenchments. Now fewer than 800 yards separated the two armies. Little did the men in Battery G know, but this position would be of immense importance in a few days.[6]

Lieutenant General Ulysses S. Grant pondered the situation in late March 1865. For nine months the Army of the Potomac had been besieging Richmond and Petersburg. Lee's lines were stretched to the breaking point; his 40,000 men were stationed

Major William Sperry of the Sixth Vermont captured the howitzers and ordered them turned on the enemy, for which he was awarded the Medal of Honor (USAMHI).

along a forty mile front. With deserters pouring in each day, Grant knew it was time to move. He now planned to launch the campaign to finally capture Richmond and end the Civil War. The plan was set in motion on March 29, as the Cavalry and Fifth Corps marched to the left and on April 1 attacked and captured the strategic crossroads at Five Forks while the Confederate commander was engaged in having a fish bake rather than attending to his men. Now one of Lee's lines of retreat was cut off. Unable to flank the defenses, Grant ordered a direct frontal assault on Petersburg itself. At 4:00 on the morning of April 2, the Army of the Potomac would charge. This time Richmond was going to fall, no matter what the cost.[7]

Major Andrew Cowan's Sixth Corps Artillery Brigade were assigned to provide supporting fire for the assault. After receiving notice of the charge, Captain Adams went to General Horatio Wright with a mission he had been considering since his arrival at Petersburg. When the infantry charged, they would capture the enemy's cannon. These guns could be used to support the infantry charge and if need be repel any Confederate counterattack. Captain Adams proposed, "with his characteristic daring," to take a section of his battery on foot and charge the lines with the infantry. Once inside the fortifications they would capture the cannons and use them on their former owners. If this failed, the detachment would "spike and render them useless, as circumstances might warrant." Meanwhile the remainder of the command would stay behind and use Battery G's own ordnance rifles as support. Corporal Edward P. Adams called it "a movement so full of hazard." Before granting permission to the captain, General Wright "warned him of its extreme danger." Adams would not back down and finally Wright gave his consent and the captain hurried back to the battery to prepare the men for the mission.[8]

Captain George W. Adams laid his plan before the cannoneers of Battery G. He would take only volunteers with him, knowing full well that this charge could be a costly one. Adams stressed the extreme importance and danger of the mission; no one would be looked down upon who did not volunteer. The captain explained this to the artillerists and then called for the men. One cannoneer recalled, "It was a dangerous enterprise, but the men were eager for a trial." Battery G at this time was an odd mixture of detached soldiers, transferred men from the Second Rhode Island, and the artillerists of Batteries C and G; only forty of the men present were originally members of the battery. Every member of the battery instantly stepped forward to volunteer. Finally, the captain selected twenty men for the storming party, two detachments of soldiers he knew would carry out the mission. Eleven of these men were former members of Battery C.

Corporal Samuel E. Lewis served from Coventry and was one of seven cannoneers awarded the Medal of Honor for heroic actions at Petersburg.

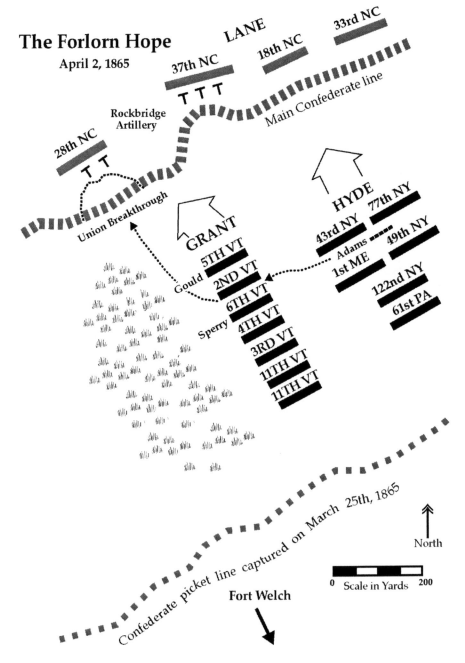

The Forlorn Hope

April 2, 1865

LANE

37th NC

18th NC

33rd NC

Rockbridge
Artillery

Main Confederate line

28th NC

Union Breakthrough

GRANT

HYDE

5TH VT

77th NY

Gould

2ND VT

43rd NY

Adams

49th NY

1st ME

6TH VT

Sperry

4TH VT

122nd NY

3RD VT

61st PA

11TH VT

11TH VT

Confederate picket line captured on March 25th, 1865

North

0   Scale in Yards   200

Fort Welch

Unlike the infantry, armed with musket and bayonet, the cannoneers would be carrying only their sponge-rammers and lanyards. Artillery spikes were also issued; if the men failed in the mission they could at least put these pieces of iron in the vents of the guns, thus rendering them inoperable. Only the noncommissioned officers had the revolvers Adams had issued in November. The veterans quietly quipped in the ranks of the hopelessness of such an attack, while others wrote their last letters. With his detachment ready, Adams left camp and moved up to the front to find a position to charge from, while Lieutenants Jacob Lamb, Reuben Rich, and Frank Waterman took command of the remaining men as they prepared the guns for action once more. Lieutenant Freeborn remained on staff duty. Although one section had been turned in the previous May, Battery G had retained its four experienced subalterns.[9]

At 10:00 that night, all of the Sixth Corps batteries began firing a heavy bombardment to soften up the Confederate defenses and to mass the noise of the infantry as they formed up. The Sixth Corps infantry moved to the front of the fortifications and formed en masse, all being in position by midnight. The position captured by the Vermonters on March 25 would be the starting point. A section of Battery H also left the entrenchments to support the charge of Wheaton's Division, much as Battery G had done at Fisher's Hill. Once the soldiers were ready, the artillery ceased fire; the corps lay down on the damp, cold ground in front of the works. Some soldiers cautiously made trips to the forts in the rear to bring hot coffee to their comrades in the ranks.[10]

Axmen would lead the assault, cutting away at the Confederate defenses so the rest of the Sixth Corps could quickly follow through the breach. A small break in the entrenchments near a marsh would be the focal point of the Sixth Corps. The infantry was ordered to load, but not cap, their weapons, thus preventing accidental firing, as the officers were to lead from the front. Silence was to be maintained at all costs, and men were threatened with death if they spoke. General Wheaton directed Captain Adams to report to Colonel Thomas W. Hyde, a Mainer, as he moved his brigade into position on the outskirts of Fort Welch; the detachment arrived at midnight.[11]

The Sixth Corps was arranged in the shape of a spear with the First Division on the right, followed by the Second, and the Third on the left. In total, some 14,000 men wearing the Greek cross would charge the works. The men were formed in echelon; the first line would smash through the defenses as the lines to the rear followed through. This same plan of attack had already benefited the Sixth Corps at Marye's Heights and Spotsylvania. Hyde's Third Brigade, Second Division, Sixth Corps, formed the point of the spear as they prepared for the mission. The brigade was in the middle of the corps line. Battery G was part of the "forlorn hope," the first to enter the works, but also very likely the first to be shot. The position of the detachment was to be in the rear of the first line of infantry; as soon as the parapet was clear, the cannoneers would work the guns. The Forty-Third and Seventy-Seventh New York would lead the column, followed by the First Maine, Forty-Ninth and One Hundred Twenty-Second New York, and the Sixty-First Pennsylvania bringing up the rear. To their left was the Sixth Corps' most famous unit, the Vermont Brigade. Captain Hazard Stevens of General Getty's staff remembered Battery G's desperate stand at Cedar Creek. Riding along as the Second Division was moving into line, Stevens saw "Captain Adams with twenty picked men of his Rhode Island Battery, provided with rammers and primers ready to turn the enemys guns upon him as soon as captured."[12]

Hyde's Brigade was to enter the entrenchments and swing left, cutting off the Boydton Plank Road and then the South Side Railroad, a major rail line and retreat route for the Confederates. It was a moonless, misty, cold night as the men clutched the ground, their thick overcoats protecting them from the morning cold. A heavy ground fog lay over the trenches; it was so thick the soldiers could not see twenty yards in front of them. Furthermore, the Confederates thought something was occurring and kept up a sporadic fire all night long. The Sixth Corps soldiers yelled back it was an "April's Fool's." The twenty artillerymen in Captain Adams' detachment went over the plan again and again with their commander: take the guns, swing them around, and begin using them against the enemy. Four o'clock came and there was no firing as Grant waited for the fog to lift somewhat so that the Union fire would not endanger the advancing columns. It was the moment of truth for the cannoneers. Adams asked the men for the final time if any wanted to depart and return to Battery G. Three men did and left seventeen to go forward. Among those who returned was Bugler Henry Seamans. After four hours of waiting, it was time to go.[13]

The first shot was fired at 4:40 in the morning by Battery E, First Rhode Island Artillery, on the extreme left of the Sixth Corps line at Fort Rice. From the start there was contention between which battery fired the first shot. The Rhode Island sources state it was Battery E, the Vermont accounts it to the Third Vermont Battery. Lieutenant Elisha Potter of Battery E wrote, "Genl. Wright was anxious that the first gun would be fired from his line on that night and instructions were sent to Battery Commanders accordingly. I was fortunate enough to fire the desired first gun." The Third was stationed at Fort Fisher, right in the middle of the attacking columns. The guns of the Third Vermont would have endangered the men right in their front going forward. The idea of the signal gun was one on each end of the line, Battery E on the left and the Seventh Maine on the right at the Ninth Corps' Fort Sedgwick. With this in mind and the confusion of battle, both the Rhode Islanders and the Vermonters claimed the honor.[14]

Immediately every gun in the Army of the Potomac began shelling the city, including the four pieces from Battery G. Because of the immense noise from all of the cannon going off at the same time, there was a ten minute delay before the men knew that it was

The Civil War Medal of Honor (Library of Congress).

actually the signal to go in. With the Fifth Vermont in the lead, the rest of the Sixth Corps followed after them, and soon 14,000 men were advancing towards the enemy lines. Dr. Stevens of New York recorded, "Without wavering, through the darkness, the wedge which was to the split the confederacy was driven home." Many batteries in the Sixth Corps Artillery Brigade fired only a dozen rounds before they had to stop so that no friendly fire would occur as the columns pushed on.[15]

As Colonel Hyde deployed his brigade, Captain Adams and his men suddenly realized they had lost contact with the New Yorkers to their right. Instead, the detachment angled to the left and followed the Green Mountain Boys as they pressed on. One of the Sixth Corps' original units, the Old Vermont Brigade had a reputation for fighting that no other brigade could match; it came at a cost. The Vermonters had the highest loss in battle of any brigade in the Union army. General Lewis A. Grant had formed his men with the Fifth Regiment in front, followed by the Second, Sixth, Fourth, Third, and two battalions of the Eleventh Vermont bringing up the rear. Grant's Brigade had the distinction of being one of the few all state brigades in the Army of the Potomac. Now the proud Green Mountain Boys rushed onward in total darkness. Grant had selected a six hundred yard long ravine that led directly to the weak point in the Confederate line. It was in this ravine that nearly 2,000 Vermonters now charged. Captain Adams saw them and ordered his seventeen men to follow the Fifth Vermont; they would be the first to strike the Confederate line. Battery G and the Vermont Brigade were intimately familiar with each other, the two having supported each other on numerous occasions from Granite Hill to Petersburg. After the Federal artillery had ceased, the lines had been very quiet, with only the occasional clanking of metal, the footsteps of the advancing columns and the flapping in the breeze of dark blue flags with the motto "Freedom and Unity" inscribed upon them. All of a sudden, the Confederate defenses came alive and men began to fall.

Speaker of the House Henry Joshua Spooner, a Rhode Island Republican and veteran of the Fourth Rhode Island, was instrumental in having the Medal of Honor awarded to Privates Potter and Corcoran.

The very guns that Battery G had been sent to capture were firing salvos of canister, knocking down many of the Vermonters. Although the Confederates were poorly equipped, they still had plenty of fight left. Lieutenant Charles Anson of the Eleventh Vermont remembered: "Rushing to their guns a terrible fire of shot and shell, grape and canister pouring into the advancing columns. Thick and fast came the cannon shot, thicker and faster came the bullets." In fifteen minutes, 1,100 members of the corps went down. Despite this, the seventeen Rhode Islanders kept pushing onward. Within minutes, the infantry was scrambling into the forts as flashes of musketry and cannon fire illuminated the early morning sky. The element of surprise had been lost, so the Federals let out a tremendous roar, fired a volley, and went in with the bayonet. A captain from the Fifth Vermont was the first to jump into the Rebel entrenchments that had stood for so long; now they simply crumbled under the pressure of the charging lines. After crossing the deadly space between the two sides, the small Rhode Island detachment was almost there. Rushing forward into the smoke filled entrenchments, the artillerists saw a prime target before them: an earthen gun emplacement. The position was located near a swamp in a woodlot. The Vermonters shouted out "Capture that battery," and the eager soldiers promptly obeyed. This is what George Adams' Rhode Islanders had been sent to accomplish.[16]

Around the fortification was a line of earthworks held by a brigade of North Carolinians commanded by James Lane, but most important was what the works contained. Covering the break in the fortifications near the swamp, the Confederates had stationed two twenty-four pound howitzers to the left side of the salient, while another howitzer, two other cannon, and an eight-inch mortar were positioned on the right of the ravine that the Vermonters charged through, presenting a deadly position for an advancing foe. These guns were from the Rockbridge Artillery of Virginia; this battery had been trained by Stonewall Jackson himself. These cannon were larger than any other piece Battery G had ever operated. The howitzers were formerly Union pieces, captured in battle by the Confederates; now they would be reclaimed by the Army of the Potomac. In the way of this goal were the Virginia cannoneers and the Twenty-Eighth North Carolina; they were all that stood in the path of the charging Vermonters and Rhode Islanders.[17]

A party of men from Company G of the Fifth Vermont had lost their way in the initial bombardment as they crossed no-man's-land, leaped onto the parapet and into the redoubt. Before being shot, Captain Charles Gould had led thirty men to the left as they went for the cannon. In an instant, the Green Mountain Boys were in the position, fighting hand to hand for its possession. In the Virginia ranks, Lieutenant Samuel Wallace was clubbed to death as Sergeant James T. Paxton was dispatched by a rifle shot. The Virginians did not abandon the guns without a fight. Lieutenant Robert Pratt of the Fifth remembered the sanguinary fight for the guns as a Virginian stood by, lanyard in hand, ready to fire in the faces of the Vermonters: "We soon got possession of the fort taking a good many prisoners. I struck a man with my saber that was just going to fire the cannon bearing on our troops. Knocked him under the gun but did not kill him. I sent him to the front as a prisoner." Two more cannoneers were killed, while six were wounded, three of them being captured. Captain Gould, the first Union soldier inside the works, called it "a short but desperate fight." Lieutenant Pratt left the cannon and prisoners as the rest of Company G re-formed and pushed further into the Confederate works.[18]

Directly in back of Gould's men was Major William Sperry of the Sixth Vermont. Sperry saw the two abandoned howitzers and knew exactly what needed to be done. He took charge of the operation and rallied a dozen men from the Vermont Brigade and ordered the two guns turned around on the fleeing mass of North Carolinians and Georgians. Major Sperry then directed some of his men from the Sixth and a few wayward members of the Eleventh Vermont to load the two pieces. Unable to find any primers among the debris of the battlefield, Sperry directed his men to fire blanks from their muskets into the vents of the cannon; twelve rounds were fired in this manner. Major Sperry would later earn the Medal of Honor for his actions in taking the guns and ordering their use on the enemy.[19]

Battery G, caught in the confusion of the battlefield, finally found their target and went in as the Vermonters fired the howitzers. The men scrambled up the steep fortification and found the Green Mountain Boys fast at work. Captain Adams lost his footing and had a difficult time mounting the works and Corporal James Barber took his hand and helped the captain up into the position. Major Sperry instantly realized what Adams and his men were there to accomplish and surrendered the position to the artillerists. His party from the Sixth and Eleventh Vermont re-formed their ranks and joined in the pursuit of the Confederates. As they did, the captured prisoners were left behind. Unable to accommodate them, the Rhode Islanders sent them to the rear.[20]

While Battery G had been waiting to charge, some of the men had worried that many of their number would be lost in the assault; fortunately the charge was almost bloodless. As the Carolinians ran away, they fired one last ragged volley. Two Coventry men were wounded in the exchange. Private Luther Cornell received a paralyzing injury from a minie ball to the right shoulder, which he would never recover from. George W. Potter was hit in the left eye, which instantly blinded him. The men had done their duty by volunteering to go. Knowing what was ahead of him, Captain Adams had no use for two severely wounded cannoneers and ordered both to the rear and the waiting surgeons; Cornell made it back on his own, while Potter required two men to help carry him. This left only Adams and thirteen men to work the guns. With the fortifications now in Union control, the men got to work.[21]

Half of the regiments in the Sixth Corps which made the charge claimed the honor of being the first Union troops to reach the Confederate line; indeed all were, in reaching their own portion of the line. As the Sixth Corps infantry drove on, they ran into stiffer Confederate resistance. In the Second Rhode Island Regiment, Sergeant William J. Babcock planted the American flag on the parapet, and was awarded the Medal of Honor. Some of the Rhode Islanders disobeyed orders and began giving out mad Narragansett Indian battle yells. The Confederates heard the commotion and instantly began to concentrate their fire against these positions; sixteen soldiers from the Second were hit, two fatally. All order was lost as the Sixth Corps soldiers broke ranks and fought in a brutal struggle with the Rebels to capture the works. Private Wilbur Fisk of the Second Vermont

Throughout his life, James Barber would be proud of his service in Battery G. Here he wears the Medal of Honor (courtesy of Midge A. Frazel).

recalled, "The old Sixth Corps had made Lee's strong line of no use to him—charging through Rebel fort, and killing Rebel soldiers with Rebel artillery, in a terribly unceremonious manner." As he galloped towards a subordinate's headquarters, A.P. Hill, a senior Confederate general, was killed.[22]

At the South Side Railroad, the Sixth Corps reformed and swung to the left, capturing hundreds of prisoners as they began to tear up the railroad. They also started to take some heavy losses as they pushed on towards Hatcher's Run. Five Confederate battle flags and tons of materiel were also captured. Nearly fifty Rebel guns were taken, including a dozen in Battery G's sector of the line, but the thirteen Rhode Islanders could man only two of them, the captured howitzers. The infantry then angled to the right and began to charge towards Petersburg itself. The officers were having a tough time trying to keep their commands together as the men were so excited in the moment of victory. It was almost every man for himself as they charged through the works, killing every Confederate in sight. The sun was starting to rise as the Confederates made a determined stand to hold their line; they directed their fire against Battery G's position. Despite a hurricane of lead, the boys from Hope stood firm. A historian recorded how the Rhode Islanders used the howitzers: "When they began to work them it was necessary to fire along the line of works in order to drive the enemy out of the embrasures at the end of the pits."[23]

As Captain Adams looked through the smoke of the battlefield, he saw "one of the most perilous exploits of the war." In the early morning light, with the unnerving noise of shouting and minie balls giving the perfect backdrop, the artillerists remained by their captured twenty-four pounder howitzers, continuing to load and fire. These thirteen men, two gun detachments, were working exactly as they had been trained for over three years. The howitzers were turned to the right and left as shot after shot was fired into the Confederate ranks: "The gun was kept hot by the rapid fire with which the little band poured into the enemy." This sustained fire and additional Union reinforcements finally pushed back the last remaining Confederate defenders.

All resistance collapsed as the Rebels ran for their lives towards Petersburg itself. The Rhode Islanders continued to work the piece until the ammunition was expended. Nearly one hundred rounds were fired from the two cannons in the brief engagement, a "deed of valor." These cannoneers remained by their guns in the midst of a furious assault and continued with the mission that they were sent to accomplish. This artillery fire was responsible for holding the Confederates back as the remaining troops came up. "The men who served this gun so nobly, standing up unflinchingly before the terrific fire of the enemy were rewarded for their bravery and daring," recorded a postwar publication about Civil War heroes.[24]

Corporal Edward P. Adams was among the members of Battery G who had been

Sixth Corps Artillery Brigade soldiers removing captured Confederate artillery from Petersburg on April 3, 1865 (Library of Congress).

This sketch, taken from George W. Potter's account of what occurred inside the Confederate fortifications on April 2, 1865, is the only illustration of what the detachment did. It shows the cannoneers forming up with the infantry of the Sixth Corps, armed with sponge-rammers and lanyards.

turned down by Captain Adams to go forward with the assault force. Despite this, he remained by his cannon as he directed its fire in the early morning fight. He would never forget the heroism of his comrades: "The Captain and his trained men with steady tread marched up with the Corps until the opportune moment when, rushing with great impetuosity they scaled the earthworks and crowned their undertaking with success, most fortunately without the loss of life." The men who remained behind could only imagine what had occurred in the works that morning; after the war, however, they would fully realize the importance of this mission and the invaluable services performed by the detachment.[25]

Among the cannoneers who fought so valiantly were seven who gave a representative cross section of the men who composed Battery G. Sergeant Archibald Malbourne was a recent Battery C transfer who was a mill worker from West Greenwich. Sergeant John H. Havron was another Battery C soldier, but he was an Irish immigrant who lived in Providence. Corporal James A. Barber was a fisherman from Westerly who joined in 1861 and was one of the few surviving Westerly boys. Private John Corcoran was a machinist from Pawtucket who had served in Battery C. Private Charles D. Ennis came from a farm in Charlestown, while Corporal Samuel E. Lewis and George W. Potter resided in Coventry. Potter was unique among the enlisted men because he had attended Brown University for two years before enlisting in Battery G in February of 1862. Despite the many openings in the ranks, Potter had never been promoted. The main cause was his failure at Brown to pass his studies in physics and algebra, skills needed to be a noncommissioned officer in the light artillery. Besides these social differences, these men were artillerists; they had to work together to insure the deadly task was performed. One historian referred to them as "Adams intrepid band of cannoneers."[26]

The action of these seventeen men who deliberately volunteered to follow their captain into the jaws of hell led Adams to nominate them all for the Medal of Honor; he felt all were deserving of the honor. Established in 1862, it was the only medal awarded for military bravery in the United States. During the Civil War, it was sometimes given to men for superfluous actions, but most of these were later rescinded in the early 1900s. In his letter, the captain wrote his men as being "worthy of medals, such as other brave men have received." On April 23, Adams sent in his nomination to Major Andrew Cowan, who endorsed it and sent it to his superior, General Wright, who added his own endorsement and forwarded it to the War Department. Finally, in April of 1866, only one year after the battle, it became official and the seventeen Rhode Islanders were awarded the medal. The official citation of each soldier stated, "For gallant conduct at Petersburg, VA., April 2, 1865. Being one of a detachment of twenty picked artillerymen who voluntarily accompanied an infantry assaulting column and who turned upon the enemy the guns captured in the assault."[27]

From the beginning, a major problem arose. Adams brought seventeen men into the assault; two were wounded and two helped their comrades to the rear. This left thirteen to work the cannons. All had been equally brave, but the War Department did not take note of the difference among the names of who went to the rear and who went into the fort. The seventeen medals were struck and engraved with the names and units of each man. On June 20, 1866, four medals were sent to Rhode Island to award Sergeants Malbourne and Havron, along with Corporals Barber and Lewis as the noncommissioned officers who had led the detachments in the action. There was no formal presentation; the medals arrived at the men's homes in simple boxes with a certificate announcing the award; this also entitled them to a small monthly increase in their meager pensions. Unfortunately, however, the officer in charge of sending out the awards had failed to mail them to the privates.

In the decade and a half immediately after the war, many of the veterans simply wanted to put the past behind them and move on with their lives. However, by the 1880s, with the resurgent interest in the Civil War, some Battery G members began to wonder where their medals had gone. They knew Adams had nominated them, but none of the fourteen privates had ever received their award. The captain could not intervene in the current matter because he had died several years earlier. George Potter never made it to the fort. However, by 1885 he had become aware that four members of the command had been awarded to that date and that Adams had nominated and all seventeen had been awarded the Medal of Honor on paper but only four had actually received it. He brought this to the attention of Henry J. Spooner, his congressman, himself a veteran of the Fourth Rhode Island. In a letter of inquiry to the Secretary of War as to why Potter and the other men had not received the award yet, Spooner wrote, "He believes himself entitled to such medal. His participation in the assault can be proven by his comrades." The War Department clerks returned to the records and noticed the mistake from 1866. They argued that only the four noncommissioned officers had been nominated, not the fourteen privates, despite the fact that Adams was clear that all were to be awarded. Potter was already a Medal of Honor recipient, but was being denied his award because of government bureaucracy. Henry Spooner, however, was a powerful House Republican and the War Department backed off and finally mailed his medal in 1886.

The following year John Corcoran applied through Congressman Spooner for his award. At the time, with veteran's rights at the forefront of politics, it was not frowned upon for a soldier to seek his own glory and what he thought was rightfully his. Unlike

Potter, Corcoran had remained by the cannon. He claimed, "I was one of the selected men from that battery who scaled the enemys works, capturing their guns, turning them upon the enemy, and rendering such other service that bronze medals were ordered for presentation to us from the government in recognition of such service." Corcoran followed the same route as Potter, through Spooner, this time including affidavits from Samuel E. Lewis and George W. Potter. Corcoran received his award in 1887.

The last cannoneer to receive the Medal of Honor was Private Charles D. Ennis; it came nearly thirty years after the war. Both Potter's and Corcoran's awards had come through a combination of their own requests and that of speaker of the house Henry Spooner. In 1892, Rhode Island's quartermaster general, Charles R. Dennis, stepped up "on behalf" of Ennis in writing to the War Department requesting his award. Dennis had personally traveled through Rhode Island, meeting with Barber, Malbourne, Lewis, Potter, and Corcoran to interview them and insure that Ennis was truly a worthy recipient: he was. The award came a few months later. This was the last Medal of Honor awarded to a member of Battery G. Even though seventeen men had been nominated and awarded the medal, only seven would actually receive it and the final outcome would take nearly three decades. When he was investigating Potter's case, Spooner actually went to the War Department and upon inquiring was shown a drawer containing all of the Medals of Honor, inscribed with the names of each member of Battery G upon it. The medals were there, but "was laid away & quite corroded in the case."

After Ennis was sent his medal, the War Department issued special orders allowing any Battery G veteran who had been named by Adams to write in and receive the award. The problem was that most of them were either dead or had left the conflict behind in their youth and simply did not care anymore. Captain George W. Adams himself wrote as to why the Medal of Honor had not been awarded to all earlier: "It is possible that these soldiers have been overlooked, this particular service having been performed so near the close of the war."[28]

The small redoubt where the early morning action had taken place is the most decorated earthwork in American military history; ten men were awarded the nation's highest award for bravery for their actions involved in capturing the cannons, seven Rhode Islanders and three Vermonters. The seven Medals of Honor awarded to Battery G represent the most issued to a single command for one engagement in the Civil War and the most to any artillery battery in the history of the United States Army.[29]

The act that Battery G performed this day did not go unnoticed by the senior commanders, who endorsed the nominations. In his official report, General Wright wrote, "This detachment, which had been carefully supplied by Major Adams with reamers, lanyards, and friction primers, was of great service in the operations subsequent to the assault in turning the captured guns upon the enemy's columns and works, thereby adding much to the demoralization of the Rebel forces." Major Cowan recorded the following: "When the assault was found to be successful Major Adams, with his detachment of cannoneers, succeeded in turning some of the guns of the enemy on their retreating columns, doing good execution and assisting to demoralize them materially." As was the case throughout its history, only a few citizens of Rhode Island ever learned of this uncommon act of bravery rendered by Battery G. The only official notice of it ever printed in the state was a report by Corporal Edward Adams, who recounted, "The moral effect of this deed of daring was felt not only on the men of Battery G, but upon the army, it was inspiring and awakened the greatest enthusiasm." Again it was a New York newspaper that commented on the Rhode Islanders, which was picked up by the *Providence Journal*. This small two inch block of print simply stated Captain Adams planned and led the assault "which contributed to its success." Three weeks later the paper printed a small column listing the men who had taken part in the assault.[30]

Private George W. Potter left behind the only written record of the assault from Battery G's perspective:

> I served with my company through all the campaigns of the Army of the Potomac up to and including the assault on Petersburg where I was shot in the left temple, and the sight of my left eye nearly destroyed. On the evening of April 1, 1865, about twenty of us volunteered to go forward under the leadership of our company commander, George W. Adams, with the charging column the following morning. Just before daylight we formed with our detachment in the front line and, at the booming of the signal gun, started. We were successful, and on reaching the line of works our little squad took charge of the guns. We brought with us lanyards, sponge-staffs, and other tools as we thought necessary. It was a grand undertaking, well executed, and many of the enemy bit the dust from their own guns. Captain Adams of Company G, who led us received a brevet-major's commission for his share in the work. I was shot down in the charge, and still suffer from the wound, but I have a medal of honor to show what my portion was in the days work. The inscription on it is as follows: "The Congress to George W. Potter, Battery G, First Rhode Island Light Artillery."[31]

Captain Adams already had a brevet of major for his actions at Cedar Creek. Instead of receiving the Medal of Honor himself, the War Department rewarded his bravery with the brevets of lieutenant colonel and colonel for his planning and executing of the mission. The new brevet colonel wasted no time in sewing on his eagles, the emblem of his rank, but he was still paid at the rank of captain.[32]

At 5:30 on the morning of April 2, General Wright reported the trenches secured as his infantry prepared to make the final push forward to attack the inner fortifications around Fort Gregg to capture and seal off the vital escape routes. The detachment of Battery G was relieved of duty and sent to the rear. After the charge was over there was still much to be done. The Sixth Corps continued to pursue the Confederates, and the light artillery continued their barrage as well. Since early in the morning Batteries G and H had been taking part in the fighting. With their work over, Captain Adams and the men that could be gathered together returned to their battery to carry on the fight. As soon as Adams had started Battery G moving forward to support the battle, a mud stained and powder grimed officer rode up to him requesting help. Even from a distance this officer was known throughout the army for his brightly trimmed red and gold officer's jacket. With a flowing mustache, he requested that Battery G come to his battery's rescue. The officer was Captain Crawford Allen, a former lieutenant in Battery G. After being promoted to adjutant following Marye's Heights, Allen was given the captaincy of Battery H in September of 1863. Although in the field since the spring of 1864, this was Battery H's first battle. They had been sent out to support General Wheaton's charge, but had been caught in the furious cross-fire as the Confederates fired everything they had to stop the Federal advance. All morning they had been in combat, losing four killed and a half dozen wounded.[33]

The four twelve pounder Napoleons were out of range to hit the targets near the last remaining Confederate defenses at the Turnbull House; where an annoying, sporadic Confederate response had been coming from. This was Lee's headquarters and was in the path leading directly to Petersburg. Without infantry support, Major William Poague had gathered every available Confederate gun still on the field and concentrated their fire against the advancing Sixth Corps infantry; he was trying to buy precious time for James Longstreet's surviving Confederates to move to the left and support the efforts near the Appomattox River. This was accomplished, but at some loss. One battery was in an enfilading position and could fire right down the length of Battery H. Adams placed Battery G alongside Battery H and he personally sighted the four, three-inch ordnance rifles for 1,700 yards. Some return Confederate fire landed in Battery G's position and Lieutenant Rich received a slight wound, the last combat casualty for the battery. After returning an accurate, sustained fire for five minutes, the Confederate guns withdrew. General Wheaton wrote, "If these guns, occupying one of their intrenched works and thoroughly enfilading our lines, had not been silenced, they might have materially retarded our advance." These were the last shots Battery G fired in anger during the war.[34]

The artillerists returned to the Confederate entrenchments to remove the captured artillery and send it to City Point, site of army headquarters. Battery G helped to drag in the three howitzers, ten Napoleons, three ordnance rifles, a Parrott, and an imported English Blakely rifle. The guns were turned over to the Third Vermont Battery, which took them to the rear. The Confederates had been routed from their entrenchments and were evacuating Richmond and Petersburg as Grant finally ordered his men to stop and wait for further orders; they were going to march west and finally force Lee to surrender.[35]

On the morning of April 3, the Sixth Corps led the Army of the Potomac in the pursuit of the Army of Northern Virginia. Sheridan's Cavalry was the vanguard, constantly skirmishing with the Southerners. At every bridge and river crossing, the Confederates fought bitterly for their survival, but they could not stop the Federal pursuit. On the afternoon of April 6, the last large pitched battle of the war was fought at Sailor's Creek. With Wheaton's Division in the lead, the Sixth Corps "ran as fast as legs could carry them" as they rushed into action to engage the enemy and stop the Confederate forces. Battery H was at the head of the column and moved forward just as the last Confederates were fleeing, Batter H managed to unlimber and fire fifteen rounds. These shots were the last fired in anger by the Army of the Potomac's light artillery.

Battery G did not make it into the fight that resulted in the capture of a third of Lee's Army, but arrived on the field just as the Confederates retreated. General Horatio Wright ordered the remaining batteries not to move forward and engage, "as a dictate of humanity." Furthermore, the general claimed the storming of Petersburg and Sailor's Creek as the Sixth Corps greatest fight. This decisive victory sped Lee's force on its way as the Rhode Islanders again continued on in the muddy spring weather. The horses, as usual, suffered from the campaign; nine died during the pursuit. The supply lines were strained from Petersburg, as the Army of the Potomac marched rapidly; the men had to forage off the land. The rough roads and the return of the mud to Virginia greatly hampered the progress of Battery G; this did not stop the men from carrying on westward through southern Virginia.[36]

A week after leaving the Petersburg lines, the Sixth Corps arrived in the small, pastoral village of Appomattox on April 9. That morning Lee had surrendered the Army of Northern Virginia. It was finally over; one of the greatest armies ever to march into battle faded into history. Upon hearing the news, General Wheaton mounted his horse and rode over to his two Rhode Island batteries and told them what had just occurred.

The news was electrifying to the cannoneers: "Men shouted, threw up their hats, hugged each other and rolled over in excess of joy." Wheaton then ordered Captains Adams and Allen to fire one hundred blank charges as a sign of victory. The general had to repeat the orders three times because the noise the Rhode Islanders were making was too immense. Finally the men began firing the cannon; each shot echoed off the surrounding hills as the artillerists from the smallest state ended what had begun four years earlier. It was almost four years to the day when Colonel Charles Tompkins received orders to prepare the Providence Marine Corps of Artillery for service. Since that time, Rhode Island had sent nine additional batteries to the front; scores of young men in red trimmed jackets laid down their lives for this day. The United States was finally restored, and freedom was given to those held in bondage for so long. General Wright recalled, "The surrender of General Lee's forces was announced to the army, and was received with great enthusiasm by the soldiers, who looked upon this as the result of all their privations, and as the virtual ending of the struggle which had enveloped the country for four years, in which they had willingly rushed their lives and fortunes." As the last shots were fired something dawned on the soldiers. The enemy they had been fighting for so long was not a foreign power, but Americans. Now with the carnage over, American met American as the two sides exchanged handshakes and the Federals gave what little food they had to their fellow countrymen.[37]

The news of Lee's surrender was received in Westerly via telegram on the morning of April 10. The *Narragansett Weekly* reported, "Westerly was jubilant over the news of General Lee's capture throughout Monday little else was talked of. In the afternoon, flags were flying, the church and factory bells rung and groups of boys paraded the streets with such house bells and other noisy apparatus as they could lay hands on." That afternoon in neighboring Hopkinton, home to four Battery G soldiers, there was a militia review; the citizens paraded through the entire town, eventually ending in downtown Westerly. As the group marched triumphantly down the highway, flags flew everywhere as the local citizens finally realized that the carnage was over. In Ashaway, a detachment of discharged soldiers on horseback joined them while they stopped at the Hopkinton Academy to listen to several speeches. The school itself had to shut down during the war because most of the students and their principal left to fight; only half came home alive. As the procession made its way to Westerly they passed by several graveyards containing the remains of nearly fifty veterans who had died in the service.[38]

The Army of Northern Virginia had surrendered, but another large Confederate force lurked in North Carolina. Grant dispatched Sheridan with his cavalry and the Sixth Corps to link up with William Tecumseh Sherman and force them to surrender. The Sixth Corps left Appomattox on April 11 in a driving rainstorm and marched south. All around them the local inhabitants were in stunned disbelief that Lee had surrendered. On the fifteenth, sad news was received; President Abraham Lincoln had been assassinated. The president had carried the nation through the war, while the soldiers in Battery G had already shown their faith by unanimously voting for him in November. Although his decisions sometimes resulted in fatal mistakes for the battery, he had done the best that could be done as the United States fell apart.

Despite being stationed in Louisiana, Lieutenant George L. Gaskell still kept abreast of affairs in his old battery. Like nearly all Federal soldiers, he was deeply saddened by Lincoln's death. Gaskell wrote, "Toward him we have even looked at like a father." The eighteenth was a national day of mourning as Battery G and the Sixth Corps artillery fired salutes every half hour throughout the day. This was the last time the guns were used by Adams' Rhode Island Battery. Finally, after marching for two weeks, the Sixth Corps arrived at Danville, Virginia, where they received news that Johnston had surrendered to Sherman on April 28. Although the war was over, the discipline problems in Battery G still persisted. On April 26, Corporal Virgil M. Posey, who had held his rank since December of 1861 was reduced to private for "gross neglect of his duty."[39]

With the two main Confederate forces having surrendered in the eastern theatre, Battery G and the Sixth Corps remained encamped at Danville. On the third of May, the battery boarded a train to Wellsville, where the Sixth was being sent to protect the local citizens against reprisal guerilla attacks. With little to do, all of the officers in Battery G went on a furlough to Washington. Frank Waterman received a commission as first lieutenant and went to assume his duty with Battery F in Richmond. Lieutenant Jacob Lamb had fought two pitched battles to try to save Battery C, one at Cedar Creek with canister and the other with pen and ink with the War Department. He was finally recognized for his bravery in the Shenandoah Campaign with a promotion to captain and transfer to Battery E, then in the Washington defenses. The recently promoted First Lieutenant Reuben H. Rich remained on duty to command the battery. After four months of trying to justify their rank, First Sergeant John B. Peck and Quartermaster Sergeant Christopher Carpenter of Battery C were discharged as "supernumerary noncommissioned officers."[40]

At Wellsville, the men found mountains of stores, such as cornmeal and hams, which were liberally taken. Only the infantry took part in the duty, patrolling the railroad and insuring the local inhabitants remained loyal to the United States. The Sixth Corps left Wellsville on the sixteenth, passing through Petersburg on the eighteenth. The soldiers all took view of the entrenchments as they marched to Richmond. Battery G and the Sixth Corps did the Overland Campaign in reverse, marching up to Fredericksburg, over battlefields that would never be forgotten. The mud continued to be a problem, but the rate of march was slow and not tiring, allowing the men to take in the sights and remember the history they had made on the now calm fields before them.[41]

Finally, on June 2 the Sixth Corps arrived back in Washington. Between May 23 and May 24 the Army of the Potomac and Army of Georgia marched proudly in review before President Andrew Johnson and other dignities. However, the Sixth Corps was not present, being on campaign. To offset any slight to these veterans a special review was held on June 8. New clothing and white gloves were issued. For the men in Battery G this was their last official act as soldiers in the United States Army. The Sixth Corps, commanded by General Wright, marched past their commander in chief and General Grant. Of the twenty-five corps that served in the war, the Sixth was known as having the best fighters and had seen some of the bloodiest service. Formed on the Peninsula, they fought at Antietam and Fredericksburg, assaulted Marye's Heights and fought in the bloody engagement near Salem's Church at Chancellorsville, and then made the long march to Gettysburg. They held a critical junction in the Wilderness, while the beloved Uncle John Sedgwick was killed at Spotsylvania. The Overland Campaign severely tested the men, but they saved Washington and later won everlasting glory in the Shenandoah Valley. Storming into Petersburg they helped to hasten the end of the war. The artillerists of Battery G were part of these actions.[42]

With their duties officially over, Captain Adams, along with his three officers and First Sergeant Marcus M. Streeter, began the process of preparing the battery for mustering out. The four three inch ordnance rifles, which had only been used at the storming of Petersburg and to fire salutes, were turned into the Ordnance Department, along with the horses which had steadily pulled the guns. Every man who served in the unit was to be accounted for, and their records had to be known and forwarded to the adjutant general before the battery was released. Next to each name was the record of his service. Some were awarded the nation's highest honors; others had died a hero's death or perished from horrible illness; many more were discharged for disability; and others had taken the cowards' way out and deserted. Quartermaster Sergeant George F. Russell also went over his books, checking the clothing records of the men. Those who had not overdrawn on the accounts were paid the balance of their forty-two dollar per year allowance. The men were allowed to take their uniforms and other tokens of their service home. With all of these tasks complete, Battery G was ready to go home.[43]

Taps

*Rhode Island has always been justly proud of her batteries, whose worth was known
not only through our armies but to those of the enemy as well. Of no battery,
can she speak of with more pride than Battery G.*
—*Providence Journal*, October 17, 1883

Battery G's service in the war had lasted three and a half long and brutal years and
half of its command had become casualties in the struggle. Now it was all over. Now Boots
and Saddles was called one last time in the South. After remaining in camp at Washington for a week the paperwork was complete and all was in order. It was June 14, 1865. For
three years, seven months, and twelve days Battery G, First Rhode Island Light Artillery,
had been part of the United States Army; now they were going home. In company with
Battery H, Adams' Battery left Washington early on the morning of the fourteenth and
arrived in Philadelphia on the fifteen, where they were again treated to a fine meal. At 3:00,
the commands entered another train to New York, where the steamer *Neptune* was boarded.
Finally on the morning of June 16 they arrived home, docking at Fox Point. It was a total
reversal from when the first detachment of the battery left the city in silence on the afternoon of December 2, 1861.

A cannon shot, fired by the Providence Marine Corps of Artillery echoed through
downtown Providence, letting all know that the Rhode Islanders were finally home. The
two commands received a welcome from the Burnside Zouaves and Adjutant General
Edward C. Mauran, in addition to "the warm greetings of anxious friends," as thousands
of Rhode Islanders flocked the streets to see who had come home. The men in the two batteries presented a stark contrast to the zouaves, who had never left the state. Battery G had
seen service from Yorktown to Appomattox, and the faded red on their mounted services
jackets stood out against the magnificent crimson of the militia. In total, three officers and
135 enlisted men returned home; only twenty of them had originally left in December of
1861. The battery was commanded this day by First Lieutenant Benjamin Freeborn. Enlisting as a private in 1861, Freeborn had risen through the ranks, had been wounded at Gettysburg, and now commanded the unit for a short time. Before coming home, Captain
Adams had received a regular commission as major, replacing his first brevet. The move
was only a reward for the service he had given; there was no more regiment of light artillery
to command. Likewise, First Sergeant Streeter was promoted to second lieutenant on June
12 as a symbolic effect only; he was given a commission, but was not allowed to be mustered in to the rank because the war was over. After another meal and the customary grand
speeches by the state officials, Adams dismissed the men until June 26.[1]

Battery G was officially mustered out of the United States Army on June 24, 1865. On
the twenty-sixth, the artillerists assembled in Exchange Place for the last time to receive
their rightfully earned honorable discharges and final payments from Captain Horace W.
Freely of the Third United States Infantry. This was the last time that any of these men

ever saw each other as a collective body. The officers gave a few last parting words as comrades shook hands for the last time. For over three years they had fought together through the seething hell of the Civil War as brothers in the light artillery; now they returned to their farms, factories, and other walks of life. In their army careers they had depended upon each other for survival while working the guns; now these veterans simply departed and walked away, back to their prewar lives to pick up the pieces.[2]

The eleven remaining Westerly boys were welcomed back without much fanfare. They simply took a train south from Providence and quietly went home after their years of service. Westerly more than made up for the lack of a homecoming on the Fourth of July with a large celebration for all the men from the town who served in the conflict. The Westerly Rifles led the parade through downtown, while the "Heroes of the War," as the veterans were dubbed, marched alongside. The artillerists of Battery G made their first public display in a parade and their last as well. However, the war was over, victory had been won and many just wanted to get on with their lives: only four Battery G veterans marched.[3]

The war was over, but some things would never be the same again. There would be no replacing men like Charles V. Scott, William H. Lewis, Thomas F. Mars, or the others that gave "the last full measure of devotion." Every survivor was forever touched by the conflict in good and bad ways. Two hundred and seventy-three officers and men served in Battery G, plus ninety-four soldiers attached from other units. In total, seventeen were killed in action or died of wounds, while twenty-six perished from other causes. Half of these artillerists died from the horrid disease faced on the Peninsula. These losses were felt severely. The desertion factor had a serious impact upon Battery G, with twenty-one leaving permanently, and many more going absent without leave for brief periods of time. Despite all this, though, those that remained served honorably on many fields.[4]

With his battery officially mustered out of the service, Major Adams delivered the small swallow tailed battery guidon to the state house on Benefit Street, in the care of Gov-

After the war, Albert Cordner moved to North Dakota, and as his business card can attest, operated a successful stable business.

ernor James Y. Smith. During the war, the guns of Battery G had unlimbered fifty-three times in combat. The battles emblazoned upon the small flag, authorized by General Grant were a testament to the fury Battery G fought through: Yorktown, Fair Oaks, Malvern Hill, Antietam, Fredericksburg, Marye's Heights, Gettysburg, Mine Run, Wilderness, Spotsylvania, Cold Harbor, Petersburg, Opequon, Fisher's Hill, and Cedar Creek. They were also heavily engaged and contributed immensely at Granite Hill and Cool Spring, but these were considered skirmishes and not recorded in the history books. Corporal Edward Adams best described the contributions of Battery G to the Union war effort: "This battery shared all the perils and glories of the Army of the Potomac."[5]

The eight batteries of the First Rhode Island Light Artillery Regiment never served together as a regiment. They did, however, fight through every engagement with the Army of the Potomac in Pennsylvania, Maryland, and Virginia, while others fought in North Carolina, Ohio, Kentucky, and Tennessee. At every one of these engagements the batteries had a pivotal role, from Batteries A and B holding Cemetery Ridge during Pickett's Charge, to Battery D at the Battle of Knoxville, Tennessee, and the storming of the Confederate lines at Petersburg by Battery G. Battery A fired the first light artillery shots at Bull Run and Battery H fired the final shots at Sailor's Creek. In total, eighty-seven officers and 1,977 men served in the batteries during the war, in addition to several hundred detached infantry serving for short periods. Over 250 officers and men paid the supreme sacrifice. Battery G sustained the highest number of these honored dead. Broken down by battery, the numbers do not seem very devastating; but considering that each battery had at most 130 men on duty during the majority of their service, and no more than 300 ever on the rolls, the losses were high. The First Rhode Island Light Artillery Regiment suffered one of the highest losses of artillery in the Civil War. In 1867 an imposing granite monument was erected in Exchange Place in Providence, the site where all Rhode Island units left for the war. On it were listed the names of over two thousand Rhode Islanders who died in the war. By 1890 monuments to Batteries A, B, and E were erected at Gettysburg and one to Battery F in North Carolina. In 1917, the remaining, aged veterans again gathered at the Benefit Street Arsenal to dedicate a plaque commemorating the batteries and the building as the place where the Rhode Island batteries had been recruited some fifty years earlier.[6]

The artillerists from Rhode Island who fought in the Civil War continued the long held tradition of artillerists from the smallest state. At each battle they fought in, they were always mentioned favorably in both official and unofficial dispatches from the front. Lieutenant Colonel William F. Fox, in his *Regimental Losses in the Civil War,* wrote:

> The Rhode Island troops were prominent by reason of the fine regiment of light artillery furnished by that State. The light batteries of the command were remarkable for their efficiency, and the conspicuous part assigned them in all the battles of the Army of the Potomac. As a whole they were unsurpassed, and they made a record which reflected credit on their State. A comparison of their losses in action with those of other batteries tells plainly the dangers which they braved.[7]

Several factors made the Rhode Island Light Artillery such an effective combat force. According to one prominent historian they "maintained a good standing in regimental cohesion." Because most of the batteries served together in the Army of the Potomac, qualified officers could be promoted from the ranks and sent to other batteries to increase knowledge of artillery theory. In addition Rhode Island's excellent prewar education system had given the men the important math skills needed to operate the guns. Although their weapons had limitations, the artillerists of Battery G overcame the obstacles and proved what well placed artillery fire could accomplish. The most important factor, however, was Colonel Charles H. Tompkins and the Providence Marine Corps of Artillery; it was in their roots that one of the finest regiments of artillery to ever serve in the United States Army was created.[8]

After the last battery was mustered out, the Providence Marine Corps of Artillery again became a resort for the elite; many of the regimental officers again became privates. The old arsenal on Benefit Street became a repository for war relics and served as the headquarters for the Rhode Island Grand Army of the Republic. In 1875, the Marine Artillery was simply redesignated as Rhode Island Battery A. In 1898, the corps again took the field, during the Spanish-American War, but did not leave the state. In 1903 with the passing of the Militia Act, the units of the Rhode Island Militia were federalized. In World War One, Battery A formed the nucleus of the One Hundred and Third Field Artillery Regiment. Under this designation, they served on the Western Front in World War I and in the South Pacific during World War II. Today the artillerists from Rhode Island carry on the struggle and have fought in Iraq during the war on terror.

The tradition of the Providence Marine Corps of Artillery continues to live on. From the fields of Antietam and Gettysburg, to the Meuse-Argonne, the Solomon Islands, and Baghdad, the Rhode Islanders have been there. Fifteen years after the Japanese surrender, General Harold Barker recorded, "The genuine achievement and heroic traditions established by Rhode Island Artillery in our previous Wars resulted in setting a standard that was second to none." On their red regimental flag are numerous battle honors, but the ones most proud of are those won through the blood and fury of the Civil War.[9]

During the war, the artillerists of Battery G had been part of a revolution in warfare; in only four years, field artillery had evolved five centuries. In 1861, the majority of Union batteries were still using what amounted to an implement capable of throwing a projectile several hundred yards. It was Rhode Islanders who introduced the future of rifled artillery into the United States Army. This change in technology allowed commanders to engage targets miles away and use artillery in ways never before seen before. Despite this, the drill manual remained the same during the war, but the tactics in which the field artillery was used on the battlefield changed immensely. It was the last of the old style of war and the beginning of the modern.

Although the artillery pieces in use during the conflict were severely hampered by faulty ammunition and the inability to provide indirect fire, the cannoneers of Battery G, First Rhode Island Light Artillery, took was what given to them and never looked back. Throughout the war, the men of Battery G were able to take the war to the enemy with their superior firepower. With superb aiming by the noncommissioned officers and proper fuze settings by the Number Six Men, the artillery became an offensive weapon. Despite the fact that the guns inflicted only 10 percent of the total casualties during the war and although Battery G's total destruction to the enemy will never be known, what the battery accomplished was quite amazing.

On the bloody fields of Antietam the men fought in their first real engagement and effectively engaged the enemy. At First Fredericksburg they helped to cover the first bridgehead landing in American military history and later covered the retreat of the defeated Federal army. Under the command of Captain George W. Adams the battery flourished; he had a distinct taste for battle and instilled this in his men in combat. They effectively worked the guns on every battlefield where Adams commanded. During the Battle of Marye's Heights, the battery took part in a savage artillery duel that allowed the infantry to charge the hill by taking pressure off the advancing lines. At Granite Hill, Battery G effectively shelled the Confederate wagon train in its retreat to Virginia. Spotsylvania tested the men as they fought for ten hours straight in adverse conditions against an enemy they could not see. Throughout the Shenandoah Valley Campaign at Cool Spring, Opequon, Fisher's Hill, and Cedar Creek, Battery G distinguished itself, providing the needed firepower to defeat the foe and provide critical support for the Sixth Corps' infantry. Indeed, in this campaign, on more than one occasion, Battery G's support turned the tide of battle in favor of the Union. In the last charge at Petersburg, the battery did something truly amazing, advancing with an assaulting infantry force to capture the guns and turn them on the enemy. Captain Adams and his Rhode Islanders helped to usher in the modern era of field artillery as the king of battle.[10]

The Civil War devastated Rhode Island. In 1860, the state had a population of 175,000 and sent 24,000 men to the war in eight infantry, three heavy artillery, three cavalry, and one light artillery regiments. In addition, a battalion of cavalry, company of hospital guards, and 1,500 men for the Regular Army, Navy and Marine Corps were also provided. Of this number, over 2,000 never returned. These losses were felt throughout Rhode Island. Washington County, located in southern Rhode Island, was home to many of the men in the battery. The county sent 2,717 men to war and five hundred of them died. The prewar military age population in Rhode Island was 35,000 men: 69 percent of the eighteen to forty-five age group went to war.

Some outside of this bracket fought as well. Private George Norton of Battery G was over sixty when he volunteered; he paid for his advanced age by being discharged on the Peninsula and later dying of the disease contracted there. Every Rhode Islander knew of

Grand Army of the Republic veterans from Richmond and Charlestown gather in this 1890s image of the Burnside Post in Shannock. Among the Battery G veterans present are Artificer Welcome Tucker (front right arrow), thrice wounded Corporal Daniel Hoxsie (white arrow), and Private Charles D. Ennis (back right arrow), who wears his Medal of Honor (courtesy the Richmond Historical Society).

someone who had lost a husband, son, brother, or father on the field of battle. The Rhode Island troops were present at every major engagement during the war, except some in Tennessee and Georgia. They fought with the same reputation that had carried them through the Revolution, while new laurels and honors were added to the flags with the fouled anchor carried by these soldiers. The small mill villages of the fringes of the state is where the war hit home the most; everywhere in their small graveyards would rest the soldiers who laid down their lives to free a people held in bondage and to restore the United States flag to its proper place.[11]

With the carnage over, the men again resumed their lives. Some returned to their old occupations, while others moved west to new lands and opportunities. Still others returned home sick or maimed for life from the service they had seen. As a hundred small homecomings were celebrated across the small state of Rhode Island, Private William A. Baker walked the short distance from Fox Point to his Providence home. Reunited with his family, the forty-nine-year-old soldier did not have long to live. He died on July 21, 1865, of disease contracted in the service. Emmons B. Weston was another Battery G soldier who met an early death. Weston was a sailor from Providence and was eighteen when he joined the service in 1863. His father served in the Third Rhode Island Heavy Artillery and died of disease at Andersonville. Returning home Emmons promptly returned to his profession and caught a merchant steamer to England. He was only employed for several months before being killed in an accident in Liverpool in November of 1865.[12]

In 1867, Rhode Island published a large book commemorating the services of the officers from the state. In it, John Russell Bartlett wrote of Battery G's commander Adams: "He gained during his connection with the army, a distinguished reputation for knowledge of his profession, military skill, and great bravery." These were fitting words to a man who had served his state and country well. Brevet Colonel George Adams went home a sick man, ill with rheumatism contracted in the service. He opened a mercantile in Providence, and later spent several years in New York before moving to Bristol in 1880, where he married again. Constantly sick from his wartime illness, Adams traveled to Arkansas, seeking relief in the hot springs, but to no avail.

Although he had his problems with drinking and gambling, Adams came to Battery G at a critical moment, turned the unit around, and led them through the rest of the war; serving credibly and honorably. He was the officer who thought of the mission at Petersburg and insured it was carried out. Captain Adams died of rheumatism and a cerebral hemorrhage on October 13, 1883. After a large funeral procession in Bristol he was laid to rest at Juniper Hill Cemetery. During its history, the battery was commanded by Charles D. Owen, Horace S. Bloodgood, and George W. Adams. No man left a greater mark on the command then their third captain. Battery G would always be remembered as Adams' Battery. The captain was eulogized by the *Providence Journal:* "His cheerful and cheering words when all seemed the darkest, on the long march, or the losing fight, will long be cherished by many a comrade of those days. His presence had a charm in it that will never be forgotten. He was brave, loyal, and generous. Let that be a farewell to a good soldier gone to rest."[13]

Private and later Lieutenant George L. Gaskell remained in service until October of 1865 with the Fourteenth Rhode Island; the regiment saw no field service. The Civil War was responsible for abolishing slavery, and it also abolished many prejudices, such as Gaskell's views towards blacks. In time, he grew to respect his soldiers and they later testified on his behalf to receive a pension. Like many of the veterans, Gaskell's was the subject of strong scrutiny from the Pension Bureau, who thought the old soldiers were trying to steal

The veterans of the Stillman D. Budlong Post of the Grand Army of the Republic gather in West-erly for a Memorial Day Parade in this 1895 image. Among the Battery G veterans present are Cor-poral James Barber (upper right arrow) and Private John S. Babcock (upper left arrow) (courtesy Kris VanDenBossche).

money from the government they had served so faithfully by making up claims. Any young clerk reading the letters and diaries of the cannoneers in Battery G regarding the horrible diseases or the terrible wounds suffered during the desperate stand at Cedar Creek would know that the old men were not lying but telling a disturbing truth.

Instead of returning to Rhode Island, Gaskell remained in the South where he opened a grocery business. During Reconstruction, he became a Republican and served as the mayor of Plaquemine, Louisiana. He later removed to Chattanooga, Tennessee, where he became a dealer in "Staple and Fancy Groceries." Gaskell continued to write his sister while raising a family. His years of service outside of Rhode Island led him to never return to his native state: "I do not expect to ever return North to live should I change from here it would be to go still farther South." This long sojourn in the South had also destroyed his body. Gaskell suffered a severe injury on the Peninsula by being thrown from his horse at Malvern Hill. Fearful of medical treatment, he never went to the hospital. The service with the Four-teenth Rhode Island had exposed him to "recurrent malarial fevers" which continued for the rest of his life. The government would not pay Gaskell on the first injury, because there was no record, but did agree on the fevers. In 1890, the Gaskell family again moved north, to Cincinnati; here the old soldier lived for the rest of his life. He died in 1926.[14]

In addition to losing his horse at Marye's Heights and being wounded at Cedar Creek,

James Barber takes a break in his retirement years at Watch Hill in Westerly (courtesy Providence Public Library, Special Collections [C. Fiske Harris Collection]).

Private James Matthewson of Scituate lost his two brothers in the service. Calvin Matthewson of the Third Rhode Island Cavalry drowned coming home from Louisiana, and Nicholas was killed at Fredericksburg charging up Marye's Heights with the Seventh Rhode Island. George W. Cole rose to the rank of captain in the Fourteenth Rhode Island and after the war returned to the teaching profession and taught in Pawtucket and Coventry, later becoming an insurance agent. Like many, Benjamin Freeborn became caught in the rush of "western fever" and moved to St. Louis, where he managed a railroad. In his remarkable rise from private to acting captain, Freeborn could not escape a fate that occurred to many artillerists during the war; he was thrown from his horse in 1874 and died. Sergeant Archibald Malbourne moved to Scituate, where he became the foreman in a large cotton mill. When he died in 1912, he was honored for his years of hard work by being buried in a corner of the mill property.[15]

Amanda Scott was the widowed mother of Brevet Captain Charles V. Scott; she had lost her only son to the war, as had the mother of Lieutenant Benjamin E. Kelley. Mrs. Scott fought hard to get a small pension for her son's service. She firmly believed that Scott ranked as a first lieutenant, instead of a second. A letter from a pension officer reported, "The War Department fail to show that he at any time held the ranks of 1st Lieut. The rank confirmed by brevet is not a pensionable rate." Amanda Scott mourned her loss for the rest of her life, while living on a fifteen dollar per month pension. Even Scott's cause for promotion was taken from him; another Battery A veteran claimed responsibility for saving the cannon at Bull Run, thus robbing Lieutenant Scott of the honor.[16]

Another survivor left behind because of Battery G's actions was Jane Lewis, mother of the fallen Bugler William H. Lewis. For the rest of her days she continued to receive a small mother's pension from the government, while cherishing her son's letters and looking with sadness at the only possession of his to return home, his elaborate coat pierced by the fatal ball that killed him. Her ex-husband, William B. Lewis, continued with his old ways of lying and after the war assumed his son's identity as a member of Battery G to gain membership in the Grand Army of the Republic, an organization open only to honorably discharged veterans He forged a discharge, and was granted membership. When he died in 1880, the elder Lewis was buried in an exclusive Grand Army plot in Providence's North Burial Ground, designed only for Civil War veterans. Today the chronic liar lies among true Rhode Island heroes, while his brave son still rests in the soil he died defending.[17]

Quartermaster Sergeant William B. Westcott was promoted to first lieutenant in 1865 and briefly commanded Battery B in the Appomattox Campaign. He later rose to prominence in the Masons and became a successful pharmacist in Providence. Private Albert D. Cordner returned to Charlestown. In 1872, he abandoned his wife and children and moved to North Dakota, where he remarried; his first wife was granted a divorce for abandonment. He operated a successful whip manufacturing firm and stable before dying in 1912. When Corporal Samuel E. Lewis went forward on April 2, 1865, he did so as a quiet, unassuming Yankee farmer who went to war because it was the right thing to do to preserve the Union. After the war, he returned to his ways, largely forgetting about his role in the conflict. He never sought fame and his decoration never brought him any. Lewis lived in rural western Coventry until his death in 1907. He never applied for a government pension and died in poverty. A wealthy neighbor discovered his plight, and saw to it that the hero was buried with dignity in Providence.[18]

Private George W. Potter never returned to Brown; he was the only student of the college to be awarded the Medal of Honor. He moved to nearby Sterling, Connecticut, where he, like many others, continued to till the rocky soil of New England while coping daily with the blinding wound which brought him his medal. Potter managed to save some money, so when he died in 1918, he was buried under a large monument, capped by a life sized cannon. In 1911, his house in Sterling burned down, and along with it went his original Medal of Honor. This small item of bronze and ribbon meant more to Potter than anything else, as along with his service as a cannoneer in Battery G. He wrote, "Is it

James Chase survived a stint in Libby Prison to command his own battery. He returned home to become a merchant and served over fifty years in the Rhode Island Militia (courtesy Phil DiMaria).

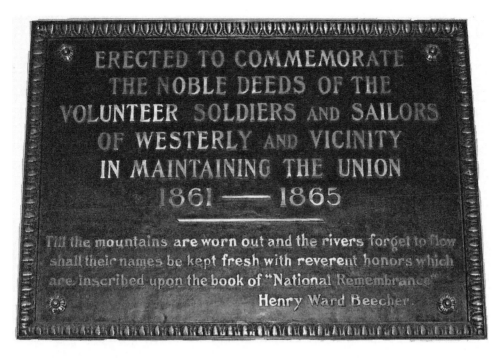

ERECTED TO COMMEMORATE
THE NOBLE DEEDS OF THE
VOLUNTEER SOLDIERS AND SAILORS
OF WESTERLY AND VICINITY
IN MAINTAINING THE UNION
1861 — 1865

Till the mountains are worn out and the rivers forget to flow
shall their names be kept fresh with reverent honors which
are inscribed upon the book of "National Remembrance"
Henry Ward Beecher

This plaque, placed at the Grand Army Hall in Westerly, is the only monument to the Westerly Boys who sacrificed all they had to save their country.

possable or me to get another Medal as I wish after I am gone that my son can have it as he is a loyal son of a veteran."[19]

It was Lieutenant Elmer Corthell's strict attention to detail and gunnery classes that made Battery G such a potent force in the 1864 and 1865 campaigns. After the war, he tried to remain in the Regular Army as an artillery officer, but was rebuffed. Instead, he returned to Brown University, earned a master's degree and had a fifty-year career as a civil engineer around the world. Indeed the mathematical skills he learned in the artillery service proved just as versatile in the civilian world as well. While the war made one officer, it destroyed another. Lieutenant Otto L. Torslow was a brave officer, but alcohol destroyed his army career. He returned to Providence, where he worked in the mercantile trade. By 1886, Torslow retired to a Soldier's Home in Hampton, Virginia, and spent the rest of his years trying to gain a government pension. The adjutant general's office kept on denying him, not being able to find any record of his service. After the war some of the men took up the state's offer of free housing for disabled soldiers by moving to the Rhode Island Soldiers Home in Bristol; among the designers was Corporal William B. Thurber, who had passed his time on the Peninsula painting the local flora and fauna. Some Battery G veterans took up the state's offer for crippled and poor soldiers to move to the new facility. Corporal Jeremiah P. Healey remained there for the rest of his life.[20]

Battery G's first two senior officers led similar but different lives after the war. After resigning his commission at Fredericksburg, Captain Charles D. Owen opened a mercantile business in Providence. Only marginally successful, he moved to Cranston and managed a large textile mill. When Owen left his battery that cold winter day, he also left the war behind him; he never took an active role in veteran's affairs. Owen made Battery G, but it took the leadership of George Adams to make them a potent battlefield weapon. Captain Owen lived until 1915. Battery G's original senior lieutenant also left the command in the winter of 1862, but he never stopped rising.

William B. Rhodes beat Battery D back into shape, which showed when they contributed to the Confederate defeat at Knoxville, Tennessee. In light of this action, Rhodes was promoted to captain of Battery E and commanded the unit throughout the Overland Campaign to Petersburg; he was brevetted major for the actions. With a growing family at home and the war nearly over, Rhodes resigned in March of 1865 and returned to Warwick. The return was wrought with sadness, as Rhodes' brother was killed in action in Texas. His postwar career flourished as he divided his time between New York and Providence, running the New York Cotton Exchange. He made major gains in this work, while becoming active again in the Rhode Island Militia, Grand Army of the Republic, Warwick Town Council, and as a Master Mason. The father of six children, it was Rhodes' experience with rifled artillery that had produced such splendid effects on the battlefield.[21]

Medal of Honor recipient Sergeant John H. Havron moved to New Orleans, where he lived in poverty and died in 1910. He was remembered by the United States Army in the 1980s when a road was named in his honor at Fort Sill, Oklahoma, where Rhode Island artillerists still go for training. Havron was similar to many of his fellow Irishmen who served in Battery G; they simply faded away to work miniscule, obscure jobs in Providence after the war. Their service in the Civil War had proven that they were loyal Americans, willing to die for their adopted country. The population was finally accepted as they found their status taken over by the recently freed slaves who traveled north seeking advancement. The immigrant-soldiers were finally rewarded for their sacrifice in 1886 when the Rhode Island General Assembly granted them the right to vote.[22]

More than others, the forty-eight men who joined from the southwestern Rhode Island

The members of Battery G who were awarded the Medal of Honor received these special grave markers as a testament to their service. Private Potter is buried at Swan Point in Providence under a life-size cannon.

towns of Charlestown, Hopkinton, Richmond, and Westerly suffered after the war; nearly all returned home sick and broken by their army experiences. Many remained in the same neighborhoods they had grown up in; the economic growth of the area had exploded during the war and would continue well into the twentieth century. Nathan Champlin, like many of the men from the area, also returned ill, but was heartbroken to discover his wife had committed adultery while he was in the army. He never complained about the wounds suffered at Cedar Creek, but rather the stomach and back pains that were endured sleeping many nights on the ground in horrible conditions.[23]

Champlin was neighbors with several of his comrades in Battery G who remained in the local area after the war. After losing a brother at Cedar Creek, First Sergeant Nathaniel R. Chace was promoted to lieutenant and joined Battery B. He was mustered out and returned to Westerly to resume farming. This came to a halt in 1887 when he lost all use of his left hand in a boating accident. In his later years, Chace became completely blind, requiring constant attention. He blamed the loss of his vision to diseases contracted in the service. Government doctors agreed with him, and in 1900 Chace received a twenty dollar per month pension until his death in 1927. When he went to the last muster, Lieutenant Chace was the last surviving Westerly boy.[24]

Sergeant Alexander B. Sisson and Private Charles E. Sisson were the twin brothers who had both been severely wounded in the early morning fight for the guns. Alexander lived only until 1875, while his brother survived him by thirty-eight years. William H. Burton was injured at both Marye's Heights and Cedar Creek. The injuries crippled him and he was unable to perform work as a blacksmith; he lived out his life in poverty with his wife and he never received a government pension. Private Burton broke his neck and died in 1880 at age forty and was buried in the pauper's lot at the Cross Mills village cemetery. Corporal Daniel Hoxsie as well returned home injured and spent his life as an invalid; he had suffered three severe wounds at Marye's Heights, Cold Harbor and Battery G's desperate stand at Cedar Creek. When he died in 1901, his widow was left with forty dollars and a dilapidated old farmhouse.[25]

As they had done in their service in Battery G, Welcome and Peleg Tucker and their brother-in-law Charles Ennis remained together after the war, operating a successful blacksmith shop in Wood River Junction. Peleg and Ennis lived together on the same farm with their wives, who were sisters; both men assisted in building the house. In his later years, the usual bouts of rheumatism from his three years of service in Battery G started to affect Peleg. He hired an additional hand to help him in the shop when Charles moved to nearby Potter Hill to take up farming. Like many, Tucker took an active role in both politics and religious affairs. Originally a Democrat, Tucker later became a Republican, but he was a radical for his time. In his later years he voted for the candidate he best thought should hold the office, regardless of his party affiliation; his son served on the town council in Charlestown. The *Wood River Advertiser* wrote of him: "Though a man of few words, he was interested in passing events and was an intelligent observer of the progress of the times." Corporal Tucker died of tuberculosis in 1907, leaving behind two sons, a magnificent Congregational Church which he had built in Wood River Junction, and a proud record of service as a member of Battery G. Like many veterans, he was interred with full military honors, and a packed congregation attended the service; many of his comrades in the Grand Army came from Providence to pay their last respects to the old soldier.[26]

Private John D. Wells of Westerly never recovered from the severe injuries he received at Marye's Heights. He was discharged from the Veterans Reserve Corps, married, and tried to resume farming, but it was to little avail. He carried the scars of the battle on his face and legs. Wells was deaf in one ear, and his kidneys always gave him problems. Still, he tried to work odd jobs to support his family. In 1871 he received a meager eight dollar per month pension from the government he had served so faithfully. He tried frequently to gain an increase to the small amount; his old friends from Battery G, including Welcome C. Tucker and Daniel Hoxsie, wrote to the Pension Bureau to help their comrade receive an increase. By 1890, it was granted, and Wells received twelve dollars for his wounds. He lived on in agony until 1925. His grave was marked by a small government marker giving his name and unit, while the flag of the country he defended continues to fly over it to this day. Eunice Wells asked to be granted a widow's pension only a week after her husband's death. Mrs. Wells was supported by the government until her death in 1936.[27]

Westerly had contributed the most men to Battery G outside of Providence, sending twenty-nine of her sons into the ranks. Of these, three were killed in action and fourteen received wounds, some more than once. In addition, five were discharged for disability, while two deserted. Only five soldiers survived the conflict unscathed. The war had a profound impact on the soldiers from Westerly. According to town council president Edward G. Champlin, the soldiers returned home with a "decidedly favorable character previous to their enlistment." Some men, however, were the subject of "sad demoralization" because of the unspeakable things they had seen and done in the war. Private John S. Babcock was among the Westerly soldiers who had an unlucky Civil War experience. He was wounded at Marye's Heights, only to be captured two months later by Mosby's Rangers, and he was hit again at Cedar Creek. After being discharged, Babcock returned to Westerly and resumed work in a textile mill. Frederic Denison, a Baptist minister and a veteran himself, wrote of the sacrifice the town gave: "Westerly poured out much precious blood upon the country's altar. Some of the most valued lives in the town were given as a sacrifice." In total, forty men from Westerly died in the war.[28]

Prior to the Civil War, a large granite vein was discovered in Westerly. It was said that this blue tinged stone was among the most beautiful granite in the world. A decade after the conflict ended, the ring of chisels and hammers in the granite quarries encircling the town could be heard for a half century as hundreds of monuments and memorials to the conflict were chiseled out of Westerly granite to be placed at Antietam and Gettysburg, and many sites in between. Some Battery G veterans labored on these tasks, but no monument was ever erected to their battery. In 1890, the survivors from the town gathered to dedicate an impressive Grand Army of the Republic Hall. Named after a veteran of their regiment, the soldiers from Battery G were largely represented on the rolls as they met biweekly to honor their fallen brothers. Meeting in a large hall in the impressive structure that was flanked with flags and two howitzers, they served as a daily reminder to all of the sacrifice given, until 1934, when the last Westerly soldier passed to the last muster.[29]

Of all the Westerly men who went into Battery G, Corporal James A. Barber was a fitting tribute to all of them, earning the Medal of Honor at Petersburg. After the war, Barber returned home and married, raising seven sons. He continued to live as a sailor and operated a lifeboat station at Watch Hill. He further became a prominent member of the Stillman D. Budlong Post of the Grand Army of the Republic. The badge of the organization was shaped much like the highest award for military bravery. At Budlong Post events, Barber always wore two medals on his jacket. These were his Grand Army of the Republic badge and the Medal of Honor. Beginning in 1916 all recipients began to receive a special ten dollar per month pension in recognition of their services. In 1921, Barber was invited to a special gathering of medal recipients at Arlington National Cemetery for the dedication of the Tomb of the Unknown Soldier. Unfortunately, his poor health prevented him from attending the ceremonies. Corporal Barber died in June of 1925 at age eighty-four and was buried in Westerly near several members of his battery. Shortly before his death, the *Westerly Sun* wrote, "Westerly is honored by having such a man, with such a record as a citizen."[30]

Unlike many of their comrades who spread to the wind when the war was over, many of the Westerly Boys returned to their small villages. Here they could walk the same old dirt trails to each other's homes to remember what they had seen and done. It had taken over three years of their lives. Not everyone from the detachment had made it through, but those who did had quite the stories to tell their grandchildren, from the terrible ordeal of the summer of 1862, the mire and muck of the Mud March, the deadly first shot at Marye's Heights, the epic march to Gettysburg, the horrors of the fighting at Spotsylvania, the terrible carnage and bravery at Cedar Creek, to the glory of that last charge in April of 1865. The twenty-nine who had served in the First Detachment were among the bravest and had given all that could be given to the Union and to each other.

With the war over, the veterans of Battery G, First Rhode Island Light Artillery, put the war behind them. They had done their part in the War of the Rebellion and unlike many, left it behind with their youths. No postwar reunions ever took place and no memorials were ever erected. Except for listing service in the battery on their gravestones, the veterans largely forgot about their role in the conflict. Captain Adams attempted to gather material for a book, but never completed it. After the war, each Rhode Island regiment and battery were given an official historian by the adjutant general's office to write a brief account of the service of their unit. In Battery G, the appointment went to Corporal Edward P. Adams, a painter from East Providence. Adams received no support from his comrades and had to rely on his own writings and records from the Rhode Island adjutant general. By 1892, Corporal Adams had prepared a six page sketch of Battery G's history. This became the only published account of their service and exploits.[31]

The war was brought to mind in memory and on each Decoration Day as the surviving veterans mustered and placed flowers on the graves of the dead soldiers. Many Battery G veterans did join the local posts of the Grand Army of the Republic. Each Rhode Island community had one as the veterans met often to remember the conflict and their fallen comrades, while fighting for their rights in pension reform. The officers of Battery G, as they had done during the war, joined an even more elite organization, the Military Order of the Loyal Legion of the United States. Organized in similar lines to the Grand Army of the Republic, membership in the legion was only open to commissioned officers and their firstborn heirs. Eventually six Battery G officers joined.[32]

In the 1870s the veterans of the First Rhode Island Light Artillery Regiment banded together to form a veterans organization, as nearly every other Rhode Island regiment did. From the start, the organization presented problems. Because the eight batteries of the First Rhode Island Light Artillery Regiment served individually of their regiment and never fought as a single unit, there was no level of regimental cohesion as seen in the other regiments from the state. With this in mind, each battery formed its own veterans organization; again, Battery G did not, but some of its members joined the overall regimental organization. Throughout the 1880s the old soldiers prepared to write a grand history of their regiment. This had begun with the First Rhode Island Infantry in 1862 and would continue unabated until nearly every Rhode Island regiment had a history. Again, the batteries presented a problem; no two shared a single history and a book about the regiment as a whole would have been impossible to write. While Colonel Tompkins maintained a regimental headquarters, it was on paper only. The individual batteries reported directly back to Adjutant General Edward Mauran in Providence. With this in mind, the Rhode Island general assembly passed legislation in 1892 calling for each battery to write its own history, which would be paid for by the state. By the close of the decade, it was accomplished. Again, Battery G fell by the wayside as its veterans failed to record the war outside of their wartime diaries and letters, carefully preserved by family members as mementoes of the Great Rebellion.[33]

In 1913, a fiftieth anniversary reunion was held at Gettysburg as the veterans North and South again gathered to meet as united Americans who once had fought each other to the death on the hollowed ground they now walked upon. The battle had a special meaning for the veterans of Batteries A, B, and E, all of which fought in the struggle and lost immensely. Their positions were all marked by monuments erected in the 1880s. As they had not fought upon the main battlefield, Battery G and their brothers in Battery C were not allocated the funds from the Rhode Island General Assembly to erect a monument in their reserve positions; instead a simple iron tablet from the War Department marked the headquarters position of Colonel Charles Tompkins' Sixth Corps Artillery Brigade. The cannoneers of Battery G had been engaged during the skirmish near Fairfield on July 5, earning them the battle honor "Gettysburg" for its history. No marker was placed at Granite Hill, however. Now, fifty years after the battle, the state they had faithfully served paid the way of any Rhode Island veteran who wanted to travel to the battlefield for the reunion. The veterans of Battery G responded and six went South. Again, it was mostly the men from the southwestern corner of Rhode Island. Among the Battery G soldiers present were three of the seven Medal of Honor recipients, including James Barber and George Potter. For four days they toured the battlefield and reminisced about the days in their youth when they gained glory on the fields of the South as members of the Rhode Island Light Artillery. It was the last time Boots and Saddles was called.[34]

As time passed, the ranks of Battery G thinned each year. As they died, many of their funerals were celebrated in the small clapboard structures of western Rhode Island or at churches in Providence. As with many veterans of the war, their simple headstones were inscribed "A member of Battery G, 1st RI Light Artillery." The three years they had spent working together in the brotherhood of the light artillery had been the most important event of their lives. The seven men who earned the Medal of Honor were marked with distinction from their comrades in death as well. Their graves are marked by a special government issued headstone with the Medal inscribed upon its top: only 3,467 Americans share this honor. Although most were buried in the soil of their native state, some were forever left in the South. In a small corner of the National Cemetery in Winchester, Virginia, are six members of Battery G, five of whom fell in the early morning fight for the guns at Cedar Creek.[35]

The last veteran of Battery G was Private Charles D. Ennis of Charlestown. Enlisting in August 1862, Ennis served throughout the war, never being reported absent for duty. The private was among the artillerists recognized for choosing to go forward into the jaws of hell at Petersburg. He had a varied life after the war and ended it by farming in the Potter Hill section of Westerly, where he and several other Battery G veterans became members of the Burnside Grand Army Post; Ennis was also its last survivor. He died of "senile debility" on December 29, 1930, at the age of eighty-seven. The following day the *Westerly Sun* printed his obituary on the front page. Civil War veterans were becoming increasingly scarce and each passing made headlines. Ennis had lived a full life as a soldier, blacksmith, and farmer and had raised two sons. Despite this, his entire existence was remembered by his three years' service in the Civil War as a member of Battery G. Of these three years, only a brief thirty minutes would be remembered: his participation as a member of the assault party on April 2, 1865. The headline to his obituary was "Given Medal for Bravery in Civil War. Cited for 'Gallantry in Action' at Battle of Petersburg."

Private Ennis was buried in Carolina, Rhode Island, near three of his brothers in arms. Only one member of the Grand Army of the Republic was left in Westerly to attend his comrade's funeral; soon he would be gone and the world would look to another war. The old man who once proudly wore a Greek cross on his hat was laid to rest by Rhode Island artillerymen of a much more recent war, this one not on the fields of Virginia, but across the Atlantic. With his death, the last direct connection to the history accomplished by him and his fellow soldiers was gone. Only scraps of paper and faded memories would remain.[36]

These Boys of Hope truly showed their foe what Rhode Islanders could do. The men earned their place in history at Antietam, Marye's Heights, and Cedar Creek, while their charge on Petersburg made heroes of the command. Throughout its history, Battery G was plagued by drunkenness, deserters, incompetent officers, and those who went absent without leave for long periods of time; thus robbing the command of much needed manpower. These men did not diminish what those who remained accomplished. During their three years and a half years of war, this gallant battery was at the forefront of battle with the Army of the Potomac. On the battlefields of Pennsylvania, Maryland, Virginia, and West Virginia, the Rhode Islanders were able to take a new piece of technology, the rifled cannon, and employ it to great effect on many bloody fields. In doing so they helped take the war to the enemy and restored the United States as a united country, free of slavery. They were the officers, cannoneers, and drivers of Battery G, First Rhode Island Light Artillery.

Appendices

I: *Roster of Battery G, First Rhode Island Light Artillery*

The following roster of Battery G was compiled from the muster rolls and service records at the Rhode Island State Archives and the National Archives. This is a listing of all the officers, noncommissioned officers, and enlisted men who served in the unit. The format is as follows: Name, residence, age upon enlistment, occupation, enlistment date, and service details. While many of the men joined the battery during the early recruiting expedition, they did not sign their names to the books until the date given. For officers, the date is when the officer received his commission to serve in Battery G or, for the case of the officers from Battery C, when they were commissioned into that battery. All Battery C soldiers were transferred to Battery G on December 29, 1864. All batteries are those of the First Rhode Island Light Artillery Regiment. It should be noted that some men listed as in their forties could have been older as some lied about their ages in order to enlist. For brevity's sake, the following abbreviations have been utilized:

Rank

Pvt: Private
Art: Artificer
Mus: Musician
Corp: Corporal
Sgt: Sergeant
1st Sgt: First Sergeant
QM Sgt: Quartermaster Sergeant
Wag: Wagoner
Bvt: Brevet rank
2nd Lt: Second Lieutenant
1st Lt: First Lieutenant
Capt: Captain
Maj: Major
Lt Col: Lieutenant Colonel
Col: Colonel

Other

Arty: Artillery
Bat: Battery
Co: Company
KIA: Killed in action
MWIA: Mortally wounded in action
Trans: Transferred
Wd: Wounded
Wds: Wounds

Commissioned Officers

CAPTAINS

Owen, Charles D. Providence, 19, Student, Dec. 2, 1861. Promoted from 1st Lt. Bat. A. Resigned Dec 26, 1862.

Bloodgood, Horace S. Providence, 22, Student, Dec. 29, 1862. Promoted from 1st Lt. Bat. B. Resigned April 23, 1863.

Adams, George W. Providence, 29, Merchant, April 25, 1863. Promoted from 1st Lt. Bat B. Bvt. Maj. Oct 19, 1864, for gallantry at Cedar Creek. Participated in the Assault on Petersburg, April 2, 1865. Bvt Lt. Col. and Col. for gallantry at Petersburg, April 2, 1865. Promoted to Maj. 1st RI Lt. Arty. June 12, 1865. Mustered out June 24, 1865.

FIRST LIEUTENANTS

Allen, Crawford A., Jr. Promoted from 2nd Lt. Bat. G. Wd. May 3, 1863, at Marye's Heights. Trans. to Sixth Corps Arty. Brigade May 30, 1863, as adjutant. Promoted to Capt. Bat. H, Sept 30, 1863.

Corthell, Elmer D. Providence, 20, Student, Nov. 1, 1863. Promoted from 2nd Lt. Bat. A. Promoted to Capt. Bat. D, Oct 21, 1864, for gallantry at Cedar Creek.

Freeborn, Benjamin. Oct. 21, 1864. Promoted from 2nd Lt. Bat E. Acting Capt. June 12–24, 1865. Mustered out June 24, 1865.

Lamb, Jacob H. Newport, 43, Merchant, Sept. 28, 1863. Trans. from Bat. C. Bvt. Capt. for gallantry at Cedar Creek. Promoted to Capt. Bat. E, Mar. 5, 1864.

Rhodes, William B. Warwick, 29, Jeweler. Oct. 2, 1861. Trans. to Bat. D. Dec. 26, 1862.

Rich, Reuben H. Mar. 5, 1865. Promoted from 2nd Lt. Bat. G. Wd. April 2, 1865 at Petersburg. Mustered out June 24, 1865.

Sears, Edward H. Providence, 21, Student, June 6, 1861. Trans. from Co. D. 2nd R.I. Vols. Nov. 1861. Resigned Nov. 21, 1862, to take position as paymaster in the U.S. Navy.

Torslow, Otto L. Nov 18, 1862. Promoted from 2nd Lt. Bat. G. Wd. May 3, 1863, at Marye's Heights. Resigned June 28, 1864.

Second Lieutenants

Allen, Crawford A., Jr. Providence, 20, Student, Nov. 18, 1861. Promoted to 1st Lt. Bat. G, Nov. 18, 1862.

Chase, James E. Mar. 12, 1863. Promoted from Sgt. Bat G. Promoted to 1st Lt. Bat. B, April 26, 1864.

Hoar, Allen. May 14, 1863. Promoted from Sgt. Bat G. Detached to Sixth Corps Arty. Brigade, May 1864. Promoted to 1st Lt. Bat. H, May 17, 1864.

Kelley, Benjamin E. Nov 18, 1862. Promoted from 1st Sgt. Bat. G. MWIA May 3, 1863, at Marye's Heights. Died of wds. May 3, 1863, at Falmouth, VA.

MacMillan, Andrew T. Providence, 20, Student, July 26, 1863. Trans. from Bat. C. Never served with Bat. G, having been captured Sept. 20, 1864. Resigned Feb. 22. 1865.

Rich, Reuben H. Providence, 22, Machinist, April 23, 1863. Trans. from Bat. C. Promoted to 1st Lt. Bat. G. Mar. 5, 1865.

Scott, Charles V. Providence, 20, Machinist, April 30, 1864. Promoted from Sgt. Bat. A. Wd. at Cold Harbor, June 3, 1864. Bvt. 1st Lt. Aug. 25, 1864, for gallantry at Cold Harbor. MWIA Oct. 19, 1864, at Cedar Creek. Died of Wds. at Winchester, VA, Jan. 21, 1865. Posthumously promoted to Bvt Capt. for gallant conduct at Cedar Creek Feb. 1, 1865.

Streeter, Marcus M. June 12, 1865. Promoted from 1st Sgt. Bat. G. Mustered out June 24, 1865.

Torslow, Otto L. Providence, 30, Soldier, Nov. 12, 1861. Promoted to 1st Lt. Bat. G, Nov. 18, 1862.

Waterman, Frank A. Providence, 18, Farmer, May 10, 1864. Promoted from Sgt. Bat. D. Promoted to 1st Lt. Bat. F, May 16, 1865.

Noncommissioned Officers

First Sergeants

Chace, Nathaniel R. Promoted from Sgt. May 14, 1863. Promoted to 2nd Lt. Bat. B, Oct. 21, 1864.

Hoar, Allen. Promoted from Sgt. Nov. 18, 1862. Promoted to 2nd Lt. Bat. G. May 14, 1863.

Kelley, Benjamin E. Providence, 20, Student, Dec. 2, 1861. Promoted to 2nd Lt. Bat G. Nov. 18, 1862.

Peck, John B. Pawtucket, 25, Machinist, Aug. 25, 1861. Trans. from Bat. C. Mustered out May 2, 1865. Never served as 1st Sgt, having been deemed supernumerary to Bat. G.

Streeter, Marcus M. Promoted from Sgt. Promoted to 2nd Lt. Bat. G, June 12, 1865.

Quartermaster Sergeants

Carpenter, Christopher. West Greenwich, 25, Grocer, Aug. 14, 1862. Trans. from Bat. C. Mustered out May 2, 1865. Never served as QM Sgt., having been deemed supernumerary to Bat. G.

Field, J. Russell. Providence, 36, Merchant, Nov. 1, 1861. Reduced to the ranks June 9, 1862.

Russell, George F. Promoted from Sgt. Mustered out June 24, 1865.

Westcott, William B. Promoted from Sgt. June 9, 1862. Promoted to 2nd Lt. Bat H, April 26, 1864.

Sergeants

Bogman, Charles H. Providence, Clerk, Dec. 2, 1861. Reduced to the ranks June 9, 1862.

Bowler, Henry H. Providence, Clerk, Dec. 1, 1861. Discharged for disability Jan. 23, 1863.

Brown, Samuel T. Promoted from Pvt. Mustered out June 24, 1865.

Buckley, Thomas. Warwick, 22, Wagoner, Feb. 11, 1864. Trans. from Bat. C. Mustered out June 24, 1865.

Chace, Nathaniel R. Promoted from Pvt. Promoted to 1st Sgt.

Chase, James E. Providence, 22, Clerk, Dec. 2, 1861. Promoted to 2nd Lt. Bat. G, Mar. 12, 1863.

Freeborn, Benjamin. Promoted from Pvt. Promoted to 2nd Lt. Bat. E. April 4, 1863.

Havron, John H. Providence, 19, Farmer, Aug. 25, 1861. Trans. from Bat. C. Participated in the assault on Petersburg, April 2, 1865. Mustered out June 24, 1865. Medal of Honor Recipient.

Hoar, Allen. Promoted from Pvt. Wd. Sept. 17, 1862 at Antietam. Promoted to 1st Sgt.

Jennings, Charles. Promoted from Corp. Detached to Sixth Corps Arty. Brigade as ordnance sergeant. Mustered out June 24, 1865.

Kent, Jacob F. Warwick, 22, Clerk, Dec. 2, 1861. Discharged Sept. 15, 1862. Died Dec. 5, 1862, of tuberculosis at Warwick.

Malbourne, Archibald. West Greenwich, 22, Operative, Aug 13, 1862. Trans. from Bat. C. Participated in the Assault on Petersburg, April 2, 1865. Mustered out June 24, 1865. Medal of Honor Recipient.

Mars, Thomas F. Promoted from Mus. Oct. 5, 1862. Reduced to Mus. April 8, 1863.

McCarthy, Charles. Providence, 20, Boiler Maker, Aug 25, 1861. Trans. from Bat. C. Mustered out June 24, 1865.

Potter, William W. Promoted from Corp. Acting as QM Sgt. April-Nov. 1864. Mustered out June 24, 1865.

Russell, George F. Promoted from Corp. Wd. Oct. 19, 1864 at Cedar Creek. Promoted to QM Sgt. Dec. 2, 1864.

Short, William F. Pawtucket, Aug 25, 1861. Trans. from Bat. C. Mustered out June 24, 1865.

Sisson, Alexander B. Promoted from Corp. Wd. Oct. 19, 1864 at Cedar Creek. Reduced to the ranks Dec. 29, 1864. Mustered out June 24, 1865.

Steinhaur, Kirby. Providence, 35, Farmer, Oct. 10, 1861. Promoted to 2nd Lt. Bat H Sept. 1, 1862.

Streeter, Marcus M. Promoted from Corp. Promoted to 1st Sgt. Nov. 3, 1864.

Sullivan, Edward G. Promoted from Pvt. Died of disease at Petersburg, VA, Mar. 22, 1865.

Westcott, Gilbert O. Promoted from Art. Oct. 5, 1862. Reduced to Art. April 1863.

Westcott, William B. Warwick, 21, Clerk, Dec. 2, 1861. Promoted to QM Sgt. June 9, 1862.

CORPORALS

Adams, Edward P. Promoted from Pvt. Mustered out June 24, 1865.

Barber, James A. Promoted from Pvt. Participated in the Assault on Petersburg, April 2, 1865. Mustered out June 24, 1865. Medal of Honor Recipient.

Brown, David. Pawtucket, 30, Seaman, Nov. 23, 1861. Wd. May 3, 1863, at Marye's Heights. Wd. Oct. 19, 1864, at Cedar Creek. Mustered out June 24, 1865.

Chace, Henry E. Promoted from Pvt. KIA Oct. 19, 1864, at Cedar Creek.

Cole, George W. Coventry, 26, Teacher, Nov 11, 1861. Discharged for disability Dec. 2, 1862. Promoted to Capt. 14th RI Heavy Artillery, Nov. 10, 1863.

Cole, James A. Scituate, 21, Farmer, Nov 11, 1861. Died of typhoid at Fort Monroe, Virginia. Sept. 18, 1862.

Conners, Charles. Promoted from Pvt. Captured by Mosby's Rangers July 24, 1863. Mustered out Mar. 14, 1865.

Curley, Patrick. East Providence, 27, Shoe Maker, Aug 25, 1861. Trans. from Bat. C. Mustered out June 24, 1865.

Griffith, Henry. Keene, NH, 27, Farmer, Dec. 3, 1861. Participated in the Assault on Petersburg, April 2, 1865. Mustered out June 24, 1865.

Hall, Alvin E. Promoted from Pvt. Mustered out June 24, 1865.

Hazelton, Edgar. Promoted from Pvt. Discharged for disability May 25, 1863.

Hoxsie, Daniel. Promoted from Pvt. Wd. June 3, 1864, at Cold Harbor. Wd. Oct. 19, 1864, at Cedar Creek. Reduced to the ranks Dec. 29, 1864. Trans. to the VRC. Mustered out Aug. 8, 1865.

Jennings, Charles. Warren, 22, Clerk, Nov. 20, 1861. Reduced to the ranks, Feb. 1, 1862. Re-promoted to Corp. Promoted to Sgt.

Keating, John. Providence, 18, Weaver, Aug. 25, 1861. Trans. from Bat. C. Promoted to Corp. Mustered out June 24, 1865.

Larkin, Henry. Promoted from Pvt. Mustered out June 24, 1865.

Lawton, Nicholas W. Warwick, 27, Farmer, Aug. 15, 1862. Trans. from Bat. C. Mustered out June 24, 1865.

Lewis, Samuel E. Coventry, 20, Farmer, Aug. 25, 1861. Trans. from Bat. C. Participated in the Assault on Petersburg, April 2, 1865. Mustered out June 24, 1865. Medal of Honor Recipient.

Lewis, William H. Providence, 16, Student, Nov. 5, 1861. Reduced to Mus. June 9, 1862.

Mann, Edward K. Promoted from Pvt. June 9, 1862. Mustered out May 11, 1865.

Peckham, Orrin S. Providence, 18, Farmer, Jan 6, 1862. Trans. from Bat. C. Mustered out June 24, 1865.

Polsey, Virgil M. Pawtucket, 19, Teacher, Dec. 22, 1861. Reduced to the ranks April 26, 1865. Mustered out June 24, 1865.

Potter, William W. Coventry, 19, Bookkeeper, Nov. 22, 1861. Reduced to the ranks, Feb. 1, 1862. Re-promoted to Corp. Wd. Sept. 17, 1862 at Antietam. Promoted to QM. Sgt.

Randall, Henry. Providence, 19, Teamster, April 7, 1862. Trans. from Bat. C. Participated in the Assault on Petersburg, April 2, 1865. Mustered out April 14, 1865.

Russell, George F. Providence, 28, Box Maker, Dec. 3, 1861. Promoted to Sgt.

Sisson, Alexander B. Promoted from Pvt. Wd. May 3, 1863 at Marye's Heights. Promoted to Sgt. Dec. 2, 1863.

Stephens, William H. Newark, NJ, 22, Machinist, Aug. 25, 1861. Trans. from Bat. C. Promoted to 2nd Lt. Bat. B, June 12, 1865.

Streeter, Marcus M. Providence, 20, Machinist, Nov. 5, 1861. Promoted to Sgt.

Tennant, Benjamin D. Promoted from Pvt. Mustered out June 24, 1865.

Thurber, William B. Promoted from Pvt. Mustered out June 24, 1865.

Tucker, Peleg D. Promoted to Pvt. Reduced to Art. at own request.

Enlisted Men

MUSICIANS

Baker, Francis B. Promoted from Pvt. Nov. 1864. Mustered out Mar. 11, 1865.

Lewis, William H. Reduced from Corp. June 9, 1862. MWIA Oct. 19, 1864, at Cedar Creek. Died of wds. Oct. 21, 1864.

Mars, Thomas F. East Providence, 24, Carriage Maker, Nov. 24, 1861. Promoted to Sgt. Oct. 5, 1862, for gallantry at Antietam. Reduced from Sgt. April 8, 1863. MWIA May 3, 1863, at Marye's Heights. Died of wds. May 9, 1863, at Washington.

Russell, Thomas. Providence, 36, Musician, Dec. 20, 1861. Deserted Jan 30, 1864, while on furlough in Providence.

Seamans, Henry C. Promoted from Pvt. Mustered out June 24, 1865.

Schmidt, Louis. Providence, Musician, Dec. 18, 1861. Discharged for disability Jan. 1, 1863.

ARTIFICERS

Bowers, William. Providence, 42, Farmer, Sept. 4, 1861. Trans. from Bat. D. Discharged for disability Sept. 26, 1862.

Butts, James. Warren, 36, Harness Maker, Dec. 6, 1861. Served as Wagoner. Mustered out June 24, 1865.

Buzberger, John. Providence, 40, Farmer, Dec. 23, 1861. Discharged for disability Feb. 17, 1862.

Capen, Elisha M. East Providence, 24, Farmer, Nov. 2, 1861. Mustered out Nov. 22, 1864.

Ellis, Albert. Providence, 37, Teamster, Nov. 16, 1861. Mustered out June 24, 1865.

Hull, Augustus. Providence, 20, Farmer, Dec. 5, 1861. Mustered out Dec. 17, 1864.

McManus, Charles. New York City, NY, 23, Weaver, Dec. 17, 1861. Died of disease Sept. 21, 1863 at Washington.

Shea, Dennis. Chelsea, MA, 36, Blacksmith, June 10, 1863. Trans. from Bat. C. Mustered out June 24, 1865.

Tucker, Peleg D. Appointed from Corp. Mustered out June 24, 1865.

Tucker, Welcome C. Charlestown, 25, Machinist, Aug 7, 1862. Mustered out June 24, 1865.

Westcott, Gilbert O. Warwick, 30, Clerk, Nov. 4, 1861. Promoted to Sgt. Oct. 1862. Reduced to Art. Mustered out Dec. 3, 1864.

Wilbur, William B. Providence, 27, Farmer, Aug. 16, 1862. Served as Stable Sgt. in charge of artificer detachment. Died of disease at Warrenton, VA, Aug. 10, 1863.

Wright, Matthew P. Hopkinton, 23, Blacksmith, Mar. 3, 1862. Mustered out Mar. 3, 1865.

PRIVATES

Adams, Edward P. East Providence, 25, Painter, Nov. 18, 1861. Promoted to Corp.

Adamson, James R. Providence, 30, Sailor, Nov. 22, 1861. Wd. Oct. 19, 1864, at Cedar Creek. Mustered out Nov. 22, 1864.

Andrews, Martin. Coventry, 28, Farmer, Aug. 14, 1862. Trans. from Bat. C. Mustered out June 24, 1865.

Austin, George D. Westerly, 33, Carder, Aug. 7, 1862. Wd. May 3, 1863, at Marye's Heights. Discharged on account of wds. June 22, 1863.

Austin, Ira B. Westerly, 21, Operative, Mar. 17, 1862. Wd. May 3, 1863, at Marye's Heights. Mustered out June 24, 1865.

Austin, Nathaniel C. Westerly, 19, Farmer, Nov. 11, 1861. Wd. May 3, 1863, at Marye's Heights. Discharged on account of wds. June 22, 1863.

Ayres, Nathaniel C. Providence, 43, Engineer, Nov. 22, 1861. Mustered out Nov. 22, 1864.

Babcock, John S. Westerly, 22, Operative, Mar. 15, 1862. Wd. May 3, 1863, at Marye's Heights. Captured by Mosby's Rangers July 24, 1863. Wd. at Cedar Creek, Oct. 19, 1864. Mustered out Mar. 14, 1865.

Baker, Francis B. Warwick, 18, Student, Mar. 11, 1862. Promoted to Mus. Nov. 1864.

Baker, Frederick A. Pawtucket, 20, Laborer, Mar. 22, 1864. Trans. from Bat. C. Mustered out June 24, 1865.

Baker, William A. Providence, 45, Machinist, Nov. 18, 1861. Mustered out June 24, 1865. Died of disease contracted in the service, July 21, 1865.

Barber, Ellery. Westerly 20, Clerk, Nov. 18, 1861. Mustered out June 24, 1865.

Barber, James A. Westerly, 22, Sailor, Nov. 11, 1861. Wd. May 3, 1863 at Marye's Heights. Promoted to Corp.

Barber, Manley P. Westerly, 28, Teamster, Nov. 15, 1861. Wd. Sept. 17, 1862, at Antietam. Mustered out June 24, 1865.

Barden, Joseph F. Foster, 19, Machinist, Aug. 14, 1862. Trans. from Bat. C. Mustered out June 24, 1865.

Barney, Beriah. Woonsocket, 44, Butcher, Dec. 14, 1861. Discharged for disability Oct. 30, 1862.

Bogman, Charles H. Reduced from Sgt. Trans. to Bat. E, Mar. 16, 1863.

Boutwell, Loammi. Providence, 40, Harness Maker, Nov. 5, 1861. Discharged for disability, Feb. 17, 1862.

Bowen, Esek K. Scituate. 44, Farmer, Nov. 18, 1861. Discharged for disability Feb. 17, 1862.

Bowen, George W. Providence, 18, Machinist, Nov. 29, 1861. MWIA Oct. 19, 1864, at Cedar Creek. Died of wds. at Baltimore, Dec. 3, 1864.

Bowling, John. Boston, MA, 26, Carriage Maker, June 22, 1863. Mustered out Sept. 7, 1864.

Braman, James H. South Kingstown, 30, Nov. 15, 1861. Died of typhoid Sept. 11, 1862, at Philadelphia, Pennsylvania.

Braman, Marcus L. Providence, 22, Shoemaker, June 20, 1863. Mustered out June 24, 1865.

Brennan, Patrick. North Providence, 31, Laborer, Dec. 1, 1861. MWIA. May 3, 1863, at Marye's Heights. Died of wds. April 28, 1864, at Providence, RI.

Briggs, Edward C. Coventry, 20, Laborer, Nov. 11, 1861. Died of disease Sept. 28, 1862, at Washington.

Brogan, Edward. North Providence, 18, Laborer, Aug. 8, 1862. Trans. from Bat. C. Mustered out June 24, 1865.

Brown, Elizer H. Providence, 34, Joiner, Nov. 4, 1861. Died of pneumonia Mar. 22, 1862 at Washington.

Brown, Patrick. Providence, 34, Laborer, Dec. 16, 1861. Mustered out June 24, 1865.

Brown, Samuel T. Warwick, 19, Laborer, Aug. 25, 1861. Trans. from Bat. C. Promoted to Sgt.

Burke, John. Providence, 20, Boot Maker, Mar. 15, 1862. Deserted May 4, 1864.

Burns, Andrew. Providence, 18, Operative, May 29, 1862. Trans. from Bat. C. Mustered out May 25, 1865.

Burton, William H. Richmond, 21, Operative, Aug. 7, 1862. Wd. May 3, 1863, at Marye's Heights. Wd. Oct. 19, 1864, at Cedar Creek. Mustered out June 24, 1864.

Bush, Alexander. Providence. Aug. 9, 1863. Trans. from Co. H. 2nd RI Vols. Dec. 9, 1863. Mustered out June 24, 1865.

Bymer, George A. New York City, NY, 19, Clerk, Nov 8, 1862. Trans. from Bat. C. Mustered out June 24, 1865.

Byrnes, Thomas. East Greenwich, 31, Laborer, June 5, 1861. Trans. from Co. H, 2nd R.I. Vols. Dec. 9, 1863. Mustered out June 6, 1864.

Byron, Patrick O. Providence, 21, Mar.18, 1862. Mustered out Mar. 18, 1865.

Cabe, John. South Kingstown, 25, Oct 20, 1862. Trans. to the VRC April 15, 1864.

Callahan, James. Pawtucket, 18, Weaver, June 5, 1861. Trans. From Co. F, 2nd R.I. Vols. Dec. 9, 1863. Captured May 12, 1864, at Spotsylvania. Died at Andersonville, GA, July 23, 1864.

Callahan, Michael. Providence, 25, Shoemaker, Dec 3, 1861. Wd. Dec. 11, 1862, at First Fredericksburg. Mustered out Dec. 17, 1864.

Campbell, Neil. Providence, 41, Painter, Dec. 2, 1861. Discharged for disability Oct. 11, 1862.

Camsteen, Henry. South Kingstown, 26, Oct. 18, 1861. Deserted December 1861.

Canning, John. Providence, 17, Stonecutter, Nov. 8 1861. Died of disease at Washington, Dec. 23, 1862.

Capp, Joshua. Providence, 19, Miller, June 30, 1863, Deserted Oct. 23, 1863.

Capron, John H. Portsmouth, 34, Machinist, Aug. 7, 1862. Wd. May 3, 1863, at Marye's Heights. Mustered out June 24, 1865.

Carrew, Thomas. Providence, 45, Sailor, Nov. 27, 1861. Discharged for disability July 17, 1862.

Carrigan, Patrick. Providence, 25, Molder, Dec. 6, 1861. Killed after being kicked by a horse at Falmouth, VA, Dec. 17, 1862.

Carroll, James. Providence, 23, June 25, 1863. Deserted Dec. 9, 1863.

Casey, John. Cranston, 35, Weaver, Feb. 23, 1864. Trans. from Bat. C. Mustered out June 24, 1865.

Chace, Henry E. Westerly, 27, Cabinetmaker, Nov. 6, 1861. Promoted to Corp.

Chace, Nathaniel R. Westerly, 22, Farmer, Nov. 2, 1861. Promoted to Sgt. June 9, 1862.

Chace, William A. Pawtucket, 22, Laborer, July 9, 1863. Trans. from Co. F, 2nd RI Vols. Dec. 9, 1863. Mustered out June 24, 1865.

Champlin, Nathaniel. Charlestown, 32, Operative, Aug. 7, 1862. Deserted Jan. 1863 and returned to unit May 1863. Wd. Oct. 19, 1864, at Cedar Creek. Discharged for disability May 5, 1865.

Champlin, Samuel. Westerly, 34, Fisherman, Nov. 27, 1861. Wd. May 3, 1863, at Marye's Heights. Wd. Oct. 19, 1864, at Cedar Creek. Mustered out Nov. 22, 1864.

Chapman, Daniel L. Westerly, 27, Stonecutter, Dec. 19, 1861. Discharged for disability Dec. 16, 1862.

Chapman, Thomas F. Westerly, 33, Stonecutter, Dec. 11, 1861. Wd. Oct. 19, 1864, at Cedar Creek. Mustered out June 24, 1865.

Church George P. Westerly, 27, Farmer, Mar. 16, 1862. Deserted May 24, 1862.

Clarkin, Henry. Warwick, 35, Laborer, Aug. 6, 1862. Trans. from Bat. C. Mustered out June 24, 1865.

Coffery, Michael. Providence, 42, Laborer, Nov. 20, 1861. Died of disease at Harpers Ferry, Oct. 18, 1862.

Collins, John. Warwick, 22, Spinner, Oct. 4, 1861, Mustered out June 24, 1865.

Conley, William. Providence, 17, Stonecutter. Nov. 18, 1861. Died of disease Oct. 3, 1863, at Washington.

Conners, Charles. Providence, 19, Farmer, Mar. 10, 1862. Promoted to Corp.

Connery, John. Providence, 17, Stonecutter, Nov. 2, 1861. Died of disease Dec. 23, 1862, at Washington.

Corcoran, John. Pawtucket, 21, Machinist, Feb. 17, 1864. Trans. from Bat. C. Participated in the Assault on Petersburg, April 2, 1865. Mustered out June 24, 1865. Medal of Honor Recipient.

Cordner, Albert D. Charlestown, 26, Mechanic, Mar. 3, 1862. Mustered out Mar. 3, 1865.

Cornell, Luther. Coventry, 22, Farmer, Mar. 17, 1862. Wd. May 3, 1863, at Marye's Heights. Participated in the Assault on Petersburg, April 2, 1865. Wd. April 2, 1865, at Petersburg. Mustered out June 24, 1865.

Cosley, Patrick. East Providence, 29, Shoemaker, Dec. 22, 1863. Trans. from Bat. C. Mustered out June 24, 1865.

Craven, John. Providence, 43, Laborer, Feb. 15, 1862. Discharged for disability, Dec. 16, 1862.

Dean, Charles W. East Providence, 24, Carpenter, Dec. 18, 1861. Discharged for disability Sept. 18, 1863.

Deane, Marshall. Providence, 39, Operative, May 13, 1862. Trans. from Bat. C. Mustered out June 24, 1865.

Dobson, Joseph D. North Providence, 23, Machinist, Dec. 3, 1861. Discharged for disability Dec. 16, 1862.

Douglas, William C. Westerly, 28, Laborer, Dec. 16, 1861. KIA Oct. 19, 1864, at Cedar Creek.

Drake, Horace F. Bristol, 22, Oct. 20, 1862. Discharged for disability Aug. 21, 1863.

Durfee, Albert C. Foster, 25, Teamster, Mar. 21, 1862. Wd. and captured Oct. 19, 1864, at Cedar Creek. Mustered out April 20, 1865.

Durham, Charles C. Providence, 35, Shoemaker, Nov. 9, 1861. Discharged for disability Feb. 15, 1862.

Ennis, Charles D. Charlestown, 19, Farmer, Aug. 7, 1862. Participated in the Assault on Petersburg, April 2, 1865. Mustered out June 24, 1865. Medal of Honor Recipient.

Farnsworth, Henry. East Providence, 45, Farmer, Nov. 22, 1861. Died of disease at Hampton, VA, Sept. 20, 1862.

Fenner, George D. Johnston, 21, Farmer, Mar. 3, 1862. Sent to hospital where detached to Co. I,

2nd United States Infantry. KIA May 13, 1864, at Spotsylvania.

Field, J. Russell. Reduced from QM Sgt. Promoted to 2nd Lt. Bat. E Jan 10, 1863.

Forrest, Edward. Hopkinton, 41, Operative, Mar. 3, 1862. Wd. and captured Oct. 19, 1864, at Cedar Creek. Mustered out July 27, 1865.

Franklin, Warren P. Providence, 38, Sailor, Feb. 11, 1864, Trans. from Bat. C. Participated in the Assault on Petersburg, April 2, 1865. Mustered out June 24, 1865.

Freeborn, Benjamin. Providence, 26, Clerk, Dec. 4, 1861. Promoted to Sgt. June 9, 1862.

Gardner, Charles G. Barrington, 33, Farmer, Nov. 30, 1861. Detached to 6th Corps Arty. Brigade. KIA Oct. 19, 1864, at Cedar Creek.

Gaskell, George L. Coventry, 21, Sailor, Dec. 3, 1861. Served as guidon bearer and orderly to the commanding officer. Wd. July 1, 1862, at Malvern Hill. Discharged Dec. 1863 to accept commission as 2nd Lt. in the 14th RI Heavy Artillery.

Gigle, Joseph. Providence, 28, Teacher, June 23, 1863. Deserted Oct. 18, 1863.

Goran, John. Providence, 20, Farmer, Dec. 22, 1863. Trans. from Bat. C. Mustered out June 24, 1865.

Goulding, John. Providence, 20, Machinist, Dec. 22, 1863. Trans. from Bat. C. Mustered out June 24, 1865.

Gray, William. Providence, 29, Farmer, Oct. 31, 1861. Discharged for disability Oct. 11, 1862.

Greene, William R. Warwick, 17, Farmer, Nov. 11, 1861. Discharged for disability Jan. 1, 1863.

Griesinger, William. Charlestown, 31, Operative, Aug. 7, 1862. Mustered out June 24, 1865.

Grieves, John. Providence, 40, Operative. Mar. 24, 1862. Mustered out Mar. 24, 1865.

Guhl, Karl. Boston, MA, 33, Tailor, June 25, 1863. Trans. from Bat. C. Participated in the Assault on Petersburg, April 2, 1865. Mustered out June 24, 1865.

Hagerdon, Jacob. Providence, Aug. 7, 1862. Deserted Sept. 24, 1862.

Haley, Patrick. Providence, 18, Laborer, Mar. 4, 1862. Trans. from Bat. C. Mustered out May 20, 1865.

Hall, Alvin E. 18, Providence, Student, Nov. 5, 1862. Trans. from Bat. C. Promoted to Corp.

Hallam, John. Westerly, 32, Boot Maker, Dec. 6, 1861. Mustered out Dec. 10, 1864.

Harper, Thomas. Providence, 23, Aug. 20, 1863. Detached to 6th Corps Arty. Brigade. Wd. and captured Oct. 19, 1864, at Cedar Creek. Mustered out June 24, 1865.

Hazelton, Edgar. Cumberland, 18, Teamster, Dec. 16, 1861. Promoted to Corp.

Healey, Jeremiah P. Providence, 18, Farmer, Mar. 8, 1862. Wd. May 3, 1863, at Marye's Heights. Mustered out Mar. 8, 1865.

Heap, Henry. Providence, 32, Stonecutter, Nov. 7, 1861. Discharged for disability Jan. 23, 1863.

Heiman, Frederic. Providence, 27, Dec. 5, 1863. Trans. from Bat. C. Mustered out June 24, 1865.

Heine, William. Boston, MA, 25, Laborer, June 30, 1863. Trans. from Bat. C. Mustered out June 24, 1865.

Henrys, Caleb. Cranston, 42, Teamster, Dec. 18, 1861. Discharged for disability Nov. 1862.

Henshaw, Edwin B. Providence, 18, Clerk. July 9, 1863. Trans. from Co. D, 2nd RI Vols. Dec. 9, 1863. Mustered out Oct. 31, 1864.

Hidelbrand, August. South Kingstown, 32, Oct. 18, 1861. Deserted December 1861.

Higgins, John. South Kingstown, 23, Oct. 18, 1861. Deserted December 1861.

Higgins, Patrick. Providence, 28, Spinner, Dec. 12, 1861. Mustered out June 24, 1865.

Hoar, Allen. Warren, 24, Sailor, Nov. 20, 1861. Promoted to Sgt. June 9, 1862,

Holland, Hazard. South Kingstown, 29, Feb. 28, 1862. Discharged for disability April 21, 1862.

Holly, Richmond. East Providence, 18, Farmer, May 22, 1862. Trans. from Bat. C. Mustered out May 25, 1865.

Hopkins, Albert E. Providence, 18, Dec. 5, 1863. Trans. from Bat. C. Mustered out Mar. 15, 1865.

Hopkins, Palmer L. Charlestown, 23, Carriage Maker, Aug. 7, 1862. Discharged for disability April 27, 1863.

Horton, James H. Glocester, 32, Stonecutter, Dec. 2, 1861. Wd. June 3, 1864 at Cold Harbor. Mustered out May 20, 1865.

Hoxsie, Daniel. Richmond, 31, Operative, Aug. 7, 1862. Wd. May 3, 1863, at Marye's Heights. Promoted to Corp.

Hudson, Charles W. Smithfield, 23, Lawyer, Aug. 4, 1862. Died of typhoid Aug. 24, 1862, at Philadelphia.

Hughes, James. North Kingstown, 23, Laborer, Oct. 20, 1862. Trans. from Bat. C. Mustered out May 25, 1865.

Hutchins, Thomas. Warwick, 18, Operative, Mar. 17, 1862. Wd. Oct. 19, 1864, at Cedar Creek. Mustered out Aug. 15, 1865.

Jenks, George B. Pawtucket, 21, Painter, Aug. 25, 1861. Trans. from Bat. C Mustered out June 24, 1865.

Johnson, Edward. Providence, 35, Teamster, June 25, 1863. Deserted Mar. 25, 1864. Returned to unit April 1864. Mustered out June 24, 1865.

Johnston, John K. Westerly, 24, Farmer, Aug. 7, 1862. KIA May 3, 1863 at Marye's Heights.

Jones, William. Providence, 42, Wheelwright, Nov. 5, 1861. Mustered out June 24, 1865.

Keating, John. Providence, 18, Weaver, Aug. 25, 1861. Trans. from Bat. C. Promoted to Corp. April 1865.

Kelly, Frank A. Providence, 23, Miller, Aug. 25, 1861. Trans. from Bat. C. Promoted to Corp. April 1865.

Kent, Josiah F. East Providence, 36, Farmer, Nov. 5, 1861. Detached to 6th Corps Arty. Brigade. Mustered out Nov. 18, 1864.

Kenyon, Jonathan. Charlestown, 38, Bookkeeper, Nov. 29, 1861. Discharged for disability Dec. 3, 1864.

Kershaw, Edwin B. Providence. July 9, 1863. Trans. from Co. D, 2nd RI Vols. Dec. 9, 1863. Mustered out June 24, 1865.

King, George G. Coventry, 44, Farmer, Aug. 22, 1862. Trans. from Bat. C. Mustered out June 24, 1865.

Kingsley, Michael. Providence, 35, Laborer, Nov. 22, 1861. Deserted Mar. 22, 1862.

Kronke, John P. Providence, 24, Sailor, July 8, 1863. Trans. from Bat. C. Participated in the Assault on Petersburg, April 2, 1865. Mustered out June 24, 1865.

Krull, Henry. New York City, NY, 25, Machinist, June 30, 1863. Participated in the Assault on Petersburg, April 2, 1865. Mustered out June 24, 1865.

Larke, Edward. Providence, July 9, 1863. Trans. from Co. D, 2nd RI Vols., Dec. 9, 1863. Wd. Oct.19, 1864 at Cedar Creek. Mustered out Aug. 24, 1865.

Larkin, Henry. Richmond, 18, Weaver, Aug 15, 1862. Promoted to Corp. Mustered out June 24, 1865.

Lavender, George. Burrillville, 21, Laborer, Nov. 18, 1861. Captured by Mosby's Rangers July 24, 1863. Mustered out Nov. 28, 1864.

Lavender, Nelson. Burrillville, 19, Farmer, Dec. 1, 1861. Mustered out Dec. 2, 1864.

Laverty, Joseph. Providence, 21, Machinist, Dec. 22, 1863. Trans. from Bat. C. Mustered out June 24, 1865.

Logan, Matthew. Providence, 21, Dec. 29, 1861. Mustered out June 24, 1865.

Magnusen, Peter A. Providence, 48, Machinist, Dec. 3, 1861. Discharged for disability Oct. 29, 1862.

Mann, Edward K. Providence, 21, Machinist, Oct. 31, 1861. Promoted to Corp.

Matthewson, James A. Scituate, 17, Farmer, Dec. 2, 1861. Wd. Oct. 19, 1864, at Cedar Creek. Mustered out June 24, 1865.

McCabe, James. Providence, 36, Cabinetmaker, Dec. 6, 1861. Deserted Feb. 24, 1862.

McCaffery, John. Scituate, 18, Operative. June 20, 1862. Trans. from Bat. C Mustered out June 24, 1865.

McCardle, Owen. Providence, 22, Seaman, Dec. 20, 1861. Deserted Feb. 1863 and returned to unit. Detached to 6th Corps Arty. Brigade. Trans. to the US Navy April 27, 1864.

McCormick, Patrick. Cumberland, 21, Laborer, June 20, 1862. Trans. from Bat. C Mustered out June 24, 1865.

McDonald, James. Providence, 19, Farmer. Mar. 8, 1862. MWIA Oct. 19, 1864, at Cedar Creek. Died of wds. Nov. 1, 1864.

McDonald, James. Richmond, 25, Operative, Aug. 7, 1862. Wd. Oct. 19, 1864, at Cedar Creek. Mustered out June 24, 1865.

McDonald, James T. Newark, NJ, 29, Farmer, Dec. 22, 1863. Trans. from Bat. C Mustered out June 24, 1865.

McGrath, John. Boston, MA, 22, Clerk, June 22, 1863. Deserted Sept. 24, 1863.

McGuire, George. Providence, 42, Operative, Nov. 8, 1861. Discharged for disability Mar. 11, 1863.

McLaughlin, Bernard F. Providence. Dec. 10, 1861. Deserted Jan. 13, 1862.

McNally, James. Westerly, 28, Operative, Aug. 16, 1862. Mustered out June 24, 1865.

Mitchell, Samuel C. Westerly, 18, Blacksmith, Nov. 18, 1861. Wd. May 3, 1863, at Marye's Heights. Trans. to the VRC, Feb. 15, 1864.

Murray, Michael. Providence, 19, Operative, May, 16, 1862. Trans. from Bat. C. Mustered out May 16, 1865.

Myony, Matthew. Providence, June 25, 1863. Detached to 6th Corps Arty. Brigade. Wd. Oct. 19, 1864, at Cedar Creek. Mustered out May 29, 1865.

Nicholas, Henry H. Warwick, 20, Farmer, Aug. 6, 1862. Trans. from Bat. C. Mustered out June 24, 1865.

Nichols, Lafayette G. Johnston, 37, Clerk, Aug. 16, 1862. Detailed to Conscript Camp at New Haven, CT July 1863. Mustered out June 24, 1865.

Niles, Nathaniel. Westerly, 40, Farmer, Aug. 5, 1862. Discharged for disability Oct. 29, 1862.

Norton, George R. Providence, 61, Laborer, Nov. 27, 1861. Discharged for disability April 14, 1862. Died of disease contracted in the service Feb. 22, 1869.

O'Brien, Patrick. Providence, 21, Sailor, Mar. 18, 1862. Wd. Oct. 19, 1864 at Cedar Creek. Mustered out Mar. 18, 1865.

O'Brien, Patrick. Cumberland, 28, Sailor, June 30, 1863. Trans. to the US Navy April 27, 1864.

Osmond, William. Providence, June 20, 1863. Deserted Dec. 9, 1863.

Partlow, Hazard. Richmond, 21, Farmer, Aug. 7, 1862. Mustered out June 24, 1865.

Place, Joseph B. West Greenwich, 40, Blacksmith, Aug. 13, 1862. Trans. to Bat. D.

Place, Stephen W. Glocester, 26, Teamster, Dec. 17, 1861. Wd. Oct. 19, 1864 at Cedar Creek. Discharged for disability May 5, 1865.

Platt, John. Cumberland, 41, Spinner, June 26, 1863. Mustered out June 24, 1865.

Pomeroy, Elijah. Providence, 43, Baker, Nov. 16, 1861. Died of disease at Portsmouth Grove Hospital, Sept. 12, 1862.

Potter, Daniel. Coventry, 21, Farmer, Aug. 14, 1862. Trans. from Bat. C. Mustered out June 24, 1865.

Potter, George W. Coventry, 18, Student, Feb. 26, 1862. Participated in the Assault on Petersburg, April 2, 1865. Wd. April 2, 1865, at Petersburg. Mustered out June 24, 1865. Medal of Honor Recipient.

Potter, German. Providence, 18, Farmer, Aug. 25, 1861. Trans. from Bat. C. Mustered out June 24, 1865.

Quigley, James. Smithfield, 19, Laborer, Aug. 6, 1862. Trans. from Bat. C. Mustered out June 24, 1865.

Rathbun, John G. Westerly, 21, Farmer, Aug. 7, 1862. Mustered out June 24, 1865.

Rathbun, John L. Exeter, 41, Farmer, Dec. 7, 1861. Captured June 1, 1862, at Fair Oaks, VA. Died Oct. 18, 1862, at Baltimore, MD, of disease.

Reynolds, Patrick. Providence, 47, Teamster, Nov. 6, 1861. Discharged for disability Oct 31, 1862.

Rice, Charles H. Coventry, 27, Farmer, Aug. 14, 1862. Trans. from Bat. C .Mustered out June 24, 1865. Died of disease contracted in the service at Hopkins Hollow, RI, Jan. 20, 1868.

Riley, Peter. Cranston, 35, Laborer. Nov. 11, 1861. Wd. Sept. 17, 1862, at Antietam. Discharged on account of wds. at Baltimore, MD, Feb. 24, 1863.

Ripley, Silas R. Westerly, 27, Spinner, Oct. 13, 1862. Deserted Jan. 1863. Returned to unit May 1863. Wd. Oct. 19, 1864 at Cedar Creek. Mustered out June 24, 1865.

Robinson, George. Providence, 30, Teamster, Nov. 25, 1861. Trans. to the VRC Aug. 5, 1863.

Russell, Thomas. Providence, 18, Clerk, Dec. 20, 1861. Deserted Jan. 30, 1864.

Ryan, Cornelius. Providence, 20, Operative, May 26, 1862. Trans. from Bat. C. Mustered out May 25, 1865.

Salpaugh, Jacob H. New York City, NY, 33, Laborer, Nov. 23, 1861. Died of typhoid at Falmouth, VA, Dec. 11, 1862.

Sampson, William B. Providence, 28, Teamster,

Nov. 25, 1861. Discharged for disability Oct 9, 1862.

Saunders, Albert R. Foster, 33, Farmer, Dec. 18, 1861. Discharged for disability Oct. 9, 1862.

Saunders, Henry A. Providence, 32, Farmer, Aug. 27, 1863. Trans. from Co. I, 2nd RI Vols. Dec. 9, 1863. Mustered out June 24, 1865.

Schwartz, Benno. New York City, NY, 23, Tailor, June 27, 1863. Deserted near Centreville, VA, Oct. 18, 1863.

Seamans, Henry C. Providence, 16, Cigar Maker, Dec. 17, 1861. Promoted to Mus. Oct. 21, 1864.

Searll, Richard W. Providence, 35, Wheelwright, June 11, 1863. Trans. from Bat. C. Mustered out June 24, 1865.

Short, William F. Pawtucket, 24, Operative, Aug. 25, 1861. Trans. from Bat. C. Participated in the Assault on Petersburg, April 2, 1865. Mustered out June 24, 1865.

Simmons, George N. North Providence, 25, Teamster, Dec. 16, 1861. Detached to Conscript Camp near New Haven, CT. Mustered out June 24, 1865.

Sisson, Alexander B. Westerly, 18, Farmer, Nov. 18, 1861. Promoted to Corp. June 9, 1862.

Sisson, Charles E. Westerly, 18, Farmer, Nov. 27, 1861. Wd. Oct. 19, 1864, at Cedar Creek. Mustered out June 24, 1865.

Smith, Henry. East Providence, 45, Mason, Oct. 3, 1861. Discharged for disability April 21, 1862.

Smith, James Y. North Providence, 42 Teamster, Nov. 27, 1861. Discharged for disability Dec. 26, 1861.

Smith, John. South Kingstown, 42, Operative, Dec. 21, 1861. Wd. Sept. 17, 1862, at Antietam. Discharged for disability Feb. 21, 1863.

Smith, Joseph. Westerly, 18, Machinist, Nov. 6, 1861. Wd. Sept. 17, 1862, at Antietam. Deserted Jan. 30, 1864.

Snell, Joseph. Smithfield, 34, Spinner, Aug. 6, 1862. Trans. from Bat. C. Mustered out June 24, 1865.

Sprague, Nathan C. Cumberland, 37, Blacksmith, Nov. 4, 1861. Reduced from Artificer. Mustered out Nov. 28, 1864.

Starboard, Simeon H. Davisville, ME, 35, Engineer, June 3, 1863. MWIA Oct. 19, 1864, at Cedar Creek. Died of wds. Jan. 1, 1865, at Winchester, VA.

Stephens, Daniel C. Glocester, 18, Farmer, Nov. 20, 1861. Deserted Feb. 1, 1864, at Providence, RI.

Stephens, George W. Charlestown, 31, Shoemaker, Dec. 12, 1861. Died of typhoid at Washington, Sept 9, 1862.

Stillman, Thomas L. Westerly, 29, Wheelwright, Aug. 14, 1862. Mustered out June 24, 1865.

Sullivan, Edward G. Coventry, 18, Farmer, Feb. 16, 1862. Promoted to Sgt. Mar. 9, 1864.

Sullivan, John. Providence, 18, Machinist, Nov. 1, 1864. Mustered out June 24, 1865.

Sullivan, Maurice. Westerly, 18, Laborer, Aug. 8, 1862. Trans. from Bat. C. Mustered out June 24, 1865.

Sullivan, Patrick. Smithfield, 23, Laborer, Aug. 6, 1862. Trans. from Bat. C. Mustered out June 24, 1865.

Sullivan, Patrick O. Westerly, 27, Laborer, Aug. 14, 1862. Mustered out May 25, 1865.

Sunderland, Joseph W. South Kingstown, 18, Farmer, Nov. 16, 1861. MWIA May 3, 1863, at Marye's Heights. Died of wds. at Washington, April 20, 1864.

Tabor, William O. Richmond, 24, Operative, Mar. 17, 1862. Died of typhoid January 27, 1863, at Washington.

Taft, James A. Providence, 34, Laborer, Dec. 16, 1861. Participated in the Assault on Petersburg, April 2, 1865. Mustered out June 24, 1865.

Taft, John. Providence, 30, Weaver, Dec. 21, 1861. Died of disease Jan. 24, 1862, at Washington.

Tanner, Charles. Providence, 18, Weaver, Jan. 9, 1862. Died of disease Sept 25, 1862, at Washington.

Tanner, Horace B. Hopkinton, 25, Farmer, Aug. 25, 1861. Trans. from Bat. C. Participated in the Assault on Petersburg, April 2, 1865. Mustered out June 24, 1865.

Tennant, Benjamin D. Hopkinton, 41, Mason, Nov. 12, 1861. Promoted to Corp.

Thurber, William B. Providence, 19, Jeweler, Nov. 18, 1861. Promoted to Corp.

Tillinghast, Henry C. West Greenwich, 26, Machinist, Aug. 14, 1862. Trans. from Bat. C. Mustered out June 24, 1865.

Travers, Augustus F. Providence, 21, Clerk, Aug. 8, 1863. Trans. from Co. I, 2nd RI Vols. Dec. 9, 1863. KIA Oct. 19, 1864, at Cedar Creek.

Tucker, Henry J. Scituate, 19, Operative, Mar. 17, 1862. Mustered out June 24, 1865.

Tucker, Peleg D. Charlestown, 27, Operative, Aug. 7, 1862. Promoted to Corp.

Wade, George D. Scituate, 19, Farmer, Nov. 14, 1862. Trans. from Bat. C. Mustered out June 24, 1865.

Walworth, James W. Westerly 30, Stonecutter, Dec. 11, 1861. Detached to Conscript Camp near New Haven, CT. Wd. Oct. 19, 1864, at Cedar Creek. Mustered out Dec 17, 1864.

Waters, James. Providence, 39, Laborer, Nov. 6, 1861. Discharged for disability July 31, 1863.

Watson, Hazard. South Kingstown, 30, Farmer,

Nov. 11, 1861. Deserted July 5, 1863, at Gettysburg. Later returned. Discharged for disability Dec. 30, 1863.

Webb, Charles H. Coventry, 18, Spinner, Nov. 11, 1861. Discharged for disability Feb. 15, 1862.

Webber, Frank. North Providence, 27, Laborer, June 25, 1863. Trans. to VRC. April 15, 1864. Mustered out Sept. 26, 1864.

Webster, Levi F. Providence, 28, Laborer, June 20, 1863. Deserted Oct. 23, 1863.

Welden, Frank. Smithfield, 24, Machinist, Mar. 24, 1862. Mustered out June 24, 1865.

Wells, John D. Westerly, 23, Farmer, Dec. 9, 1861. Wd. May 3, 1863, at Marye's Heights. Trans. to the VRC Aug. 1863.

Westcott, James F. Cumberland, 28, Painter, Nov. 30, 1861. Mustered out Dec. 3, 1864.

Weston, Emmons B. Providence, 18, Sailor, Oct. 13, 1863. Trans. from Bat. C. Mustered out June 24, 1865.

Wiley, John A. Coventry, 23, Farmer, Aug. 14, 1862. Trans. from Bat. C. Mustered out June 24, 1865.

Williams, Jason L. Coventry, 21, Teacher, Dec. 16,

1861. Died of disease at Portsmouth Grove Hospital, July 31, 1862.

Williams, John. Providence, 25, Laborer, Dec. 9, 1863. Trans. from Co. F, 2nd RI Vols. Trans. to US Navy April 18, 1864.

Williams, Thomas. Warren, 40, Tinsmith, Nov. 4, 1861. Discharged for disability Sept. 21, 1863.

Wilson, George. Providence, 34, Shoemaker, Nov. 1, 1861. Deserted Feb. 1, 1864, at Providence, RI. Returned to unit April 1864. Mustered out June 24, 1865.

Wilson, Thomas. Providence, 36, Cigar Maker, Nov. 28, 1861. Detached to 6th Corps Arty. Brigade. Mustered out June 24, 1865.

Wilson, William. Providence, 29, Merchant, June 22, 1863. Wd. Oct. 19, 1864, at Cedar Creek. Mustered out June 24, 1865.

Wood, Albert. Exeter, 22, Operative, Aug. 7, 1863. Trans. from Bat. C. Mustered out June 24, 1865.

Young, Jesse. Coventry, 42, Laborer, Dec. 3, 1861. Deserted May 27, 1862, and returned to unit Nov. 27, 1862. Sentenced to be shot. Sentence Commuted. Mustered out Dec. 17, 1864.

II: Roster of Attached Men

The following is the roster of those men who were detached from their original units to serve a period in Battery G. This roster is far from complete, as many infantrymen would join for a week or two and then be returned to their units. The roster is taken from the *Revised Register of Rhode Island Volunteers* and the muster rolls at the National Archives. All pertinent information pertaining to these men, including unit, dates attached and returned, and casualty data, has been entered. The abbreviations used remain the same.

Ancona, John D. Tenth NY Bat. May 13, 1863–Sept. 7, 1864. Served at Sixth Corps Arty. Brigade.

Anderson, Alexander. Co. K, Twelfth NJ Vols. April 1863–May 13, 1863. Trans. to Bat. A.

Anderson, John. Co. E, Fourth NY Heavy Art. April 27, 1864–June 12, 1864.

Baldwin, William H. Tenth NY Bat. Jan. 1864–Sept. 7, 1864.

Barton, Augustus. Co. K, Twelfth NJ Vols. Mar. 6, 1863–May 13, 1863. Wd. May 3, 1863 at Marye's Heights.

Billings, Charles. Fourth ME Bat. Mar. 18, 1865–June 24, 1865.

Brown, Frederick. Tenth NY Bat. May 13, 1863–Sept. 7, 1864.

Campbell, John J. Co. I, Sixty-Seventh NY Vols. April 22, 1864–June 24, 1865.

Campbell, William. Co. K, Twelfth NJ Vols. Mar. 16, 1863–May 13, 1863. Trans. to Bat. A.

Carroll, Edward. Co. G, Fourth NY Heavy Art. April 27, 1864–June 12, 1864.

Carroll, Peter. Trans. to Bat. E Mar. 23, 1865.

Castle, Henry. Co. G, Fourteenth CT Vols. Mar. 17, 1863–May 13. 1863. Trans. to Bat. A.

Colvin, Henry. Trans. to Bat. E Mar. 23, 1865.

Creamer, Simon W. Co. K, Twelfth NJ Vols. Mar. 16, 1863–May 13, 1863. Trans. to Bat. A.

Crows, Ivan. Tenth NY Bat. May 13, 1863–Sept. 7, 1864.

Cullen, Patrick. Tenth NY Bat. May 13, 1863–Sept. 7, 1864.

Curten, Frederick. Tenth NY Bat. May 13, 1863. Deserted July 9, 1863.

Dawson, William. Tenth NY Bat. May 13, 1863–Sept. 7, 1864

Devolve, Albert. Co. F, Ninth NY Heavy Art. Oct. 28, 1864–Jan. 1, 1865.

Duncombe, John. Co. C, Fourth NY Heavy Art. April 27, 1864–June 12, 1864.

Eddy, Osborne. Trans to Bat. E Mar. 23, 1865.

Friend, Edward. Fourth Maine Bat. Mar. 18, 1865–June 24, 1865.

Gordon, Thomas J. Co. E, Twelfth NJ Vols. Mar. 17, 1863–May 13, 1863. Trans. to Bat. A.

Gould, Charles H. Co. F, Ninth NY Heavy Art. Oct. 28, 1864–Jan. 1, 1865.

Granger, Leman B. Co. C, Fourth NY Heavy Art. April 27, 1864–June 12, 1864.

Gray, Albert C. Tenth NY Bat. May 13, 1863–Sept. 7, 1864. Served as Sgt.

Harrington, Thomas. Trans. to Bat. E. Mar. 23, 1865.

Hart, Isaac. Fourteenth NY Heavy Art. Mar. 6, 1864–Sept. 7, 1864.

Hoffman, Solon. Co. K, Twelfth NJ Vols. Mar. 16, 1863–May 13, 1863. Trans. to Bat. A.

Holton, Jesse. Co. K, Twelfth NJ Vols. Mar. 16, 1863–May 13, 1863.

Hughes, John. Co. I, First DE Vols. Mar. 16, 1863–May 13, 1863. Trans. to Bat. A.

Hunt, Charles E. Trans. to Bat. E. Mar. 23, 1865.

Jones, Charles. Co. F, Ninth NY Heavy Art. Oct. 28, 1864–Jan. 1, 1865.

Keating, M.M. Tenth NY Bat. May 13, 1863–Sept. 7, 1864.

King, George. Tenth NY Bat. May 13, 1863–Sept. 7, 1864.

Kneeland, Edward. Fourth ME Bat. Mar. 18, 1865–June 24, 1865.

Lawrence, Charles H. Co. D, One Hundred and Eighth NY Vols. Mar. 17, 1863. KIA May 3, 1863, at Marye's Heights.

Lewis, Elias. Co. F, Ninth NY Heavy Art. Oct. 28, 1864–Jan. 1, 1865.

Lewis, Patrick. Tenth NY Bat. May 13, 1863–Sept. 7, 1864.

Leudvan, Edwin. April 1863–May 13, 1863. Trans. to Bat. A.

Ludham, Charles. Tenth NY Bat. May 13, 1863–Sept. 7, 1864.

Martin, Dennis. Tenth NY Bat. May 13, 1863–Sept. 7, 1864.

Martin, Edward. Tenth NY Bat. May 13, 1863–Sept. 7, 1864.

Martin, Patrick. Tenth NY Bat. May 13, 1863–Sept. 7, 1864.

Mason, Lawrence. Fourth ME Bat. Mar. 18, 1865–June 24, 1865.

McClathchey, John. Tenth NY Bat. May 13, 1863–Aug. 21, 1864. Trans to the VRC.

McCune, James. Co. K, Fourth NY Heavy Art. April 27, 1864–June 12, 1864.

McGuire, Owen. Co. F. Ninth NY Heavy Art. Oct. 28, 1864–Jan. 1, 1865. Served as Wag.

McKee, Leman H. Co. C, Fourth NY Heavy Art. April 27, 1864–June 12, 1864.

McNally, Felix. Tenth NY Bat. May 13, 1863–Sept. 7, 1864.

Melvin, William. Co. F, Ninth NY Heavy Art. Oct. 28, 1864–Jan. 1, 1865.

Middleton, Emerson E. Co. C, Twelfth NJ Vols. April 1863–May 13, 1863.Trans. to Bat. A.

Miller, Charles. Co. F, Ninth NY Heavy Art. Oct. 28, 1864–Jan. 1, 1865.

Molloy, M. Tenth NY Bat. May 13, 1863–Sept. 7, 1864.

Morse, Nelson. Co. F, Fourth NY Heavy Arty. April 27, 1864–June 12, 1864.

Morris, Thomas. Co. F, One Hundred and Eleventh NY Vols. April 1863–May 13, 1863. Trans. to Bat. A.

Mulligan, William F. Co. F, Twelfth NJ Vols. Mar. 16, 1863. KIA May 3, 1863 at Marye's Heights.

Murnin, Dennis. Tenth NY Bat. May 13, 1863–Sept. 7, 1864.

Murphy, James. Co. F, Ninth NY Heavy Art. Oct. 28, 1864–Jan. 1, 1865.

Nicodemus, Andrew. Co. F, Ninth NY Heavy Art. Oct. 28, 1864–Jan. 1, 1865.

Osborne, Horace O. Co. F, Ninth NY Heavy Art. Oct. 28, 1864–Jan. 1, 1865.

Patterson, Duncan. Tenth NY Bat. May 13, 1863–Sept. 7, 1864. Captured July 24, 1863, by Mosby's Rangers. Wd. May 12, 1864, at Spotsylvania.

Phillips, Abner S. Trans. to Bat. E Mar. 23, 1865

Powers, Howard. Fourth ME Bat. Mar. 18, 1865–June 24, 1865.

Ragin, M. Tenth NY Bat. May 13, 1863–Sept. 7, 1864.

Riley, Charles. Co. F, Ninth NY Heavy Art. Oct. 28, 1864–Jan. 1, 1865.

Rodgers, M.A. Tenth NY Bat. May 13, 1863–Sept. 7, 1864.

Rogan, Michael J. Co. C, Fourth NY Heavy Art. April 27, 1864–June 12, 1864.

Rogers, Augustus. Co. K, Sixty-Second NY Vols. Wd. Oct. 19, 1864, at Cedar Creek. Sent to hospital where deserted in Dec. 1864.

Sexton, John. Tenth NY Bat. May 13, 1863–Sept. 7, 1864.

Shields, William. Tenth NY Bat. May 13, 1863–Sept. 7, 1864.

Shoemaker, Isaac. Co. F, Ninth NY Heavy Art. Oct. 28, 1864–Jan. 1, 1865.

Small, Newcome E. Fourth ME Bat. Mar. 18, 1865–June 24, 1865.

Smith, Randall A. Co. F, Ninth NY Heavy Art. Oct. 28, 1864–Jan. 1, 1865.

Sneidiker, John. Co. K Twelfth NJ Vols. Mar. 16, 1863–May 13, 1863. Trans. to Bat. A.

Starkey, Lewis W. Co. F, Ninth NY Heavy Art. Oct. 28, 1864–Jan. 1, 1865.

Stewart, Richard. Tenth NY Bat. May 13, 1863–
Sept. 7, 1864.

Sullivan, Patrick. Tenth NY Bat. May 13, 1863–
Sept. 7, 1864.

Tandorf, Morris. Co. G, Twelfth NJ Vols. Mar.
16, 1863–May 13. 1863. Trans. to Bat. A.

Tearnan, Charles.

Teeter, Lawrence. Ninth NY Heavy Art. Oct. 28,
1864–Jan. 1, 1865.

Toye, Alfred. Tenth NY Bat. May 13, 1863–Sept.
7, 1864.

VanLour, Henry.

Van Zandt, Nicholas. Co. G, Twelfth NJ Vols.
April 4, 1863–June 13, 1864. Wd. May 3, 1863,
at Marye's Heights. Trans. to Bat. A.

Vestburg, Ira. Co. C, Fourth NY Heavy Art. April
27, 1864–June 12, 1864.

Vogel, Henry. Co. F, Twenty-Fourth NJ Vols.
April 1863–May 13, 1863. Trans. to Bat. A.

Walcott, George W. Ninth NY Heavy Art. Oct.
28, 1864–Jan. 1, 1865.

Wheeler, Daniel A. Tenth NY Bat. May 13, 1863–
Sept. 7, 1864.

White, Thomas. Tenth NY Bat. May 13, 1863–
June 1864.

Willis, James. Co. F, Ninth NY Heavy Art. Oct.
28, 1864–Jan. 1, 1865.

Woolston, Levi. Co. B, Twenty-Fourth NJ Vols.
April 1863–May 13, 1863. Trans. to Bat. A.

Wyman, Davis. Fourth ME Bat. Mar. 18, 1865–
June 24, 1865.

Young, Charles. Tenth NY Bat. May 13, 1863–
Sept. 7, 1864.

III: *Casualties of Battery G,*
First Rhode Island Light Artillery

Battle	Killed/Mortally Wounded	Wounded	Missing or Captured	Total
Yorktown, April 1862	0	0	0	0
Fair Oaks, June 1, 1862	0	0	2	2
Malvern Hill, July 1, 1862	0	1	0	1
Antietam, Sept. 17, 1862	0	5	0	5
First Fredericksburg, Dec. 11–15, 1862	0	1	0	1
Marye's Heights, May 3, 1863	7	20	0	27
Gettysburg Campaign, June-July, 1863	0	0	4	4
Mine Run, Nov. 30, 1863	0	1	0	1
Wilderness, May 4–8, 1864	0	0	0	0
Spotsylvania, May 9–21, 1864	1	1	1	3
Cold Harbor, June 1–7, 1864	0	3	0	3
Petersburg, June 16-July 9, 1864	0	0	0	0
Cool Spring, July 18, 1864	0	0	0	0
Opequon, Sept. 19, 1864	0	0	0	0
Fisher's Hill, Sept. 22, 1864	0	0	0	0
Cedar Creek, Oct. 19, 1864	9	20	3	32
Storming of Petersburg, April 2, 1865	0	3	0	3
Total	17	55	10	82

Died of Other Causes	26
Resigned Commission	4
Veterans Reserve Corps	7
Deserted	23
Discharged for Disability	44
Total Loss	186
Horses killed in action	80
Rhode Islanders in Battery G	273
Attached Men	94
Total Enrollment	367
Percent Casualties	51%

IV: Enlistments by Town

The following is a listing of the communities that the men in Battery G enlisted from. The numbers are garnered from the muster rolls and bounty receipts housed at the Rhode Island State Archives. Only those towns which contributed men to Battery G are included; Rhode Island had thirty-five towns in 1861. The residence is given according to that in the descriptive book, town records, or Ken Carlson's "Men of Rhode Island to Arms!"

Town	Number	Town	Number	Town	Number
Barrington	1	Glocester	3	Warren	3
Bristol	1	Hopkinton	4	Warwick	14
Burrillville	2	Johnston	2	West Greenwich	4
Charlestown	9	Newport	1	Westerly	29
Coventry	15	North Kingstown	2	Woonsocket	1
Cranston	3	North Providence	5	Maine	1
Cumberland	6	Providence	113	Massachusetts	5
East Greenwich	1	Richmond	6	New Hampshire	1
East Providence	10	Scituate	6	New Jersey	2
Exeter	2	Smithfield	4	New York	5
Foster	3	South Kingstown	9		

V: Occupations of Battery G Soldiers

The soldiers in Battery G represented a crossroads in mid–nineteenth century America, as the country moved from an agricultural to a manufacturing based economy. These artillerists came from all walks of life and the skills that they had as civilians carried over into their army positions, tailoring uniforms for a perfect fit, completing paperwork, blacksmithing, and using mathematics to calculate ranges were all skills utilized daily in the battery. This list is taken from the Battery G Descriptive Book at the Rhode Island State Archives.

Trade	Number of Soldiers Represented	Trade	Number of Soldiers Represented
Baker	1	Mason	2
Blacksmith	5	Mechanic	1
Boilermaker	1	Merchant	3
Bookkeeper	2	Miller	2
Boot/Shoemaker	9	Molder	1
Box Maker	1	Musician	2
Butcher	1	Painter	4
Cabinetmaker	2	Operative	23
Carder	1	Sea Trades	13
Carpenter	1	Soldier	1
Carriage Maker	4	Spinner	6
Cigar Maker	2	Stonecutter	8
Clerk	15	Student	11
Engineer	2	Tailor	2
Farmer	56	Teacher	4
Grocer	1	Teamster	13
Harness Maker	2	Tinsmith	1
Jeweler	2	Wagoner	1
Joiner	1	Weaver	8
Laborer	32	Wheelwright	3
Machinist	21	Not Stated	2

Chapter Notes

Note: The following abbreviations are used throughout the notes.

ANB	Antietam National Battlefield
CCB	Cedar Creek Battlefield
CL	Clark Library
CSL	Connecticut State Library
EPH	East Providence Historical Society
FRSP	Fredericksburg-Spotsylvania National Military Park
GNMP	Gettysburg National Military Park
HAFE	Harpers Ferry National Historic Park
HL	Hay Library, Brown University
LOC	Library of Congress
LPL	Langworthy Public Library
MNB	Manassas National Battlefield
NA	National Archives
PHS	Pettaquamscutt Historical Society
PPL	Providence Public Library
RG	Robert Grandchamp collection
RIHS	Rhode Island Historical Society
RISA	Rhode Island State Archives
RNB	Richmond National Battlefield
STH	Sterling, Connecticut, Town Hall
USAMHI	United States Army Military History Institute
WML	Westerly Memorial Library

Introduction

1. Mathias P. Harpin, *The High Road to Zion* (Pascoag: Corey's Comp Shop, 1976), 146; Walter F. Beyer and Oscar F. Keydel, eds. *Deeds of Valor: How America's Heroes won the Medal of Honor* (Detroit: Perrien-Keydel, 1901), 515–516. Sixteen Rhode Islanders were awarded the Medal of Honor during the war; nine of them were awarded for heroism on April 2, 1865. Seven went to Battery G and two to the color sergeants of the Second Rhode Island Infantry for their actions carrying the flags that day.

2. *Wood River Advertiser,* April 16, 1907.

3. *Providence Journal,* May 26, 1862; Edward P. Adams, "Battery G, First Rhode Island Light Artillery," *Revised Register of Rhode Island Volunteers* (Providence: E.L. Freeman, 1895), 900–906.

4. Harold R. Barker, *History of Rhode Island Combat Units in the Civil War* (Providence: NP, 1964), 112–113; *In Memoriam: George William Adams* (Providence: NP, 1883), 10–11. Captain Adams was the first to attempt to write a history of Battery G, but his personal papers and rough draft were destroyed after his death in 1883. General Barker was the next to attempt it, but he died before he could delve seriously into the project.

5. Philip Van Doren Stern, *An End to Valor: The Last Days of the Civil War* (Boston: Houghton Mifflin, 1958), 153–155.

6. Frederick H. Dyer, *A Compendium of the War of the Rebellion,* vol. 3 (New York: Thomas Yoseloff, 1959), 1633.

7. L. VanLoan Naisawald, *Grape & Canister: The Story of the Field Artillery of the Army of the Potomac, 1861–1865* (Mechanicsburg, PA: Stackpole Books, 1999).

8. Naisawald, *Grape and Canister,* xvi-xvii; Joseph T. Glatthaar, "Battlefield Tactics," in *Writing the Civil War: The Quest to Understand,* ed. James M. McPherson and William J. Cooper, Jr. (Columbia: University of South Carolina Press, 1998), 65–67; Paddy Griffith, *Battle Tactics of the Civil War* (New Haven: Yale University Press, 1989), 170–172; *Martinsburg Journal,* June 22, 2007.

9. Griffith, *Battle Tactics,* 171. While this author agrees much with Griffith's thesis, he still follows the old theory that it was the smoothbore, not the rifle, that held the main advantage on the battlefield. This author maintains it was the new rifled cannon, not the old smoothbore pieces, that proved to be of so much use. Griffith wrote, "Direct fire at extreme long range was too lightweight, and indirect fire too inaccurate to have an effect." While commanders often shelled a line blindly with little effect, a few well-placed shots from a rifled cannon, as will be seen in this study, often was the decisive factor on the battlefield Griffith (*Battle Tactics,* 177).

10. James N. Arnold, "The Importance of Local History," *Narragansett Historical Register* 1 (1882), 81.

Chapter 1

1. John J. Richards, *Rhode Island's Early Defenders and Their Successors* (East Greenwich: Rhode Island Pendulum, 1937), 14–15; Anthony Walker, *So Few the Brave* (Newport: Seafield Press, 1981), 109–110; Thomas J. Abernethy, "Crane's Rhode Island Company of Artillery," *Rhode Island History* (Winter 1970), 46–51. One of the distinct helmets is now housed at the Varnum Museum in East Greenwich. The Artillery Company of Newport served in the Civil War as an infantry company.

2. Providence Marine Corps of Artillery, Records, RIHS; Barker, *Rhode Island Combat Units,* 3–5. Arthur M. Mowry, *The Dorr War, or the Constitutional Struggle in Rhode Island* (Providence: Preston & Rounds, 1901), 1–222.

3. Robert Anderson, *An Artillery Officer in the Mexican War, 1846–7,* ed. Eba Anderson Lawton (New York: Knickerbocker Press, 1911), 309–317; Barker, *Rhode Island Combat Units,* 3–5; George B. Peck, *Historical Address: Rhode Island Light Artillery in the Civil and Spanish Wars* (Providence: Rhode Island Printing Company, 1917), 4–7. In the Mexican War, artillery heroes were popular in American culture. Captain Duncan Ringgold, who pioneered the use of flying artillery, was killed at Palo Alto and Major John Rovers Vinton of Providence, who served in the Third United States Artillery, fell at Vera Cruz. Vinton was buried under an elaborate monument in Swan Point Cemetery, the grave being surmounted by the cannonball that killed him. The Providence Marine Corps of Artillery was present at the funeral and prior to the Civil War wore a uniform stylized after that adopted by Ringgold for the Regulars.

4. Entry for February 22, 1861, Providence Marine Corps of Artillery, Records Book 1861–1868, RIHS; *Memoirs of Rhode Island Officers Who Were Engaged in the Service of Their Country during the Great Rebellion with the South*, ed. John R. Bartlett (Providence: Sydney S. Rider & Brothers Press, 1867), 108–110, 372–373. Bartlett's book is one of the finest postwar accounts written by a Rhode Islander. Although not a participant in the conflict, Bartlett and a team of associates interviewed the surviving officers of the Rhode Island Regiments, or the families of the deceased to produce the handsomely illustrated tome. See *Autobiography of John Russell Bartlett* (Providence: Brown University, 2006), 59.

5. Edwin W. Stone, *Rhode Island in the Rebellion* (Providence: Knowles, Anthony, 1864), xvi–xix; William Sprague to Abraham Lincoln, April 11, 1861, Abraham Lincoln Papers, LOC.

6. *Providence Journal*, April 19, 1861, and July 12, 1861; *Revised Register of Rhode Island Volunteers*, vol. 2 (Providence: E.L. Freeman, 1895), 707–710. The *Revised Register* is composed of two volumes. The first consists of men who served in Rhode Island infantry units, while the second lists those who fought in the artillery and cavalry. All references to the *Revised Register* are taken from volume two unless otherwise noted.

7. James C. Hazlett, Edwin Olmstead, and M. Hume Parks, *Field Artillery Weapons of the Civil War* (Chicago: University of Illinois Press, 2004), 147–157; Stone, *Rebellion*, xx; Roy P. Bastler, ed. *The Collected Works of Abraham Lincoln*, vol. 4 (New Brunswick: Rutgers University Press, 1953), 352–353. Ever since Tompkins' Battery left on April 18, 1861, there has been a continued, heated debate as to whether they were truly the first group of Federal militia to leave in response to the call. The unit most historians cite is the Sixth Massachusetts. After the war, the veterans of the two groups decided to call a truce. The Rhode Islanders had been the first to answer the call, leaving on the morning of April 18, while the Bay Staters left that afternoon. However Tompkins remained at Easton for a week, allowing the Sixth Massachusetts to be the first group of Northern troops to enter Washington. Thus the honor of being first goes to the First Rhode Island Battery. See *Providence Journal*, December 15, 1889.

8. Theodore Reichardt, *Diary of Battery A* (Providence: N. Bang Williams, 1865), June 19, 1861. Reinchardt's narrative is the diary he kept in the field, afterwards cited as Reichardt, Diary, date of entry; Augustus Woodbury, *A Narrative of the Campaign of the First Rhode Island Regiment in the Spring and Summer of 1861* (Providence: Sydney S. Rider, 1862), 1–7, 56–68, 232–233; *Memoirs of RI*, 373.

9. *Memorial of Colonel John S Slocum* (Providence: R.A. and J.A. Reid, 1886), 61–68; George W. Field to Father, July 25, 1861, RG; Reichardt, Diary, July 21, 1861. The Bull Run Gun is now displayed at the Rhode Island State House; the motto is inscribed on the barrel.

10. Barker, *Rhode Island Combat Units*, 4–5; John H. Rhodes, *History of Battery B, First Rhode Island Light Artillery* (Providence: Snow and Farnum, 1894), 1–13; Peck, *Historical Address*, 6–15; Special Orders Number 75, Adjutant General's Papers, RISA.

11. J. Rhodes, *Battery B*, 11–13; Margaret Gardner, "Sketch of Alfred G. Gardner," Alfred G. Gardner Letters, HL.

Chapter 2

1. J. Albert Monroe, *Battery D, First Rhode Island Light Artillery at the Second Battle of Bull Run* (Providence: Providence Press, 1886), 6–7.

2. Battery G, First Rhode Island Light Artillery, Monthly Returns, May-August 1863, Rhode Island State Archives.

3. William F. Barry, William H. French, and Henry J. Hunt, *Instructions for Field Artillery* (New York: NP, 1860), 46–47.

4. Monroe, *Second Bull Run*, 6–7; Augustus V. Kautz, *The 1865 Customs of Service for Officers of the Army* (Philadelphia: J.B. Lippincott, 1865), 223–260.

5. Kautz, *Customs of Officers*, 17–195; Monroe, *Second Bull Run*, 8.

6. John D. Billings, *Hardtack and Coffee: The Unwritten Story of Army Life* (Lincoln: Nebraska University Press, 1993), 169; August V. Kautz, *The 1865 Customs of Service for Enlisted Men of the Army* (Philadelphia: J.B. Lippincott, 1865), 131–149.

7. Kautz, *Customs of Enlisted Men*, 165–171.

8. Monroe, *Second Bull Run*, 8–9; Kautz, *Customs of Enlisted Men*, 116–131.

9. Kautz, *Customs of Enlisted Men*, 103–115; William Marvel, *The First New Hampshire Battery: 1861–1865* (South Conway, NH: Lost Cemetery Press, 1985), 11–12.

10. *Providence Journal*, August 10, 1861; Barry et al., *Field Artillery*, 363–371.

11. Kautz, *Customs of Enlisted Men*, 68–91.

12. Billings, *Hardtack and Coffee*, 171; Monroe, *Second Bull Run*, 7–8; John H. Rhodes, *History of Battery B, First Rhode Island Light Artillery* (Providence: Snow and Farnum, 1894), 2–3.

13. J. Rhodes, *Battery B*, 180–181; Billings, *Hardtack and Coffee*, 182–183.

14. Barry et al., *Field Artillery*, 74–78.

15. Barry et al., *Field Artillery*, 74–78; Augustus Buell, *The Cannoneer: Recollections of Service in the Army of the Potomac* (Washington: National Tribune, 1897), 215–216.

16. J. Rhodes, *Battery B*, 3; Barry et al., *Field Artillery*, 127–135: 294–295.

17. Barry et al., *Field Artillery*, 74–78.

18. Ibid., 273–279.

19. J. Albert Monroe, *Battery D, First Rhode Island Light Artillery at the Battle of Antietam* (Providence: Providence Press, 1886), 17–21; Kautz, *Customs of Officers*, 343; J. Howard Wert, "Brown's Battery B," RG. This poem tells of a Rhode Island Battery in action at Gettysburg and fully captures the essence of the artillery in combat.

20. Barry et al., *Field Artillery Providence Journal*, November 9, 1861.

21. J. Rhodes, *Battery B*, 171.

22. Barry et al., *Field Artillery*, 6–14; Hazlett, Olmstead, and Parks, *Field Artillery Weapons*, 23–24; Buell, *The Cannoneer*, 20–22: 57–58.

23. Barry et al., *Field Artillery*, 6–14; Hazlett, Olmstead, and Parks, *Field Artillery Weapons*, 109–125; Buell, *The Cannoneer*, 20–22: 146–147.

24. George W. Field to Father, July 25, 1861, RG; John D. Imboden, "Incidents of the First Bull Run," in *Battles & Leaders [B&L]*, vol. 1, 229–239; William Reynolds to William F. Barry, November 7, 1861, Rhode Island State Archives. In 1984 during an archaeological dig in Manassas, Virginia, James projectiles were found three miles from where the Rhode Islanders had fired the guns. They came from only one source: Battery A, First Rhode Island Light Artillery.

25. Barry et al., *Field Artillery*, 6–14; Hazlett, Olmstead, and Parks, *Field Artillery Weapons*, 88–93; Buell, *The Cannoneer*, 20–22.

26. Jack W. Melton and Lawrence E. Pawl, *Guide to Civil War Artillery Projectiles* (Gettysburg: Thomas Publications, 1996), 53–60; Field to Father, July 25, 1861, RG.

27. Melton and Pawl, *Artillery Projectiles*, 29–35.

28. Ibid., 20–40.

29. Monroe, *Second Bull Run*, 8–9; Kautz, *Customs of Enlisted Men*, 116–131.

30. Kautz, *Customs of Enlisted Men,* 103–115; William Marvel, *The First New Hampshire Battery: 1861–1865.* (South Conway, NH: Lost Cemetery Press, 1985), 11–12.

31. *Providence Journal,* August 10, 1861; Barry, Hunt, French, *Field Artillery,* 363–371.

Chapter 3

1. *Supplement to the Official Records of the Union and Confederate Armies* 63: 654, ed. Janet B. Hewett, Jocelyn Pinson, Julia H. Nichols et al. (Wilmington, NC: Broadfoot Publishing, 1998). Captain Cutts was a native Rhode Islander who fought at Bull Run with the First Rhode Island. A Brown graduate, he used his political connections to jump in rank from private to captain in the Eleventh United States. Initially assigned as the mustering officer in Rhode Island, he later joined Ambrose Burnside's staff and later took the field with his regiment. He was awarded the Medal of Honor for gallantry at the Wilderness and retired from the army as a lieutenant colonel.

2. Adams, "Battery G," 900.

3. First Rhode Island Light Artillery, Muster in Book for Batteries, Benefit Street Arsenal.

4. Edward C. Mauran, *Disbursements of the Adjutant General* (Providence: NP, 1863), 9; Monroe, *Antietam,* 2–3; Phillip S. Chase, *Battery F, First Rhode Island Light Artillery, in the Civil War* (Providence: Snow and Farnum, 1892), 2–6.

5. P. Chase, *Battery F,* 2–6; Adams, "Battery G," 900; Cyrus Walker, "History of Scituate, RI," RG.

6. Charles S. Nichols, "Memoirs," LPL; Robert F. Shea, "Aspects of the History of Westerly During the Civil War" (Master's thesis, University of Rhode Island, 1957), 19–24.

7. *Driftways into the Past: Local History of Richmond, Rhode Island* (Westerly, RI: Utter, 1977), 5: 15: 269–271.

8. Frederic Denison, *Westerly and Its Witness* (Westerly: Utter, 1878), 201–212, 269; George R. Dowding, *Military History of Westerly, 1710–1932* (Westerly: Blackburn & Benson, 1932). Frederic Denison would go to war as the chaplain of the First Rhode Island Cavalry and the Third Rhode Island Heavy Artillery. He would be known as the "Fighting Chaplain," and after the war would write many important papers on the role of Rhode Island in the Civil War.

9. "Muster Roll of Captain Henry Card's Company I," Westerly Rifles Records, WML; *Narragansett Weekly,* November 14, 1861, and May 10, 1863; First Rhode Island Light Artillery, Muster Rolls, RISA. While twenty-one Westerly men would join during the initial recruiting drive, and eventually seven more would enlist, it is evident from the muster rolls that Westerly would serve a far more important role as the recruiting center of southern Rhode Island for the regiment. With its easy railroad connections to Providence, and a bustling commercial district, it would have represented an easy locale for recruits to enlist from. This is evidenced by the number of men who claimed residence in another town but enlisted in Westerly, as was the case of Battery G's Private George W. Potter. A resident of Coventry, he enlisted at Westerly.

10. Mauran, *Disbursements,* 16.

11. Adams, "Battery G," 900; Battery F, First Rhode Island Light Artillery, Recruiting Poster, RG; *Providence Press,* November 18, 1861; Kautz, *Customs of Officers,* 342.

12. Battery F, Recruiting Poster, RG; Rhode Island Paymaster General, Receipts, 1861–1865, RISA; *Narragansett Weekly,* December 19, 1861. Battery G was quite the cosmopolitan organization. It had members from Canada, England, Germany, Ireland, Italy, Scotland, Switzerland, and Wales. The majority of these men were quite literally right off the boat and found their way to Providence, where they enlisted and are credited from by this author. Other immigrants from New York, Boston, and other metropolitan areas had settled in their areas and were residents, but not U.S. citizens yet. They are credited to where they gave their place of residence.

13. Rhode Island Volunteers, Muster Rolls, RISA.

14. George R. Norton, Memorial Marker, North Burial Ground, Providence, RI; Henry Seamans to Mrs. Lewis, November 30, 1864, CSL.

15. Battery G, First Rhode Island Light Artillery, Descriptive Book, RISA; Henry Barney, *A Country Boy's First Three Months in the Army* (Providence: N. Bang Williams, 1880), 6–12.

16. Henry S. Burrage, *Brown University in the Civil War: A Memorial* (Providence: Providence Press, 1868), 355; Charles D. Owen, Service File, NA; *Providence Press* December 2, 1861; J. Albert Monroe, *The Rhode Island Artillery at the First Battle of Bull Run* (Providence: Sydney S. Rider, 1878), 15–30; William Ames, "Civil War Letters," ed. William Greene Roelker; *Rhode Island History* (January 1941): 20–22.

17. George Lewis, *History of Battery E, First Rhode Island Light Artillery* (Providence: Snow and Farnum, 1892), 405–406; *Memoirs of RI,* 421–23; Earl J. Fenner, *The History of Battery H, First Rhode Island Light Artillery* (Providence: Snow and Farnum, 1894), 101–104; Burrage, *Brown University,* 345; John A. Tompkins to Henry Hunt, October 1, 1864, Hunt Papers, LOC.

18. Otto L. Torslow, Service File, NA; *Memoirs of RI,* 439–440.

19. *Westerly Sun,* June 26, 1925; Battery G, Descriptive Book, RISA; George W. Field to Father, November 7, 1861, RG.

20. Battery G, Descriptive Book, RISA.

21. *Providence Press,* December 9, 1861; Woodbury, *First Rhode Island,* 171.

22. Entry for November 25, 1861, Providence Marine Corps of Artillery Records, Records Book 1861–1868, RIHS.

23. Entry for February 22 and November 30, 1861, Providence Marine Corps of Artillery, Records Book 1861–1868, RIHS.

24. Battery G, First Rhode Island Light Artillery, Clothing Book, RIHS; *Providence Press,* December 2, 1861.

25. *Providence Journal,* November 27, 1861, and December 2, 1861.

26. Special Orders 136, November 30, 1861, RISA; Adams, "Battery G," 900; Frederic Denison, *Sabres and Spurs: The First Rhode Island Cavalry in the Civil War* (Central Falls, RI: First Rhode Island Cavalry Veterans Association, 1876), 31; *Providence Journal,* December 9, 1861, and January 30, 1862; J. Rhodes, *Battery B,* 3–5.

27. Charles D. Owen, Muster Roll of 1st Detachment, Battery G, 1st RILA, December 2, 1861, RISA; Entry for December 3, 1861 in Providence Marine Corps of Artillery, Records Book 1860–1868, RIHS; *Narragansett Weekly,* December 5, 1861. Battery G is sometimes referred to as the Eighth Rhode Island Battery, as it was the eighth battery recruited in the state, but the seventh in the regimental line.

Chapter 4

1. Battery G, First Rhode Island Light Artillery, Morning Reports, December 8 and 9, 1861, NA; Battery G, Descriptive Book, RISA. Webb would serve as a staff officer in the First Rhode Island Light Artillery for a year before becoming a brigadier general of volunteers. He would be best remembered for commanding the Philadelphia

Brigade as they held the Angle during Pickett's Charge at Gettysburg, where he was wounded and awarded the Medal of Honor.

2. George L. Gaskell to Mary Call, December 27, 1861, USAMHI *Revised Regulations,* 159–403; Battery G, Clothing Book, RIHS.

3. Adams, "Battery G," 900; Hazlett, Olmstead, and Parks, *Field Artillery Weapons,* 116–117.

4. Kris VanDenBossche, ed., *Pleas Excuse all bad writing: A Documentary History of Rhode Island during the Civil War Era, 1861–1865* (Peace Dale, RI: Rhode Island Historical Document Transcription Project, 1993), 31–32; Elisha Hunt Rhodes, *All for the Union: The Civil War Diary and Letters of Elisha Hunt Rhodes,* ed. Robert Hunt Rhodes (Woonsocket: Andrew Mobray, 1985), 41; *Providence Press,* December 18, 1861. Clearly the author of the letter had yet to realize that Owen was to be the captain of Battery G. Once all of the battery was mustered into the service, Owen was formally commissioned on December 21, 1861, but had been acting with the rank of captain since the battery was recruited.

5. Denison, *First Cavalry,* 31; James Cutts and William B. Rhodes, Muster Roll of Lt. William B. Rhodes' Detachment, December 18, 1861, RISA.

6. Introduction to George L. Gaskell Letters, USAMHI; William Chenery, *The Fourteenth Regiment Rhode Island Heavy Artillery in the War to Preserve the Union* (New York: Negro University Press, 1960), 291–292, 327.

7. Cutts and Rhodes, Muster Roll of Lt. William B. Rhodes' Detachment; George L. Gaskell to Mary Call, December 16, 1861, USAMHI. An ambulance was a light duty wagon used to carry quartermaster stores; one was usually always allocated specifically to carry officers' equipment.

8. Gaskell to Call, December 27, 1861.

9. James A. Barber, Diary, January 1–5, 1862, PPL. This is only one copy of the Barber Diary, covering 1862, which survives at the Providence Public Library. The other two, covering 1863 and 1864, are at the Hay Library. Upon his retirement from Brown University, Dr. Robert H. George began to collect letters and diaries of Rhode Island Civil War soldiers in preparation for a book relating to the conflict. He traveled to Westerly, interviewed two granddaughters of James Barber, and was granted permission to borrow the 1862, 1863, and 1864 diaries for his project. Dr. George completed a rough draft of his manuscript, but General Harold Barker beat him in publishing his *History of Rhode Island Combat Units in the Civil War* in 1964. After this, Dr. George lost interest in the Civil War project. During his research process he had taken copious notes on 3x5 index cards, mostly relating to Brown students who served in the Civil War. George took a special note of the Medal of Honor recipients from Rhode Island and collected information on their deeds. Upon his death in 1979, Dr. George's family donated all of his research material to Brown University. Today it resides at the University Archives, Hay Library, Brown University. Apparently the library did not notice that George had borrowed them from the Barber family and retains them in their possession to this day, where they can be viewed by researchers. It remains a mystery how the 1862 diary became separated and ended up in the Special Collections of the Providence Public Library. It is clear that this small, leather-bound, battered book is the one Barber wrote in during the war. The 1863 and 1864 volumes are fair copies, transcribed from his field notes. Unlike many postwar writings, however, Barber simply rewrote for his children what had occurred in the war as he had seen it in the war years; he never changed any of it to fight a postwar battle against his enemies—he had none. This makes it one of the best accountings of the war this author has ever seen and was the key source for this project (Albert Straight to Pardon Tillinghast, January 4, 1862; R.G. Billings, *Hard-tack and Coffee,* 108–142; Gaskell to Call, December 27, 1861).

10. Reichardt, Diary, January 5, 1862; Albert Straight to Father, January 20, 1862, RG; *Providence Journal,* January 15 and January 23, 1862.

11. Billings, *Hardtack and Coffee,* 61–63; George L. Gaskell to Mary Call, January 14, 1862, USAMHI; Barber, Diary January 14–17, 1862.

12. General Orders Number 2, 3, and 4, Battery G, First Rhode Island Light Artillery, Orders Book, NA; Reichardt, Diary, July 9, 1861.

13. Billings, *Hardtack and Coffee,* 164–197; Field to Father, October 21, 1861, RG; John E. Tobey, "Day Planner, Army of the Potomac Style" *CRRC,* 251–254.

14. Gaskell to Call, January 14, 1862.

15. Henry Farnsworth, Battery G Clothing Book, RIHS; Battery G, Morning Report, January 17, 1862, NA.

16. Barber, Diary, January 21–24, 1862; *OR, Series III, I,* 253; *Revised Regulations,* 544–46; George W. Field to Father, October 21, 1861, RG.

17. General Orders, Number 5, Battery G, NA; Barber, Diary, February 1, 1862.

18. Adams, "Battery G," 900; Barber, Diary, February 7–18, 1862; Battery G, Morning Report, March 1, 1862, NA; *Narragansett Weekly,* March 6, 1862; Straight, Diary, gun ranges.

19. Charles H. Webb, Discharge Papers, GNMP; Battery G, Monthly Return, February 1862, RISA.

20. Barber, Diary, March 7–9, 1862; George L. Gaskell to Mary Call, March 10, 1862, USAMHI.

21. Barber, Diary, May 11–15, 1862; George L. Gaskell to Mary Call, March 21, 1862, USAMHI.

22. Battery G, Descriptive Book, RISA; Constance Cordner Anderson to Author, September 9, 2007.

23. Barber, Diary, March 16–21, 1862.

24. George B. McClellan, "The Peninsular Campaign," in *B&L,* vol. 2, 160–70; Francis A. Walker, *History of the Second Army Corps in the Army of the Potomac* (New York: Charles Scribner's Sons, 1887), 3–11; George B. McClellan, *Report on the Organization and Campaigns of the Army of the Potomac* (New York: Sheldon & Company, 1864), 55–57. A three-inch ordnance rifle and ten-pounder Parrott each had fifty rounds contained in the limber chest. A Napoleon had thirty-two, while a twenty-pounder Parrott had only twenty-four rounds.

25. Walker, *Second Corps,* 3–11; Albert Straight to Father, March 20, 1862, RG.

26. Gaskell to Call, March 21, 1862; Barber, Diary, March 23–25, 1862; Reichardt, Diary, March 25, 1862; Sixth Corps Artillery Brigade Ordnance Returns, June–July 1863, Hunt Papers, LOC. There is some contention as to what type of cannon Battery G used after the twenty-pounders were turned in. A plaque at Gettysburg gives it as being ten-pounder Parrotts. This is wrong, as this is the armament of Battery C, First Rhode Island Light Artillery. All of the sources are unanimous that Battery G used ordnance rifles throughout its service.

27. Barry et al., *Field Artillery,* 42–45; Barber, Diary, March 28, 1862; Battery G, Clothing Book entries for March 29, 1862, RIHS; Billings, *Hardtack and Coffee,* 51–54.

28. Gaskell to Call, March 21, 1862; Barber, Diary, March 29–31, 1862; Adams, "Battery G," 900; Albert D. Cordner, Diary, March 30-April 2, 1862, FRSP.

29. Battery G, Morning Report, April 2, 1862, NA; Cordner, Diary, April 2, 1862; Barber, Diary, April 2, 1862.

Chapter 5

1. McClellan, "The Peninsular Campaign," 168–174.

2. Warren L. Goss, "Yorktown and Williamsburg," in

B&L,vol. 2, 189–195; Cordner, Diary, April 4, 1862; Barber, Diary, April 5–8, 1862; Albert Straight to Pardon Straight, April 12 and 28, 1862, RG.

3. Walker, *Second Corps,* 13–16; Barber, Diary, April 16, 1862.

4. J. Rhodes, *Battery B,* 78–79.

5. Silas W. Wood to Benjamin Pendleton, April 29, 1862, RIHS; Cordner, Diary, April 5–16, 1862.

6. Barber, Diary, April 17, 1862; Cordner, Diary, April 17, 1862; Stone, *Rebellion,* 55–63.

7. Adams, "Battery G," 900; George L. Gaskell to Mary Call, April 23, 1862, USAMHI; Cordner, Diary, April 16-May 5, 1862.

8. Barber, Diary, April 25–30, 1862; Thomas Aldrich, *The History of Battery A, First Rhode Island Light Artillery, in the War to Preserve the Union, 1861–1865* (Providence: Snow and Farnum, 1904), 74–75.

9. Barber, Diary, April 25–30, 1862; Albert Straight to Parents, April 28, 1862, RG.

10. Goss, "Yorktown and Williamsburg," 189–195.

11. James A. Barber, Diary, January 27, 1863, HL; George L. Gaskell to Mary Call, May 11, 1862, USAMHI.

12. Barber, May 13–21, 1862; *Narragansett Weekly,* May 5, 1862.

13. Gaskell to Call, May 11, 1862.

14. Cordner, Diary, May 9–12: 22, 1862.

15. David B. Patterson to Mother, May 29, 1862, RNB; Barber, Diary, May 31, 1862; Cordner, Diary, May 31–June 1, 1862; Jesse Young, Court-Martial Record, NA. The comment about Torslow wanting to fight in a battle is taken from testimony he gave at Jesse Young's court-martial.

16. Cordner, Diary, May 31-June 1, 1862; Edward E. Cross, *Stand Firm and Fire Low: The Civil War Writings of Colonel Edward E. Cross,* ed. Walter Holden, William E. Ross, and Elizabeth Slomba (Hanover, NH: University Press of New England, 2003), 24–25.

17. Walker, *Second Corps,* 19–40; Joseph E. Johnston, "Manassas to Seven Pines," in *B&L,* vol. 2, 213–217.

18. Walker, *Second Corps,* 19–40; Cross, *Stand Firm,* 24–26.

19. Cordner, Diary, May 31-June 1, 1862; Aldrich, *Battery A,* 81–83; Nelson Ames, *History of Battery G, First Regiment New York Light Artillery* (Marshalltown, IA: Marshall, 1900), 30–33. Apparently the situation to cross the river got worse as each unit went over. According to William C. Barker of Battery A, the mud was "about two feet deep." It took Battery A only four hours to go through. As each unit passed, however, the road became more problematic, with the worst situation being for Battery G (William C. Barker to Annie Barker, June 9, 1862, RIHS).

20. *OR, 11,* 791–798; Cordner, Diary, May 31-June 1, 1862; *Providence Journal,* 1862.

21. *OR, 11,* 791–798; J. Rhodes, *Battery B* 88–89; John Sedgwick, *Correspondence of John Sedgwick,* vol. 2, ed. William D. Sedgwick (Baltimore: Butternut and Blue, 1999), 51–57. There is some contention as to what time Battery G arrived on the field. According to Private Chester F. Hunt of Battery B, Owen's men were on the field between nightfall and early morning. He wrote, "The 2nd and 8th RI Battery together with Sedgwicks Division got up on Saturday night we got ours section up soon after dark but most of them was stuck in the mud so a whole regiment was detailed to go back and most of them help out but they were all up before morning" (Chester F. Hunt to Mother, June 9, 1862, Navarro College Collections). Battery A and Battery G, First New York, were on the field by nightfall; but as Battery G was the last unit in line, it took them all night to make the journey. Because times varied according to the pocket watch of the individual officer, the author has decided to use the latest possible time recorded by the soldiers due to the nearly impossi-

ble situation in getting the guns through the Chickahominy Swamp.

22. Gustavus W. Smith, "Two days of Battle at Seven Pines," in *B&L,* vol. 2, 220–263; *OR, 11,* 791–798; *Providence Journal,* July 1, 1862; Battery G, Morning Reports, June 1–2, 1862, NA.

23. *OR 11,* 791–798; Barber, Diary, June 1, 1862; Albert Straight to Parents, June 7, 1862, RG.

24. Henry Farnsworth and John L. Rathbun, Service Files, NA; Young, Court-Martial. Unfortunately no member of Battery G left any record of the journey of Torslow's caissons, but they rejoined the battery immediately after the battle and were present directly after with the men's personal equipment. A member of Battery A, which also left their equipment on the opposite bank of the river wrote on June 1, "All our wagons + baggage, forge + Battery wagons remained in camp" (Daniel W. Marshall, Diary, May 31-June 1, 1862, Marshall Papers, LOC).

25. George L. Gaskell to Mary Call, June 8, 1862, US-AMHI; Cordner, Diary, June 2–3, 1862; Barber, Diary, June 8–10, 1862; G. Smith, "Two days of Battle at Seven Pines," 220–63.

26. Gaskell to Call, June 8, 1862.

27. Barber, Diary, June 12, 1862; *Providence Journal,* July 1, 1862; J. Franklin Dyer, *The Journal of a Civil War Surgeon,* ed. Michael B. Chesson (Lincoln: University of Nebraska Press, 2003), 23–24.

28. George T. Stevens, *Three Years in the Sixth Corps* (Albany: S.R. Gray, 1866), 73–76; Dyer, *Journal of a Civil War Surgeon,* 28–30; George L. Gaskell to Mary Call, June 8: June 17: June 20, 1862, USAMHI; Henry Newton to Louisa Newton, undated letter Peninsula Campaign, HL.

29. Henry Heap, Pension File, NA.

30. Barber, Diary, June 11, 1862; General Orders 8, Battery G, NA; J. Russell Field, Charles Bogman, and William H. Lewis, Service Files, NA; Lewis, *Battery E,* 502.

31. Cordner, Diary, June 9–16, 1862; Gaskell to Call, June 17, 1862.

32. Cordner, Diary, June 11–16, 1862; James Horton in Battery G, Clothing Book, RIHS.

33. Gaskell to Call, June 17, 1862; William Thurber, Sketches, RIHS; Battery G, Morning Report, June 17, 1862, NA; *Providence Journal,* July 1, 1862.

34. Barber, Diary, June 26, 1862; Fitz John Porter, "Hanover Court House and Gaine's Mill," in *B&L,* vol. 2, 319–331.

35. Porter, "Hanover Court House," 332–343; William F. Franklin, "Rear-Guard Fighting during the Change of Base," in *B&L,* vol. 2, 366–382; Barber, Diary, June 27–30, 1862; L. Gaskell to Mary Call, July 3, 1862, USAMHI; *Memoirs of RI,* 375–376.

36. Cordner, Diary, June 27–30, 1862; Reichardt, Diary, June 28, 1862; Gaskell to Call, July 3, 1862; *Providence Journal,* July 9, 1862.

37. Gaskell to Call, July 3, 1862; Walker, *Second Corps,* 63–77; Barber, Diary, June 30, 1862; Cordner, Diary, June 30, 1862.

38. Fitz John Porter, "The Battle of Malvern Hill," in *B&L,* vol. 2, 416–424; Gaskell to Call, July 3, 1862; Charles Tompkins to Edward C. Mauran, July 7, 1862, RISA.

39. Porter, "Malvern Hill," 416–424; *OR, 11,* 82–85; Barber, July 1, 1862; Peter Hunt to Mother, July 5, 1862, EPH; Gaskell to Call, July 3, 1862.

40. Gaskell to Call, July 3, 1862; George L. Gaskell, Pension File, NA.

41. J. Rhodes, *Battery B,* 106–107; Barber, Diary, July 2–7, 1862; Gaskell to Call, July 3, 1862.

42. Battery G, Clothing Book, RIHS; Cordner, Diary, July 3–7, 1862; Barber, Diary, July 8, 1862; George L. Gaskell to Mary Call, July 14, 1862, USAMHI.

43. David B. Patterson to Mother, June 22, 1862, RNB. "Bars" refers to the shoulder insignia officers used to show

their ranks (*New York Times*, July 7 and 28, 1862, August 14, 1862).

44. George L. Gaskell to Mary Call, July 14 and July 23, 1862, USAMHI; Barber, Diary, July 15–30, 1862.

45. Cordner, Diary, July 6–16, 1862; Jean Barber to Author, September 2, 2007.

46. Reichardt, Diary; July 23-August 14, 1862; Gaskell to Call, July 14 and July 23, 1862; J. Rhodes, *Battery B*, 80–81.

47. Gaskell to Call, July 14 and July 23, 1862; Cordner, Diary, July 28-August 7, 1862.

48. Cordner, Diary, July 28-August 7, 1862; Battery G, Morning Reports, August 7 and 17, 1862, NA.

49. Barber, Diary, August 14, 1862; "Muster Roll of Detachment of Rects. for Battery G, 1st Regt R.I; Arty, Aug. 11, 1862," RISA.

50. *Wood River Advertiser*, April 16, 1907; United States 1850 and 1860 Census information for the Tucker family, courtesy of Kris VanDenBossche; Charles T. Straight, *Battery B, First RI Light Artillery, August 13, 1861-June 12, 1865* (Pawtucket: NP, 1907), 16.

51. Cordner, Diary, August 16–21, 1862; Barber, Diary, August 16–23, 1862; Battery G, Morning Reports, August 16–21, 1862, NA; Stone, *Rebellion*, 84.

Chapter 6

1. George B. McClellan, "From the Peninsula to Antietam," in *B&L*, vol. 2, 545–555; Barber, Diary, August 31-September 4, 1862; Cordner, Diary, August 30–September 5, 1862.

2. James Longstreet, "The Invasion of Maryland," in *B&L*, vol. 2, 663–665.

3. Ibid., 663–665.

4. McClellan, "From the Peninsula to Antietam," 545–555; Walker, *Second Corps*, 93; Cordner, Diary, September 6–13, 1862.

5. Henry Kyd Douglass, "Stonewall Jackson in Maryland," in *B&L*, vol. 2, 620–627.

6. Barber, Diary, September 14–16, 1862; Cordner, Diary, September 14–16, 1862; William B. Rhodes to Ezra Carmen, March 21, 1896, ANB. Captain Owen insisted he forded the Antietam on the morning of September 17, while William Rhodes and Albert Cordner claimed it was in the middle of the night.

7. Barber, Diary, September 17, 1862; Jacob D. Cox, "The Battle of Antietam," in *B&L*, vol. 2, 632–41.Walker, *Second Corps*, 101–108; Jennings C. Wise, *The Long Arm of Lee* (Lynchburg, VA: J.P. Bell, 1915), 297–303.

8. Monroe, *Antietam*, 6–11; "Greene's Division, Twelfth Army Corps," Carmen Papers, ANB.

9. *OR 19*, 275–276; Cox, "Antietam," 643–645; Walker, *Second Corps*, 101–108; E. Rhodes, *All for the Union*, 73.

10. *OR 19*, 325–326; Barber, Diary, September 17, 1862; Mumma Farm Files, Carmen Papers, ANB.

11. *OR 19*, 325–326; George L. Gaskell to Mary Call, September 24, 1862, and May 7, 1863, USAMHI; Barber, Diary, September 17, 1862; Tully McCrea, *Dear Belle: Letters from a Cadet & Officer to His Sweetheart, 1858–1865*, ed. Catherine S. Creary (Middletown, CT: Wesleyan University Press, 1965), 151–153. An officer in Battery I, First United States, McCrea is clear that his battery and those along the West Woods line had no choice but to fire into the Second Corps.

12. William D. Child to Ezra Carmen, March 26, 1896, ANB.

13. Cox, "Antietam," 643–645; Reichardt, Diary, September 17, 1862; William C. Barker to Henry Barker, September 19, 1862, RIHS.

14. Reichardt, Diary, September 17, 1862; *OR 19*, 308–09; *Providence Journal*, September 26, 1862.

15. *Memoirs of RI*, 439–440; *OR 19*, 325–326; William B. Rhodes to Ezra Carmen, March 14, 1896, ANB.

16. *OR 19*, 326; Rhodes to Carmen, March 21, 1896.

17. *OR 19*, 323–324; Walker, *Second Corps*, 109–112; Cox, "Antietam," 643–645; Reichardt, Diary, September 17, 1862.

18. *OR 19*, 326; Ezra Carmen, "Battery G, 1st R.I; Artillery," ANB; Kent M. Brown, *Cushing of Gettysburg: The Story of a Union Artillery Commander* (Lexington: University Press of Kentucky, 1993), 126.

19. Cox, "Antietam," 643–647; Walker, *Second Corps*, 113–116.

20. *OR 19*, 326; Wise, *Long Arm*, 305–308; This quote is taken from a plaque hanging in the visitor's center of the Antietam National Battlefield.

21. *OR 19*, 326; Barber, Diary, September 17, 1862; Battery G, Descriptive Book, RISA; Clarence R. Geir and Stephen R. Potter, eds., *Archaeological Perspectives on the American Civil War* (Gainesville: University Press of Florida, 2000), 348–359; "Antietam Archaeological Records," Carmen Papers, ANB; George L. Gaskell to Mary Call, September 28, 1862, and October 4, 1862, USAMHI. During a series of archaeological digs in the area of Piper's Farm in the 1990s, numerous Dyer and Hotchkiss shell fragments were found in the area. As Battery G was one of the units equipped with three-inch ordnance rifles, which fired this ammunition, and Captain Owen reported using it in his *OR* report it is highly likely that some of these relics were fired by Battery G from its position near Bloody Lane.

22. *OR 19*, 326; Walker, *Second Corps*, 115–119.

23. Cox, "Antietam," 649–656; *OR 19*, 455–457; George H. Allen, *Forty-Six Months in the Fourth RI Volunteers* (Providence: J.A. and R.A. Reid, Printers, 1887), 142–148.

24. *OR 19*, 326; Peter Riley, Service File, NA; George L. Gaskell to Mary Call, September 24, 1862, USAMHI; Melton and Pawl, *Artillery Projectiles*, 53–57.

25. Reichardt, Diary, September 17, 1862; Amos M.C. Olney to Sisters, September 27, 1862, RIHS.

26. *Providence Journal*, September 19, 1862; *Narragansett Weekly*, October 9, 1862. These were all Regular Army batteries in the Mexican War. Magruder and Bragg became Confederate generals. Sherman is Thomas West Sherman of Newport, Rhode Island, who commanded troops in South Carolina and Louisiana during the Civil War.

27. *Narragansett Weekly*, October 9, 1862.

28. Cordner, Diary, September 18, 1862; Battery G, Morning Reports, September 18 and 19, 1862, NA; Allen, *Forty-Six Months*, 142–148.

29. Cordner, Diary, September 17, 1862; Gaskell to Call, September 24, 1862; *Providence Press*, September 18, 1862.

30. Walker, *Second Corps*, 127–128; Barber, Diary, September 20-October 5, 1862; George L. Gaskell to Mary Call, September 24, 1862, September 28, 1862, and October 4, 1862; USAMHI; Cordner, Diary, September 20-October 3, 1862.

31. Battery G, Monthly Return, September 1862, RISA; George L. Gaskell to Mary Call, October 4, 1862; *Narragansett Weekly*, November 10, 1862; Battery G, Descriptive Book, RISA.

32. George L. Gaskell to Mary Call and to George B. Gaskell, separate letters, both October 10, 1862, and to Call, October 4, 1862, USAMHI; Cordner, Diary, October 5–20, 1862.

33. Walker, *Second Corps*, 128–131.

34. George L. Gaskell to Mary Call, October 21, 1862, USAMHI; *Narragansett Weekly*, November 10, 1862; Michael Coffery, Service File, NA; Cordner, Diary, October 21–27, 1862; Barber, Diary, October 19, 1862. Coffery

is now buried in the National Cemetery at Winchester, Virginia.

35. Cordner, Diary, October 27–29, 1862; Barber, Diary, October 28-Novenber 9, 1862; Battery G, Clothing Book, RIHS.

Chapter 7

1. *OR 21*, 46–61.

2. Barber, Diary, November 10–18, 1862; Cordner, Diary, November 10–18, 1862.

3. *Memoirs of RI*, 439–440; General Orders 11, Battery G, NA; Battery G, Clothing and Descriptive Book, RIHS and RISA.

4. Billings, *Hardtack and Coffee*, 73–89; Cordner, Diary, November 18–21, 1862.

5. William Miller, "A Hot Day on Marye's Heights," in *B&L*, vol. 3, 97–99; Barber, Diary, November 25–26, 1862.

6. Cordner, Diary, November 28-December 9, 1862; Barber, Diary, December 4–9, 1862.

7. Cordner, Diary December 7–11, 1862; Battery G, Descriptive Book, RISA; *OR 21*, 208; Barber, Diary, December 10, 1862.

8. *OR 21*, 209–210; Barber, Diary, December 11, 1862.

9. Cordner, Diary, December 11, 1862; *Providence Journal*, December 25, 1862.

10. Reichardt, Diary, December 12, 1862; Straight, Diary, December 12, 1862.

11. Straight, Diary, December 13, 1862; Walker, *Second Corps*, 146–193; Peter Hunt to Daniel Hunt, December 16, 1862, EPH.

12. Barber, Diary, December 13, 1862.

13. *OR 21*, 209: 362; Cordner, Diary, December 14–15, 1862; Barber, Diary, December 14, 1862. This entry concludes the 1862 Diary of James A. Barber at the Providence Public Library.

14. *OR 21*, 209: 362; Anon., "Cannons at Kenmore: A Civil War Walking Tour of Kenmore Plantation & Washington Avenue," FRSP.

15. *OR 21*, 209: 362.

16. Rhodes, Diary, December 14, 1862.

17. W. Rhodes, Diary, December 14, 1862; Cordner, Diary, December 29, 1862.

18. Battery G, Morning Reports, December 13–15, 1862, NA.

19. *OR 21*, 209–210; William B. Rhodes, Diary, December 14–15, 1862, USAMHI; Stone, *Rebellion*, 188; *Providence Journal*, December 25, 1862; Anon., "Cannons at Kenmore."

20. Reichardt, Diary, December 15, 1862; W. Rhodes, Diary, December 16, 1862; *Narragansett Weekly*, March 6, 1862.

21. *OR 21*, 209–210; Charles Tompkins to Edward C. Mauran, December 19, 1862, RISA; Battery G, Descriptive Book, RISA; *Providence Journal*, December 16, 1862; *Narragansett Times*, December 19, 1862. The casualty figures for Rhode Island at Fredericksburg were appalling. The Second Rhode Island lost eight wounded; Fourth, one killed and nine wounded; Seventh Regiment, forty-four dead, 136 wounded, forty missing in action; Twelfth Rhode Island, twenty-four killed, ninety-four wounded; Battery A, five wounded; Battery B, three dead and thirteen wounded; Battery C, one dead; Battery D, one wounded; Battery E two killed and two wounded; and Battery G, one wounded. The total loss was 384, not counting men in the Regulars or other state units.

22. Melton and Pawl, *Artillery Projectiles*, 53–57; *OR 21*, 209–210.

23. *Providence Journal*, December 25, 1862; Cordner, Diary, December 17, 1862; Rhodes, Diary, December 17, 1862.

24. W. Rhodes, Diary, December 20–21, 1862; Stone, *Rebellion*, 378–380; *Memoirs of RI*, 406–407.

25. W. Rhodes, Diary, December 24–26, 1862; Owen, Service File, NA; Cordner, Diary, December 22–27, 1862; William Rhodes, Service File, NA.

26. James A. Barber, Diary, January 1–3, 1863, HL; Cordner, Diary, December 20–31, 1862; William H. Lewis to Mother, May 21, 1863, CSL.

27. *Providence Journal*, December 25, 1862.

28. William O. Tabor, Service File, NA; William O. and Phebe Tabor, Memorial Markers, Wood River Cemetery, Richmond, Rhode Island.

29. VanDenBossche, *Pleas Excuse*, 1–2, 5–22.

30. George L. Gaskell, letters, USAMHI; Barber, Diary, December 14, 1862; Peleg Peckham to David R. Kenyon, January 4, 1863, LPL. This author has reviewed the correspondence of over 300 Rhode Island soldiers. When there is a mention of abolition it is always negative; only one soldier wrote that he was for the Emancipation Proclamation.

31. William Barker to Henry Barker, January 14, 1863, RIHS.

32. Horace S. Bloodgood, Service File, NA; Horace Bloodgood, Student File, HL; Barber, Diary, January 5–12, 1863; Peter Hunt to Howard Hunt, January 10, 1863, EPH.

33. General Orders 1 and 2, Battery G, NA. Each time a new officer took command a new set of order numbers began, but they were written in the same book.

34. Bogman and Field, Service Files, NA; Kris VanDenBossche to Grandchamp, December 17, 2006; Lewis, *Battery E*, 146–152.

35. Cross, *Stand Firm*, 60–62; Peter Hunt to Mother, January 18, 1863, EPH; J. Rhodes, *Battery B*, 151–152; Barber, Diary, January 17–20, 1863.

36. Barber, Diary, January 20–24, 1863; Allen, *Forty-Six Months*, 167–169.

37. J. Rhodes, *Battery B*, 151–152; Barber, Diary, January 20–24, 1863; Frederick M. Sackett to Mother, January 24, 1863, RIHS.

38. Charlotte Dailey, *Report upon the Disabled Rhode Island Soldiers* (Providence: Alfred Anthony, 1863), 7–52. In Mrs. Dailey's report she located the following sick or injured soldiers from Battery G: Nathaniel Champlin, George D. Fenner, John G. Rathbun, Peter Riley, and Silas R. Ripley.

39. J. Rhodes, *Battery B*, 151–160; Battery G, Morning Report, February 10, 1863, NA; Barber, Diary, February 2 and February 22, 1863.

40. J. Rhodes, *Battery B*, 156–58; Barber, Diary, February 12–29, 1863.

41. Jesse Young, Court-Martial Records, NA; Barber, Diary, February 13, 1863.

42. Young, Court-Martial. Young was the only Rhode Island soldier to be sentenced to death during the war.

43. Barber, Diary, March 1–17, 1863.

44. Battery G, Morning Report, March 19, 1862, NA; Billings, *Hardtack and Coffee*, 119–121: 254–262.

45. J. Rhodes, *Battery B*, 162; Barber, Diary, April 1–15, 1863; Battery G, Descriptive Book, RISA.

46. Barber, Diary, April 4–8, 1863; Thomas F. Mars, Service File, NA; George L. Gaskell to Mary Call, May 7, 1863, USAMHI; Peter Hunt to Mother, April 20, 1863, EPH.

47. Horace Bloodgood, Service File, NA. During his term as commander Bloodgood failed to communicate with the Rhode Island Adjutant General, evidenced by four months of missing reports at the Rhode Island State Archives.

Chapter 8

1. Darius N. Couch, "The Chancellorsville Campaign," in B&L, vol. 3, 156–157; John Gibbon, *Personal Recollections of the Civil War* (New York: G.P. Putnam's, 1928), 110–114.

2. Budlong, Diary, April 28, 1863; William H. Lewis to Mother, April 26, 1863, CSL.

3. Couch, "Chancellorsville,"158–165; Lewis, *Battery E*, 162–172.

4. Couch, "Chancellorsville,"163–170.

5. George L. Gaskell to Mary Call, April 30, 1863, US-AMHI.

6. George W. Adams, Service File, NA; *George W. Adams*, 1–3; Burrage, *Brown University*, 338–339; *Memoirs of RI*, 414–415.

7. J. Rhodes, *Battery B*, 8, 352; *Narragansett Times*, November 1, 1861; David B. Patterson to Mother, June 13, 1862, R1HS; *OR 21*, 267–268. Adams was originally commissioned as a captain in January of 1863 and sent home to recruit Battery I for the First Rhode Island Light Artillery Regiment. Battery I never was mustered into the service, its members having been sent to fill the ranks of the depleted batteries in the field and the officers transferred to other commands as well. According to official records, Captain Adams assumed command of Battery G on April 30, 1863. All of the veterans' accounts from the unit state it was May 2; therefore, this is the date used.

8. Walker, *Second Corps*, 202–212: 231–237; Gibbon, *Personal Recollections*, 110–114; *Memoirs of RI*, 376–377.

9. Barber, Diary, May 2, 1863.

10. Benjamin G. Humphrey, "Recollections of Marye's Heights and Salem Church," in B&L, vol. 6, 219–230. This battle is also referred to as Second Fredericksburg to differentiate it from the December 13, 1862, battle. The Rhode Islanders, however, referred to it as Marye's Heights, as do most government resources. Therefore the name Marye's Heights will be used.

11. J. Rhodes, *Battery B*, 168–170; Barber, Diary, May 3, 1863; T. Fred Brown to Charles Morgan, May 8, 1863, Hunt Papers, LOC; Budlong Diary, May 3, 1863; *OR 25*, 820–824.

12. J. Rhodes, *Battery B*, 69–70; Brown to Morgan, May 8, 1864; Straight, Diary, May 3, 1863.

13. E. Rhodes, *All for the Union*, 97; *OR 25*, 614–615.

14. *Providence Journal*, May 8, 1863; George L. Gaskell to Mary Call, May 7, 1863, USAMHI; E. Rhodes, *All for the Union*, 97.

15. William H. Lewis to Mother, May 21, 1863, CSL; Lorraine Tarket-Arruda and Gayle E. Waite, *Historical Cemeteries of Charlestown, Rhode Island* (Hopkinton: The Authors, 2008), 8; Barber, Diary, May 3, 1863.

16. Royall W. Figg, *"Where Men Only Dare to Go!" or The Story of a Boy Company* (Richmond: Whilet and Shepperson, 1885), 114–128; Robert K. Krick, *Parker's Virginia Battery* (Berryville, VA: Virginia Book Company, 1975), 123–126; Barber, Diary, May 3, 1863.

17. *Providence Journal*, May 8, 1863; Gaskell to Call, May 7, 1863; Barber, Diary, May 3, 1863; George W. Adams to Charles H; Morgan, May 7, 1863, Hunt Papers, LOC.

18. Patrick Lyons, Journal, May 3, 1863, PHS. Lyons still uses the old name for Battery G—the Eighth Rhode Island Battery.

19. *Providence Journal*, May 8, 1863; Barber, Diary, May 3, 1863.

20. Barber, Diary, May 3, 1863.

21. Anon, "Guns at Kenmore."

22. Adams to Morgan, May 7, 1863; Wilbur Fisk, *Hard Marching Every Day: The Civil War Letters of Private Wilbur Fisk, 1861–1865* , ed. Emil and Ruth Rosenblatt (Lawrence: University Press of Kansas, 1992), 77–80.

23. Adams to Morgan, May 7, 1863; James L. Bowen, *History of the Thirty-Seventh Regiment Mass Volunteers in the Civil War of 1861–1865* (Holyoke: Clark W. Bryan, 1884), 145–149; Henry Woodhead, ed., *Chancellorsville* (Alexandria: Time Life Books, 1996), 124; George W. Bicknell, *History of the Fifth Regiment Maine Volunteers, Comprising Brief Descriptions of Its Marches, Engagements, and General Services from the Date of Its Muster In, June 24, 1861, to the Time of Its Muster Out, July 27, 1864* (Portland: Hall L. Davis, 1871), 217–224.

24. Huntington W. Jackson, "Sedgwick at Fredericksburg and Salem's Heights," in B&L, vol. 3, 227–30 OR 25, 350–351: 820–824.

25. Krick, *Parker's Virginia Battery*, 126–28; *New York Times*, May 6, 1863.

26. John D. Wells, Pension File, NA; Lewis to Mother, May 21, 1863.

27. Gibbon, *Personal Recollections*, 115–116; Gaskell to Call, May 7, 1863. After dying at a hospital in Washington, Mars was buried at the Soldiers Home Cemetery in the northern reaches of the city. Here he was laid alongside three other Battery G soldiers who died of disease: Elizer H. Brown, John Connery, and John Taft (*Revised Register*, 1064).

28. Benjamin E. Kelley, Service File, NA Dyer, *Journal of a Civil War Surgeon*, 76; *Narragansett Weekly*, May 14, 1863; *Memoirs of RI*, 439–440; Stone, *Rebellion*, 239; VanDenBossche, *Pleas Excuse*, 119–120; *Narragansett Times*, December 26, 1862; Lewis to Mother, May 21, 1863; Richard Waterman to Mrs. Sackett, May 4, 1863, RIHS; *Providence Journal*, May 8, 1863. There is some argument as to when Kelley died, either late on the night of the third or early in the morning of May 4. Most accounts state he lived some twelve hours after receiving the wound, which occurred around 10:30 on the morning of May 3. Therefore this author has taken it to be May 3. Today Lieutenant Kelley lies buried at Swan Point in Providence under a barely legible marble stone.

29. Aldrich, *Battery A*, 177.

30. *Narragansett Weekly*, May 14, 1863; Barber, Diary, May 3, 1863; Battery G, Morning Report, May 4, 1863, NA.

31. *Providence Journal*, May 8, 1863; George W. Adams to Edward C. Mauran, May 13, 1863, RISA; Barber, Diary, May 3, 1863; William H. Lewis to Mother, June 22, 1863, CSL.

32. *OR 25*, 309–310; Gaskell to Call, May 7, 1863.

33. Jackson, "Sedgwick," 231–232; *Memoirs of RI*, 377; *Providence Press*, May 11, 1863; John A. Tompkins to Henry J. Hunt, May 10, 1863, Hunt Papers, LOC.

34. Jackson, "Sedgwick," 231–232; E. Rhodes, *All for the Union*, 98–102; Barber, Diary, May 5–6, 1863; Adams to Morgan, May 7, 1863.

35. Adams, "Battery G," 903; Barber, Diary, May 21, 1863.

36. George W. Adams to Edward C. Mauran, May 4 and May 13, 1863, RISA; Battery G, Descriptive Book, RISA.

37. Battery G, Monthly Return, May 1863, RISA; General Orders Number 5, Battery G, NA.

38. Battery G, Monthly Return, May 1863, RISA.

39. Henry J. Hunt, "The First Day at Gettysburg," in B&L, vol. 3, 257–260; *Instructions for Making Muster Rolls, Mustering into Service, and Periodical Payments* (Washington: Government Printing Office, 1863), 26–28; Artillery Returns, March-May 1863, Hunt Papers, LOC; Buell, *The Cannoneer*, 22–24: 57–58. While Hunt insisted on the term "brigades" to try to get general officers for his artillery arm, the most proper term would have been artillery battalions, as the Army of Northern Virginia had created with great effect in late 1862.

40. Hunt, "First Day at Gettysburg," 257–260.

41. Peck, *Historical Address*, 6–10.

42. Special Orders Number 129, Army of the Potomac, May 12, 1863, Hunt Papers, LOC.

43. Barber, Diary, May 9–21, 1863; Battery G, Monthly Return, May 1863; Reichardt, Diary, July 3, 1863.

44. General Orders Number 6, Battery G, NA; George Soule to Cousin Hatter, June 3, 1863, USAMHI.

45. Barber, Diary, May 12–13, 1863; Frederick Phisterer, *New York in the War of the Rebellion* (Albany: J.B. Lyon, 1912), 358.

46. George L. Gaskell to Henry Call, June 2, 1863, US-AMHI; Barber, Diary, May 31, 1863.

47. William H. Lewis to Mother, June 6, 1863, CSL.

Chapter 9

1. Barber, Diary, June 4–13, 1863; Hunt, "First Day at Gettysburg," 261–264; William H. Lewis to Mother, June 22, 1863, CSL.

2. Frederick M. Edgell to George W. Adams and Richard Waterman, Special Orders 164, June 18, 1863, RG; Adams, "Battery G," 903; Stone, *Rebellion*, 260; *OR 27*, 162–164. The long retold story, as written by Corporal Adams in his sketch, was that it was Battery G's performance at Marye's Heights that brought about their transfer. He wrote, "For the qualities shown at the second battle of Fredericksburg, General Sedgwick requested the Battery to be attached to his Corps (the 6th). Accordingly it was detached from the 2d Corps, where it had been since the formation of the Corps, and placed in the 6th where it remained until the close of the war."Adams fails to note that the battery had initially served in the Artillery Reserve for a month before the transfer. In addition, Sedgwick had known Battery G since January of 1862 when they served with him on the Potomac, the Peninsula and Antietam. Here Sedgwick had observed the battery in combat as part of his division. When he was forced to give up several batteries after Chancellorsville, the Sixth Corps needed additional ones when reinforcements were received in June. The most logical explanation is that Tompkins and Sedgwick knew two batteries—most important for Tompkins, they were ones of his own regiment, and Battery G, which Sedgwick personally knew—were sitting in the Reserve and their transfer was authorized by General Henry Hunt. A forage cap worn by a member of Battery G is now preserved by the Cranston Historical Society at the Sprague Mansion in Cranston, Rhode Island. Some members of the unit, including William H. Lewis, wore a distinctive emblem on their hats. It consisted of a small pair of crossed cannons, over "G and I" followed by "R I" on either side of the cannons. See the image of Bugler Lewis in this volume for further detail.

3. Patterson to Mother, June 13, 1862.

4. E. Rhodes, *All for the Union*, 105–106; Straight, Diary, June 7, 1863; John W. Chase, *Yours for the Union: The Civil War Letters of John W Chase: First Massachusetts Light Artillery*, ed. John S. Collier and Bonnie B. Collier (New York: Fordham University Press, 2004), 229–231, 246, 250–252. Chase served in the First Massachusetts Battery, part of the Sixth Corps Artillery Brigade (Daniel A. Handy to Jeannie Handy, July 1, 1863).

5. Barber, Diary, June 26–29, 1863.

6. G. Stevens, *Sixth Corps*, 239–41; *OR 27*, 694–695; Barber, Diary, June 29, 1863.

7. Augustus Woodbury, *The Second Rhode Island Regiment* (Providence: Valpey, Angell, 1875), 184–193; Hunt, "First Day," 255–271.

8. Hunt, "First Day," 271–284.

9. *OR 27*, 694–695; Woodbury, *Second Rhode Island*, 194–195; Barber, Diary, July 1–2, 1863.

10. Henry J. Hunt, "The Second Day at Gettysburg," in *B&L*, vol. 3, 296–313; Straight, Diary, July 2, 1863; Benjamin Freeborn to Edward C. Mauran, July 5, 1863, RISA.

11. Barber, Diary, July 2, 1863; *OR 27*, 695; Woodbury, *Second Rhode Island*, 194–196. There are many different recordings of the amount of miles marched by the Sixth Corps on July 2. They range from thirty-four to forty. This is because the corps was so spread out that they marched the further distance. Corporal Adams reported thirty-seven miles in his *Revised Register* sketch. They marched with the Third Division and were one of the first Sixth Corps units to arrive on the field, around 4:00. Therefore this author has taken Captain Adams' initial report of thirty-five miles to mark the distance marched.

12. Bicknell, *Fifth Maine*, 243–246; Barber, Diary, July 2–3, 1863; George S. Greene, Reports, RG. Although a native of Warwick, Greene commanded five New York regiments and had acted as a civil engineer in New York before the war. Commissioned as the colonel of the Sixtieth New York, he was promoted to brigadier and led competently at Cedar Mountain and Antietam in command of a division when he was reduced to brigade command. After leading his men to victory at Gettysburg, the Twelfth Corps went west. Greene followed and was wounded at Wahautchie, Tennessee, and later marched to the sea with Sherman. He returned to engineering after the war and is buried in Warwick. He was the oldest Federal field commander at Gettysburg and was called "Old Man" or "Pap Greene" by his men.

13. Henry J. Hunt, "The Third Day at Gettysburg," in *B&L*, vol. 3, 369–383; Wise, *Long Arm*, vol. 2, 660–694; Reichardt, Diary, July 3, 1863; Straight, Diary, July 3, 1863. The Gettysburg Gun is now on display at the Rhode Island State House, along with the Bull Run Gun and the battle flags of the Rhode Island Regiments.

14. *Memoirs of RI*, 378–379; David L. Ladd and Audrey J. Ladd, eds., *Gettysburg in Their Own Words: The Batchelder Papers*, vol. 1 (Dayton: New Hampshire Historical Society, 1995), 445–446.

15. *OR 27*, 696; Barber, Diary, July 3, 1863; Bicknell, *Fifth Maine*, 246. Bicknell wrote, "The stone breastworks saved our men wonderfully." He also called the position "one of great importance."

16. Hunt, "The Third Day at Gettysburg," 369–383.

17. Straight, Diary, July 3, 1863; *OR 27*, 695; Barber, Diary, July 3, 1863.

18. Straight, Diary, July 3, 1863; John W. Busey, *These Honored Dead: The Union Casualties at Gettysburg* (Hightstown, NJ: Longstreet House, 1996), 307–309. Many legends have grown up surrounding this cannon in recent years; among them is that the Confederates actually shot the round into the muzzle. For more information see John H. Rhodes, *History of Battery B*.

19. *OR 27*, 695; Battery G, Descriptive Book, RISA; Andrew Cowan to John P. Nicholson, December 5, 1903, GNMP.

20. Barber, Diary, July 5, 1863; G Stevens, *Sixth Corps*, 253–256; Edmund Halsey, *Brother Against Brother: The Lost Civil War Diary of Lt Edmund Halsey*, ed. Bruce Chadwick (Secaucus, NJ: Carroll Communications, 1997), 149; Simon Baruch, "A Surgeon's Story of Battle and Capture," GNMP; Nichols, "Narrative."

21. Kent M. Brown, *Retreat from Gettysburg: Lee, Logistics, and the Pennsylvania Campaign* (Chapel Hill: University of North Carolina Press, 2005), 188–192; John E. Divine, *35th Battalion Virginia Cavalry* (Lynchburg, VA: H.E. Howard, 1985), 36; Frank M. Myers, *The Commanches: A History of White's Battalion, Virginia Cavalry* (Baltimore: Kelly, Piet, 1871), 204–205; Jubal A. Early, *War Memoirs: Autobiographical Sketch and Narrative of the War Between the States*, ed. Frank A. Vandiver (Bloomington: Indiana University Press, 1960), 280; *OR 27*, 663.

22. Early, *War Memoirs*, 280; *OR 27*, 493.

23. Fisk, *Hard Marching*, 115–120; Charles G. Howe to Sir, March 24, 1864, GNMP; Charles C. Morey, Diary, July 5, 1863, GNMP; Barber, Diary, July 5, 1863.

24. Alton J. Murray, *South Georgia Rebels: The True Wartime Experiences of the 26th Regiment, Georgia Volunteer Infantry, Lawton-Gordon-Evans Brigade, Confederate States Army, 1861–1865* (St. Mary's, GA: Murray, 1976), 138–141; Joseph Hilton to Lizzie Lachilson, July 18, 1863, GNMP; Barber, Diary, July 5, 1863; William H. Moore, "Narrative," GNMP; Brown, *Retreat from Gettysburg*, 191–193.

25. Brown, *Retreat from Gettysburg*, 188–192; Bicknell, *Fifth Maine*, 247. The site of the fight at Granite Hill has been the subject of continued digging survey by Civil War relic hunters. From the intersection of the Cashtown and Fairfield roads, numerous friction primers have been located to mark the position of the Louisiana Guard Battery, while their shell fragments have been found to the rear of Granite Hill, indicating the rounds flew off target. Hotchkiss shell fragments and lead sabots have been found in the valley between Granite Hill and the town of Fairfield, proof that Battery G, First Rhode Island Light Artillery, was present. In addition, twelve-pounder fragments have been found that mark the position of Harn's Third New York Battery. In the woodlot where the infantry fight took place, numerous buttons, buckles, and hundreds of minie balls are indicative of the heavy fighting that took place there. This author is indebted to Dean Thomas for the above information and for showing him the location of the battle.

26. Fisk, *Hard Marching*, 115–120; Joseph G. Bilby, *Three Rousing Cheers: A History of the Fifteenth New Jersey from Flemington to Appomattox* (Hightstown, NJ: Longstreet House, 2001), 83–84; Halsey, *Brother Against Brother*, 149. According to Bilby, it was Companies B and D of the Fifteenth that went into the woods.

27. Alanson A. Haines, *History of the Fifteenth Regiment New Jersey Volunteers* (Gaithersburg, MD: Butternut Press, 1987), 97–98; Dayton F. Flint to Sisters, July 6, 1863, GNMP. Flint's account of the skirmish is brief, but is well suited for the type of fighting that marked the retreat from Gettysburg: "We were chasing the enemy all day yesterday, our company being one which was skirmishing in advance."

28. Fisk, *Hard Marching*, 115–120; Early, *War Memoirs*, 280–281; Samuel Toombs, *New Jersey Troops in the Gettysburg Campaign, from June 5 to July 31, 1863* (Orange, NJ: Evening Mail Publishing House, 1888), 315–316; Camille Baquet, *History of the First Brigade, New Jersey Volunteers, from 1861 to 1865* (Trenton: State of New Jersey, 1910), 97; Adams, "Battery G," 903. In Toombs' book on New Jersey, he lists only one killed in action and no wounded. Based on talks with various NPS Rangers and historians, this author has determined the Union casualty figures for the Granite Hill fight. The best estimate for Confederate total losses were those of the Twenty-Sixth Georgia, as they performed the only fighting. One of the only confirmed killed was First Lieutenant Charles Walker of the Twenty-Sixth, who was killed in the woodlot. There may have been casualties from Battery G and the Third New York shelling of the wagon train, but they were never reported separate of the total Confederate loss for the three days of battle. See Murray, *South Georgia Rebels*, 138–141, and Bilby, *Three Rousing Cheers*, 83–84.

29. *OR 27*, 493: 669–670: 695; Early, *War Memoirs*, 280–281.

30. Richard E. Winslow, *General John Sedgwick: The Story of a Union Corps Commander* (Novato, CA: Presidio Press, 1982), 109; Charles S. Wainwright, *A Diary of Battle: The Personal Journals of Colonel Charles S. Wainwright, 1861–1865*, ed. Allan Nevins (Gettysburg: Stan Clark Mil-

itary Books, 1992), 257–258. It is interesting to note that, although this incident occurred, no member of Battery G, including the usually dictative James Barber, ever wrote about it.

31. *OR 27*, 695; George L. Gaskell to Mary Call, July 9, 1863, USAMHI.

32. J. Chase, *Yours for the Union*, 258–261; Daniel A. Handy to Jennie Handy, July 11, 1863, RIHS; Barber, Diary, July 7–12, 1863; *OR 27*, 695.

33. *Providence Journal*, July 16, 1863; P. Chase, *Battery F*, 92–93.

34. *OR 27*, 695; J. Chase, *Yours for the Union*, 269–273; Sedgwick, *Correspondence*, 144–145.

35. *Providence Journal*, July 23, 1863; Silas W. Wood to Benjamin W. Pendleton, January 12, 1863, RIHS; *Narragansett Weekly*, October 1862-July 1863; Cordner, Diary, October 15–30, 1862; George L. Gaskell to Mary Call, July 26, 1863, USAMHI. A dozen Rhode Island soldiers, all from different units were unanimous in their feelings that the Twelfth Regiment won a great deal of glory, despite breaking and running under fire at Fredericksburg. No doubt they took over a hundred casualties, but their performance left many soldiers disgusted that these men were fellow Rhode Islanders. One artillery officer watching on as the Twelfth broke was so outraged that he wrote, "The R.I. 12th ran like the devil. I would like to put about 20 rounds of canister into their ranks officers and all. Damned hounds" (Peter Hunt to Daniel Hunt, December 16, 1862, EPH).

36. Gaskell to Call, July 26, 1863; Coates, McAfee, and Troiani, *Don Troiani's Regiments*, 229; Lewis to Mother, June 6, 1863.

37. Battery G, Monthly Return, July 1863, RISA.

Chapter 10

1. *Revised Register*, 748; *Narragansett Weekly*, July 9, 1863; George B. Peck, *Camp and Hospital* (Providence: The Society, 1884), 1–10; Battery G, Descriptive Book and Battery G, Monthly Return, August 1863, RISA.

2. George L. Gaskell to Mary Call, August 27, 1863, USAMHI.

3. Barber, Diary, September 9–15, 1863.

4. Barber, Diary, September 30-October 2, 1863.

5. Adams, Service File; William H. Lewis to Mother, September 26, 1863, CSL.

6. *Narragansett Weekly*, June 26, 1862 and July 3, 1862; Shea, "Aspects of Westerly," 37–39.

7. Barber, Diary, October 9–19, 1863; Billings, *Hardtack and Coffee*, 148–149; Lewis to Mother, June 6, 1863.

8. Stevens, *Sixth Corps*, 276–280; William H. Lewis to Mother, October 17, 1863, CSL.

9. Otto L. Torslow, Court-Martial Records, NA.

10. Torslow, Court-Martial; *Revised Regulations*, 486; Battery G, Monthly Returns, October and November 1863, RISA.

11. Torslow, Court-Martial.

12. Torslow, Court-Martial; Barber, Diary, October 28, 1863.

13. Barber, Diary, November 22, 1863; E. Rhodes, *All for the Union*, 112–123; William H. Lewis to Mother, October 29, 1863, CSL; Battery G, Descriptive Book, RISA.

14. Lewis to Mother, October 29, 1863; Burrage, *Brown University*, 369; *Providence Journal*, July 27, 1864; Battery G, Monthly Return, November 1863, RISA.

15. George L. Gaskell to Mary Call, November 20, 1863, USAMHI.

16. Gaskell to Call, November 20, 1863.

17. William H. Lewis to Mother, November 21, 1863, CSL.

18. William H. Lewis to Mother, November 27, 1863, CSL; Gaskell to Call, November 20, 1863; *OR 29,* 796–797; Barber, Diary, November 25, 1863.

19. Martin T. McMahon, "From Gettysburg to the Coming of Grant," in *B&L,* vol. 4, 88–91; *OR 29,* 796–797: 800.

20. *OR 29,* 796–797: 800; Barber, Diary, November 28–30, 1863; Adams, "Battery G," 903; McMahon, "From Gettysburg to Grant," 88–91.

21. McMahon, "From Gettysburg to Grant," 88–91; John F.L Hartwell, *To My Beloved Wife and Boy at Home: The Letters and Diaries of Orderly Sergeant John F L Hartwell,* ed. Ann Hartwell Britton and Thomas J. Read (Madison: Farleigh Dickinson University Press, 1997), 164–165.

22. Barber, Diary, November 30-December 6, 1863; E. Rhodes, *All for the Union,* 125–127.

23. Chenery, *Fourteenth Rhode Island,* George L. Gaskell to Mary Call, November 10, 1863 and April 30, 1864, USAMHI.

24. G. Stevens, *Sixth Corps,* 289–291; Barber, Diary, December 9–18, 1863; Martin T. McMahon to Charles H. Tompkins and Elisha H. Rhodes, December 15, 1863, RIHS; Woodbury, *Second Rhode Island,* 524.

25. Barber, Diary, December 18, 1863.

26. Barber, Diary, December 8, 1863-January 2, 1864; Battery G, Monthly Return, December 1863, RISA. It is evident that Barber maintained a vast wartime diary. The 1862 diary survives at the Providence Public Library, while two volumes covering 1863 and 1864 survive at the Hay Library.

27. Barber, Diary, December 30–31, 1863.

28. Barber, Diary, January 2-February 18, 1864; J. Rhodes, *Battery B,* 52.

29. Battery G, Monthly Return, February 1864, RISA.

30. Patrick Brown, Court-Martial Records, NA; Barber, Diary, March 17, 1864.

31. Battery G, First Rhode Island Light Artillery, Guard Book, NA.

32. William H. Lewis to Mother, March 20, 1864, CSL; Hartwell, *To My Beloved Wife,* 209; J. Chase, *Yours for the Union,* 321–23.

33. E. Rhodes, *All for the Union,* 133–134; Barber, Diary, April 18, 1864; William H. Lewis to Mother, April 26, 1864, CSL.

34. Barber, Diary, April 19-April 30, 1864; Paymaster General of Rhode Island to James A. Barber, April 16, 1864, RISA.

35. Battery G, Monthly Return, April 1864, RISA; Battery G, Morning Report, April 30, 1864, NA.

Chapter 11

1. Charles V. Scott, Pension and Service Files, NA; Monroe, *First Bull Run,* 28–31.

2. Barber, Diary, May 1-May 4, 1864; E. Rhodes, 134–136; *OR 36,* 771.

3. Alexander S. Webb, "Through the Wilderness." *B & L,* vol. 4, 152–153; Hartwell, *To My Beloved Wife,* 221; *OR 36,* 106–116. The Sixth Corps entered the campaign with 22,584 infantry and 900 artillery.

4. J. Chase, *Yours for the Union,* 331–332; Lewis, *Battery E,* 277.

5. Evander M. Law, "From the Wilderness to Cold Harbor," in *B&L,* vol. 4, 118–128; E. Rhodes, *All for the Union,* 135–137; Fisk, *Hard Marching,* 214–221.

6. Warren Wilkinson, *Mother May You Never See the Sights I Have Seen: The Fifty-Seventh Massachusetts Veteran Volunteer Infantry in the Last Year of the Civil War* (New York: Harper Collins, 1990), 66–68; Wilderness Bat-

tle Maps, FRSP; *OR 36,* 753. Barber, Diary, May 5–6, 1864; Hartwell, *To My Beloved Wife,* 222. E. Rhodes, *All for the Union,* 135–141.

7. Law, "Wilderness to Cold Harbor," 127–128; *OR 36,* 754–755; E. Rhodes, *All for the Union,* 141–142.

8. Law, "Wilderness to Cold Harbor,"127–129; Barber, Diary, May 9, 1864.

9. Martin T. McMahon, "The Death of General Sedgwick," in *B&L,* vol. 4, 175; Sedgwick, *Correspondence,* 210–221; Barber, Diary, May 9, 1864; *Memoirs of RI,* 379. Charles Tompkins is placed near General Sedgwick by McMahon's "Death" and a postwar painting by Julian Scott of the Third Vermont that illustrates the colonel beckoning for a stretcher bearer to bring the general to the rear.

10. Law, "Wilderness to Cold Harbor,"127–130; Gregory A. Mertz, "Upton's Attack." *Blue & Gray* (Summer 2001): 12–25; Fisk, *Hard Marching,* 218–222; Barber, Diary, May 11, 1864.

11. Norton Galloway, "Hand-to-hand fighting at Spotsylvania," in *B&L,* vol. 4, 170–174; Fisk, *Hard Marching,* 220–221.

12. Barber, Diary, May 12, 1864.

13. Buell, *The Cannoneer,* 190–191; Fisk, *Hard Marching,* 220–221; E. Rhodes, *All for the Union,* 142–145.

14. Barber, Diary, May 12, 1864; William D. Matter, *If It Takes All Summer: The Battle of Spotsylvania* (Chapel Hill: University of North Carolina Press, 1988), 249–250.

15. Barber, Diary, May 12, 1864; *OR 36,* 756: 771; Fenner, *Battery H,* 54–55; Adams, "Battery G," 903.

16. Battery G, Monthly Return, May 1864, RISA; State of Rhode Island, *Report of the Joint Committee on the Erection of the Monument at Andersonville, GA* (Providence: E.L. Freeman, 1903), 53.

17. Barber, Diary, May 12, 1864.

18. George D. Fenner, Service File, NA; E. Rhodes, *All for the Union,* 146–147; Barber, Diary, May 14–18, 1864; *OR 36,* 756.

19. *OR 36,* 756:772; J. Chase, *Yours for the Union,* 335–337. Barber, Diary, May 14–18, 1864; Battery G, Monthly Return, May 1864, RISA.

20. Barber, Diary, May 18–21, 1864; Law, "Wilderness to Cold Harbor," 134–135.

21. Law, "Wilderness to Cold Harbor," 134–138; *OR 36,* 772; *Providence Journal,* May 10–25, 1864; Charles E. Perkins to Sister, May 29, 1864, USAMHI.

22. *OR 36,* 757; J. Chase, *Yours for the Union,* 337–338; Martin T. McMahon, "Cold Harbor," in *B&L,* vol. 4, 213–217.

23. Barber, Diary, May 31-June 2, 1864. Except for Barber's diary and Captain Adams' reports in the *OR,* not one Battery G soldier recorded what happened during the Overland Campaign.

24. McMahon, "Cold Harbor," 216; Barber, Diary, May 31–June 2, 1864; E. Rhodes, *All for the Union,* 150–153; Battery G, Monthly Return, May 1864, RISA.

25. McMahon, "Cold Harbor," 217–220.

26. *OR 36,* 772; Barber, Diary, June 3–12, 1863; Charles H. Tompkins to Edward C. Mauran, June 4, 1864, RISA; City of Providence to Charles V. Scott, June 15, 1864, RIHS.

27. Barber, Diary, June 3–12, 1863.

28. Barber, Diary, June 17–25, 1864; Pierre G.T. Beauregard, "Four Days of Battle at Petersburg," in *B&L,* vol. 4, 540–44

29. J. Chase, *Yours for the Union,* 343–347; Battery G, Monthly Return, June 1864, RISA; VanDenBossche, *Pleas Excuse,* 190–192; Battery G, Monthly Return, June 1864, RISA.

30. *OR 40,* 514–515: 521; Barber, Diary, June 19–23, 1864.

31. P. Chase, *Battery F,* 37.

32. Daniel C. Stevens and George Wilson, Court-Martial Records, NA.

33. Wilson, Court-Martial.

34. Stevens, Court-Martial.

35. Torslow, Service File; Barber, Diary, June 28, 1864.

36. *OR 40,* 521; G. Stevens, *Sixth Corps,* 367–368.

Chapter 12

1. Jubal Early, "Early's March to Washington in 1864," in *B&L,* vol.4, 492–499; John F. Ward to Mother and Father, June 30, 1864, HAFE.

2. *OR 37,* 282–283; Barber, Diary, July 1864; Battery G, Monthly Return, July 1864, RISA.

3. Lewis, *Battery E,* 339; Buell, *The Cannoneer,* 263–264.

4. G. Stevens, *Sixth Corps,* 372–374; Buell, *The Cannoneer,* 269–271.

5. *OR 37,* 282–283; E. Rhodes, *All for the Union,* 160–163.

6. Buell, *The Cannoneer,* 274–277; VanDenBossche, *Pleas Excuse,* 192–194.

7. *OR 37,* 282–283; Robert J. Trout, *Galloping Thunder: The Stuart Horse Artillery Battalion* (Mechanicsburg, PA: Stackpole Books, 2002), 534–545.

8. *Providence Journal,* July 27, 1864.

9. *OR 37,* 282–283; James B. Ricketts, Third Division, Sixth Corps, Memoranda Book, July 18, 1864, MNB. The Shenandoah River flows north, emptying into the Potomac at Harpers Ferry. Traveling south is therefore called "going up the Valley."

10. John F. Ward to Mother and Father, July 21, 1864, HAFE; Thomas F. Wildes, *Record of the One Hundred and Sixteenth Regiment Ohio Volunteers in the War of the Rebellion* (Sandusky: I.F. Mack, 1884), 129–131; Scott C. Patchan, *Shenandoah Summer: The 1864 Valley Campaign* (Lincoln: University of Nebraska Press, 2007), 60–89. This battle is sometimes referred to in the Federal record as the Battle of Snicker's Gap. However, most sources cite it as Cool Spring and that name is used here. Today the Cool Spring Battlefield is open to the public and preserved by a peaceful group of Cistercian Monks in Berryville, Virginia. An interesting note is that the order began in Cumberland, Rhode Island, and was forced to relocate due to a fire in the 1950s.

11. Peter J. Meaney, *The Civil War Engagement at Cool Spring, July 18, 1864: The Largest Battle Ever Fought in Clark County, Virginia* (Berryville, VA: Meaney, 1979), 32–33. As was the case with every battle fought by Battery G, this author has visited and walked each site and can attest to the difficulty in bringing artillery up this ridge. He firmly believes that while history is past, it can still be experienced by walking the ground; and it is absolutely necessary for a writer to do so, so he can better understand exactly what the participants recorded.

12. *Memoirs of RI,* 415–416; *Providence Journal,* July 27, 1864. It is interesting to note that the *Providence Journal* reported on Battery G only a dozen times during the war. Only four letters were sent directly to the paper, while the others, such as this piece, were picked up from Washington and New York papers and later reprinted in the *Journal.* No Battery G soldier makes reference to writing to the *Journal* and the letters received were anonymous, thus making any identification of the writer impossible. Albert Cordner wrote frequently to Westerly's *Narragansett Weekly,* but they never carried any of his stories. The only Battery G letter in that paper was one written by George L. Gaskell to a friend in Westerly; added to this were only two brief reports from Marye's Heights and Cedar Creek.

13. William C. Walker, *History of the Eighteenth Connecticut Volunteers in the War for the Union* (Norwich: Gordon Wilcox, 1886), 286–288; Ricketts, Memoranda Book, July 18, 1864; E. Rhodes, *All for the Union,* 165–169; Bowen, *Thirty-Seventh Mass Volunteers,* 362–364.

14. Adams, "Battery G," 904; Geier and Potter, *Archaeological Perspectives,* 73–93; *OR 37,* 283; Wildes, *One Hundred and Sixteenth,* 131; Hartwell, *To My Beloved Wife,* 257. Just as they did at the dig at the Piper Farm at Antietam, archaeologists have located shell fragments fired from Battery G's position on the east bank of the Shenandoah within the Confederate positions on the left bank. This evidence, combined with the sources recorded by the soldiers, makes it more than clear that the artillery fire from Battery G was working as it should have been, supporting the efforts of Ricketts and Thoburn. While it is very important to have the direct sources of the soldiers who were present, the archaeological record adds another important factor by providing physical evidence for the historical record; the two complement each other in unbreakable support of the author's thesis that field artillery had developed into the offensive weapon. The monks at the monastery where Cool Spring is located maintain a small collection of artifacts they have found over the years, including numerous pieces of burst Hotchkiss shell. It could have come from only one source: Battery G, First Rhode Island Light Artillery.

15. Patchan, *Shenandoah Summer,* 87–104; Haines, *Fifteenth New Jersey,* 229–230. Even though the Rhode Islanders saved the day during the daylight hours, at night it became a bit of an annoyance for some Federal soldiers who were trying to rest amid the cannonade and the occasion picket shot as the artillery rounds overflew the ridge Battery G was stationed on and landed in a field to the rear of the hill. Chaplain Edward M. Haynes of the Tenth Vermont wrote, "The scene closed for the night with an artillery dual conducted from two commanding ridges on opposite banks of the river, very much to the annoyance of our infantry which had been dropped into an open field stretching back behind the ridge occupied by our batteries" (Edward M. Haynes, *A History of the Tenth Regiment Vermont Volunteers* (Lewiston, ME: Journal Steam Press, 1870),90–92).

16. Meaney, *Cool Spring,* 32. This author has carefully reviewed a dozen sources from Union infantrymen who fought at Cool Spring, from both Thoburn's men on the west bank of the Shenandoah and those of the Sixth Corps who did not cross. All of these sources are unanimous in one regard: without the support of Batteries C and G, First Rhode Island Light Artillery, Thoburn's Division would have been crushed and driven into the Shenandoah River. It was only because of the timely arrival of the guns that the battle did not become a crushing defeat for the Federal army. The best correlation for what Battery G was able to accomplish at Cool Spring is the 1965 Battle of the Ia Drang Valley in Vietnam. In circumstances very similar to Thoburn's, a small American platoon was cut off and surrounded by the North Vietnamese. They were able to stay alive only because the artillery was used as an offensive shield to keep the enemy at bay and allow a relief mission to reach the survivors. This is dramatized with remarkable historical accuracy in the 2000 film *We Were Soldiers.*

17. Charles E. Perkins to Sister, July 30, 1864, US-AMHI.

18. E. Rhodes, *All for the Union,* 165–169; J. Chase, *Yours for the Union,* 160–163; *Memoirs of RI,* 415.

19. J. Chase, *Yours for the Union,* 357–363; Battery G, Monthly Return, August 1864, RISA; Battery G, Clothing Book, RIHS; *OR 36,* 771–772: *37,* 282: *40,* 521. During the war it was very rare for an officer to receive a brevet promotion as quickly as Scott did. Oftentimes it would get bogged down in senate committees and would not reach

the secretary of war's desk for some time; brevets were awarded by the federal government, not the state. Most brevet promotions did not come until 1865, when every officer in the Union Army who wanted one could apply "for gallant and meritorious services" performed during the war. There is no indication that any Battery G officer ever applied for one of these promotions; every brevet awarded to a member of Battery G came as a result of bravery in combat, not political favor. Scott's actions during his first thirty days in Battery G must have been of tremendous consequence, as his first brevet came so quickly. No image of Scott survives as an officer, just an 1862 image as a private in Battery A. See Gibbon, *Personal Recollections,* 371–377.

20. William H. Lewis to Mother, August 28, 1864, CSL.

21. Phisterer, *New York in the War of the Rebellion,* 355–356: 358; George Perkins, *Three Years a Soldier: The Diary and Newspaper Correspondence of Private George Perkins, Sixth New York Independent Battery, 1861–1864,* ed. Richard N. Griffin (Knoxville: University of Tennessee Press, 2006), 273: 380–381; Barber, Diary, August 9: 13–16, 1864. The men from the Tenth New York Battery had been transferred to the Fifth New York, Fifth Massachusetts, and Rhode Island Batteries C and G. The first detachments reported back to Washington and the Sixth New York Battery in June, while those from Battery G were the last to depart. The Sixth would fight in the Shenandoah as part of the Cavalry Corps.

22. Barber, Diary, August 9:13–16, 1864; Battery G, Monthly Return, August and September 1864, RISA; Peleg D. Tucker, Bounty Records, courtesy of Mike Stewart.

Chapter 13

1. John F. Ward to Father and Mother, July 29, August 10, and August 27, 1864, HAFE.

2. Wesley Merritt, "Sheridan in the Shenandoah Valley," in *B&L,* vol. 4, 503–510.

3. Hartwell, *To My Beloved Wife,* 286–290; Aldace F. Walker, *The Vermont Brigade in the Shenandoah Valley, 1864* (Burlington: Free Press Association, 1869), 103–104. This battle is also referred to as Third Winchester by Confederate sources. Some Federal commanders initially referred to it by that name as well. In order to separate it from the previous two battles near the city, which were both Federal defeats, Sheridan issued orders in December 1864 that the engagement would be named Opequon and this was what commanders were to paint on their colors. Following the National Park process of naming battles after the winner, and the fact that "Opequon" was inscribed on Battery G's guidon, this author will call the engagement Opequon.

4. *OR 43,* 149–153: 271–272; Walker, *Vermont Brigade,* 103–104; Frank M. Flinn, *Campaigning with Banks in Louisiana, '63 and '64, and with Sheridan in the Shenandoah Valley in '64 and '65* (Boston: W.B. Clarke, 1889), 183–185.

5. *OR 43,* 149–153: 271–272; *Memoirs of RI,* 380.

6. Thomas J. Watkins, Reminiscences, courtesy of Scott C. Patchan.

7. Barber, Diary, September 19, 1864.

8. *OR 43,* 149–153: 271–272; Barber, Diary, September 19, 1864.

9. Paul Mathless, ed., *Shenandoah, 1864* (Richmond: Time Life Books, 1998), 94.

10. Flinn, *Campaigning,* 188–191.

11. *OR 43,* 149–153: 271–272; Barber, Diary, September 19, 1864.

12. Barber, Diary, September 20–22, 1864; Merritt, "Sheridan in the Shenandoah," 510–513.

13. Scott C. Patchan, "Fisher's Hill," *Blue & Gray* (Winter 2008), 22–26, 43–45; Barber, Diary, September 22, 1864.

14. Fisk, *Hard Marching,* 257–260.

15. Hartwell, *To My Beloved Wife,* 287–290; Barber, Diary, September 22, 1864. It has been written that only one out of every fifteen shells actually worked properly in combat. Judging by both accounts, it would appear that Battery G's were working properly at Fisher's Hill. Indeed, throughout its service, the record would seem to indicate that this statement is somewhat false, as much of Battery G's ordnance, as has been seen, worked properly in combat.

16. Barber, Diary, September 22, 1864; *OR 43,* 153–157: 271–273: 277–279; George W. Getty to Charles A. Whittier, October 1, 1864, Getty Papers, LOC.

17. *OR 43,* 153–157: 271–273: 277–279; Battery G, Morning Report, September 22, 1864, NA;J . Chase, *Yours for the Union,* 363–365.

18. Barber, Diary, September 23–27, 1864; *Memoirs of RI,* 380–381.

19. Barber, Diary, September 23–27, 1864; George W. Adams to Charles V. Scott, September 27, 1864, RIHS.

20. Kris VanDenBossche, ed., *Write Soon and Give Me All the News* (Peace Dale, RI: Rhode Island Historical Document Transcription Project, 1993), 262–263.

21. Barber, Diary, September 25-October 14, 1864; George C. Sumner, *Battery D, First Rhode Island Light Artillery, in the Civil War, 1861–1865* (Providence: Rhode Island Print Company, 1897), 141–142.

22. *OR 43,* 156–157; J. Chase, *Yours for the Union,* 367–369.

23. Merritt, "Sheridan in the Shenandoah," 513–517; Barber, Diary, October 15–18, 1864; Buell, *The Cannoneer,* 283.

24. Merritt, "Sheridan in the Shenandoah," 516–521; Barber, Diary, October 19, 1864; John K. Bucklyn, *Battle of Cedar Creek* (Providence: Sydney S. Ryder, 1883), 1–13; Elmer L. Corthell to Edward C. Mauran, December 9, 1864, RISA; Charles E. Perkins to Sister, October 20, 1864, USAMHI.

25. Scott C. Patchan, "Cedar Creek," *Blue and Gray* (Summer 2007), 40–41.

26. Patchan, "Cedar Creek," *Blue and Gray* (Summer 2007), 40–41; *OR 43,* 276–278; Edwin Hobson, Report of Cedar Creek, CCB.

27. Henry Seamans to Mrs. Lewis, October 21 and November 30, 1864, CSL.

28. Bucklyn, *Cedar Creek,* 11–13; G. Stevens, *Sixth Corps,* 419–420; Thomas W. Bicknell, *A History of Barrington, Rhode Island* (Providence: Snow and Farnum, 1898), 507; Barber, Diary, October 19, 1864.

29. *Narragansett Weekly,* November 10, 1864; Abijah P. Marvin, *History of Winchendon* (Winchendon, MA: N.P., 1868), 506. The most logical conclusion is that the Chace's were originally from Winchendon, Massachusetts, and moved to Westerly in the years before the war. Nathaniel Chace stayed there the rest of his life. If a soldier was originally from another place but died in the service in another state, a memorial notice was usually carried where he originated.

30. Buell, *The Cannoneer,* 300–301; *Narragansett Weekly,* November 10, 1864; Scott, Service File. There is contention as to which Sisson brother was the sergeant. Most sources, including both government and personal, identify him as Alexander Sisson, not Charles. The misidentification is easy to understand, as there were few identical twins at this time and even fewer who served in the same battery. Based on the strong evidence, it was Alexander; this author has decided to refer to him as being the sergeant and his brother, Charles, as a private.

31. *Providence Journal,* October 24, 1864; *Memoirs of RI,* 381–382.

32. Adams, "Battery G," 904; *Narragansett Weekly*, November 10, 1864; Hazard Stevens, "The Battle of Cedar Creek: October 19, 1864," *Civil War Papers Read before the Commandery of the State of Massachusetts, Military Order of the Loyal Legion of the United States*, vol. 1 (Boston: E.H. Gilson, 1900), 206–207.

33. Isaac O. Best, *History of the 121st New York State Infantry* (Chicago: James H. Smith, 1921), 193–198; *Memoirs of RI*, 381–382; John D. Ingraham to Parents, October 23, 1864, CCB; Hartwell, *To My Beloved Wife*, 298–300; Barber, Diary, October 19, 1864; *Memoirs of RI*, 382. According to Ingraham, the One Hundred and Twenty-First lost fifty men in their stand.

34. Barber, Diary, October 19, 1864; Bucklyn, *Cedar Creek*, 13–15; G. Stevens, *Sixth Corps*, 419; Haines, *History of the Fifteenth New Jersey*, 276–278.

35. Benjamin F. Cobb, "My Last Battle," CCB.

36. Hobson, Cedar Creek Report, CCB; Frederick D. Bidwell, *History of the Forty-Ninth New York Volunteers* (Albany: J.B. Lyon, 1916), 74–76; *Narragansett Weekly*, November 10, 1864.

37. Buell, *The Cannoneer*, 306. In both Buell and Best's *121st New York*, the authors mention Battery C, First Rhode Island Light Artillery, as the ones being overrun. Battery G was engaged right near Battery C and the topography described by both fits the route Battery G used in their retreat. In addition, Battery C suffered only three dead and twenty wounded compared to Adams' Battery's massive casualties. While these authors have mentioned Lamb's Battery C, this author has fit it into the narrative of Battery G, as they fought side by side and the narrative is the same.

38. Bilby, *Three Rousing Cheers*, 206–207; *Memoirs of RI*, 381–382: 416.

39. Bucklyn, *Cedar Creek*, 16–20; Barber, Diary, October 19, 1864. Sheridan would be celebrated in poem, song, and painting for his "ride" on his black horse, Rienzi, from Winchester to Cedar Creek. Both Wright and Sheridan deserve credit for their performances in re-forming the line at Cedar Creek. Without the Sixth Corps' desperate early stand, the entire line would have collapsed. Unfortunately, since Wright commanded only the corps and not the army, he received hardly any credit for what he did. Wright could not, however, re-form the entire line, as his men were spent and needed motivation to go in again. Sheridan's actions were re-forming the shattered force, reorganizing it, and ordering the counterattack. His appearance was electrifying to many Federal soldiers. For further discussion of the argument, see Eric J. Wittenberg, *Little Phil: A Reassessment of the Civil War Leadership of General Phillip H Sheridan* (Washington: Brassey's, 2002), 75–78.

40. *Memoirs of RI*, 381–382; H. Stevens, "Cedar Creek," 230–231; Buell, *The Cannoneer*, 301–302. Buell writes that Battery G went into action at 2:30. Since 3:00 is the most quoted time of Sheridan's counterattack, this author has decided to use the latter time.

41. Bucklyn, *Cedar Creek*, 20–23; Barber, Diary, October 19, 1864.

42. *Memoirs of RI*, 381–382: 416; *George W Adams*, 6; Buell, *The Cannoneer*, 306; *The Union Army: A History of Military Affairs in the Loyal States, 1861–65; Records of the Regiments in the Union Army-Cyclopedia of Battles-Memoirs of Commanders and Soldiers*, vol. 1, *Maine, New Hampshire, Vermont, Massachusetts, Rhode Island, Connecticut, Pennsylvania, and Delaware* (Wilmington, NC: Broadfoot Publishing, 1997), 254.

43. Lewis, Service File; Seamans to Mrs. Lewis, October 21 and November 30, 1864. The elaborate jacket of William H. Lewis is now housed at the Pamplin Park Museum in Petersburg, Virginia. He remains buried at Winchester National Cemetery.

44. Battery G, Morning Report, October 20, 1864, NA; Simeon Starboard, Service File, NA; Charles Tompkins to Edward C. Mauran, November 14, 1864, RISA; *The Medical and Surgical History of the War of the Rebellion*, vol. 2 (Washington: Government Printing Office, 1883), 295.

45. Battery G, Morning Report, October 20, 1864, NA; Simeon Tompkins to Mauran, November 14, 1864. The casualty figures, as they are throughout this entire volume, are based on the author's research in the National Archives, soldiers' letters, newspaper reports, and casualty returns. Battery B suffered the highest regimental loss at Gettysburg, followed by G at Cedar Creek, Battery A at Gettysburg, and Battery D at Antietam. Contrary to popular belief, 95 percent of Civil War surgeries were done using anesthesia.

46. *Providence Journal*, October 24, 1864 and October 27, 1864; *Narragansett Weekly*, October 27, 1864, and November 10, 1864; J. Chase, *Yours for the Union*, 369–72. It is clear that Captain Adams was a prodigious letter writer, writing constantly to the Rhode Island adjutant general and writing his official reports. Unfortunately, only a half dozen of his after-action reports survive today in the *OR*. Most disappointing for the researcher is that those from Marye's Heights, Cedar Creek, and the Assault on Petersburg are missing. This author was very fortunate to find, while examining Henry Hunt's papers at the Library of Congress, Adams' original May 8, 1863, report for the Chancellorsville Campaign, which was not in the *OR*. A possible reason for the missing Cedar Creek report is that Battery G had been so chewed up in the fighting one was never written; or it was sent to a different department because the command was operating outside the parameters of the Army of the Potomac, where such reports, normally to General Hunt, were usually sent. Either way, James Barber's accounts of the battle are the only direct, firsthand account from a Battery G veteran.

47. *Narragansett Weekly*, November 10, 1864; Abijah P. Marvin, *History of Winchendon* (Winchendon, MA: N.P., 1868), 506. The most logical conclusion is that the Chaces were originally from Winchendon, Massachusetts, and moved to Westerly in the years before the war. Nathaniel Chace stayed there the rest of his life. If a soldier was originally from another place, but died in the service in another state, a memorial notice was usually carried where he originated.

48. Tompkins to Mauran, November 14, 1864. There are very few monuments to Union forces in the Shenandoah Valley today, with the exception of those to Vermont, Massachusetts, New Hampshire, and Connecticut at the Winchester National Cemetery. In 1891 a group of veterans from the Sixth Corps as a whole dedicated a monument in the cemetery to honor the Sixth Corps service in the Valley. Nearby are the graves of the Rhode Island men who fell fighting in 1864.

49. Barber, Diary, October 20–24, 1864; J. Rhodes, *Battery B*, 284: 353.

50. *Memoirs of RI*, 416–417.

51. Barber, Diary, October 27-November 2, 1864. There is evidence from a number of sources that this resolution was passed. However, the original is not on file at the Rhode Island State Archives or the state library in the state house.

52. *Providence Journal*, September 28, October 25, November 7, and November 8, 1864. These are all letters from Rhode Island soldiers urging the people of the state to vote for Lincoln. Barber, Diary, November 2–November 9, 1864. *Narragansett Weekly*, November 17, 1864.

53. Barber, Diary, December 31, 1864; Battery G, Morning Report, November 15, 1864, NA; J. Chase, *Yours for the Union*, 373–378.

54. E. Rhodes, *All for the Union*, 186–191; Barber, Diary, November 26, 1864; Seamans to Mrs. Lewis, November 30, 1864.

55. Battery G, Monthly Return, November 1864, RISA; James E. Taylor, *With Sheridan up the Shenandoah Valley in 1864* , ed. Dennis E. Frye (Dayton: Morningside, 1989), 583–586.

Chapter 14

1. Barber, Diary, December 8–10, 1864.
2. *Narragansett Weekly,* September 1, 1864; J. Rhodes, *Battery B,* 316–322; Barber, Diary, December 15–20, 1864. Adams was very fortunate that the consolidation went smoothly. In October, when the Fourth and Seventh Rhode Island Regiments were consolidated, the men from the Fourth nearly mutinied rather than serve in the Seventh and had to be kept under close guard. Many of the veterans never considered themselves members of the Seventh and continued to refer to themselves as the Fourth Rhode Island.
3. Jacob Lamb to Charles E. Bailey, December 19, 1864, RISA; VanDenBossche, *Write Soon,* 262–263; Special Orders 464, December 23, 1864, RISA.
4. John B. Peck, "Battery C, First Rhode Island Light Artillery," in *Revised Register of Rhode Island Volunteers* (Providence: E.L. Freeman, 1893), 791–797; Peter Hunt to Brother, July 4, 1862, EPH; *Revised Register,* vol. 1, 748–749.
5. Battery G, Monthly Return, December 1864, RISA; Battery G, General Orders 49 and 50, NA; Barber, Diary, December 28, 1864.
6. *Revised Register,* 810; Hopkins Hollow Cemetery, Coventry, RI. William Rice died in 1872.
7. Battery G, Monthly Return, December 1864, RISA; Barber, Diary, December 28, 1864; Battery G, General Orders 49 and 50, NA. Private Henry Clarkin was an Irish immigrant who lived in Warwick and had been transferred from Battery C to G. He was one of the defiant ones, and in death he still claimed allegiance to Battery C. On his headstone in West Warwick's St. Mary's Cemetery, Clarkin is listed as being a member of Battery C, not G. This too is rare, as few Catholic soldiers recorded their regimental information on their headstone.
8. Batteries C and G, First Rhode Island Light Artillery, Muster Rolls in regard to Special Orders 464, December 23, 1864, RISA; Reuben H. Rich, Pension File, NA.
9. Lewis, *Battery E,* 439–442; Walker, *Vermont Brigade,* 118.
10. Batteries C and G, First Rhode Island Light Artillery, Muster Rolls in regard to Special Orders 464, December 23, 1864, RISA.
11. Jacob Lamb to James Y. Smith, November 19, 1864, RISA.
12. Torslow, Pension and Service File; State of Rhode Island, *Acts and Resolves of the General Assembly of the State of Rhode Island and Providence Plantations, January Session, 1865* (Providence: H.H. Thomas, 1865), 280–281. Based on Torslow's casualty sheet and information from the Providence papers, this author believes Torslow's wounds were not life threatening but he inflated their severity to get more pension money. His heavy drinking and fall from his horse at Warrenton were greater injuries than the Marye's Heights wound.
13. Scott and Lewis, Pension Files; Seamans to Mrs. Lewis, November 30, 1864; Irene P. Williams, "William H. Lewis," November 19, 1864, CSL. This poem was found among Lewis' letters at the Connecticut State Library.
14. *Memoirs of RI,* 417.
15. Scott, Service File; *Medical and Surgical History,* vol. 12, 511; Samuel F. Chaefin to Charles V. Scott, February 1, 1865, RIHS. This letter was never received by Scott and was forwarded to his mother (Grace Church Cemetery Records, PPL; *Providence Journal,* January 21-February 1, 1865); *Memoirs of RI*). Scott is recorded to have been buried in Grace Church Cemetery, but no headstone was recorded by James N. Arnold in his 1904 survey of Rhode Island graves, nor was one found on numerous trips by this author.

Chapter 15

1. Adams, "Battery G," 905; E. Rhodes, *All for the Union,* 197–199.
2. Battery G, Monthly Return, January 1865, RISA; Albert C. Durfee, Pension File, NA.
3. E. Rhodes, *All for the Union,* 201–208; J. Chase, *Yours for the Union,* 393–394.
4. *Revised Register,* 958–992; Lewis, *Battery E,* 500–549; Battery G, Monthly Return, March 1865, RISA.
5. E. Rhodes, *All for the Union,* 211–214; George W. Adams to Edward C. Mauran, March 31, 1865, RISA. Sullivan is still buried at Poplar Grove National Cemetery near Petersburg, Virginia.
6. George G. Benedict, *Vermont in the Civil War,* vol. 1 (Burlington: Free Press Association, 1888), 574–579; G. Stevens, *Sixth Corps,* 430–432.
7. Hazard Stevens, *The Storming of the Lines of Petersburg by the Sixth Corps, April 2, 1865* (Providence: Snow and Farnum, 1904), 12–18; Benedict, *Vermont Civil War,* 585–587.
8. *OR 46,* 901–905; *Memoirs of RI,* 417; *History of Providence County, Rhode Island,* vol. 1, ed. Richard M. Bayles (New York: W.W. Preston, 1891), 243–246. Whether he knew it or not, what Captain Adams attempted to do had already been accomplished once in American military history. During Washington's December 26, 1776, attack against Trenton, a small force of American artillerymen followed a battalion of Virginians in the vanguard of the assault. It was almost exactly what Battery G was ordered to accomplish at Petersburg in April of 1865, almost a century later. According to David Hackett Fischer, "These men [of 1776] went into battle armed with drag ropes, handspikes, and hammers. Their orders were to seize the Hessian cannon at the start of the battle and turn them against the enemy. If this plan failed, their job was to disable the Hessian guns by driving iron handspikes into the touch holes and breaking them flush with the gun tube" (David Hackett Fischer, *Washington's Crossing* (New York: Oxford University Press, 2004), 223–225, 244–246). In addition, Fischer makes it very clear that during the battle the Americans used their small smoothbore cannon as an offensive weapon against the Hessians. Firing muskets was impossible in the snowstorm, so the three batteries that Washington brought with him provided his only firepower and were able to overwhelm the German defenders. This information is critical because it proves artillery was used as an offensive weapon during the Revolution and Mexican Wars, but was lost in the decades leading up to the Civil War, only to be discovered during the current conflict by intelligent officers, such as George W. Adams who knew how to work their guns.
9. *OR 46,* 1009–1011; State of Rhode Island, *Annual Report of the Adjutant General of the State of Rhode Island for the Year 1865* (Providence: Providence Press, 1866), 776; Thomas W. Hyde, *Following the Greek Cross, or Memories of the Sixth Army Corps* (Boston: Houghton Mifflin, 1894), 249–252. The *Providence Journal* of April 28, 1865, gives the names of seventeen of the men who volunteered for the charge. They were Sergeants John Havron and Archibald Malbourne, and Corporals James A. Barber, Henry Griffith, Samuel E. Lewis, and Henry Randall. The privates were James Callahan, John Corcoran, Charles D.

Ennis, William P. Franklin, Carl Guhl, John P. Kronke, Henry Krull, George W. Potter, William F. Short, James A. Taft, and Horace B. Tanner. There are two different listings in print identifying the men who followed Adams. The original was printed in the *Providence Journal* on April 28, 1865, and was later reprinted in the *1865 Adjutant General's Report*, but not in the *Revised Register of Rhode Island Volunteers*. Both of these lists contain seventeen names, the number identified by Adams. In his 1892 history of Battery E, George Lewis names twenty men. The other privates are listed as Luther Cornell, German Potter, Cornelius Ryan, and Henry Seamans. It is known that twenty men were called for, but three left right before the assault began. James Callahan could not have gone forward, because he died at Andersonville after being captured at Spotsylvania. The only other Callahan in Battery G, Private Michael Callahan, was mustered out with the original members in December 1864. The name of Luther Cornell is on Lewis' list only; however both Adams and Andrew Cowan wrote that two privates were wounded during the charge. George W. Potter was one of them; the only other private wounded that day was Luther Cornell. Therefore this author has decided to follow conventional wisdom and add Cornell's name to the list of those who went. The most probable explanation is that German Potter and Cornelius Ryan, like Seamans, backed out at the last moment and returned to Fort Fisher. This is not to say that they were not brave soldiers, they just decided not to go forward into the jaws of hell.

10. Charles H. Anson, "Assault of the Lines of Petersburg, April 2d, 1865." *War Papers Read before the Commandery of the State of Wisconsin, Military Order of the Loyal Legion of the United States*, vol. 1 (Milwaukee: Burdick, Armitage & Allen, 1891), 86–87; Fenner, *Battery H*, 103.

11. *OR 46*, 901–905; Hyde, *Greek Cross*, 249–252; H. Stevens, *Storming the Lines*, 19–21; A. Wilson, Greene, *Breaking the Backbone of the Rebellion: The Final Battles of the Petersburg Campaign* (Mason City, IA: Savas, 2000), 259.

12. Hyde, *Greek Cross*, 249–252; Anson, "Assault on Petersburg," 88–91; *The Sixth Corps*, May 11, 1865; Hazard Stevens, "Storming of the Lines at Petersburg," *The Shenandoah Campaigns of 1862 and 1864 and the Appomattox Campaign, 1865* (Boston: Military Historical Society of Massachusetts, 1907), 421–422.

13. *OR 46*, 901–905; Hyde, *Greek Cross*, 249–252; H. Stevens, *Storming the Lines*, 19–21; E. Rhodes, *All for the Union*, 216–218; Beyer, and Keydel, *Deeds of Valor*, 515–516.

14. Elisha Potter to Lieutenant Phillips, April 8, 1865; Hunt Papers, LOC; VanDenBossche, *Pleas Excuse*, 197–99.

15. John P. Campbell to Mary Campbell, April 15, 1865, USAMHI; G. Stevens, *Sixth Corps*, 434–436.

16. Anson, "Assault on Petersburg," 91–92; Greene, *Breaking the Backbone*, 259; Benedict, *Vermont Civil War*, 585–590, 593–596. After the war, General Grant and Colonel Hyde would fume constantly over which brigade had been given the honor of being the point of the spear to pierce the Confederate line. It is not known which was given the honor; but Lewis Grant had much to do with the planning and execution of the mission, and his Vermonters were always at the front. In the end, both commanders' arguments proved true, as both brigades were in the middle of the Sixth Corps' line and both leading regiments struck at the same time. In either case, Battery G was to follow the leading regiment and then strike after the parapet was clear.

17. Robert Driver, *The 1st and 2nd Rockbridge Artillery* (Lynchburg, VA: H.E. Howard, 1987), 120–123; Wise, *Long Arm*, vol. 2, 913, 917; Hazlett, Olmstead, and Parks, *Field Artillery Weapons*, 182–190; James H. Lane, "Defence of Fort Gregg," *SHSP* 3 (1887), 19–22. The Rockbridge Artillery was the only unit in this sector of the line using twenty-four pound howitzers. This type of gun is identified by Beyer and Keydel but is mistaken as a "twenty-four pound Napoleon." The Rockbridge Artillery had three of these weapons. Wise writes that howitzers were stationed at intervals along the line. Captain Elisha Wales of the Second Vermont attacked a redoubt to the right of the ravine, capturing four pieces, while Sperry's party captured two—the twenty-four pound howitzers taken over by Adams' men.

18. Benedict, *Vermont Civil War*, 585–597; Greene, *Breaking the Backbone*, 300–301; Driver, *Rockbridge Artillery*, 120–123; Robert Pratt to Sydney Pratt, April 9, 1865, and Robert Pratt, Diary, April 2, 1865 (both courtesy of Tom Ledoux). Pratt wrote that he entered the works at 5:04, which would indicate it took nearly twenty-four minutes to cross the 800 yards between the two lines. The actions of Battery G occurred sometime after this; but, as will be seen, Wright reported the trenches secured at 5:30 am, which would have allowed Battery G only twenty-six minutes to perform its deed. Gould would be recognized as the first Union soldier to enter the Confederate works and would later be awarded the Medal of Honor.

19. *OR 46*, 969–970: 973; Linda M. Welch, "Major William Sperry"; R.G. Benedict, *Vermont Civil War*, 585–597; Beyer and Keydel, *Deeds of Valor*, 518–519.

20. Jean Barber to Author, September 2, 2007; Benedict, *Vermont Civil War*, 585–590: 593–596; Anson, "Assault on Petersburg," 95–96; Greene, *Breaking the Backbone*, 284; *OR 46*, 1,010. Unfortunately, Major Sperry's papers and his Medal of Honor were lost in a flood in Cavendish, Vermont, in the 1920s. The incident that he took part in has appeared reprinted in various accounts in at least a half dozen works. All of them say Sperry was "relieved by a section of artillery." It is very clear that this is the storming party from Battery G, as there were a section of men and they followed the Green Mountain Boys in their charge against Lane's position.

21. Luther Cornell, Pension File, NA; George W. Potter, Medal of Honor File, NA.

22. Fisk, *Hard Marching*, 320–323; H. Stevens, *Storming the Lines*, 25–28; *Narragansett Weekly*, April 20, 1865; *OR 46*, 903–905; Jeffrey D. Marshall, ed., *A War of the People: Vermont Civil War Letters* (Hanover, NH: University Press of New England, 1999), 298–300. Some of these other captured guns were also turned back on the enemy by the other soldiers of the Vermont Brigade. One of these was done by a band of Vermonters in the Third Division, Sixth Corps. The men in Battery G were the only trained artillerists who went forward with the assaulting column. Private Edwin C. Hall of the Tenth Vermont wrote, "At the 2d fort we captured 6 guns which were turned on the 'retreating Jons.'" Hall's statements seem to fit a recurring pattern that the cannon were only briefly used; instead the infantry relied upon the musket, while Battery G remained with their captured pieces.

23. Hyde, *Greek Cross*, 252–255; Beyer and Keydel, *Deeds of Valor*, 515–516.

24. *Memoirs of RI*, 417; Glenn Laxton, "The Seven," unpublished manuscript; Beyer and Keydel, 515–516. The actions of Battery G are recorded in a dozen sources. Unfortunately again, none of them are in exact chronological order to describe the exact actions and movements of Captain Adams and the cannoneers that morning. Based on all available information, the author has presented the actions of the men in the most logical order that could be ascertained. None of the information conflicts with any other, but rather flows smoothly to create the narrative of the morning's events.

25. Adams, "Battery G," 405.

26. James A. Barber, John Corcoran, Charles D. Ennis,

John H. Havron, Samuel E. Lewis, Archibald Malbourne, George W. Potter, Service Files, NA; Henry S. Burrage, *Civil War Record of Brown University* (Providence: Brown University, 1920), 47; George W. Potter, Student File, HL; Greene, *Breaking the Backbone,* 324. Malbourne's name is often erroneously misspelled as Molbone.

27. Rhode Island Medal of Honor Citations, RISA.

28. James A. Barber, John Corcoran, Charles D. Ennis, John H. Havron, Samuel E. Lewis, Archibald Malbourne, George W. Potter, Medal of Honor Files, NA; Robert H. George, "Their Caissons Kept Rolling Along," unpublished manuscript; HL, 4; Beyer and Keydel, *Deeds of Valor,* 515–516; *OR 46,* 257; *Revised Register,* 995. The same citation was used for each soldier. Unfortunately Captain Adams' original report of the incident does not exist; neither does his report from Cedar Creek. They are not at the Library of Congress or the National Archives. Contrary to popular belief, not every Civil War report was published in the *OR.* This author found Adams' report from Marye's Heights among the Hunt Papers at the Library of Congress. The closest estimate for the same number of medals that Battery G received were Victoria Medals (Britain's highest award for valor) awarded to the thirteen men from B Company, Second Battalion, Twenty-Fourth Regiment of Foot, at the 1879 Battle of Rourke's Drift, South Africa. The second highest number of medals awarded to a battery during the Civil War went to the Chicago Mercantile Battery on May 22, 1863, when six men were awarded the Medal of Honor during Grant's initial storming of Vicksburg, Mississippi. A gun detachment and some attached infantry dragged a six-pound gun up a steep ravine and began firing point blank into a Confederate fort. The charge failed, but the cannoneers were awarded medals for their bravery. Like Battery G, more men were nominated but only six received it. Battery G's record of seven Medals of Honor still stands as the most awarded during the war to one unit for one battle. For more information, see Richard B. Williams, *Chicago's Battery Boys: The Chicago Mercantile Battery in the Civil War's Western Theatre* (El Dorado Hills, CA: Savas Beattie, 2005), 113–121.

29. Beyer and Keydel, *Deeds of Valor.* Besides the seven Rhode Islanders and Major Sperry and Captain Gould of Vermont, Sergeant Jackson Sargent of the Fifth Vermont was awarded the Medal for carrying the regimental colors of the Fifth into the earthwork.

30. *OR 46,* 902: 1,010; Adams, "Battery G," 905; *Providence Journal,* April 8, 1865, and April 28, 1865.

31. *The Sotry of American Heroism: Thrilling Narratives of Personal Adventures During the Great Civil War, as Told by the Medal Winners and Roll of Honor Men* (New Haven: Butler & Alger, 1896), 616. Clearly Potter is wrong, as Adams received his brevet majority for actions at Cedar Creek and the rank was confirmed in November of 1864. As Adams was quick to add a pair of colonel's shoulder straps, he most likely adopted the double-breasted frock coat and gold oak leaves of a major at this time, while still serving as the captain of Battery G. This was an accepted and common practice during the war that brought with it great confusion. A famous example is George Armstrong Custer. At the time of his death at the Little Big Horn, he held four separate ranks. He was a full rank lieutenant colonel in the Regular Army, but he also had a Regular brevet colonelcy. In addition, he still held the rank of brigadier and brevet major general of volunteers and was addressed at this rank. Adams ended the war as a full-ranked major, with a brevet of colonel. He was addressed as Colonel Adams in most texts, while his battery was always referred to as "Adams' Battery." This author has found no material on Adams using his full rank of major, as he held the commission for only twelve days before mustering out of the service and the rank of brevet colo-

nel was the highest rank he achieved. For the most part, this author has refrained from this common practice and refers to him throughout the text as Captain Adams.

32. *Memoirs of RI,* 417. Adams' only surviving Civil War image shows him wearing the rank of brevet colonel.

33. Greene, *Breaking the Backbone,* 324; Campbell to Campbell, April 15, 1865; *Providence Press,* April 24, 1865; George B. Peck, *A Recruit Before Petersburg* (Providence: N. Bang Williams, 1880), 54.

34. Fenner, *Battery H,* 103–104; *Providence Journal,* April 28, 1865; William T. Poague, *Gunner with Stonewall: Reminiscences of William Thomas Poague,* ed. Robert K. Krick (Lincoln: University of Nebraska Press, 1998), 110–113; George W. Adams to Edward C. Mauran, April 4, 1865; Crawford Allen to Edward C. Mauran, April 22, 1865, RISA; *Providence Journal,* April 17, 1865; *OR 46,* 912.

35. *OR 46,* 1,011; *Providence Press,* April 24, 1865. According to this letter in the *Providence Press* by a member of Battery H, as soon as the Confederates were driven out of the entrenchments and the two Rhode Island batteries had defeated the Confederates, a section of both was sent forward under command of Captain Crawford Allen to bring in the guns.

36. Fenner, *Battery H,* 70–72; E. Rhodes, *All for the Union,* 218–221; J. Warren Keifer, "The Battle of Sailor's Creek," in *Sketches of War History 1861–1865: Papers Prepared for the Ohio Commandery of the Military Order of the Loyal Legion of the United States,* vol. 3 (Cincinnati: Robert Clarke, 1890), 5–13; *OR 46,* 905–908.

37. Campbell to Campbell, April 15, 1865; Fenner, *Battery H,* 78–81; *OR 46,* 907–908; E. Rhodes, *All for the Union,* 221–223.

38. *Narragansett Weekly,* April 13 and 20, 1865.

39. Fenner, *Battery H,* 82–83; E. Rhodes, *All for the Union,* 222–226; George L. Gaskell to Mary Call, April 23, 1865, USAMHI; General Orders, Number 62, Battery G, NA.

40. *The Sixth Corps* (This periodical was printed for the corps from captured presses at Danville, Virginia); Battery G, Monthly Return, May 1865, RISA; Lewis, *Battery E,* 439–442.

41. E. Rhodes, 227–234.

42. Fenner, *Battery H,* 87–90; E. Rhodes, *All for the Union,* 233–236.

43. Battery G, Monthly Returns, May and June 1865; RISA.

Chapter 16

1. Fenner, *Battery H,* 88–89; Entry for June 16, 1865, Providence Marine Corps of Artillery, Records Book 1861–1868, RIHS.

2. Adams, "Battery G," 906; *Supplement to the Official Records* 63, 656.

3. *Narragansett Weekly,* July 6, 1865.

4. Battery G, Descriptive Book, RISA; Rhode Island Cemetery Database, RIHS.

5. Adams, "Battery G," 905–906; "Battery G, 1st RI Artillery, ANB," *Providence Journal,* April 28, 1865. Today Battery G's tattered, rotted, and battle-worn guidon resides at the Rhode Island State House. Stored in an unprotected glass case since 1903, it will soon disappear forever as a result of less than desirable storage conditions.

6. Fox, *Regimental Losses,* 7–8: 472; State of Rhode Island, *The Monument in Memory of the Rhode Island Soldiers and Sailors Who Fell Victims to the Rebellion* (Providence: Providence Press, 1869), 15–17; Peck, *Historical Address,* 1–14.

7. Fox, *Regimental Losses,* 412–413.

8. Peck, *Historical Address,* 15–18; Edwin Bearss to Author, January 7, 2008.

9. Barker, *Rhode Island Combat Units,* 3–5; Everett S. Hartwell, *An Historical Sketch of the Providence Marine Corps of Artillery, 1801–1951* (Providence: Providence Marine Corps of Artillery, 1952), 1–14; William E. Kernan, *History of the 103rd Field Artillery, Twenty-sixth Division (AEF) World War, 1917–1919* (Providence: Remington Printing, 1930), 7–145; Harold R. Barker, *History of the 43rd Division Artillery, World War II, 1941–1945* (Providence: J.E. Greene, 1961), 3–7, 48–214; General Richard Valente to Author, August 26, 2006. The 103rd Field Artillery Regiment is today one of the crack units of the Rhode Island Army National Guard. The unit traces its descent from the Providence Marine Corps of Artillery and the First Rhode Island Light Artillery Regiment; a presence is still maintained at the Benefit Street Arsenal. The 103rd has won numerous awards and battle honors. Each cannon in the regiment is named after a Civil War battle where the First Rhode Island Light Artillery fought. In the recent cutbacks in defense spending, the 103rd musters only one firing battalion of three batteries. The unit was activated to service in Iraq in 2004 and 2007. Only Battery A served as artillery, while the rest of the battalion fought as infantry; one sergeant, Christopher Potts, was killed and several were wounded. In recent years there have been plans to consolidate the 103rd with a military police battalion, but it has yet to occur.

10. In the vast field of Civil War studies, this author has found only one other study that corroborates his conclusion that Civil War artillery evolved into an offensive weapon. Most historians follow the antiquated research of VanLoan Naisawald in *Grape and Canister,* which concludes that field artillery was used strictly on the defensive. Through this current study, this author has concluded that field artillery was an offensive weapon. For a Confederate study, see Peter S. Carmichael, *Lee's Young Artillerist: William RJ Pegram* (Charlottesville: University of Virginia Press, 1995), 168–172. This study does illustrate that Pegram was very similar to Captain G.W. Adams as a highly effective tactical commander. Pegram, however, mostly employed his guns with canister at close range, as was common during the Mexican War. The only effective offensive use of Confederate artillery was during the September 13–15 operations at Harpers Ferry; here they encircled the town with artillery and pounded it into submission.

11. Ken Carlson, "Rhode Island's Civil War Dead," RISA; Fox, *Regimental Losses,* 534–536; *Revised Register* J.R. Cole, *History of Washington and Kent County Rhode Island* (New York: W.W. Preston, 1889), 151. Officially Rhode Island is credited with losing 2,000 men during the war. This author has reason to believe the number is much higher, approaching 2,500. This includes those soldiers who came home and died of wounds or disease. Just because a man came home with the illness that killed him and he did not expire while mustered into service does not mean he did not die as a result of the Civil War. This author has visited each cemetery in Rhode Island and can vouch for this. Furthermore, throughout this study, whenever official records or those of the family, such as a date of death, has been recorded and is in conflict with another source, the author has taken the information provided by the relative of the soldier, such as that written upon the headstone. To the government, the soldier was just another body to put into uniform, but to the family the soldier was a living, breathing individual and they would know precisely such vital dates.

12. William A. Barker, Death Certificate, July 23, 1865, Providence City Hall; Emmons B. Weston, Memorial Marker, Grace Church Cemetery, Providence, Rhode Island.

13. *Memoirs of RI,* 418; *George W Adams,* 10–11; George W. Adams, Death Certificate, October 15, 1883, RG; *Prov-*

idence Journal, October 17, 1883; *Bristol Phoenix,* October 20, 1883. There is no doubt that Adams was one of the best officers to serve in the First Rhode Island Light Artillery. Another obituary, taken from a small memorial pamphlet remarked that "Colonel Adams was a man of marked traits of character. His energy and courage were unbounded. His personal magnetism was remarkable, attracting and attaching all with whom he came in contact with. He was a man of literary tastes, and had begun a history of Battery G, but his untimely death left this work unfinished." Today Adams is buried in Juniper Hill Cemetery in Bristol. Only a simple stone with his name and the years of birth and death mark this great man's final resting place.

14. George L. Gaskell to Mary Call, April 30, 1885, US-AMHI; Chenery, *Fourteenth Rhode Island,* 327; Gaskell, Pension File.

15. William P. Hopkins, The *Seventh Regiment Rhode Island Volunteer in the Civil War: 1862–1865* (Providence: Snow and Farnum, 1903), 401–402; Chenery, *Fourteenth Rhode Island,* 291–93; Lewis, *History of Battery E,* 379–380; Nichols Post Records, GAR Papers, RIHS. Readers wishing to visit Malbourne's grave should be warned that it is on land owned by the City of Providence that provides a watershed for the Scituate Reservoir. Permission must first be obtained through the city water board before entering the property; directions to the gravesite can also be obtained from the city as it remains quite secluded in the woods. The rest of the veterans are buried in well maintained, perpetual care cemeteries.

16. Charles V. Scott, Pension File, NA; William M. Duffey to Amanda M. Scott, January 7, 1884, RIHS; Monroe, *First Bull Run,* 21–23; Thomas Aldrich, *The History of Battery A, First Regiment, Rhode Island Light Artillery, in the War to Preserve the Union* (Providence: Snow and Farnum, 1904), 28–31. Aldrich was a chronic liar who placed himself in events that he was not even present at. Another such example is the Battle of Gettysburg. He claimed that he was at the front line of Pickett's Charge as Battery A stood and fired into the ranks of a North Carolina regiment. The incident never took place, but it has been blown out of proportion to the point of a monument on the battlefield citing Aldrich's false information. This battery had a superb reputation for battlefield prowess but was damaged after the war by Aldrich's false statements. For further information on Battery A, refer to Theodore Reichardt's *Diary of Battery A.* Published immediately after the war, the small volume has its own problems, but it is a better source of information then Aldrich's book. The cannon Charles Scott saved, now known as the Bull Run Gun, is displayed at the Rhode Island State House.

17. Prescott Post Records, RIHS. There is no record of William B. Gaskell ever being in the United States Army. After the war, a descendent of William H. Lewis donated his jacket, letters, and images to the Connecticut State Library. Unfortunately, in 2000 the jacket was sold to a private museum in Petersburg, Virginia, thus separating the interesting collection.

18. Fenner, *Battery H,* 116; Constance Cordner Anderson to Author, September 9 and 15, 2007; Samuel E. Lewis, Death Certificate, Coventry Town Hall. In the government pension index, Lewis is not listed.

19. Burrage, *Civil War Record,* 47; Potter, Medal of Honor File; George W. Potter, Will, STH. Potter's will, filed in Sterling, Connecticut, illustrates that he did not have much to his name when he died. He left everything to his wife, Lucy, including, presumably, his Medal of Honor, which has now been lost. Potter owned 73 acres worth $250.00, a house worth $50.00, one horse and one cow valued at $100.00 each, and an old carriage and harness worth $25.00. His household items, including war relics, were not included; presumably he lost them all in

the 1911 fire, although he did receive another Medal of Honor. Potter's stone cost $80.00 and ironically today he is buried near General Harold R. Barker, who had attempted to write Battery G's story.

20. George, "Caissons Kept Rolling Along," 9–10; Torslow, Service File; State of Rhode Island, *Rhode Island at the Universal Exposition, 1904* (Providence: E.L. Freeman, 1904), 15; Jeremiah P. Healey, Memorial Marker, Old North Cemetery, Bristol, Rhode Island; State of Rhode Island, *Third Annual Report of the State Board of Soldier's Relief* (Providence: E.L. Freeman, 1892), 44–51. There is little doubt that other Battery G veterans went to the Soldiers Home, but the only other confirmed members were George B. Jenks of Providence and James McNally of Westerly.

21. *Providence Journal,* June 27, 1915; Lewis, *Battery E,* 405–407.

22. Havron Family Records, courtesy of Colonel Bill Havron.

23. Nathan Champlin, Pension File, NA.

24. Budlong Post 18, Death Book, WML; Nathaniel R. Chace, Pension File, NA; *Westerly Sun,* January 9 and January 12, 1927.

25. Budlong Post 18, Death Book, WML; Burton, Service File, NA; William H. Burton, Death Record, 1880, Death Book, RISA; Daniel Hoxsie, Pension File, NA.

26. *Wood River Advertiser,* April 16, 1907; United States, 1870 Census for Tucker and Ennis families, courtesy of Kris VanDenBossche.

27. Wells, Pension File.

28. *Revised Register,* vol. 1, 726–727; John S. Babcock, Pension File, NA; Denison, *Westerly,* 220–222, 269–273.

29. Steven W. Macomber, *The Story of Westerly Granite* (Westerly: Westerly Historical Society, 1958), 8–22. Today the Westerly Granite records are housed at the Westerly Memorial Library, a former Grand Army of the Republic Hall. The large research facility houses the best collection of material relating to Rhode Island military history and was the primary research facility used by this author.

30. James A. Barber, Pension File, NA; Joseph M. Barber, ed., "Brotherhood: Abstracts of the membership of Budlong Post No. 18, GAR, Westerly, RI," in *Rhode Island Roots* (December 2001), 160–86; Budlong Post Records, WML; U.S. War Department to James A. Barber, September 30, 1921, courtesy of Midge Frazel; *Westerly Sun,* June 26, 1925; *Westerly Sun,* clippings, courtesy of Midge Frazel. Other confirmed members of Battery G who joined the Budlong Post were Ellery Barber, Nathaniel R. Chace, Daniel Champlin, Thomas Chapman, Samuel C. Mitchell, Alexander B. Sisson, Charles E. Sisson, and Maurice Sullivan. Today these men are all buried at Riverbend Cemetery in Westerly.

31. *George W Adams,* 6–7. *Revised Register,* vii, 900–906.

32. Robert B. Beath, *History of the Grand Army of the Republic* (New York: Bryan, Taylor, & Co, 1889), 418–427; Budlong Post Records, WML; Burnside Post Records, CL; Joshua H. Aubin, *Register of the Military Order of the Loyal Legion of the United States* (Boston: Edwin L. Slocomb, 1906), 3–9, 155, 172, 190–91, 203, 237. The Battery G officers who joined MOLLUS were Andrew T. MacMillan, Charles D. Owen, Reuben Rich, William B. Rhodes, Edward H. Sears, and Frank Waterman. The evidence that there were no reunions is taken from each of the battery regimental histories. Outside of the Gettysburg Reunion, the veterans of Battery G never mustered after the war as an organized unit.

33. Lewis, *Battery E;* Battery B Veterans Association, Papers, RISA; *Dedication of the Equestrian Statue of Major-General Ambrose E Burnside in the City of Providence, July 4, 1887* (Providence: E.L. Freeman, 1887), 7. Beginning in 1892, Battery E would publish their history, ending with Battery D in 1897. It is known that Battery G members joined the overall First Rhode Island Light Artillery Veterans Association, which met at the Benefit Street Arsenal. However, this organization's papers and those of the other organizations have not survived, but only those of Battery B at the RIHS. The Rhode Island General Assembly voted to pay for the first 200 copies of each history. Over the years they would be reprinted numerous times.

34. Horatio Rogers, *Rhode Island Excursion to Gettysburg* (Providence: E.L. Freeman, 1887), 1–12; *Pawtucket Evening Times,* June 28, 1913; *Report of the Rhode Island Fiftieth Anniversary of the Battle of Gettysburg Commission* (Providence: Rhode Island Printing Company, 1914), 17–24. This marker is today located on Cemetery Ridge, near the New Jersey Brigade monument and that of Father William Corby. It mislabels the two Rhode Island batteries, stating that C had ordnance rifles and Battery G the ten-pounder Parrotts. As corroborated through official ordnance returns and memoirs, the two commands' guns were reversed. The Sixth Corps Artillery Brigade was nowhere near this marker, being positioned all over the line, from the Third New York on Cemetery Hill to Battery G near Little Round Top. The Battery G veterans who went to the reunion were James and Ellery Barber, Charles D. Ennis, George W. Potter, William W. Potter, and Daniel C. Stevens.

35. Medal of Honor and Cemetery Records, Winchester National Cemetery, Winchester, Virginia. The men of Battery G buried at Winchester are Henry Chace, William C. Douglass, Charles G. Gardner, William H. Lewis, and Augustus F. Travers, who were all killed at Cedar Creek, and Michael Coffery, who died of disease at Harpers Ferry. The Medal of Honor recipients are buried as follows: Sergeant Archibald Malbourne, Scituate Historical Cemetery off Route 12, Clayville, RI; Corporal James A. Barber, Riverbend Cemetery, Westerly RI; Corporal Samuel E. Lewis, North Burial Ground, Providence, RI; Private Charles D. Ennis, White Brook Cemetery, Carolina, RI; Private John Corcoran, Oak Grove Cemetery, Pawtucket, RI; Private George W. Potter, Swan Point Cemetery, Providence, RI. Sergeant John Havron died in New Orleans in 1910; unfortunately, his grave was never marked and attempts to locate his final resting place have been futile due to the recent natural disaster events in the New Orleans area. This author has surveyed nearly every cemetery in Rhode Island and nearby Connecticut and Massachusetts in search of Battery G veterans and has burial data available for most veterans.

36. *Wood River Advertiser,* April 16, 1907; Charles D. Ennis, Death Certificate, December 29, 1930, RG; *Westerly Sun,* December 30, 1930 and January 1, 1931; *Roster of Burnside Post No 5, GAR Department of Rhode Island, Shannock, RI* (Westerly: G.H. Utter, 1894), 1–10; Burnside Post Records, CL. It is interesting to note that the veterans of Battery G died in a peculiar pattern. If they did not perish in the years immediately after the war, they lived to become aged, dying in a steady stream from 1918 to1930. Most of those from the Westerly area lived to be in their eighties. No Medal of Honor awarded to any of the Battery G veterans is known to have survived. According to records in the Robert H. George collection at the Hay Library, James Barber's was "lost due to unfortunate family circumstances."

Bibliography

The following is the bibliography of sources used in the writing of *The Boys of Adams' Battery G*. This author has compiled the following listing of primary and secondary sources directly relating to Battery G. The most important of these sources are those manuscripts and printed primary sources written by the men who fought in the Civil War. Without those, this work would not have been possible. The diaries and letters of such men as James A. Barber, Albert D. Cordner, George L. Gaskell, William H. Lewis, and the other veterans who served in and with Battery G provide a superb written record for understanding the day-to-day operations, arguments, and service of the battery. They represent the single most important and most often consulted sources. The fine series *Battles & Leaders of the Civil War* gave excellent insight into the campaigns and battles that the battery found itself participating in. Likewise, the pertinent and very important *Official Records of the War of the Rebellion* retold the story from the battlefield as the commanders saw it. This source provided invaluable information and placed the unit's movements in context with the larger battle. To the greatest extent possible, the primary sources have been utilized and cited, as they remain the single most credible accounting of the war. The secondary works gave an excellent understanding of the battles and experiences of the soldiers. They were used to gain knowledge of the larger picture of how Battery G fit into the Army of the Potomac. Together, all of the works provided the necessary information to write this, a history of Battery G, First Rhode Island Light Artillery.

Manuscripts and Unpublished Material

Adams, George W. Service File. National Archives.

_____. Student File. Hay Library, Brown University.

Allen, Crawford. Court Martial Records. National Archives.

_____. Service File. National Archives.

_____. Student File. Hay Library, Brown University.

Antietam National Battlefield. Papers. Antietam National Battlefield.

Barber Family Genealogy. Private Collection.

Barber, James A. 1862 Diary. Providence Public Library.

_____. 1863 and 1864 Diaries. Hay Library, Brown University.

_____. Medal of Honor File. National Archives.

_____. Pension File. National Archives.

_____. Service File. National Archives.

Barber, Manley. Pension File. National Archives.

Barker, Harold R. "Notes on Rhode Island Combat Units." Rhode Island Historical Society.

Barker, William C. Letters. Rhode Island Historical Society.

Barney, Beriah. Pension File. National Archives.

Baruch, Simon. "A Surgeon's Story of Battle and Capture." Gettysburg National Military Park.

Battery B Veterans Association. Books and Ledgers. Rhode Island Historical Society.

Battery G, First Rhode Island Light Artillery. Clothing Book. Rhode Island Historical Society.

_____. Reports and Letters. Antietam National Battlefield.

Battlefield Maps. Wilderness and Spotsylvania Battlefields. Fredericksburg-Spotsylvania National Military Park.

Bloodgood, Horace S. Service File. National Archives.

_____. Student File. Hay Library, Brown University.

Bogman, Charles. Service File. National Archives.

Briggs, Edward C. Service File. National Archives.

Brown, Patrick. Court Martial Records. National Archives.

Budlong, Stillman D. Diary. Westerly Memorial Library.

Budlong Post Records. Westerly Memorial Library.

Burnside Post Records. Clark Library.

Burton, William H. Pension File. National Archives.

_____. Service File. National Archives.

Callahan, James. Service File. National Archives.

Campbell, John P. Letters. United States Army Military History Institute.

Carlson, Ken. "Men of Rhode Island to Arms!" Rhode Island State Archives.

_____. "Rhode Island's Civil War Dead." Rhode Island State Archives.

Carmen, Ezra. Papers. Antietam National Battlefield.

Chace, Henry E. Service File. National Archives.

Chace, Nathaniel R. Pension File. National Archives.

Champlin, Nathan. Pension File. National Archives.

Cobb, Benjamin F. "My Last Battle." Cedar Creek Battlefield.

Corcoran, John. Medal of Honor File. National Archives.

_____. Service File. National Archives.

Cordner, Albert D. Diary. Fredricksburg-Spotsylvania National Military Park.

_____. Service File. National Archives.

Cornell, Luther. Pension File. National Archives.

Corthell, Elmer L. Student File. Hay Library, Brown University.

Cowan, Andrew. Letters. Gettysburg National Military Park.

Daley, Charlotte. Papers. Providence Public Library.

Durfee, Albert C. Pension File. National Archives.

Ennis, Charles D. Medal of Honor File. National Archives.

_____. Pension File. National Archives.

_____. Service File. National Archives.

Farnsworth, Henry. Service File. National Archives.

Fenner, George D. Service File. National Archives.

Field, George W. Letters. Private collection.

First Rhode Island Light Artillery. Regimental Records. National Archives; Rhode Island Historical Society; Rhode Island State Archives.

Fisk, Wilbur. Papers. Library of Congress.

Flint, Daniel. Letters. Gettysburg National Military Park.

Frazel, Midge. "James Barber." Unpublished Manuscript.

Johnson, Edward. Court Martial Record. National Archives.

Gardner, Alfred G. Letters. Hay Library, Brown University.

Gaskell, George L. Letters. United States Army Military History Institute.

_____. Pension File. National Archives.

_____. Service File. National Archives.

George, Robert H. Papers. Hay Library, Brown University.

_____. "Their Caissons Kept Rolling Along." Unpublished Manuscript. Hay Library, Brown University.

Getty, George W. Papers. Library of Congress.

Grand Army of the Republic. Records. Rhode Island Historical Society.

Gould, Charles H. Medal of Honor File. National Archives.

Handy, Daniel. Letters. Rhode Island Historical Society.

Havron, John H. Medal of Honor File. National Archives.

_____. Service File. National Archives.

Havron Family Genealogy. Private Collection.

Heap, Henry. Pension File. National Archives.

Hilton, Daniel. Letters. Gettysburg National Military Park.

Hobson, Edwin L. Report of Cedar Creek. Cedar Creek Battlefield.

Hoxsie, Daniel. Pension File. National Archives.

Hunt, Henry J. Papers. Library of Congress.

Hunt, Peter. Letters. East Providence Historical Society.

Ingraham, John J. Letters. Cedar Creek Battlefield.

Jackson, Daniel D. Letters. Cedar Creek Battlefield.

Kelley, Benjamin E. Service File. National Archives.

Lancaster, Jane. "The Providence Marine Corps of Artillery." Unpublished Manuscript.

Larkin, Henry. Letters. Rhode Island Historical Society.

Laxton, Glenn. "The Seven." Unpublished Manuscript.

Lewis, Samuel E. Medal of Honor File. National Archives.

_____. Service File. National Archives.

Lewis, William H. Letters. Connecticut State Library.

_____. Pension File. National Archives.

_____. Service File. National Archives.

Lincoln, Abraham. Papers. Library of Congress.

Lyon, Patrick. Journal. Pettaquamscutt Historical Society.

Malbourne, Archibald. Medal of Honor File. National Archives.

_____. Service File. National Archives.

Marshall, Daniel W. Diary. Library of Congress.

Matthewson, James A. Service File. National Archives.

Military Order of the Loyal Legion of the United States. Books and Papers. United States Army Military History Institute.

Moore, William H. Narrative. Gettysburg National Military Park.

Morey, Charles C. Diary. Gettysburg National Military Park.

National Park Service. Battlefield Study Maps and Reports. Harpers Ferry National Historic Park.

Newton, James. Letters. Hay Library, Brown University.

Nichols, Charles S. "Memoirs." Langworthy Public Library.

Olney, Amos M.C. Letters. Rhode Island Historical Society.

Owen, Charles D. Service File. National Archives.

Patterson, David B. Letters. Rhode Island Historical Society and RNB.

Peckham, Peleg. Letters. Langworthy Public Library.

Perkins, Charles E. Letters. United States Army Military History Institute.

Perry, John A. Papers. Rhode Island Historical Society.

Pratt, Robert. Letters and Diary. Private Collection.

Potter, George W. Medal of Honor File. National Archives.

_____. Service File. National Archives.

_____. Student File. Hay Library, Brown University.

_____. Will. Sterling, Connecticut, Town Hall.

Providence Marine Corps of Artillery. Records. Rhode Island Historical Society.

Rathbun, John L. Service File, National Archives.

Remington, James. Letters. Rhode Island Historical Society.

Rich, Reuben H. Pension File. National Archives.

Ricketts, James B. 1864 Memoranda Book. Manassas National Battlefield.

Riley, Peter. Pension File. National Archives.

Rhode Island Adjutant General. General and Special Orders. Rhode Island State Archives.

_____. Memoranda Books. Rhode Island State Archives.

Rhode Island Historical Cemetery Database. Rhode Island Historical Society.

Rhode Island Paymaster General. Papers. Rhode Island State Archives.

Rhode Island Quartermaster General. Papers. Rhode Island State Archives.

Rhodes, Elisha H. Papers. Rhode Island Historical Society.

Rhodes, William B. Diary. United States Army Military History Institute.

_____. Service File. National Archives.

Sackett, Frederick M. Letters. Rhode Island Historical Society.

Scott, Charles V. Orders and Pension letters. Rhode Island Historical Society.

_____. Pension File. National Archives.

_____. Service File. National Archives.

Smith, Peter C. Diary. Rhode Island Historical Society.

Soldiers and Sailors Historical Society. Papers. Rhode Island Historical Society.

Soule, George. Letters. United States Army Military History Institute.

Sperry, William J. Medal of Honor File. National Archives.

Straight, Albert. Diary and Letters. Robert Grandchamp collection.

Straight, Charles T. Letters. Robert Grandchamp collection and Gettysburg National Military Park.

Starboard, Simeon. Service File. National Archives.

Stevens, Hazard. Papers. Library of Congress.

Stinson, Dwight E. "Operations of Sedgwick's Division in the West Woods." Antietam National Battlefield.

Tabor, William O. Service File, National Archives.

Thurber, William. Sketches. Rhode Island Historical Society.

Torslow, Otto L. Court Martial Records. National Archives.

_____ Service File. National Archives.

Travers, Augustus F. Service File. National Archives.

Tucker, Welcome C. Bounty Records. Private Collection.

Walker, Cyrus. "History of Scituate, RI." Robert Grandchamp collection.

Ward, John F. Letters. Harpers Ferry National Historic Park.

Webb, Charles H. Discharge Papers. Gettysburg National Military Park.

Wells, John D. Pension File. National Archives.

Wert, J. Howard. "Brown's Battery B." Robert Grandchamp collection.

Westerly Rifles. Papers. Westerly Memorial Library.

Wilson, George. Court Martial Records. National Archives.

Wood, Silas. Letters. Rhode Island Historical Society.

Young, Jesse. Court Martial Records. National Archives.

Printed Primary Sources

Abbott, Henry L. *Fallen Leaves: The Civil War Letters of Major Henry Livermore.* Kent, Ohio: Kent State University Press, 1991.

Aldrich, Thomas. *The History of Battery A, First Regiment Rhode Island Light Artillery, in the War to Preserve the Union.* Providence: Snow and Farnum, 1904.

Alexander, Edward P. *Military Memoirs of a Confederate: A Critical Narrative.* New York: Da Capo Press, 1993.

Allen, George H. Allen, *Forty-Six Months in the Fourth R.I. Volunteers.* Providence: J.A. and R.A. Reid, 1887.

Ames, Nelson. *History of Battery G, First Regiment New York Light Artillery.* Marshalltown, IA: Marshall Printing Company, 1900.

Anderson, Robert. *An Artillery Officer in the Mexican War, 1846–7.* Edited by Eba Anderson Lawton. New York: Knickerbocker Press, 1911.

Aubin, Joshua H. *Register of the Military Order of the Loyal Legion of the United States.* Boston: Edwin L. Slocomb, 1906.

Baquet, Camille. *History of the First Brigade, New Jersey Volunteers: From 1861 to 1865.* Trenton: State of New Jersey, 1910.

Barker, Harold R. *History of the 43rd Division Artillery, World War II, 1941–1945.* Providence: J.E. Greene, 1961.

Barnard, John G., and William F. Barry. *Report of the Engineer and Artillery Operations of the Army of the Potomac from Its Organization to the Close of the Peninsular Society.* New York: D. Van Norstrand, 1863.

Barney, Henry. *A Country Boy's First Three Months in the Army.* Providence: N. Bang Williams, 1880.

Barry, Joseph. *The Strange Story of Harpers Ferry.* Harpers Ferry: NP, 1903.

Barry, William F. ,William H. French, and Henry J. Hunt. *Instructions for Field Artillery.* New York: NP, 1860.

Bartlett, John F. *Autobiography of John Russell Bartlett.* Edited by Jerry E. Mueller. Providence: Brown University, 2006.

Bastler, Roy P, ed. *The Collected Works of Abraham Lincoln.* New Brunswick: Rutgers University Press, 1953.

Battle, Cullen A. *Third Alabama! The Civil War Memoir of Brigadier General Cullen Andrews Battle, CSA.* Edited by Brandon H. Beck. Tuscaloosa: University of Alabama Press, 2000.

Battles & Leaders of the Civil War. New York: The Century Company, 1888. 4 volumes.

Bayles, Richard M. *History of Providence County, Rhode Island.* Vol. 1. New York: W.W. Preston & Co., 1891.

Beath, Robert B. *History of the Grand Army of the Republic.* New York: Bryan, Taylor, & Co, 1889.

Benedict, George G. *Vermont in the Civil War.* Vol. 1. Burlington: Free Press Association, 1888.

Bennett, Albert J. *The Story of the First Massachusetts Light Battery Attached to the Sixth Army Corps.* Boston: Deland and Barta, 1886.

Best, Isaac O. *History of the 121st New York State Infantry.* Chicago: James H. Smith, 1921.

Bicknell, George W. *History of the Fifth Regiment Maine Volunteers, Comprising Brief Descriptions of Its Marches, Engagements, and General Services from the Date of Its Muster In, June 24, 1861, to the Time of Its Muster Out, July 27, 1864.* Portland: Hall L. Davis, 1871.

Bidwell, Frederick D. *History of the Forty-Ninth New York Volunteers.* Albany: J.B. Lyon, 1916.

Billings, John D. *Hardtack and Coffee: The Unwritten story of Army Life.* Lincoln: Nebraska University Press, 1993.

_____. *The History of the Tenth Massachusetts Battery of Light Artillery in the War of the Rebellion.* Boston: Arakelyan Press, 1909.

Bowen, James L. *History of the Thirty-Seventh Regiment Mass. Volunteers in the Civil War of 1861–1865.* Holyoke: Clark W. Bryan, 1884.

Brown University. *Historical Catalogue of Brown University, 1764–1914.* Springfield, MA: F.A. Bassett, 1915.

Bucklyn, John K. *Battle of Cedar Creek.* Providence: Sydney S. Ryder, 1883.

Buell, Augustus. *The Cannoneer: Recollections of Service in the Army of the Potomac.* Washington DC: National Tribune, 1897.

Burrage, Henry S. *Brown University in the Civil War: A Memorial.* Providence: Providence Press, 1868.

_____. *Civil War Record of Brown University.* Providence: Brown University, 1920.

Busey, John W. *These Honored Dead: The Union Casualties at Gettysburg.* Hightstown, NJ: Longstreet House, 1996.

Card, Henry C. *Charter and By-Laws of the Westerly Rifles.* Westerly, RI: G.B. & J.R. Utter, 1871.

Chase, John W. *Yours for the Union: The Civil War Letters of John W. Chase, First Massachusetts Light Artillery.* Edited by John S. Collier and Bonnie B. Collier. New York: Fordham University Press, 2004.

Chase, Phillip S. *Battery F, First Rhode Island Light Artillery in the Civil War.* Providence: Snow and Farnum, 1892.

Chenery, William. *The Fourteenth Regiment Rhode Island Heavy Artillery in the War to Preserve the Union.* New York: Negro University Press, 1960.

Child, Benjamin H. *From Fredericksburg to Gettysburg.* Providence: Snow and Farnum, 1895.

Cole, J.R. *History of Washington and Kent County Rhode Island.* New York: W.W. Preston, 1889.

Cozzens, Peter, ed. *Battles and Leaders of the Civil War.* Vols. 5 and 6. Chicago: University Press of Illinois, 2004.

Cross, Edward E. *Stand Firm and Fire Low: The Civil War Writings of Colonel Edward E. Cross.* Edited by Walter Holden, William E. Ross, and Elizabeth Slomba. Hanover, NH: University Press of New England, 2003.

Dailey, Charlotte. *Report upon the Disabled Rhode Island Soldiers.* Providence: Alfred Anthony, 1863.

Dedication of the Equestrian Statue of Major-General Ambrose E. Burnside in the City of Providence, July 4, 1887. Providence: E.L. Freeman, 1887.

Delevan, John. *By-Laws of Budlong Post, No. 18, Dept. of R.I., G.A.R., Westerly, RI.* Westerly, RI: G.B. & J.R. Utter, 1881.

Denison, Frederic. *Sabres and Spurs: The First Rhode Island Cavalry in the Civil War.* Central Falls: First Rhode Island Cavalry Veterans Association, 1876.

_____. *Westerly and Its Witness.* Westerly, RI: Utter, 1878.

Dyer, J. Franklin. *The Journal of a Civil War Surgeon.* Edited by Michael B. Chesson. Lincoln: University of Nebraska Press, 2003.

Early, Jubal A. *War Memoirs: Autobiographical Sketch and Narrative of the War Between the States.* Edited by Frank A. Vandiver. Bloomington: Indiana University Press, 1960.

Favill, Josiah M. *Diary of a Young Army Officer.* Chicago: R.R. Donnelly & Sons, 1909.

Fenner, Earl J. *The History of Battery H, First Rhode Island Light Artillery.* Providence: Snow and Farnum, 1894.

Figg, Royall W. *"Where Men Only Dare to Go!" or The Story of a Boy Company.* Richmond: Whilet and Shepperson, 1885.

Fisk, Wilbur. *Hard Marching Every Day: The Civil War Letters of Private Wilbur Fisk, 1861–1865.* Edited by Emil Rosenblatt and Ruth Rosenblatt. Lawrence: University Press of Kansas, 1992.

Flinn, Frank M. *Campaigning with Banks in Louisiana, '63 and '64, and with Sheridan in the Shenandoah Valley in '64 and '65.* Boston: W.B. Clarke, 1889.

Fox, William F. *Regimental Losses in the American Civil War.* Albany: Brandow, 1898.

Fuller, Oliver P. *The History of Warwick, Rhode Island from 1642 to the Present Day.* Providence: Angell, Burlingame, 1875.

Geir, Clarence R., and Stephen R. Potter. *Archaeological Perspectives on the American Civil War.* Gainesville: University Press of Florida, 2000.

Gibbon, John. *Artillerist's Manual.* Philadelphia: J.B. Lippincott, 1860.

_____. *Personal Recollections of the Civil War.* New York: G.P. Putnam's Sons, 1928.

Griswold, S.S. *Historical Sketch of Hopkinton.* Hope Valley: L.W.A. Cole Job Printers, 1877.

Haines, Alanson A. *History of the Fifteenth Regiment New Jersey Volunteers.* Gaithersburg, MD: Butternut Press, 1987.

Hartwell, John F.L. *To My Beloved Wife and Boy at Home: The Letters and Diaries of Orderly Sergeant John F.L. Hartwell.* Edited by Ann Hartwell Britton and Thomas J. Read. Madison: Farleigh Dickinson University Press, 1997.

Haynes, Edward M. *A History of the Tenth Regiment Vermont Volunteers.* Lewiston, ME: Journal Steam Press, 1870.

Hinman, Wilbur. *Corporal Si Klegg and His Pard.* Cleveland: Williams, 1887.

Historical Sketch of Slocum Post, No. 10, Department of Rhode Island, Grand Army of the Republic. Providence: Snow and Farnum, 1892.

History of Battery B: One Hundred and Third Field Artillery, Twenty Sixth Division, April 1917–April 1919. Providence: E.L. Freeman, 1922.

History of the Fourth Maine Battery Light Artillery in the Civil War, 1861–65. Augusta: Burleigh & Flynt, 1905.

Holmes, Oliver W. *Touched with Fire: Civil War Letters and Diary of Oliver Wendell Holmes, Jr., 1861–1864.* Cambridge, MA: Harvard University Press, 1946.

Holt, Daniel M. *A Surgeon's Civil War: The Letters and Diary of Daniel M. Holt, M.D.* Edited by James M. Grenier, Janet L. Coryell, and James R. Smithier. Kent, OH: Kent State University Press, 1994.

Hopkins, William P. *The Seventh Regiment Rhode Island Volunteers in the Civil War, 1862–1865.* Providence: Snow and Farnum, 1903.

Hyde, Thomas W. *Following the Greek Cross, or Memories of the Sixth Army Corps.* Boston: Houghton Mifflin, 1894.

In Memoriam: George William Adams. Providence: NP, 1883.

Instructions for Making Muster Rolls, Mustering into Service, and Periodical Payments. Washington: Government Printing Office, 1863.

Irish, James R. *Historical Sketch of Richmond.* Hope Valley: L.W.A. Cole Job Printers, 1877.

Kautz, August V. *The 1865 Customs of Service for Enlisted Men of the Army.* Philadelphia: J.B. Lippincott, 1865.

_____. *The 1865 Customs of Service for Officers of the Army.* Philadelphia: J.B. Lippincott, 1865.

Kernan, William E. *History of the 103rd Field Artillery, Twenty-sixth Division (AEF) World War, 1917–1919.* Providence: Remington Printing, 1930.

Kirk, Hyland C. *Heavy Guns and Light: A History of the 4th New York Heavy Artillery.* New York: C.T. Dillingham, 1890.

Ladd, David L., and Audrey J. Ladd, eds. *Gettysburg in Their Own Words: The Batchelder Papers.* 3 volumes. Dayton: New Hampshire Historical Society, 1995.

Lewis, George. *History of Battery E, First Rhode Island Light Artillery.* Providence: Snow and Farnum, 1892.

Marshall, Jeffrey D., ed. *A War of the People: Vermont Civil War Letters.* Hanover, NH: University Press of New England, 1999.

Marvin, Abijah P. *History of Winchendon.* Winchendon, MA: NP, 1868.

Mathless, Paul, ed. *Shenandoah 1864.* Richmond: Time Life Books, 1998.

Mauran, Edward C. *Disbursements made by the Adjutant General.* Providence: NP, 1862.

McClellan, George B. *The Civil War Papers of George B. McClellan: Selected Correspondence, 1860–1865.* Edited by Stephen W. Sears. New York: Ticknor and Fields, 1989.

_____. *Report on the Organization and Campaigns of the Army of the Potomac.* New York: Sheldon & Company, 1864.

McCrea, Tully. *Dear Belle: Letters from a Cadet & Officer to His Sweetheart, 1858–1865.* Edited by Catherine S. Creary. Middletown, CT: Wesleyan University Press, 1965.

The Medical and Surgical History of the War of the Rebellion. Washington: Government Printing Office, 1883. 12 volumes.

Memoirs of Rhode Island Officers: Who Were Engaged in the Service of Their Country during the Great Rebellion with the South. Edited by John R. Bartlett. Providence: Sydney S. Rider & Brothers Press, 1867.

Memorial of Colonel John S. Slocum. Providence: R.A. and J.A. Reid, 1886.

Mitchell, Joseph B., ed. *The Badge of Gallantry: Recollections of Civil War Medal of Honor Winners.* New York: McMillan Company, 1968.

Monroe, J. Albert. *Battery D, First Rhode Island Light Artillery, at the Battle of Antietam.* Providence: Providence Press, 1886.

_____. *Battery D, First Rhode Island Light Artillery, at the Second Battle of Bull Run.* Providence: Providence Press, 1886.

_____. *The Rhode Island Artillery at the First Battle of Bull Run.* Providence: Sydney S. Rider, 1878.

Moore, Edward A. *The Story of a Cannoneer under Stonewall Jackson, in Which Is Told the Part Taken by the Rockbridge Artillery in the Army of Northern Virginia.* New York: Neale Publishing Company, 1907.

Munro, Wilfred H. *The History of Bristol, RI: The Story of the Mount Hope Lands.* Bristol: NP, 1881.

Myers, Frank M. *The Commanches: A History of White's Battalion, Virginia Cavalry.* Baltimore: Kelly, Piet, & Co, 1871.

Parker, Ezra K. *From the Rapidan to the James under Grant.* Providence: Snow and Farnum, 1909.

Peck, George B. *Camp and Hospital.* Providence: The Society, 1884.

_____. *Historical Address: Rhode Island Light Artillery in the Civil and Spanish Wars.* Providence: Rhode Island Printing, 1917.

_____. *A Recruit Before Petersburg.* Providence: N. Bang Williams, 1880.

Perkins, George. *Three Years a Soldier: The Diary and Newspaper Correspondence of Private George Perkins, Sixth New York Independent Battery, 1861–1864.* Edited by Richard N. Griffin. Knoxville: University of Tennessee Press, 2006.

Phisterer, Frederick. *New York in the War of the Rebellion.* Albany: J.B. Lyon, 1912.

Poague, William T. *Gunner with Stonewall: Reminiscences of William Thomas Poague.* Edited by Robert K. Krick. Lincoln: University of Nebraska Press, 1998.

Reichardt, Theodore. *Diary of Battery A.* Providence: N. Bang Williams, 1865.

Remmel, William. *Like Grass Before the Scythe: The Life and Death of Sgt. William Remmel, 121st New York Infantry.* Edited by Robert P. Bender. Tuscaloosa: University of Alabama Press, 2007.

Report of the Rhode Island Fiftieth Anniversary of the Battle of Gettysburg Commission. Providence: Rhode Island Printing Company, 1914.

Revised Register of Rhode Island Volunteers. Providence: E.L. Freeman, 1895.

Revised Regulations for the Army of the United States. Philadelphia: G.L.B. Brown, 1861.

Rhodes, Elisha Hunt. *All for the Union: The Civil War Diary and Letters of Elisha Hunt Rhodes.* Edited by Robert Hunt Rhodes. Woonsocket: Andrew Mobray, 1985.

_____. *The Second Rhode Island Infantry at the Siege of Petersburg, Virginia.* Providence: The Society, 1915.

Rhodes, John H. *History of Battery B, First Rhode Island Light Artillery.* Providence: Snow and Farnum, 1894.

Richards, John J. *Rhode Island's Early Defenders and Their Successors.* East Greenwich: Rhode Island Pendulum, 1937.

Roe, Alfred S. *The Ninth New York Heavy Artillery.* Worcester: F.S. Blanchard, 1899.

Rogers, Horatio. *Personal Experiences of the Chancellorsville Campaign.* Providence: N. Bang Williams, 1881.

_____. *Record of the Rhode Island Excursion to Gettysburg.* Providence: E.L. Freeman, 1887.

Rollins, Richard, ed. *Pickett's Charge: Eyewitness Accounts.* Redondo Beach, CA: Rank and File, 1996.

Roster of Burnside Post No. 2, G.A.R. Department of Rhode Island: Shannock, RI. Westerly: G.H. Utter, 1894.

Scott, Robert G., ed. *Abbott.* Kent, OH: Kent State University Press, 1992.

Sedgwick, John. *Correspondence of John Sedgwick.* Vol. 2. Edited by William D. Sedgwick. Baltimore: Butternut and Blue, 1999.

Spicer, William A. *The History of the Ninth and Tenth Regiments of Rhode Island Volunteers and the Tenth Rhode Island Battery in the Union Army in 1862.* Providence: Snow and Farnum, 1892.

State of Rhode Island. *Acts and Resolves of the General Assembly of the State of Rhode Island and Providence Plantations, January Session, 1865.* Providence: H.H. Thomas, 1865.

_____. *Annual Report of the Adjutant General of the State of Rhode Island for the Year 1865.* Providence: Providence Press, 1866.

_____. *The Monument in Memory of the Rhode Island Soldiers and Sailors Who Fell Victims to the Rebellion.* Providence: Providence Press, 1869.

_____. *Report of the Joint Committee on the Erection of the Monument at Andersonville, GA.* Providence: E.L. Freeman, 1903.

_____. *Report of the Senate Special Committee on Bounty Frauds.* Providence: H.H. Thomas, 1865.

_____. *Rhode Island at the Universal Exposition, 1904.* Providence: E.L. Freeman, 1904.

_____. *Third Annual Report of the State Board of Soldier's Relief.* Providence: E.L. Freeman, 1892.

Stevens, George T. *Three Years in the Sixth Corps.* Albany: S.R. Gray, 1866.

Stevens, Hazard. *The Storming of the Lines of Petersburg by the Sixth Corps, April 2, 1865.* Providence: Snow and Farnum, 1904.

Stone, Edwin W. *Rhode Island in the Rebellion.* Providence: Knowles, Anthony & Co., 1864.

The Story of American Heroism: Thrilling Narratives of Personal Adventures during the Great Civil War, as Told by the Medal Winners and Roll of Honor Men. New Haven: Butler & Alger, 1896.

Straight, Charles T. *Battery B, First R.I. Light Artillery, August 13, 1861–June 12, 1865.* Pawtucket: NP, 1907.

Sumner, George C. *Battery D, First Rhode Island Light Artillery in the Civil War, 1861–1865.* Providence: Rhode Island Print Company, 1897.

Supplement to the Official Records of the Union and Confederate Armies. Edited by Janet B. Hewett, Jocelyn Pinson, Julia H. Nichols, et al. Wilmington, NC: Broadfoot, 1998.

Tarket-Arruda, Lorraine, and Gayle E. Waite, *Historical Cemeteries of Charlestown, Rhode Island.* Hopkinton: The Authors, 2008.

Taylor, James E. *With Sheridan up the Shenandoah Valley in 1864.* Edited by Dennis E. Frye. Dayton: Morningside Books, 1989.

Taylor, John A. *Dedication Day Address, Westerly, RI, May 30, 1884.* Brooklyn, NY: Frederic Treadwell, 1884.

Toombs, Samuel. *New Jersey Troops in the Gettysburg Campaign, From June 5 to July 31, 1863.* Orange, NJ: Evening Mail Publishing House, 1888.

Tucker, William F. *Historical Sketch of Charlestown in Rhode Island from 1636 to 1876.* Westerly, RI: G.B. & J.H. Utter, 1877.

Tyler, Mason W. *Recollections of the Civil War.* Edited by William S. Tyler. New York: G.P. Putnam Son's, 1912.

VanDenBossche, Kris, ed. *Pleas Excuse all bad writing: A Documentary History of Rhode Island during the Civil War Era, 1861–1865.* Peace Dale, RI: Rhode Island Historical Document Transcription Project, 1993.

_____, ed. *Write Soon and Give me all the news.* Peace Dale, RI: Rhode Island Historical Document Transcription Project, 1993.

Vernon, Merle. *Hints to Officers in the Army and Navy.* Boston: American Tract Society, 1862.

Wainwright, Charles S. *A Diary of Battle: The Personal Journals of Colonel Charles S. Wainwright, 1861–1865.* Edited by Allan Nevins. Gettysburg: Stan Clark, 1992.

Waite, Otis F.R. *Vermont in the Great Rebellion.* Claremont, NH: Tracy, Chase, 1869.

Walker, Aldace F. *The Vermont Brigade in the Shenandoah Valley, 1864.* Burlington: Free Press Association, 1869.

Walker, Francis A. *History of the Second Army Corps in the Army of the Potomac.* New York: Charles Scribner's Sons, 1887.

Walker, William C. *History of the Eighteenth Connecticut Volunteers in the War for the Union.* Norwich: Gordon Wilcox, 1886.

War of the Rebellion: A Compilation of the Official Records of the Union and Confederate Armies. Washington, DC: Government Printing Office, 1880–1901. 128 Volumes.

Wert, J. Howard. *A Complete Handbook of the Monuments and Indicators and Guide to the Positions on the Gettysburg Battle-Field.* Harrisburg: R.M. Sturgeon, 1886.

Westbrook, Robert F. *History of the 49th Pennsylvania Volunteers.* Baltimore: Butternut and Blue, 1999.

Wildes, Thomas F. *Record of the One Hundred and Sixteenth Regiment Ohio Volunteers in the War of the Rebellion.* Sandusky: I.F. Mack, 1884.

Woodbury, Augustus. *A Narrative of the Campaign of the First Rhode Island Regiment in the Spring and Summer of 1861.* Providence: Sydney S. Rider, 1862.

_____. *The Second Rhode Island Regiment.* Providence: Valpey, Angell, 1875.

_____. *The Uprising of 1861: The Illustration of True Patriotism.* Providence: Snow and Farnum, 1895.

Woodhead, Henry, ed. *Chancellorsville.* Alexandria: Time Life Books, 1996.

Secondary Sources

Armstrong, Marion V. *Unfurl Those Colors!: McClellan, Sumner, & The Second Army Corps in the Antietam Campaign.* Tuscaloosa: University of Alabama Press, 2008.

Barker, Harold R. *History of Rhode Island Combat Units in the Civil War.* Providence: NP, 1964.

Bicknell, Thomas W. *A History of Barrington, Rhode Island.* Providence: Snow and Farnum, 1898.

_____. *The History of the State of Rhode Island and Providence Plantations.* Vol. 2. New York: American Historical Society, 1920.

Bilby, Joseph G. *Three Rousing Cheers: A History of the Fifteenth New Jersey from Flemington to Appomattox.* Hightstown, NJ: Longstreet House, 2001.

Birkhimer, William E. *Historical Sketch of the Organization, Administration, Materiel, and Tactics of the Artillery, United States Army.* New York: James J. Chapman, 1884.

Blanding, William F., and Alfred M. Williams, eds. *Men of progress: biographical sketches and portraits of leaders in business and professional life in the state of Rhode Island and Providence plantations.* Boston: New England Magazine, 1896.

Bollet, Alfred Jay. *Civil War Medicine: Challenges and Triumphs.* Tucson: Galen, 2002.

Boyle, Frank A. *A Party of Mad Fellows: The Story of the Irish Regiments in the Army of the Potomac.* Dayton: Morningside, 1996.

Brown, Howard F., and Roberta Mudge Humble. *The Historic Armories of Rhode Island.* Pawtucket: Globe Print, 2000.

Brown, Kent M. *Cushing of Gettysburg: The Story of a Union Artillery Commander.* Lexington: University Press of Kentucky, 1993.

_____. *Retreat from Gettysburg: Lee, Logistics, and the Pennsylvania Campaign.* Chapel Hill: University of North Carolina Press, 2005.

Cannan, John. *The Bloody Angle: Hancock's Assault on the Mule Shoe Salient, May 12, 1864.* Boston: Da Capo, 2002.

Carmen, Ezra A. *The Maryland Campaign of September 1862: Ezra A. Carman's Definitive Study of the Union and Confederate Armies at Antietam.* Edited by Joseph Pierro. New York: Routledge, 2008.

Carmichael, Peter S. *Lee's Young Artillerist William R.J. Pegram.* Charlottesville: University of Virginia Press, 1995.

Carpenter, Esther B. *South County Studies.* Boston: Merrymount, 1924.

Coates, Earl J., Michael J. McAfee, and Don Troiani. *Don Troiani's Regiments and Uniforms of the Civil War.* Mechanicsburg, PA: Stackpole, 2002.

Coffin, Howard. *The Battered Stars: One State's Ordeal During Grant's Overland Campaign.* Woodstock, VT: Countryman Press, 2002.

_____. *Full Duty: Vermonters in the Civil War.* Woodstock, VT: Countryman Press, 1993.

Datsrup, Boyd L. *King of Battle: A Branch History of the U.S. Army's Field Artillery.* Ft. Monroe, VA: U.S. Army, 1992.

Delauter, Roger U., and Brandon H. Beck. *The Third Battle of Winchester.* Lynchburg, VA: H.E. Howard, 1995.

Divine, John E. *35th Battalion Virginia Cavalry.* Lynchburg, VA: H.E. Howard, 1985.

Dowding, George R. *Military History of Westerly, 1710–1932.* Westerly, RI: Blackburn & Benson, 1932.

Downey, Fairfax. *The Guns at Gettysburg.* New York: David McKay, 1958.

Driftways into the Past: Local History of Richmond, Rhode Island. Westerly, RI: Utter, 1977.

Driver, Robert J. *The 1st and 2nd Rockbridge Artillery.* Lynchburg, VA: H.E. Howard, 1987.

Dyer, Frederick H. *A Compendium of the War of the Rebellion.* Vol. 3. New York: Thomas Yoseloff, 1959.

Fischer, David Hackett. *Washington's Crossing.* New York: Oxford University Press, 2004.

Frank, Joseph A. *With Ballot and Bayonet: The Political Socialization of American Civil War Soldiers.* Athens: University of Georgia Press, 1998.

Freeman, Douglass S. *Lee's Lieutenants: A Study in Command.* 3 Volumes. New York: Charles Scribner's Sons, 1942–1944.

Gallagher, Gary W. *Stephen Dodson Ramseur: Lee's Gallant General.* Chapel Hill: University of North Carolina Press, 1985.

Glatthaar, Joseph T. *Forged in Battle: The Civil War*

Alliance of Black Soldiers and White Officers. New York: Free Press, 1990.

Graham, Martin F., and George F. Skoch. *Mine Run: A Campaign of Lost Opportunities, October 21, 1863–May 1, 1864.* Lynchburg, VA: H.E. Howard, 1987.

Greene, A. Wilson. *Breaking the Backbone of the Rebellion: The Final Battles of the Petersburg Campaign.* Mason City, IA: Savas, 2000.

Griffith, Paddy. *Battle Tactics of the Civil War.* New Haven: Yale University Press, 1989.

Gottfried, Bradley M. *The Artillery of Gettysburg.* Nashville: Cumberland House, 2008.

_____. *The Maps of Gettysburg: An Atlas of the Gettysburg Campaign, June 3–July 13, 1863.* El Dorado Hills, CA: Savas Beattie, 2007.

Hagerman, Edward. *The American Civil War and the Origins of Modern Warfare: Ideas, Organization and Field Command.* Bloomington: Indiana University Press, 1988.

Hardy, Michael. *The 37th North Carolina Troops: Tarheels in the Army of Northern Virginia.* Jefferson, NC: McFarland, 2003.

Harpin, Mathias, P. *The High Road to Zion.* Pascoag: Corey's Comp Shop, 1976.

Harsh, Joseph L. *Taken at the Flood: Robert E. Lee and Confederate Strategy in the Maryland Campaign of 1862.* Kent, OH: Kent State University Press, 1999.

Hartwell, Everett S. *An Historical Sketch of the Providence Marine Corps of Artillery, 1801–1951.* Providence: Providence Marine Corps of Artillery, 1952.

Hazlett, James C., Edwin Olmstead, and M. Hume Parks. *Field Artillery Weapons of the Civil War.* Chicago: University of Illinois Press, 2004.

Hess, Earl J. *The Union Soldier in Battle: Enduring the Ordeal of Combat.* Lawrence: University Press of Kansas, 1997.

History of Providence County, Rhode Island. Vol. 1. Edited by Richard M. Bayles. New York: W.W. Preston & Co., 1891.

Hoar, Jay S. *New England's Last Civil War Veterans.* Arlington TX: Seacliffe, 1976.

Holman, Cindy A. *Milltown Militia: North Stonington Volunteers in the Civil War.* North Stonington: C.A. Holman, 1986.

Humphreys, Andrew A. *From Gettysburg to the Rapidan: The Army of the Potomac, July 1863 to April 1864.* New York: Charles Scribner's Sons, 1883.

Johnson, Curt, and Richard C. Anderson, Jr. *Artillery Hell: The Employment of Artillery at Antietam.* College Station: Texas A & M University, 1995.

Jones, Daniel P. *The Economic & Social Transformation of Rural Rhode Island, 1780–1850.* Boston: Northeastern University Press, 1992.

Konstam, Angus. *Fair Oaks 1862: McClellan's Peninsula Campaign.* Westport, CT: Praeger, 2004.

Krick, Robert K. *Parker's Virginia Battery.* Berryville, VA: Virginia Book, 1975.

Longacre, Edward G. *The Man Behind the Guns: A Biography of General Henry Jackson Hunt.* New York: A.S. Barnes, 1977.

_____. *To Gettysburg and Beyond: The Twelfth New Jersey Volunteer Infantry, II Corps, Army of the Potomac, 1862–1865.* Hightstown, NJ: Longstreet, 1988.

Macomber, Steven W. *The Story of Westerly Granite.* Westerly, RI: Westerly Historical Society, 1958.

Manderville, Frances W. *The Historical Story of Charlestown, Rhode Island, 1669–1976.* Westerly, RI: Utter, 1979.

Marvel, William. *Burnside.* Chapel Hill: University of North Carolina Press, 1991.

_____. *The First New Hampshire Battery, 1861–1865.* South Conway, NH: Lost Cemetery, 1985.

_____. *Lee's Last Retreat: The Flight to Appomattox.* Chapel Hill: University of North Carolina Press, 2002.

Matter, William D. *If It Takes All Summer: The Battle of Spotsylvania.* Chapel Hill: University of North Carolina Press, 1988.

McWhiney, Grady, and Perry D. Jamieson. *Attack and Die: Civil War Military Tactics and Southern Heritage.* Mobile: University of Alabama Press, 1982.

Meaney, Peter J. *The Civil War Engagement at Cool Spring, July 18, 1864: The Largest Battle Ever Fought in Clark County, Virginia.* Berryville, VA: Meaney, 1979.

Melton, Jack W., and Lawrence E. Pawl. *Guide to Civil War Artillery Projectiles.* Gettysburg: Thomas, 1996.

Mohr, Ralph S. *Rhode Island Footprints on the Sands of Time.* Providence: Oxford Press, 1975.

Mohr, Theodore C. *The Battle of Cedar Creek.* Lynchburg, VA: H.E. Howard, 1992.

Mowry, Arthur M. *The Dorr War or the Constitutional Struggle in Rhode Island.* Providence: Preston & Rounds, 1901.

Mudgett, Timothy B. *Make the Fur Fly: A History of a Union Volunteer Division in the American Civil War.* Shippensburg, Pa: Burd Street, 1997.

Murray, Alton J. *South Georgia Rebels: The True Wartime Experiences of the 26th Regiment, Georgia Volunteer Infantry, Lawton-Gordon-Evans Brigade, Confederate States Army, 1861–1865.* St. Mary's, GA: Murray, 1976.

Naisawald, L. VanLoan. *Grape & Canister: The Story of the Field Artillery of the Army of the Potomac, 1861–1865.* Mechanicsburg, PA: Stackpole, 1999.

Nosworthy, Brent. *The Bloody Crucible of Courage: Fighting Methods and Combat Experience of the Civil War.* New York: Carroll & Graff, 2003.

_____. *Roll Call to Destiny: The Soldier's Eye View of Civil War Battles.* New York: Basic Books, 2008.

O'Reilly, Francis A. *The Fredericksburg Campaign: Winter War on the Rappahannock.* Baton Rouge: Louisiana State University Press, 2003.

Osborne, Charles C. *Jubal: The Life and Times of General Jubal A. Early, CSA.* New York: Algonquin Books, 1992.

Parsons, Phillip W. *The Union Sixth Army Corps in the Chancellorsville Campaign: A Study of the Engagements of Second Fredericksburg, Salem Church and Banks's Ford, May 3–4, 1863.* Jefferson, NC: McFarland, 2006.

Patchan, Scott C. *Shenandoah Summer: The 1864 Valley Campaign.* Lincoln: University of Nebraska Press, 2007.

Patterson, Job N., and Elisha H. Rhodes. *Civil War Regiments from Vermont, New Hampshire, and Rhode Island.* New York: Federal, 1908.

Pfanz, Harry W. *Gettysburg: The Second Day.* Chapel Hill: University of North Carolina Press, 1987.

Pond, George E. *The Shenandoah Valley in 1864.* New York: Blue & Gray, 1959.

Pope, Thomas E. *The Weary Boys: Colonel J. Warren Keifer and the 110th Ohio Volunteer Infantry.* Kent: Kent State University Press, 2002.

Pride, Mike, and Mark Travis. *My Brave Boys: To War with Colonel Cross and the Fighting Fifth.* Hanover NH: University Press of New England, 2001.

Priest, John M. *Antietam: The Soldiers' Battle.* Shippensburg, PA: White Mane, 1989.

_____. *Before Antietam: The Battle for South Mountain.* Shippensburg, PA: White Mane, 1992.

Rhea, Gordon. *The Battle of the Wilderness: May 5–6, 1864.* Baton Rouge: Louisiana State University Press, 1994.

_____. *The Battles for Spotsylvania Court House and the Road to Yellow Tavern: May 7–12, 1864.* Baton Rouge: Louisiana State University Press, 1997.

_____. *Cold Harbor: Grant and Lee, May 26–June 3, 1864.* Baton Rouge: Louisiana State University Press, 2002.

_____. *To the North Anna River: Grant and Lee, May 13–25, 1864.* Baton Rouge: Louisiana State University Press, 2000.

Rhode Island Gazetteer. Providence: Providence Journal, 1964.

Rogers, Phil S. *Everlasting Glory: Vermont Soldiers Who Were Awarded the Congressional Medal of Honor for Service During the Civil War: 1861–1865.* Randolph Center, VT: Vermont Civil War Hemlocks, 2007.

Scoville, Samuel. *Brave Deeds of Union Soldiers.* Philadelphia: George W. Jacobs, 1915.

Sears, Stephen W. *Chancellorsville.* Boston: Houghton Mifflin, 1996.

_____. *Controversies and Commanders: Dispatches from the Army of the Potomac.* Boston: Houghton Mifflin, 1999.

_____. *George B. McClellan: The Young Napoleon.* New York: Ticknor and Fields, 1988.

_____. *To the Gates of Richmond: The Peninsula Campaign.* New York: Ticknor and Fields, 1992.

Shea, Robert F. "Aspects of the History of Westerly During the Civil War." Master's thesis, University of Rhode Island, 1957.

Shultz, David. *"Double Canister at Ten Yards": The Federal Artillery and the Repulse of Pickett's Charge.* Redondo Beach, CA: Rank and File, 1995.

Simpson, Brooks D. *Ulysses S. Grant: Triumph over Adversity, 1822–1865.* New York: Houghton Mifflin, 2000.

Stern, Philip Van Doren. *An End to Valor: The Last Days of the Civil War.* Boston: Houghton Mifflin, 1958.

Tidball, Eugene C. *No Disgrace to My Country: The Life of John C. Tidball.* Kent: Kent State University Press, 2002.

Time Life Books. *Echoes of Glory: Arms and Equipment of the Union.* Edited by Henry A. Woodhead. Alexandria: Time Life, 1995.

Trout, Robert J. *Galloping Thunder: The Stuart Horse Artillery Battalion.* Mechanicsburg, PA: Stackpole, 2002

Trudeau, Noah Andre. *The Last Citadel: Petersburg, Virginia, June 1864–April 1865.* Baton Rouge: Louisiana State University Press, 1991.

The Union Army: A History of Military Affairs in the Loyal States, 1861–65: Records of the Regiments in the Union Army, Cyclopedia of Battles, Memoirs of Commanders and Soldiers. Vol. 1: Maine, New Hampshire, Vermont, Massachusetts, Rhode Island, Connecticut, Pennsylvania, and Delaware. Wilmington, NC: Broadfoot, 1997.

Walker, Anthony. *So Few the Brave.* Newport: Seafield, 1981.

Waugh, John C. *Reelecting Lincoln: The Battle for the 1864 Presidency.* New York: Crown, 1997.

Whitehorne, Joseph W.A. *The Battle of Belle Grove or Cedar Creek.* Strasburg, VA: Book Builders, 1987.

Wilkinson, Warren. *Mother May You Never See the Sights I Have Seen: The Fifty-Seventh Massachusetts Veteran Volunteer Infantry in the Last Year of the Civil War.* New York: Harper Collins, 1990.

Williams, Richard B. *Chicago's Battery Boys: The Chicago Mercantile Battery in the Civil War's Western Theatre.* El Dorado Hills, CA: Savas Beattie, 2005.

Winslow, Richard E. *General John Sedgwick: The Story of a Union Corps Commander.* Novato, CA: Presidio Press, 1982.

Wise, Jennings C. *The Long Arm of Lee.* 2 Volumes. Lynchburg, VA: J.P. Bell, 1915.

Wittenberg, Eric J. *Little Phil: A Reassessment of the Civil War Leadership of General Phillip H. Sheridan.* Washington: Brassey's, 2002.

Wittenberg, Eric J., J. David Petruzzi, and Michael F. Nugent. *One Continuous Fight: The Retreat from Gettysburg and the Pursuit of Lee's Army of Northern Virginia, July 4–14, 1863.* El Dorado Hills, CA: Savas Beattie, 2008.

Zabecki, David T. *American Artillery and the Medal of Honor.* Bennington, VT: Merriam Press, 1997.

Zambarano, Anthony L. "The Industrial Development in Rhode Island during the Civil War Era." Master's thesis, University of Rhode Island, 1957.

Zeller, Pawl G. *The Second Vermont Volunteer Infantry Regiment, 1861–1865.* Jefferson, NC: McFarland, 2002.

Primary Articles

Adams, Edward P. "Battery G, First Rhode Island Light Artillery." *Revised Register of Rhode Island Volunteers.* Providence: E.L. Freeman, 1895.

Ames, William. "Civil War Letters." Edited by

William Greene Roelker. *Rhode Island History,* January 1941.

Anson, Charles H. "Assault of the Lines of Petersburg, April 2d, 1865." *War Papers Read Before the Commandery of the State of Wisconsin, Military Order of the Loyal Legion of the United States.* Vol. 1. Milwaukee: Burdick, Armitage & Allen, 1891.

Arnold, James N., ed. "Dedication of the Soldiers and Sailors Monument at Riverside Cemetery, South Kingstown, R. I., June 10, 1886." *Narragansett Historical Register,* (July 1886).

Barber, Joseph M., ed. "Brotherhood: Abstracts of the Membership of Budlong Post No. 18, GAR, Westerly, RI." *Rhode Island Roots* (December 2001).

Beauregard, Pierre G.T. "Four Days of Battle at Petersburg." In *Battles & Leaders of the Civil War [B&L].* New York: The Century Company, 1888. Vol. 4.

Couch, Darius N. "The Chancellorsville Campaign." In *B&L.* Vol. 3.

Cox, Jacob D. "The Battle of Antietam." In *B&L.* Vol. 2.

Douglass, Henry Kyd. "Stonewall Jackson in Maryland." In *B&L.* Vol. 2.

Early, Jubal. "Early's March to Washington in 1864." In *B&L.* Vol. 4.

_____. "Winchester, Fishers Hill, and Cedar Creek." In *B&L.* Vol. 4.

Fishburn, Clement D. "Historical Sketch of the Rockbridge Artillery, C.S. Army." *SHSP* 23 (1895).

Franklin, William F. "Rear-Guard Fighting during the Change of Base." In *B&L.* Vol. 2.

Galloway, Norton. "Hand-to-Hand Fighting at Spotsylvania." In *B&L.* Vol. 4.

Goss, Warren L. "Yorktown and Williamsburg." In *B&L.* Vol. 2.

Granger, Moses M. "The Battle of Cedar Creek." In *Sketches of War History 1861–1865: Papers Prepared for the Ohio Commandery of the Military Order of the Loyal Legion of the United States.* Vol. 3. Cincinnati: Robert Clarke, 1890.

Grant, Lewis A. "The Old Vermont Brigade at Petersburg." In *Glimpses of a Nation's Struggle: Papers Read Before the Minnesota Commandery of the Loyal Legion of the United States.* St. Paul: St. Paul Book & Stationary, 1887.

_____. "The Second Division of the Sixth Corps at Cedar Creek." In *Glimpses of a Nation's Struggle: Papers Read Before the Minnesota Commandery of the Loyal Legion of the United States.* Minneapolis: Augustus Davis, 1909.

Humphrey, Benjamin G. "Recollections of Marye's Heights and Salem Church. In *B&L.* Vol. 6.

Hunt, Henry J. "The First Day at Gettysburg." In *B&L.* Vol. 3.

_____. "The Second Day at Gettysburg." In *B&L.* Vol. 3.

_____. "The Third Day at Gettysburg." In *B&L.* Vol. 3.

Jackson, Huntington W. "Sedgwick at Fredericksburg and Salem's Heights." In *B&L.* Vol. 3.

Johnston, Joseph E. "Manassas to Seven Pines." In *B&L.* Vol. 2.

Keifer, J. Warren. "The Battle of Sailor's Creek." In *Sketches of War History, 1861–1865: Papers Prepared for the Ohio Commandery of the Military Order of the Loyal Legion of the United States.* Vol. 3. Cincinnati: Robert Clarke, 1890.

Imboden, John D. "Incidents of the First Bull Run." In *B&L.* Vol. 1.

Lane, James H. "Defence of Fort Gregg." *SHSP* 3 (1887).

Law, Evander M. "From the Wilderness to Cold Harbor." In *B&L.* Vol. 4.

Longstreet, James. "The Invasion of Maryland." In *B&L.* Vol. 2.

McClellan, George B. "From the Peninsula to Antietam." In *B&L.* Vol. 2.

_____. "The Peninsular Campaign." In *B&L.* Vol. 2.

Miller, William. "A hot day on Marye's Heights." In *B&L.* Vol. 3.

Merritt, Wesley. "Sheridan in the Shenandoah Valley." In *B&L.* Vol. 3.

McMahon, Martin T. "Cold Harbor." In *B&L.* Vol. 4.

_____. "The Death of General Sedgwick." In *B&L.* Vol. 4.

_____. "From Gettysburg to the Coming of Grant." In *B&L.* Vol. 4.

Peck, John B. "Battery C, First Rhode Island Light Artillery." *Revised Register of Rhode Island Volunteers.* Providence: E.L. Freeman, 1895.

Pendleton, William N. "The Artillery of the A.N.V. in the Last Campaign and at the Surrender." *SHSP* 9 (1881).

Perkins, Charles E. "Letters Home." Edited by Ray Henshaw and Glenn W. LaFantaise. *Rhode Island History* (November 1980).

Porter, Fitz John. "The Battle of Malvern Hill." In *B&L.* Vol. 2.

_____. "Hanover Court House and Gaine's Mill." In *B&L.* Vol. 2.

"Roll of the Rockbridge Battery of Artillery, April 10, 1865." *SHSP* 16 (1880).

Smith, Gustavus W. "Two days of Battle at Seven Pines." In *B&L.* Vol. 2.

Stevens, Hazard. "The Battle of Cedar Creek: October 19, 1864." In *Civil War Papers Read before the Commandery of the State of Massachusetts, Military Order of the Loyal Legion of the United States:* Vol. 1. Boston: E.H. Gilson, 1900.

Stevens, Hazard. "Storming of the lines at Petersburg." In *The Shenandoah Campaigns of 1862 and 1864 and the Appomattox Campaign, 1865.* Boston: Military Historical Society of Massachusetts, 1907.

Webb, Alexander S. "Through the Wilderness." In *B&L.* Vol. 4.

Secondary Articles

Abernethy, Thomas J. "Crane's Rhode Island Company of Artillery." *Rhode Island History* (Winter 1970).

Alexander, Ted. "Ten Days in July: The Pursuit to the Potomac." *North & South* (August 1999).

Arnold, James N. "The Importance of Local History." In *Narragansett Historical Register*. Vol. 1, 1882.

Chiles, Paul. "'Artillery Hell!': The Guns of Antietam." *Blue & Gray* (Winter 1998).

Ferguson, Cynthia C. "The Providence Marine Corps of Artillery in the Civil War." *Rhode Island History* (Spring 2002).

Gallagher, Gary W. "East of Chancellorsville: Jubal A. Early at Second Fredericksburg and Salem Church." In *Chancellorsville: The Battle and Its Aftermath*. Edited by Gary W. Gallagher. Chapel Hill: University of North Carolina Press, 1996.

Glatthaar, Joseph T. "Battlefield Tactics." In *Writing the Civil War: The Quest to Understand*. Edited by James M. McPherson and William J. Cooper, Jr. Columbia: University of South Carolina Press, 1998.

Grandchamp, Robert. "'My God! There go two of our men': Brown's Battery B at the Battle of Gettysburg." *Gettysburg* (January 2007).

Greene, A. Wilson. "Day of Decision at Petersburg." *Blue & Gray* (Winter 2001).

Mertz, Gregory A. "Upton's Attack." *Blue & Gray* (Summer 2001).

Patchan, Scott C. "Cedar Creek." *Blue & Gray* (Summer 2007).

_____. "Fisher's Hill." *Blue & Gray* (Winter 2008).

_____. "Shenandoah Valley, July 1864." *Blue & Gray* (Summer 2006).

Petruzzi, J. David. "He Rides Over Everything in Sight." *America's Civil War* (March 2006).

Rollins, Richard. "Confederate Artillery Prepares for Pickett's Charge." *North & South* (September 1999).

_____. "The Failure of Confederate Artillery in Pickett's Charge." *North & South* (April 2000).

Tobey, John E. "Cheese Knife and Shoulder Straps." *CRRC*.

_____. "Day Planner: Army of the Potomac Style." *CRRC*.

_____. "The Omnivorous Haversack." *CRRC*.

Willis, Rob. "Corps Badges of the Army of the Potomac." *CRRC*.

Newspapers

Bristol Phoenix
Martinsburg Journal
Narragansett Times
Narragansett Weekly
National Tribune
New York Herald
New York Times
Pawtucket Evening Times
Providence Daily Post
Providence Evening Press
Providence Journal
Savannah Morning News
The Sixth Corps
Westerly Sun
Wood River Advertiser

Index

Numbers in **bold italics** indicate pages with illustrations.